The Living Theatre

The Living Theatre
Art, Exile, and Outrage

John Tytell

Methuen Drama

First published in Great Britain in 1997
by Methuen Drama,
an imprint of Reed International Books Ltd
Michelin House, 81 Fulham Road, London SW3 6RB
and Auckland, Melbourne, Singapore and Toronto

A CIP catalogue record for this title
is available from the British Library
ISBN 0 413 70800 4

Typeset in the United States of America
Printed in England by Clays Ltd, St Ives plc

To my wife, Mellon, for the strength of her support.

To my sister, Mae, who was a street actor in the sixties.

To poet-friend Ira Cohen, catalyst.

And to all the descendants of The Living Theatre tribe.

What is the nature of an
experimental action?
It is simply an action
the outcome of which is not foreseen.

John Cage, *Silences*

Contents

Shelley's
Great-great-grandchildren:
A Preface

In New York City, just after the end of the Second World War, two young theatrical aspirants named Judith Malina and Julian Beck dreamed of a theatre that would challenge the moral complacencies of their audience and shake the world. They called the theatre they conceived The Living Theatre, because most of what they saw on the stage seemed directed toward momentary entertainment or moribund.

Julian Beck and Judith Malina would touch the lives of many artists and thinkers: among them, writers Tennessee Williams, Anaïs Nin, Jack Kerouac, and Jean Genet; musicians John Cage, Jim Morrison, and John Lennon; painters Jackson Pollock and Dalí; and philosophers Martin Buber and Michel Foucault. Their story is that of the formation of an avant-garde in New York during the 1950s and a consequent counterculture in the 1960s.

Over the course of almost fifty years, The Living Theatre has been known as the most radical, uncompromising, and experimental group in American theatrical history. Producing seventy-five plays and offering more than five thousand performances, The Living Theatre profoundly affected theatre in Europe and America while moving on the edges of society and violating many of the taboos of culture and government. The company was also particularly flamboyant and daring, both onstage and off, attracting attention around the world and unleashing a backlash of attempted suppression and arrests.

At the core of their engagement with theatre was the notion, espoused by Judith Malina and Julian Beck, that there could be no separation between art and life. As pacifists and anarchists, they distrusted the system and the violence it engendered, both in the international cataclysms of war and in everyday life. Malina and Beck were eager to use theatre as a platform for a kind of dissent traditionally smothered by the complex organism we know as modern society.

A pragmatic world has had little tolerance for moral perspectives, and the result for The Living Theatre has been a history of conflict and condemnation. Among the first of the avant-garde to protest against atomic testing, Judith Malina was arrested and Julian Beck had a lung punctured by police in Times Square.

There were many more arrests, both in America and later in Europe, where the company began performing in 1964 after being evicted from their theatre by agents of the Internal Revenue Service. By this time, the company had become a new kind of theatrical tribe, experiencing an unusual degree of bonding by living communally, using hallucinogens like LSD, and sustaining an atmosphere of sexual openness. In an unprecedented strategy, the company decided that as anarchists, they should create plays collectively; and as the company became more international, they began performing their work in German, French, Italian, and Spanish as well as English.

During the revolutionary euphoria of 1968, The Living Theatre returned to America for a national tour. The overtly political nature of plays like *Paradise Now* and the outrageousness of their communal life-styles resulted in more conflict with authority. When they went to Brazil in 1970 to perform in the streets for the poorest of the poor, the entire company was incarcerated by a highly repressive military dictatorship.

No matter what price they had to pay for their dissent, it was better "to struggle to live a utopian dream than to consent to live in hell," Julian Beck asserted in a poem. The line exists as a motto for the company members' extraordinary commitment, underlying the lonely courage of their singular persistence and their steadfast belief in the justice of their convictions.

Although The Living Theatre has served as a sort of banner for the progressive spirit, a herald of alternatives, conservatives have seen it as a threatening antagonist and the harbinger of an unsettling bohemian disorder. Were they the sacrificial saints of the counterculture, the outcast victims of their own idealism, or sacred untouchables offering themselves in a subversive ritual of redemption? The history of the company may suggest an endemic martyrdom, but it represents as well a quality that is deeply associated with the American Dream, the demand for a freedom that can never be taken for granted and that needs to be perpetually tested or contested to be enjoyed at all.

Germinations

1. Genius Incorporated

Despite the magniloquent flamboyance of its name, Genius Incorporated was a seedy Times Square club for actors, adjacent to the St. James Hotel, an inexpensive dive in the New York theatre district. Broadway theatre had been rejuvenated during the Second World War as the need for entertainment was pronounced in a time of rationing and air-raid alarms. Rodgers and Hammerstein's first collaboration, *Oklahoma!,* had begun its successful run, an expression of the optimistic self-assurance of American power.

Since most actors were unemployed most of the time, Genius Incorporated was a place to congregate, to gossip along the coffee grapevine, to browse through *Actor's Cues,* the show business newsletter edited by Leo Shull, the club's proprietor.

Late on the humid afternoon of 14 September 1943, the club was almost empty except for Shull in a porkpie hat and a diminutive seventeen-year-old girl with especially large black eyes. Wearing a red corduroy coat that was too warm for the weather, she sipped coffee and read a newspaper description of the Allied landing in Salerno.

An idle passerby looking into the window of Genius Incorporated might have euphemistically referred to the young woman in the red coat as a "victory girl," one of the unmarried women whose participation in the war effort was limited to working in factories and boosting the morale of servicemen, of whom there were more than sixteen million. The city was saturated with an awareness of the war, with soldiers constantly in transit, incessant appeals for war bonds, omnipresent propaganda posters, and grim newsreel accounts of bloody battles.

A small, thin, dark-haired high-school student with a brooding inner glow, Judith Malina—the girl in the red coat—had a certain simmering resonance that substituted for more conventional good looks. Although she knew that she was no beauty, that her nose had an unfortunate shape which she hoped one day to correct, that there was even a bit of the gypsy in her appearance, she often spent time in the demimondaine world of Genius Incorporated in the vain expectation that someone would offer her a part in a play.

Judith Malina was part of a new generation, women who had dropped out of high school because of the enormous dislocating effect of the war. A few weeks earlier, an unruly crowd of these young women, thirty thousand cheering and jeering girls, had massed outside the Paramount Theater, a few blocks from Genius Incorporated, waiting for the young Frank Sinatra to appear after a concert, and they had caused a near riot. Judith Malina was in that melee, and she felt a similar brazenness, a lust for liberty, and a repugnance for whatever seemed stifling and conventional that many other American women experienced during and after the war.

In the evening, as the sidewalks filled with office workers returning home, Malina ventured to the doorway of Genius Incorporated, munching on penny chocolates. Daydreaming, loitering, she was surprised by an acquaintance, one of the more disreputable members of the club, an itinerant theatre district person named William Marchant, Gau-Gau to his friends. Blond, blue-eyed, looking like a handsome Connecticut stockbroker down on his luck, Marchant was known as a slick talker.

This time, however, all he wanted was a share of the chocolate, complaining that he had not eaten in three days. Judith took him to the Automat instead, where she bought him spaghetti and lemon-lime pie. Full of gratitude, he offered to introduce her to an exceptional man, the most marvelous, brilliant, poetic man she would ever meet.

She distrusted the glib, smiling Marchant. His fairy-tale man seemed much too good to be true. He was aristocratic and wealthy, Marchant promised, and to satisfy her curiosity, she gave him another nickel for the telephone. Marchant returned still smiling and announced that Julian Beck, the man he had described in such glowing terms, would meet them outside Genius Incorporated.

Marchant had met Julian Beck that summer in a midtown bar. Beck had studied at Yale, which Marchant interpreted as a sign of money, class, and culture though Marchant was unaware that Beck had dropped out the previous May, disgusted with the affectations and the social rigidities of the Ivy League.

Over the telephone, Marchant had inflated Malina's status and talent, promising Julian she was the most remarkable woman he would ever meet. He introduced her as "Jody Malin," believing the pseudonym sounded less ethnic and more socially acceptable. Judith was immediately impressed by Julian's golden hair curling to his shoulders, a most unusual feature at a time when most young men had cut their hair as closely as possible for the sake of their helmets.

Sharp-featured, Julian had thick, voluptuous lips. A few inches under six feet, he was lean, weighing only 120 pounds. Eighteen, just a year older than Judith, his high, arching eyebrows gave him a look of bemused wonderment as if he were on the verge of some astounding discovery. It seemed an expression of naive optimism, but in a deeper sense, it suggested a thoroughly modern attitude, the kind of debonair bravado associated with the French playwright and film maker Jean Cocteau, who was one of Julian's idols.

Another venerated figure was Oscar Wilde, and there was a Wildean dimension to Julian that intrigued Judith. The dandy-socialist-aesthete, Wilde had jibed at human pretensions in the brilliant repartee of his comedies, but his real revolt against middle-class values was his homosexuality, a sexual subversion that made him a martyr for one form of sexual liberation. Like Wilde, Julian cultivated ways of combatting authority with bright remarks or unusual attitudes. Even his speech sounded Wildean—witty, eloquent, poised, and affected as if in midsentence he were always seeking the precise word and confident he would find it. Julian's presence was theatrical in a self-conscious, arty fashion, and there was an effeminate, sartorial elegance about him. All this appealed to Judith, the street urchin. Even more attractive was his idealism, his conception of himself in a grand, Shelleyan tradition, a poet with "golden flashing tongue from mountain peaks and the prows of cloud ships." For Judith, the evening was turning into what the French would call a *coup de foudre.*

Julian proposed seeing a film, a Joan Crawford anti-Nazi melodrama. The film was an awful example of American patriotic propaganda. Julian and Judith both laughed about it in a coffee shop afterward though its title, *Beyond Suspicion,* was a token of the instant trust and confidence they felt in each other. A brilliant conversationalist who sometimes ran the risk of being a monologist, Julian spoke about Cocteau, Russian futurism, surrealism, abstract art, and his own ambitions as a painter. Quoting from poems he had written, as well as from writers such as T. S. Eliot, James Joyce, and Gertrude Stein, he seemed too zealous, too giddy, almost maniacally possessed by his enthusiasms, his awareness of the surprising new directions of modern art.

Judith was overwhelmed by the depth and passion of what Julian knew and its evident urgency for him. She felt that her previous life had been wasted, and she knew that she had fallen in love with the wild poet whom she saw as the incarnation of beautiful, outrageous, unfettered freedom.

Leaving the coffee shop around midnight, the couple wandered around Times Square and found a market where they purchased an abundant supply of large, luscious grapes, the perfect symbol for their future Dionysian path. Boarding an open Broadway trolley, improvising scenes from Wilde's *Salomé,* they rode around Manhattan, feeling drunk with life until the first signs of dawn.

2. An Immigrant Childhood

Malina had been stunned and seduced. In the week following her cataclysmic meeting with Julian, she cut all her classes at Julia Richman High School to undertake her own crash course in modernism. Early in the morning, she read poetry—Pound, Eliot, and Cummings. Afternoons, she went to the Museum of Modern Art to see the cubist and surrealist paintings Julian had described. In the evenings, she read Gertrude Stein, Joyce's *Portrait of the Artist as a Young Man,* Gide's *Journals.* Once she had been an excellent student—attending the select Hunter elementary and junior high schools—until the sudden death of her father when she was fourteen, an event, both uprooting and traumatic, that had filled her with anomie and despair.

Her first memory was of the smell of oranges and her grandmother's wet wash in the port city of Kiel in Germany. Her mother, Rosel Zamojre, was a German Jew whose Polish parents had settled in Kiel while escaping one of many pogroms. In the history of her family, the men had been rabbis who spent long hours studying the Torah, assisted by their wives and daughters in a small cloth and lace store. Self-sacrificing and traditional, Rosel wanted to become an actress, and trained herself by memorizing the monologues of Schiller and Lessing.

But the reality was never more exotic than the Belgian lace inside the family store. When she married Max Malina, a rabbinical student, she resolved from the beginning to devote herself to her husband's career. Keeping a kosher kitchen, wearing the tra-

ditional sheitel, Rosel did embroidery and participated in amateur theatricals. The couple lived in the former dressing rooms of
a theatre that had been renovated on Breiterweg (Broadway) in
Kiel where Judith was born on 4 June 1926.

Max was sent to America to solicit funds for impoverished
rabbonim who had settled in Jerusalem, and in 1928, Rosel agreed
to emigrate with him to New York City. They settled on the upper
East Side of Manhattan, in a tenement apartment in Yorkville,
whose windows faced the Third Avenue elevated subway. As an
infant, Judith was sickly—she refused to eat and was constipated.
The rumbling of the elevated subway terrified her, and she would
scream in her sleep.

Rosel Malina's activities were domestic—cleaning, cooking,
and caring for her daughter while doing everything she could to
assist her husband. Rosel expected that her husband would
become a great rabbi, and she sacrificed her dream of acting to
that end. Nevertheless, as a release of her secret fantasy, she
would recite Schiller in the manner of the famed actor Alexander
Moissi. Her usually gentle voice would rise in pitch, and become
turbulent and tremendous, frightening little Judith to the point
that she would hide in closets.

Rosel may have projected her own dramatic ambitions on
her daughter, who at the age of seven in a high voice played the
little lamp of the Maccabees that miraculously burned without oil
at anti-Nazi rallies in Madison Square Garden, and at ten was Tiny
Tim in *A Christmas Carol* at Hunter Elementary School.

Another early experience of theatre was the Butler Davenport's free theatre on the lower East Side. Davenport's company
performed a repertory that included Shakespeare and Chekhov.
Davenport had known the transcendentalist Margaret Fuller, and
at every performance during intermission, he passionately proselytized on behalf of birth control. It was an early illustration for
Judith of mixing theatre and politics.

When Judith was ten, her parents moved downtown into a
large room with gilt windows and a crystal chandelier on the
third floor of the Broadway Central Hotel. At the annual art show

around Washington Square, she sold her pastel drawings—landscapes and portraits—in front of the Judson Church, and her first poem was published in a magazine put out by Central Synagogue, a quite remarkable effort about a magical menorah.

If, on the one hand, she was full of the playfulness of the artist, she could subordinate all her more headstrong inclinations to the worship of her father whom she saw as a saintly figure. The first dream she could remember was of a giant hand protruding through a bank of clouds. It was God's hand, moving slowly in an act of benediction, she decided, but the wrist emerged from a shirtsleeve with cuff links resembling her father's.

Rabbi Malina began every day in prayer at dawn but spent much of the rest of it denying his more mystical tendencies—losing himself in trance, for example—by working on more practical concerns as the head of a congregation. During the late thirties, Max Malina lived in a state of permanent crisis, for he had a very early knowledge of the German deportation of Jews. A constant procession of refugees told him what they knew about the concentration camps.

In 1938, at the age of twelve, Judith helped to stuff thousands of leaflets entitled "Do You Know What Has Happened to Your Jewish Neighbors?" into shampoo packets that were sent to Germany. In a vain attempt to influence the American government, Rabbi Malina met with senators, congressmen, and Mayor La Guardia, and organized committees lobbying to convince President Roosevelt to raise or suspend immigration quotas. Albert Einstein, responding to the urgency of the cause and Malina's charismatic leadership, sat on one of these committees and frequently came to the rabbi's room in the Broadway Central. It was little Judith's first contact with a great personage, and she heard her father discuss with the disheveled scientist a proposal to pay five thousand dollars for each Jew released by the Nazis—an idea Roosevelt opposed, arguing it would only strengthen the Germans.

Obsessed by the suffering in Germany and Poland, Rabbi Malina was himself suddenly stricken with leukemia and died painfully at the age of forty-two on 23 June 1940. Just fourteen, Judith was on the verge of graduating from the Hunter Model School, at that time considered one of the most select public schools in New York City. She and her mother were devastated, and Rosel would never recover from the shock of her husband's premature death.

Rosel went to work in a factory, became ill, moved into a grim furnished room, and had to apply for welfare. Judith dropped out of high school to work in a laundry but was able to resume school through the assistance of a small scholarship fund for the children of deceased rabbis. Willful, a voracious reader determined to follow her own path at the expense of her classroom assignments, she cut her classes constantly, unconcerned with her high school degree because she had already met Julian.

She knew that what she wanted most was the freedom to write and act. Art was a way to affirm her father's scholarly quests and her mother's theatrical ambitions. Already, she had spent three years rehearsing Ibsen's *Lady from the Sea* with a perverse old Village character called St. Clair Jones and his ad hoc company. She knew she needed to see theatre and dance, and since she rarely could afford such luxuries, she would sneak into performances after the first intermission.

She had been writing poems since early childhood, and several months before her meeting with Julian, she had gathered with a group of Village poets in a Wooster Street basement and read some poems. That night, she had announced herself to the world as a poet, but, equally significant, the poet Edwin Honig had begun advocating anarchism, a subject that had immediate appeal for her. Honig entered her name on a mailing list of the anarchist newsletter *Why,* which later evolved into *Resistance,* a more formidable publication.

On another night in the summer of 1943, she was walking with a former dancer, now ill and indigent. She had bought him a cup of coffee when he saw the sculptor Isamu Noguchi across the street and presented Judith to him as a promising actress. In a sense, it was an introduction of sorts to the general artistic community, even if it was slightly soiled by occurring on the street, where her friend could cadge Noguchi for a dime.

3. Privileged Childhood

Julian had been fascinated by film and theatre since early childhood. When he was seven, he had an operation for a mastoid infection that left him with a tic in his right cheek, so elocution and acting became a natural compensation. The tic disappeared by the time he was ten, but the yen for performance was by then permanent.

His parents enjoyed Broadway musical comedy and opera. They were cultured, subscribers to the *New Yorker,* conversant in modern literature and painting. Both had been born in New York City and were assimilated Jews. The son of an Austrian horse trader, Irving Beck opened a motorcycle parts business. He was good at selling and much of the time had to go out on the road.

When his first wife, Julia Dorothy Blum, died in the influenza epidemic of 1918, he married Mabel Blum, her younger sister, who helped him build his business by teaching school. Mabel was part of a large family of six sisters, four of whom became teachers, perhaps compensating for the fact that their father had been illiterate. Attractive, forceful, and extremely capable, a schoolteacher for thirty-five years, she could also be demanding and domineering, and with her husband shared high expectations for her two sons.

Five years older than Julian, Franklin was nervous, insecure, and dependent. At Irving's insistence, his second son was named Julian D. Beck after Mabel's older sister Julia Dorothy, a subtle if not formative influence. From the start, Julian was a favored son, the imaginative child who entertained his family with circus imitations at the age of four.

Sensitive, sympathetic, a dreamer, Julian was unusual. Compulsive, militant, he could be quickly enraged and was capable of impassioned argument. At the age of six, he was first brought to the Metropolitan Opera to see *Hänsel und Gretel*. When Julian was eleven, he began a log book in which he recorded the plays, concerts, and operas he had attended and the leading performers. Soon he was acting in school plays and trying to write them.

Irving Beck would rent a summer place near New Haven, which gave him the idea of sending his sons to Yale. Franklin was already at Yale when Julian began Horace Mann in the fall of 1939. An elite prep school for young gentlemen, emphasizing sportsmanship, its graduates were routinely accepted by the Ivy League colleges. Many of the students were middle-class Jews, but some, like William F. Buckley, Jr., were upper-class WASPS who were chauffeured to school.

Athletics were more important than the arts at Horace Mann. Another of Julian's classmates was a shy, withdrawn youth from Lowell, Massachusetts, named Jack Kerouac, who was at Horace Mann to strengthen its football team; the next year, he would attend Columbia. Brooding and sullen, an outsider, Kerouac was an athlete; Julian, though frail, was gregariously sunny, eager, and engaging. Kerouac had a literary inclination, writing a long, conventional detective story for the Horace Mann *Quarterly,* which also published a story by Julian.

In the spring of 1940, Julian gleefully played the role of Lady Augusta Bracknell in Oscar Wilde's *The Importance of Being Earnest.* That summer, Julian caught stage fever in a camp in Brandon, Vermont, that featured weekly dramatic presentations.

Julian believed he was living in a glorious historical moment, a golden age of science, speed, and machinery, but this feeling was compromised by the apprehensions of the war and the imminence of American participation. Julian's junior and senior years at Horace Mann were clouded by the specter of war: the surprise attack on Pearl Harbor on 7 December 1941, the ensuing national fear of invasion, the forced blackouts, Mayor La Guardia's warnings that New York City could be attacked, and the news that three or four U.S. merchant ships were being torpedoed every day.

An honors student, Julian continued to act in plays, loudly exaggerating the role of a gangster in the melodrama *Whistling in the Dark,* writing his own plays and long poems in the manner of his favorite poets, the sensuous Keats and the idealistic Shelley.

Admitted to Yale in the spring of 1942, Julian actually began his studies in New Haven that summer—all entering students were on accelerated programs so that they would be able to participate in the war effort as soon as they graduated. Franklin had already been drafted, and Julian was receiving letters from Horace Mann classmates who had chosen enlistment rather than the university.

For the most part, Julian felt constrained, smothered by the decorous propriety of Yale and the stuffy weight of its past. Julian wrote a drama column for the Yale *Daily News* in the spring of 1943. He was reading voraciously, less to satisfy course requirements than his own curiosity. Wallace Fowlie, one of the few professors he admired, had once shared a flat with the poet W. H. Auden and told Julian that Auden only read what would assist him in writing his poetry, a fact that if emulated could not have helped Julian very much as a student.

At Yale, Julian heard the Irish writers Padraic and Mary Colum lecture on Joyce and read the "Anna Livia Plurabelle" section of *Finnegans Wake,* which Julian remembered as one of the most moving occasions of his life, encouraging him to spend endless hours groping in the labyrinth of that most esoteric and convoluted work. He also heard André Breton lecture in French on surrealism. Clearly attracted to the arcane and the obscure, early on Julian idolized Gertrude Stein, whose highly experimental style intrigued him almost as much as her lesbianism.

His own attraction to men was still furtive, undeclared, and ambivalent. With men he had been unable, afraid actually, to take any initiative, partly because he found himself undesirable. At the same time, he was aware that "the sexual ride in my life was to find a strong father and to escape a strong mother," and he had discovered sex with other young men during his senior year in high school. Although his own gay nature, as he later admitted in his book *The Life of the Theatre,* was at that time a function of or related to masochist fantasy, he "recognized that sex, outside the limits proscribed by 'society,' especially with boys and men, was revolutionary."

He suddenly and quite impulsively dropped out of Yale after experiencing in the middle of his geology final the spontaneous and overwhelming epiphany that as an artist in the Joycean tradition, he could no longer serve the system. An immediate consequence of his leaving Yale was that he was called for a physical by his Manhattan draft board. Confessing his attraction to men to an examining psychiatrist, he was classified 4F. Rejection from the army was what Julian wanted—and in a very important sense, he was terribly proud of it and saw it as a form of heroism.

Soon after he received his 4F, in the summer of 1943, Julian was cajoled by his parents into seeing Dr. Frances Arkin, a Park Avenue psychiatrist with Freudian views. Stressing adjustment, and the position that homosexuality was a treatable illness, she encouraged Julian to think about women. After meeting Judith in September, he would have ample opportunity to ponder the desirability of women although he would reach no immediate conclusions on the matter.

4. The Beggar's Bar

In the fall of 1943, Julian and Judith attended the theatre frequently, sometimes going four times a week. This immersion helped Judith to realize that she did not want to work in conventional theatre, which seemed false and deceitful. With few exceptions, most of Broadway's entertainments seemed engineered to make life seem amusing and tolerable. It suffered from a peculiar cultural lag that could only accommodate the past, often at the expense of whatever was artistically valid in the present.

If Judith was suspicious of the glittering white way, it was in part because she was drawn to the darker side. A friend had brought Judith to an unusual cabaret on Morton Street in the Village where she began to work as a hat check girl. A cramped, damp basement space, customers at the Beggar's Bar were seated on beer barrels and drank eggnog while being entertained by its owner.

Valeska Gert was a *Grotesktanzerin,* a German cabaret performer who mixed elements of dance, mime, burlesque, and political satire in her act. She had played in German films in the 1930s and had acted the role of Polly Peachum in Pabst's *Threepenny Opera.* Small, puckish, her black hair in a crew cut, with mauve eye shadow around her black eyes, she dressed in what appeared to be black silk pajamas.

For the next year, the Beggar's Bar became a sort of training school. Valeska taught Judith that life was more sordid and complex than Broadway theatre could ever allow. Working as a sing-

ing waitress, Judith was fascinated by the murky, mysterious ambiance and by Valeska herself, who was an incarnate Brechtian
caricature: crude, bitter, scornful, a harlequin with a wide-
mouthed leering grimace, and glitter on her cheeks and eyelids.
Astringent, sneering, her voice could culminate in a raw, hideous
screech of pain so intense that blue veins would emerge through
her white face powder. Completely extroverted, Valeska believed
she had invented Expressionism. Her stamping feet, the discor-
dant irregularity of her movements onstage, and an abrupt
jaggedness were the visual equivalent of her Dadaist monologues
on sexual liberty, hypocrisy, greed, and the lust for money.

At the Beggar's Bar, Judith was introduced to a Dadaist principle of distortion through bodily contortion that contradicted
the graceful movements of conventional beauty. She had wanted
to act since her father's untimely death and had struggled to
learn what she could about classical stage notions of harmony or
nobility of gesture; but the false majesty of such ideas crumbled
before Gert's onslaught, whose art was so pugnaciously challenging and abrasive that it seemed closer to martyrdom than satire.

While Judith was working at the Beggar's Bar, she and Julian
had embarked on a more formal and deliberate course of study
than any university could provide. Reading Pound, Joyce, Stein,
Cocteau, Cummings, and Breton, they discussed their findings
over chess at Chumley's, a Village hideaway with no sign to ad-
vertise its presence. In the spring of 1944, they took their discussions to the woods along the New Jersey Palisades. When the
weather got warmer and he could find gasoline, Julian borrowed
his father's car and took Judith to the beaches on Long Island
where they could walk for miles reciting poems they had memo-
rized, like Shelley's "Ode to the West Wind."

Living with his indulgent parents, Julian painted in his room,
affecting the life of the artist. One key to his mood was an index
card that he had pasted on his bedroom mirror with a quotation
from James Joyce's *Portrait of the Artist as a Young Man:* "I shall
not serve that in which I no longer believe whether it call itself my
church, my fatherland, or my home." If Stephen Dedalus, Joyce's

hero, had his supercilious or impractically arrogant side, Julian was perhaps too young to be aware of it and like Stephen took himself seriously.

Julian began to speak of needing a studio in which to paint even though he had no means to pay rent. Irving Beck suggested that Julian work for him; but after Julian's first week, when his son tried to unionize the other employees, he realized an allowance might be more prudent than a job. At the same time, Julian complained to Judith that his parents did not understand him, nor did they accept the possibility of his becoming an artist. This was to become a perennial complaint, though only Judith would sympathize with him.

Mabel Beck only wanted Julian to return to Yale, in part because she had met Judith. Although she was on her very best behavior at their meeting and even though she was a rabbi's daughter, the Becks sensed her rebellious, artistic nature and feared it. Judith's presence in his inner family circle made Julian painfully aware of his father's conservative nature (which Judith called reactionary). Irving Beck was a Hoover Republican who feared Roosevelt was going to sell socialism to American workers and control businessmen. Preventing any immediate clash over politics, Mabel Beck reminded her husband that Dr. Arkin, the psychiatrist he was paying, had encouraged Julian to consort with women.

Although the conventional world might have seen Julian as courting Judith, he had not disavowed his homosexuality, only broadened his sexual orientation. In one of the bars on the "bird circuit," a group of dressy, midtown gay bars on the East Side with names like the Blue Parrot or the Golden Pheasant, where men would cruise each other, Julian met a thirty-year-old man named Bill Simmons, who became a role model.

Son of a Provincetown fisherman, Simmons was a handsome, dark-haired industrial designer with impeccable taste. Brash, a clever conversationalist, expansive, and extremely sociable, Simmons had the appeal of a more sophisticated older man, and the two became close friends. Simmons also painted and had a comprehensive knowledge of surrealism. He would introduce Julian to a number of other young painters, including William Baziotes, and began bringing him to gallery openings. Julian tended to lionize older, accomplished men. In April 1944, he left his parents' upper West Side apartment to move into a furnished room and then into Simmons's East Side apartment.

While this complicated relations with Judith, it did not eliminate them. Julian only worried about the impression she would make on Simmons, criticizing her wardrobe as well as what she said. When she offered a perceptive remark about Gertrude Stein one night when they were with Simmons, Julian complimented her, but the attention made her feel on display and under perpetual scrutiny. She understood that a competition of some sort was in progress and felt dismayed when Julian announced that Simmons had rented a cottage in Provincetown for the summer that the men would share, ostensibly providing Julian with the inspiration to paint.

Just before they left, late in May, Julian attended the opening of the fifteenth anniversary show at the Museum of Modern Art as Simmons's guest. Noticing the French cubist master Fernand Léger admiring a photograph of Frank Lloyd Wright's Bear Run house, Julian told Léger in French how stupendous he thought his work was, and how he had been moved by his large *Diners,* which then hung in the second floor foyer of the museum. On the following afternoon, Julian and Simmons spent four hours in Léger's studio, absorbing the homely wisdom of the French painter who looked like a simple potato farmer. Excited, they went uptown to visit Baziotes. For Julian, the afternoon confirmed the direction he most wanted to take—the path of the painter.

5. A Provincetown Summer

Julian's Provincetown summer was a period of wild abandon and discovery. Located in the center of town, on Captain Jack's Wharf, the cottage was simple, without electricity or telephone, but its balcony overlooked the water. The two men played tennis, went bicycling, swam in the ocean, and basked on giant sand dunes. Both were painting, Julian in his first real flowering in an abstract mode, writing poetry, and reading it to each other.

Julian received a letter from Judith, hurt that she was not invited, feeling tangential to Julian's concerns. Unconsciously, she may have sensed that Julian's painting threatened her own theatrical ambitions.

His brother, Franklin, stationed in Camp Pickett, Virginia, wrote to him asking whether he expected "to make a living through the sale of beauty?" That sounded like the voice of his father, a voice Julian preferred to ignore. He wrote his parents a daily postcard, and his mother responded frequently, relating the dismaying news that a neighbor's son was missing in action. She was usually supportive and encouraging, grandiosely advising him to "paint and write always what your heart shrieks for," and then signing off with her "feverish, tropical, malarial devotion."

In her own youth, Mabel had written and painted, and now she hoped to recover her creativity vicariously through her son. Clearly, Julian represented qualities that were now lost to her; but it was just as certain that Julian was in Provincetown because he needed to escape from any influence as smotheringly effusive as Mabel's.

In 1944, Provincetown was still a fishing town with hardly any tourism. Fishermen, mostly of Portuguese descent, would slosh through its narrow streets in high hip boots, dangling strings of lobster, mackerel, and perch from their belts. A number of writers and artists had discovered the unspoiled beauty of the town.

One of them was Tennessee Williams, who rented a cottage on Commercial Street next to the one shared by Julian and Bill Simmons. A boyish thirty-three, Williams was a southerner with a dazed, dreamy expression, a low, deep drawl, and an elaborate, hesitant manner of speaking; he had been writing poetry and stories since his adolescence.

Only one of his plays, *Battle of Angels,* about a sexually irresistible young writer in a small southern town, had been produced. Since it had closed in Boston two weeks after opening, he still had no literary reputation. That summer Williams worked on what would become *The Glass Menagerie,* a play based on his sister's mental decline that would open in Chicago the following winter and become his first real success.

Gracious, with a woeful, resigned, plaintive air, Williams was convinced that he was destined to die young. He was gay though guarded about his sexuality. Since the war years were a period of considerable covertness about what the natives of Provincetown regarded as deviance, a natural bond between Williams, Simmons, and Julian formed. Homosexual men were by definition outside of the mainstream; in Provincetown in 1944, any young man who exhibited signs of sexual flamboyance risked being beaten on the street. Nevertheless, the combination of summer weather and geographical location, the fact that Provincetown was the end of a promontory stretching into the Atlantic, was liberating and intoxicating.

Sometimes, Julian cooked for Williams or swept his flat, seeing him almost daily. Williams introduced Julian to Paul Goodman, whom he called the finest writer in America. Earlier in the summer, Williams and Goodman had had an abortive affair, one of numerous, brief homosexual liaisons in which Williams was involved. Soft-spoken, easygoing, and shy, with a cowlick in his brown hair, glasses, an aquiline nose, and a gleeful leer on his face, Goodman was somehow appealingly childish and engaging. While Julian was not attracted to either Williams or Goodman, he did feel an affinity with Goodman, who reminded him of his own essentially cerebral nature. A genuine intellectual, a bit pedantic at times, with a Ph.D. from the University of Chicago, Goodman had something to say and the talent to write it down.

Through Williams, Julian met a number of other people who would subsequently matter in his world. One was Harold Norse, a young poet only a few years older than he, who knew W. H. Auden and whose best friend, Chester Kallman, had been Auden's lover. The illegitimate son of a Russian Jewess, Norse had been gay since childhood. Short and pugnacious, he had been a dancer, and his tough guy pose was only a Brooklyn mannerism.

Valeska Gert, whom Julian had already met through Judith's work at the Beggar's Bar, was in Provincetown most of the summer, willing to participate in whatever spontaneous theatricals Julian could improvise. Other members of Julian's circle that summer included Bill Cannastra, one of Williams's lovers, a Harvard law student with a daredevil disregard for safety and propriety, who prowled around at night spying in windows; and Charles Henri Ford, a poet who edited the surrealist literary journal called *View*.

An important figure for all the artists in Provincetown that summer was the painter and teacher Hans Hofmann who, with his wife, had set up a studio. An older German artist, Hofmann was a large man with an imposing ego. He had known Picasso and Matisse, and he commanded an encyclopedic knowledge of modernism and a rigorous pedagogical training. In New York City, he had established his own academy where many younger painters studied with him.

One of the people in Hofmann's set was Howard Putzel, whom Julian had already met at Peggy Guggenheim's gallery, Art of This Century. An epileptic, owlish and rotund, with a face perpetually reddened by alcohol, his thin hair slicked back, and his clothes always rumpled, Putzel was an art dealer, and he encouraged Julian's painting.

Julian felt he was a cynosure in a vital group of artists. Scornful of tradition, he had painted the dining room table in the cottage lemon yellow, the color fancied by the decadents, the aesthetes around Oscar Wilde in the London of the 1890s when the rallying cry was "art for art's sake." He was reading Yeats's poems and those of Rilke and Robinson Jeffers, Thomas Mann's *Joseph and His Brothers,* and Henry James's *Portrait of a Lady.* Only nineteen, he wrote in his journal, "No one doubted that it would not be very long before my then rising comet burst over the world of art."

Julian was hoping to enter some of his work in a large group show in Provincetown that summer. Jackson Pollock, another young painter to whom he had been introduced by Williams, was not as encouraging as Putzel. When Julian showed the compact, muscular, balding painter one of his paintings, Pollock exclaimed it was the worst he had ever seen and asked what it supposedly depicted. When Julian's response proved unconvincing, the man who was about to become the leading American abstract expressionist insisted that no painter "could make a mark without drawing something."

Julian's craftsmanship was his weak point, and Pollock had clearly hit on something. The fact that he said anything at all was unusual. Quite unlike Julian, he was a diffident, solitary man with little verbal facility. Many of his contemporaries in the New York art world saw his impenetrable silences as a sign of mental deficiency. Pollock had been institutionalized and was in analysis because of periodic drinking binges. Alcohol could make him voluble but also violent and menacing, and he had been ejected from many of the bars in lower Manhattan. Like Julian, however, Pollock was plagued by doubts about his own abilities, including his own draftsmanship. Like Julian, he had been categorized 4F by his draft board. Also like Julian, his mother had dominated his childhood.

Pollock was in Provincetown because his wife, Lee Krasner, was a disciple of Hans Hofmann's. Not especially attractive, she was older than Pollock, forceful, aggressive, and controlling. Intensely competitive, Krasner and Pollock were not getting along well. Six months earlier, he had come into his own as a painter with a one-man show at Peggy Guggenheim's. He had been praised by art critic Clement Greenberg and in *Harper's Bazaar* by James Johnson Sweeney, leading the Museum of Modern Art to purchase his painting *She-wolf.* The recognition had caused him to behave bizarrely, urinating in a fireplace at a party, jerking tablecloths off restaurant tables, and flinging an easel at Hans Hofmann at another party in Provincetown early in July. Pollock had been banned from Hofmann's studio, a fact that magnified the distance between Pollock and his wife.

Frequently, during the summer, Pollock would appear at the cottage shared by Julian and Bill Simmons in a semidrunken state. Part of the cottage was used for spontaneously organized little theatricals. The atmosphere was redolent of homosexuality, mostly because Simmons was self-consciously gay and eager to proselytize. Every night, a group of six to eight men would gather there to drink and talk. The balcony was reserved for sexual encounters. In August, as the weather grew warmer, Pollock would appear at any time of day or night. He had been struggling to repress homosexual inclinations for years, but on various occasions that August, whenever he felt sufficiently enraged at his wife or drunk enough to lose himself, he participated in what Julian would subsequently categorize as drunken sexual idylls. According to Julian, the sex was usually disappointing, and Pollock was too drunk to perform adequately. Several times, Lee Krasner came searching for him, and either Julian or Simmons would pretend that he was not there. For Julian, these meetings were unsatisfactory because of their sordid, forced nature and because Pollock was so evidently wrestling with obsessive problems that caused him so much pain he had to drink himself to the precipice of oblivion. Furthermore, the act they had consummated was a sort of blind groping, more lurchingly desperate than loving.

At the end of August, Provincetown was wracked by a devastating hurricane. Unsettled by the experience with Pollock, Julian found it hard to leave. He had scheduled visits with Dr. Arkin in September, and he pleaded with his father for more time, using his painting as an excuse. Irving Beck remonstrated with Mabel, who was always more sympathetic to Julian's needs. Irving Beck was unwilling to pay Dr. Arkin for services his son would not utilize, and he was afraid of the future burden of a son who was now insisting on his need for an independent studio space. Once again, Julian was persuasive, and he was allowed to remain during September.

6. An Athenian Gallery

With Pollock and Howard Putzel, Julian believed he had made valuable connections in the art world that could help establish him as a painter. The only important gallery showing work by young Americans in New York was Peggy Guggenheim's Art of This Century. Putzel worked for Guggenheim, and Pollock had shown his work there.

The design of Art of This Century was itself a stunning statement for the new with turquoise floors, ultramarine canvas sails breaking up the four rooms, and pictures suspended from ropes or protruding from curving gumwood walls on moveable, cantilevered arms or sawed-off baseball bats. In 1944, Guggenheim's gallery was the place to exhibit for any aspiring artist, and it soon became the showcase for the abstract expressionists.

Guggenheim had a deserved reputation as an ogress of the

art world, and she looked the part. Garish, with a flashy cheapness, she would flirt compulsively with any man, even if he was gay. Her own talk was freely sexual, and she lived to shock. She had slept with Tanguy and Samuel Beckett in Paris, and was notorious for a succession of one-night stands with lesser-known men.

In October of 1944, after returning from Provincetown, Beck attended William Baziotes' opening and in November, Robert Motherwell's at Art of This Century. Julian was drawn to the work of the abstract expressionists because of the sense of mystery in their canvases and the absence of recognizable images. Their work could seem unfathomable—and, as the painter Adolph Gottlieb admitted, obsessively subterranean—with rough, unfinished surfaces; uneven textures; and dripped paint. As the critic Harold Rosenberg argued, painters did not need preconceived notions and whatever image emerged resulted from an emotional encounter with the canvas.

It was the emotional release that appealed to Julian as well as a generational identification. The abstract expressionists may have been the last generation of painters to have been completely separated from the establishment. Many of them were on the political left and feared the Nazi movement that had almost overwhelmed Europe. Barnett Newman felt the world was coming to an end during the war. Adolph Gottlieb remembered painting with "a feeling of absolute desperation." His generation "felt like derelicts," he maintained, and "everything felt hopeless and we had nothing to lose."

Charming and ingratiating, Beck fit in with Peggy Guggenheim's gay enclave. She had formed an alliance of sorts with Kenneth Macpherson, an English homosexual who had in his youth been the poet H.D.'s lover and who had married the poet Bryher for mutual convenience. With Macpherson, Guggenheim had moved into a duplex apartment in an East Side brownstone where they occupied separate floors. Guggenheim threw large parties, some of which Julian attended in the winter of 1944 and the spring of 1945, along with Jackson Pollock and Lee Krasner, Ethel and William Baziotes, and Robert Motherwell. Macpherson brought his own entourage of young gay men, whom he termed his "Athenians" and with whom Peggy would flirt.

Howard Putzel had left Art of This Century to begin his own gallery, and Guggenheim hired a new assistant, a scholarly, austere man named Marius Bewley, who spoke in a clipped, precise but assumed British accent. Bewley had once intended to become a priest, and he appeared to have stepped out of the pages of a Henry James novel—he seemed so poised one could not tell whether or not his consummate taste was the result of delicacy, breeding, or effeteness.

In his early thirties, Bewley at first was another mentorial figure for Julian, just as Simmons or Putzel had been. In the heated sexual atmosphere created by Guggenheim and Macpherson, all this changed when Bewley fell in love with him. The affair was complicated for Julian who realized how important Art of This Century could be for his own fledgling ambitions as a painter. Bewley convinced Peggy Guggenheim to include several of Julian's paintings in the "Autumn Salon" in 1945, so Julian's work was displayed along with that of Pollock, Motherwell, Baziotes, Gottlieb, and Willem de Kooning—all by then painters of some reputation. Julian felt he had been discovered.

When Julian invited Judith Malina to the gallery, however, he did not count on Guggenheim's reaction. Peggy Guggenheim disliked women whom she found boring. Bluntly, she would tell them that they didn't count for very much. She saw Judith as merely a high-school girl with book bag and bobby socks. She fully sympathized with Bewley who felt threatened by Judith and who in a petulant fit in December destroyed one of Julian's drawings in front of Guggenheim. Shortly after that incident, Julian received an extraordinary typed note from Guggenheim:

> After careful consideration of your new problem in changing your sex I have decided it would be better for you not to be connected with this very Athenian gallery. It can do you no good, and possibly great harm, and with all my maternal and friendly interest for you I feel obliged to ask you to take away

your drawings. I deeply regret this step as I like your work exceedingly well, but one cannot allow art to come first in life in such deliberate matters.

The note was angry and calculated, and it closed an important door for Julian.

7. Piscator

Judith may have well projected the image of the feckless teenager, but she had been working at the Beggar's Bar for over a year when Peggy Guggenheim ended relations with Julian in the winter of 1945. Judith needed to save a thousand dollars to register for an acting program, the Dramatic Workshop at The New School, run by Erwin Piscator, a radical German director and Bertolt Brecht's sometime collaborator.

In Germany, Piscator had been one of Rosel Malina's idols, and acting was the vocation she had forfeited for the sake of her husband's rabbinical career. She thought her daughter was exceptional—a potential Sarah Bernhardt or Rachel—and encouraged her to pursue acting. For Rosel, this may have been an act of wish fulfillment, but it was certainly a departure from convention. Nice Jewish girls, particularly if their fathers were in the rabbinate, were expected to become modestly unassuming mothers. While they could teach like Mabel Beck and her sisters, or work in a family business, they were not supposed to compete with men, voice opinions, or perform on the stage.

Judith was different. A year earlier, in part responding to what she knew about Julian's Provincetown summer, she had

tried to hitchhike to New Orleans, and had been arrested for va-
grancy in Virginia and jailed overnight in a verminous cell. It
began an early understanding of the vulnerability of the dispossessed, and it left her with a determination to act against her
powerlessness.

Energy of this sort could be released at the Beggar's Bar or
by stage acting. Her audition for Piscator in January of 1945 was
very much a demonstration of ecstatic energy. Instead of performing something from Ibsen or Chekhov, she wrote a long
poem called "Lunar Bowels." In it, she visualized herself trapped
inside the moon while yearning to return to earth:

> *voluminous universe*
> *against my cheek and thigh*
> *and pain of all space*
> > *against my breast surge*
> > *and then———*
> > *MOON*
> *my foot upon the moon*
> *my foot upon the slippery moon*
> *moon globular and light*
> *ungravitated*
> > *dance*
> > > *and*
> > > > *leap*
> *a hundred feet!*

Judith believed her poem, which continued for another fifty
lines, was written in the spirit of Pound and Cummings; it was an
unsuccessful imitation, but it expressed a terrific reaching, an explosive desire to be a comet on the stage and perform with gal-
vanic impact. As she recited or shouted it, raising her voice like
Valeska Gert's, she threw herself around like a gyrating rubber
doll. After her performance, she wished she had prepared something more conventional, a speech from *The Doll's House,* for example. Piscator was impressed by the energy she displayed and

admitted her even though he realized the pretentiousness of the performance.

Piscator would become a formative influence on Judith. A descendant of the German Lutheran clergyman who translated the Bible during the Reformation, Piscator had spent three years in the trenches during the First World War. He blamed the war on capitalism and joined the German Communist party in 1919. In Berlin, he worked with a Dadaist group that included the painter George Grosz and Brecht.

In 1927, Piscator became the director of the old Nollendorf Theatre in Berlin and with Brecht staged a version of *The Good Soldier Schweik,* a clinical history of the Austrian war machine that had done much to precipitate the First World War. Instead of the indirection of most plays about the war, Piscator bluntly depicted the mechanics of war propaganda, police spying, mobilization, and bombardment. He understood that world events, as well as one's personal life, were what constituted the most effective theatrical spectacle. The play dramatized the adventures of a Sancho Panza–like peasant who has been conscripted and has witnessed the absurdities of the war; however, what made *Schweik* into a theatrical milestone was its production. An illustration of what Piscator called "epic theatre," the *Schweik* production used an elaborate technology of complex lighting, lantern slides, Grosz's animated drawings projected on screens, placards, radios, and costumed puppet characters on two conveyor belts. The technology was Piscator's way of bringing theatre into the modern world but also a way of overpowering his audience.

In 1928, as the Weimar Republic was collapsing and economic chaos swept Germany, Piscator was greeted as a cultural hero by the radicals and democrats who sought to preserve socialism in the face of an encroaching fascism. Piscator himself wrote no plays but staged productions with a highly interpretative approach similar to the way a film director creates cinema. He agreed with the Russian director Meyerhold who had declared the need for a "tendentious drama with one object only—to serve the Revolution." Piscator's ambition was to find the sort of images that could appeal to unsophisticated audiences, a panoramic presentation that exploited the propagandistic potentials of theatre. The theatre, he believed, had to become a tribune where the people could speak.

When the Nazis assumed power in Germany, Piscator made films in Russia, coming to the United States at the invitation of the Group Theatre to stage Theodore Dreiser's *American Tragedy.* Hoping to inspire a "vanguard army" of political theatres, he remained. The New School in Greenwich Village seemed like the ideal place from which to launch such a venture, with a faculty dominated by artists and intellectuals who had left Europe to escape fascism, and a lively student body that seemed less interested in careers than the excitement of learning.

Judith Malina began studying at Piscator's Dramatic Workshop in February 1945 with classes in acting, voice control, theatre criticism and history, designing, pantomime, and dance. The schedule was demanding with classes from morning until evening. The faculty was highly diversified and international, and included Lee Strasberg and Stella Adler from the Group Theatre, and critic John Gassner. Judith played Cassandra in *Agamemnon* and had a role in *The Sheep-Well* by Lope de Vega.

After watching Piscator direct for three days, Judith decided that she wanted to direct also. Piscator thought the choice frivolous. As a teacher and director, Piscator was known for his cruelty to actors, and furthermore he distrusted women in the arts because they lacked "staying power"—that is, they had children. Stubborn, ambitious, Malina was persistent, and Piscator allowed her into his directing class although he felt she would be limited by what he once termed her "rough edges." Later, he would praise her self-analytical objectivity: "Malina takes one eye in her hand and holds it at arm's length to see what she's doing."

Aloof, obsessive, often abrupt, aristocratic in bearing and manner, full of a barely suppressed hurt rage and an affected grandeur, Piscator was intolerably egotistic and self-possessed. Judith was intimidated and admitted that she could never fully express herself to him. At the same time, Piscator stressed informality in his Dramatic Workshop, believing that actors needed to know each other well in order to achieve harmony onstage. Judith performed in Nikolai Pogodin's *Aristocrats,* a Russian constructivist play, and as the leader of a chorus in Sartre's *The Flies.*

Piscator maintained that an important part of an actor's training was political commitment and compared the actor with too much technical training to "the centipede who walks along smoothly on his one hundred feet until someone asks him which foot he moves first," confusing him to the point where he cannot walk. For Piscator, art was treacherous and dispensable. His aim was to destroy the need for it, and this led to a personal conflict with Brecht.

In May 1945, Brecht and Max Ernst visited the Dramatic workshop in a room at The New School surrounded by the murals of Thomas Hart Benton. Ernst chose one of Judith's classmates to play a sleeping beauty in *The Dreams That Money Could Buy,* a film he was making, a role for which Judith knew she was physically unfitted, as she was slight and much too short. Still, she felt heartbroken that Ernst had not even noticed her.

Piscator, who had a reputation for being commercially unreliable, pressed Brecht to select some of his students for a production of *The Private Life of the Master Race,* but Brecht felt he needed famous actors and a Broadway production to call attention to his play. The incident damaged an historical partnership.

The most joyous event of the summer of 1945 was the night in mid-August that Julian and Judith went to Times Square to celebrate the official end of the war. Crowned with streamers, kissing strangers, they were caught in a euphoric wave of hope for the world. There was, however, a dark shadow: a month earlier, in a desert location near Los Alamos, New Mexico, an extraordinary team of scientists led by J. Robert Oppenheimer had detonated a prototype of the atomic bomb, releasing the most potentially destructive energy ever imagined.

Piscator had allowed Julian to audit his classes, which motivated him to resume his undergraduate education at City College.

Mabel Beck had been pressuring her son to return to Yale, which Julian had decided was too bourgeois. Irving Beck's attitude to his son's painting had improved since Julian's work had been shown at Peggy Guggenheim's "Autumn Salon," and he agreed to pay for a studio where Julian could paint in privacy if he went to City College. This school was known as the proletarian Harvard on the Hudson because of an outstanding faculty and a heterogeneous, though highly motivated student body; and Julian would study there from the spring of 1946 through 1948. He did well in his literature and foreign language classes but performed perfunctorily in required subjects and the sciences.

Living at home, so to some extent still governed by parental expectations, Julian still dressed like a dandy and played the role of an Edwardian gentleman. No matter how gallant he appeared, he felt somehow humiliated as a student because his more extravagant impulses had to be curtailed, and much of his creativity was now directed toward completing academic requirements. At the same time, he could seem self-righteous and vengeful as in his attitude toward Ezra Pound, who had collaborated with the Italian fascists and was brought to Washington, D.C., for trial. To his classmates, Beck insisted that Pound "was a corrupt and infectious being" who should be executed so as to rid the world of an "evil influence." This was the view of a young Jew who had been affected by the war, but it was one he would eventually revise, especially pertaining to the issue of execution.

Judith and Julian were still attending the theatre with regularity. In the spring of 1946, they were left speechless and enchanted by Katharine Cornell in Jean Anouilh's *Antigone* and by Judith Anderson in *Medea*. Both Judith and Julian were equally overwhelmed by the Old Vic with Laurence Olivier in *Oedipus Tyrannos*. Theatre was their preoccupation, but as Piscator had taught, Broadway was treacherous, a place committed more to financial success than any ideals in which a person could believe. According to Piscator, actors could not grow or evolve on Broadway.

After three years of speculation and dreaming, Judith and Julian were ready for the first steps leading to an experimental, repertory company in which they could direct or act in plays they thought were important. The idea of repertory—of staging a series of plays reflecting different interests and various kinds of exploration—was crucial and a sign of the sort of commitment that Piscator maintained was missing from Broadway.

Judith and Julian's intention was to begin with a play by Cocteau, and they wrote to him for permission to stage his *Antigone, Orpheus,* or *The Infernal Machine.* They wrote some fifty letters to artists they admired, among them W. H. Auden; Martha Graham; the actress Eva Le Gallienne who had started her own repertory company on Fourteenth Street; the scenic designer Aline Bernstein; and Stella Adler, who with Harold Clurman had been one of the main figures in the Group Theatre in the 1930s. Judith wrote to E. E. Cummings, requesting permission to stage *Him,* stating in perhaps overinflated terms that she hoped her theatre would be a place of nobility, poetry, beauty, and magic. Finally, Julian placed an advertisement for a "literate theater group" in the *Saturday Review of Literature,* asking for actors and soliciting plays.

Theatre was what connected Judith and Julian, and together they had begun a collection of memorabilia, including old playbills and photographs of actors, which they kept in a trunk in Julian's studio. One of Judith's particular interests, for example, was Sarah Bernhardt, whose fearsome determination, physicality, and emotional extravagance resembled her own. But the figure whom she most revered was Rachel, the nineteenth-century star of the Comédie Française, whose classic purity as an actress contrasted to Bernhardt's more decadent posturing. Rachel had been an impoverished Jewish child who mixed easily with the upper clases who venerated her, though her sympathies would remain with the people. A free spirit who could consort with royalty, in 1848 during the revolutionary turmoil that seized Europe, she recited "La Marseillaise"—the battle cry of the revolution—on the stage of the Comédie Française, and the audience went wild. Rabbi Malina had had a photograph of Rachel that Judith found in his study after his death, magnifying her importance. To a certain extent, poring over this collection was a learning process for Judith and Julian, a way to mine an extended fantasy of identification.

8. Searching for Love

Using bold capital letters, Judith wrote in the notebook she kept at the Dramatic Workshop that "THERE IS NO FACT OF HUMAN NATURE ALIEN TO MYSELF." This citation from Terence may help explain her pursuit of Julian who remained noncommittal, elusive, and fundamentally ambivalent about his need for women. He was still in analysis with Dr. Arkin, listening to her advice to deny his homosexual yearnings and marry.

In the summer of 1946—when Julian was off hiking in the Sierras—Judith entered into her first serious sexual relationship with a thirty-year-old student of Piscator's. Born in an Austrian castle, Harald Brixel was handsome, tall, and sophisticated. His father had noble blood, and Harald was aristocratic, proud, strict in his correctness, and arrogant. Brixel loved opera and music, and in the winter of 1946–47, frequently took Judith to the Metropolitan Opera where he made her follow musical scores, disciplining her hand with his pencil every time her eye strayed to the stage.

She was still seeing Julian. Even if he felt threatened by her affair with Brixel, he professed to understand. They continued to pursue the dream of their repertory theatre, which seemed a small step closer to realization when Cocteau replied to Julian's letter with permission to stage *The Infernal Machine*.

During the spring of 1947, Judith was more often with Harald than with Julian. The affair was romantically colored by her mother's opposition. As a result of the war, Rosel Malina hated anything Germanic, and felt that Harald would only deceive her daughter and exploit her innocence and use her sexually. Judith exchanged daily letters with Brixel and would listen to his recordings of Wagner's *Tristan and Isolde.* But there were problems between the lovers: a mannered European, Harald was unable to understand American casualness and interpreted Judith's exuberance as unsophisticated. At the end of the spring semester, he returned to Vienna to pursue a musical career.

Though Judith felt deserted by the man she believed was the love of her life, she was resilient enough to plunge into work. She was inspired by her reading of Hallie Flanagan's *Arena,* an account of how the Works Progress Administration sponsored a national network of regional theatres to employ actors and artists during the Depression, and to give voice to the common people.

The arduous work, however, was rehearsing the role of Zenobia in the Onstage Company's dramatization of *Ethan Frome.* When the play opened at the Cherry Lane—a theatre on a horseshoe-shaped curving street in the Village—Julian sent fourteen long-stemmed roses. She performed for three weeks in July, at the same time rehearsing the role of a woman who had lost two sons in the war in the verse drama *The Dog beneath the Skin,* by W. H. Auden and Christopher Isherwood.

Periodically, she was troubled by a form of stage fright. She had started "breaking" at the Dramatic Workshop, an involuntary laughter that disturbed the rhythm of any performance. Though it could have provided little comfort, renowned nineteenth-century performers like Edwin Booth, Ellen Terry, and Henry Irving suffered from a similar condition, as did the great Russian director Stanislavsky and Laurence Olivier. Art, as William James had asserted, was like religion in that it depended on a "willing suspension of disbelief," and "believability" was an instrinsic problem for the theatre, as the ridiculousness of certain roles and lines made it difficult for some performers to concentrate. Judith understood that the absurdity so often implicit in an anachronistic role could create a vulnerability that paradoxically empowered the actor, and she felt intoxicated by the communal aspect of theatre with "everyone working for the same end."

Judith saw much more of Julian in the summer of 1947, despite the hours spent performing and rehearsing. One day they went to Coney Island, walking at the edge of the water with their shoes in their hands, singing, and then wading in the sea. On another weekend at Marsh Pond in the Berkshires—a favorite spot that Julian had discovered as a Boy Scout—Julian spoke of their future together. Early in August, they became lovers as well as best friends, but marriage was something Judith wanted and Julian dreaded.

For most of August, Judith was onstage in *The Dog beneath the Skin*. Modest, self-effacing, calling himself only half a playwright, Isherwood himself addressed the cast. At a party after the play closed, a film maker told Julian he was looking for scripts; and subsequently, Julian and Judith began to collaborate on one, reading Cocteau's *Diary of a Film* for inspiration. They were also seeing a series of mostly German films from the 1930s at the Museum of Modern Art, including Pabst's *Threepenny Opera* with Valeska Gert, and Leni Riefenstahl's *Olympiad* with Adolph Hitler smiling under the Nazi flag.

Carl Dreyer's film *The Passion of Joan of Arc* so moved Judith that she cried throughout it. The then little-known Antonin Artaud—whose lean, ascetic face with its deep burning eyes was captured in overwhelming close-ups—played the spiritual monk who supports the defiant Joan as she mounts the stake. The film struck some chord in Judith that made her break down, weeping almost out of control for the next few days.

Julian had been unsuccessfully searching for a suitable theatre space. He had also shown some of his paintings to Sam Kootz, an art dealer sponsoring many of the abstract expressionists. Kootz felt that Julian's work was insufficiently commercial and that it would not sell. It was a judgment that might have been applied to Julian's entire future.

Perennially optimistic, Julian was not discouraged. The rejection, however, made him volatile and more sensitive than ever. Judith had been pressuring him to declare his love and decide on marriage. She knew that there existed what she called peculiarities in their relationship and that Julian had been to some extent damaged by his mother's incessant pampering, but she felt it was necessary to force the issue or there would be no resolution. At the same time, Judith suffered the gnawing worry that in marriage she might lose her identity as her mother had and the possibility of becoming an artist. At the same time, she knew that only getting away from her mother could give her the space she needed as an artist.

Just before Halloween, at the Yale-Harvard game in New Haven, with Julian sophomorically drunk, they quarreled fiercely over the question of marriage, and all possibilities seemed scrambled, then held in abeyance. What kept them in touch with each other were the responses to the letters they had written from poets E. E. Cummings and Alfred Kreymborg, and from set designer Robert Edmund Jones. The tie that still held them together, however slim it seemed, was the mutual dream of their own theatre.

Cummings lived in a cramped apartment on Patchin Place in the Village, and they visited him, full of awe and anticipation, on a rainy afternoon at the end of October. Engaging, full of stories about Lost Generation writers, Cummings entertained them for several hours with Dubonnet, cake, and talk about architecture, burlesque, and his play *Him*, which he was willing to allow them to stage.

A week later, they saw Robert Edmond Jones. A symbolist who believed that designers should never be too explicit, Jones realized that the stage could never duplicate the mimetic exactness of film. Instead of historical accuracy, Jones was interested in an evocation that resulted in a total immersion in the design process, painting every detail of the set himself, and draping and pinning every costume. He was famous for a version of *Macbeth* in the early 1920s that featured an enormous trio of masks above an almost empty stage.

In their initial letter to Jones, Beck and Malina quoted key

passages from an essay he had written for *Theatre Arts* magazine that described the qualities he sought. Realistic theatre
was less than a century old, but already it was sterile, Jones argued. Without experimentation, there could be no renewal, and
experiment was less a matter of money than eagerness and
imagination. Jones told Judith and Julian they could do theatre
without money, that they should keep their productions small,
that they could use sofa cushions for sets if no other resources
were available.

Jones's own work had become slick and conventional, but he
admired Julian's drawings and designs for *The Infernal Machine*
and even offered the use of his magnificent studio as a theatre.
Although they never took advantage of the offer, it was generous.
Jones encouraged them, and his notions of design would become
a model for Julian in the future.

Matters with Kreymborg were more complicated. When Judith and Julian first visited, Kreymborg was delighted to hear that
they wanted to perform one of his plays. Sixty-four years old,
Kreymborg had written poetry and lived in Greenwich Village
most of his life. Kreymborg knew Piscator, and was a champion of
experiment and poetry in the theatre, exactly the qualities Judith
and Julian hoped to combine.

Kreymborg read to them from *The Wooden Horse,* a cumber-
some, archaic play he was writing about the Trojan War. Later, in
Washington Square, he told them about his experiences with
Eliot, Pound, H.D., and O'Neill at the Provincetown Playhouse.

A week later, he called Judith on the pretext that he had completed his play and wanted her to hear its conclusion. When she
arrived, he read her a recently completed love poem and claimed
to have fallen in love with her. The situation was awkward because Kreymborg, who could have been her grandfather, became
fumblingly ardent; yet he represented ideas that were important
to Judith. *Esquire* had just published "No More War," one of his
dramatic poems, and he was working for the third-party candidacy of Henry Wallace, who in 1947 seemed like an alternative
to the Republican old-boy smugness of Dewey and the machine-

oiled politics of Truman. The poem against war and the stand for Wallace were issues Judith could respect, though she wondered about Kreymborg's veracity when he boasted about ghostwriting Woodrow Wilson's campaign speeches. Kreymborg's worst feature was the dominating arrogance of his conversation, which rarely permitted space for another speaker. As an artist, even if a very minor one, he was thirty years past his prime. His work had always suffered from a stilted, unnatural quality. He was a figure of the past, and because of his romantic delusions, Judith knew a certain distance would be necessary.

9. To Have or to Have Not

The meetings with Cummings, Jones, and Kreymborg could not disguise the unhealed split between Judith and Julian, and what she referred to as their "strained situation" caused by the "breach" at the Yale-Harvard game. To escape Julian in the winter of 1948, she found work as a psychiatric aide in an asylum in Hartford, Connecticut.

The Hartford Institute for Living was for the wealthy, a facility without walls, and with beautiful grounds and ample opportunities for athletics. Stressing readjustment and rehabilitation, the institute's treatment resulted in what Judith saw as a cosmetic cure. The four months she spent working there were a protracted lesson in the relativity of sanity and the ways society could categorize and ostracize the ill.

At the institute, she saw suffering daily: gurgling, spitting patients emerging from shock treatment; others lying naked on linoleum floors in a catatonic stupor, or wandering the halls as they gestured and grimaced in heated conversation with hallucinations. One night, afraid that she might fall asleep while on duty, she learned from a nurse's aide how to use Benzedrine, tearing off a piece of the drug-soaked paper from an inhaler, which she then dropped into Coca-Cola.

In her own room for the first time in her life, she read André Gide's *Journals,* then *Beowulf* and *The Canterbury Tales* because Julian was reading them at City College; she also struggled with *Tristram Shandy* because Julian recommended it. She sent Julian a handmade Valentine's Day card, cutting a heart, a snail, and a butterfly out of an old *Vogue*—obvious symbols.

In the middle of March, she visited Julian, examining their collection of theatre memorabilia in his studio. Julian's fear of commitment seemed to be assuaged by the coming of spring. Early in April, Judith left the institute, returned to New York, and found work at an aptitude testing service. In a dilapidated Fifth Avenue mansion, she marked and filed papers, and administered tests.

With Julian, she went to the office of a lawyer who presented them with the papers incorporating The Living Theatre, an embossed stock book, and a corporate seal. The step seemed empty because there was as yet no physical basis for their plans.

Dismissed without explanation from her job with the aptitude service, Judith found another one in a book-and-card shop whose wares bore platitudinous messages, where she read obscure historical novels when the store was quiet, which got her fired again. She was distressed by a recurrence of her mother's physical complaints of fatigue and insomnia. Rosel Malina refused to discuss the situation and dreaded the imminent prospect of hospitalization. Judith accompanied her mother to the Mount Sinai clinic for cancer tests, and reading Thomas Mann's essay on *Faust* made little sense to her in the surrounding babel of languages.

Mother and daughter were infected with a depression that settled in their "stomachs like a strong phantom," aggravated by the fact that Julian, finished with his semester at City College, had arranged for a bicycle trip in Vermont. Judith interpreted the holiday as a desertion at the moment when she most needed Julian's support. His weakness, she concluded, was a lack of warmth, a reluctance to accept intimacy that protected him like a shield. Julian could be clever, diplomatic, coquettish, she realized, but also still seemed trapped behind a dark veil that Dr. Arkin had been unable to rip away and that prevented him from seeing clearly.

Hospitalized and then discharged after a mastectomy, Rosel's condition worsened. Unable to eat because of the stress, Judith lost weight. The saving grace in the situation was work in the theatre. When she visited Kreymborg, he asked her to stage his "No More War" poem for the Wallace political action committee. Still keeping Kreymborg at arm's length, she agreed to direct the piece, though she knew that finding actors to work without pay would be difficult. The atmosphere at the Wallace headquarters on Park Avenue was unsatisfying, unconvincing, and amateurish. Although Wallace himself sounded like a droning civil servant—dull, repetitious, humorless, an uninspired compromise—Judith was enthusiastic about his candidacy and wanted to help.

One distraction that summer was a new friend, Pierre Garai, whom Julian had met at City College. A tall, elegant Frenchman, with dark, sallow skin and doe eyes, Garai wanted to write fiction. Pretentious and snobbish, he had published a review of Albert Camus's novel *The Plague* in the *New Leader*. Garai would accompany them to Jones Beach on the bus or by car when they could borrow Irving Beck's Oldsmobile. Garai loved to declaim the poetry of Algernon Swinburne, and with Julian would recite "A Forsaken Garden," drunk on Swinburne's luxuriance of sound. Julian soon became infatuated with Garai, probably because Garai's pose of elitist arrogance was something he recognized in himself, a mirror image he needed to pursue. When Judith mocked Julian's flirtation with her own feminine overtures to Garai, she was bewildered by an antagonism she found inexplicable and unwarranted. She thought that Garai wanted her to fall in love with him and declare that love, so that he could then scorn and repudiate it. The incipient though unconsummated triangle foreshadowed future competitions for third parties that would complicate Judith and Julian's relationship.

Arch, outspoken, Garai was a catalyst, and his conversation often acted as a stimulant. Once, when he left them on Jones Beach to return early to the city, Judith and Julian hitchhiked over a hundred miles to Southampton to see a production of *Romeo and Juliet.* Sunburned, after eight different rides, they arrived in the second act to see José Ferrer overplaying the role of Romeo, and they spent the night at the home of an actor friend whom they had met during an intermission. The incident was typical of a youthful giddiness that often swept Judith and Julian together. As Judith would later remember it in her *Diary,* if she and Julian seemed irresponsible or thoughtless at times, "we at least loved ourselves and adored our hopes and lived for the moment and for the future and felt the whole wide universe was ours." Rather than being simply facile, the attitude was part of the celebration of youth. For many, the late forties may not have represented a pinnacle of human achievement, but for Julian the age possessed "all the glory the world would ever contain," and he sought to enjoy it.

Julian spent much of the summer of 1948 in his studio painting. Judith thought some of the work seemed forced but admitted she could hardly gauge it objectively. She was occupied with Gide's *Journals* and copied into her own a passage on the unique properties drama afforded when it avoided reality and turned in a more experimental manner "towards effects that belong to it alone."

For money, she found a job selling French fashion magazines to Seventh Avenue designers but lost it in a week, more interested in studying French and working on her own play *Damocles.* When she found another job as a salesclerk at Barnes & Noble, she was dismissed again, this time caught on the sales floor reading Kafka's "Metamorphosis".

By the middle of August, the change in Julian that she had

noticed in the spring was more apparent, and they were using his studio as a love nest, talking about marriage and a baby. In Boston to see museums and visit the Keats collection at Harvard, they quarreled again. Judith realized that she felt periodic fits of dislike for Julian, whose temper was explosive whenever they fought, and who could become rough and vulgar. Returning to the studio, they made love again, and Judith decided that at twenty-three, Julian was much too young, and that he also lacked both tenderness and fragility. Yet, the following morning, she admitted to her *Diary* that she felt like a high-school girl in love.

In the sculpture garden of the Museum of Modern Art, they met Pierre Garai who spoke about *The Kinsey Report,* which had alleged a high incidence of homosexuality in American life, and Gore Vidal's *The City and the Pillar,* one of the first American fictions to openly depict gay life. Pierre speculated on the universality of homosexuality, provoking a denunciatory tirade from Julian. That evening, they saw Marlene Dietrich in *The Blue Angel,* in an audience that seemed to consist primarily of gay young men in seersucker suits, Julian observed, as subtle confirmation of Pierre Garai's insinuations. When Pierre and Julian left together for another Vermont bicycle trip, Judith again felt abandoned, especially because this time she suspected she was pregnant.

Judith had completed writing her play *Damocles,* and she knew that she had already given birth to a publishable poem. *Neurotica,* an important little magazine, had taken a love poem about Julian and transformed it into prose. She read an article in *Neurotica* entitled "Why Homosexuals Marry," while struggling with the awareness that although she feared marriage to Julian quite as much as he did to her, "there seems little else left open for me."

10. A Child Bride and a Little Boy A-Wooing

In the fall of 1948, after they had known each other for five years, the seesaw struggle over marriage was settled when Judith confirmed that she was indeed pregnant. At first, Julian maintained his ambivalence about marriage—thinking the child could be raised in the spirit of free love. Shocked—no one could even utter a dirty word in her presence—Rosel Malina threatened to place her head in an oven unless he took the proper course and married her daughter. Julian agreed, though perhaps not without trepidation, and introduced his parents to Rosel.

Instead of relief, Judith felt considerable irritation because of the necessary preparations. She chafed at the "endless banalities of the marketplace," and at what she considered Irving Beck's affluence and his reactionary political opinions, feeling discomfort because he had a live-in domestic.

The actual ceremony took place at City Hall minutes before closing time on 22 October 1948, in a room papered with roses for war brides. Judith was twenty-two and Julian a year older. No parents were present, and they had no wedding rings. When the justice of the peace requested them, Julian removed the keys from his key ring and used it despite the justice's obvious displeasure at the broken band. The spontaneous informality of the act, however, suggested that the dandified bachelor persona was moulting, ready for a change.

He must have been nervous though. When he had to sign the marriage register, he broke his pen, blotting his name and Judith's with black ink, an ambiguous symbol at best. Later, at dinner with the Becks, Judith wept at the table. She felt completely drained, washed away, and bleached. After dinner, she returned to her mother's room since Rosel would not allow her daughter to live with Julian prior to a religious ceremony.

A week after the hastily improvised City Hall process, the Becks drove Judith and her mother to Danbury, Connecticut, where they were married a second time by Rabbi Jerome Malino, Judith's first cousin. The rabbi—who had a congregation in Danbury but was also ominously a chaplain at the Danbury Penitentiary—declared the marriage an act of affirmation in a world that often destroyed all faith in man. With a Gideon Bible next to their bed, the newlyweds spent the night in a hotel and took the bus the following morning to New Haven, spending the day with acting students in the Yale theatre.

They returned to the city in time for the election. More important to them than Truman's victory was the fact that they had found a basement on Wooster Street that they hoped to use as a theatre space.

Even more encouraging was a trip they made to Rutherford, New Jersey, to visit William Carlos Williams. One of the three or four most important modern American poets, Williams was still unrecognized by the larger public and very conscious of his failure to have found the audience that someone like Eliot had found. Living modestly in a working-class area, he had retired from his pediatric practice. Williams was cheerful, unassuming, with the excited exuberance of a teenager, and Julian was mystified by the lack of any characteristic that would distinguish his personality as that of a writer. Stern, stoic, resigned, his wife Flossie sat in an overstuffed chair looking like a figure in a Grant Wood painting.

Judith and Julian wanted to stage Williams's *Many Loves.* After telling them about acting in Kreymborg's *Lima Beans* with the Provincetown Players, Williams gave them the genesis of his own play. When he was an intern at the French Hospital in Man-

hattan, a husky two-hundred-pound laborer who had been injured while helping to build Pennsylvania Station was brought to
the emergency room. Undressing him, the nurses discovered that
he was wearing pink lace lingerie with bows and silk stockings.
Later, an older man, obviously genteel and wealthy, came to the
hospital and paid for everything. The laborer and his patron
would become models for the homosexual relationship between
the producer and the director in Williams's play; and, to some
extent, the fact that Julian was so drawn to it reveals his interest
in subject matter previously considered taboo.

As a couple—no matter how condescendingly Dr. Williams
treated his wife—they had endured and in that sense provided
Judith and Julian with a testimonial of sorts. At first, however,
Judith was quite unsure about the solidity of her marriage. They
had planned to live in Julian's ice blue room in the Becks' apartment. Living with her in-laws, with her husband at school most
mornings, proved more oppressive than Judith had anticipated,
and she broke down in frequent spasms of weeping. Her marriage
seemed like a puppet play in which she was the child bride with
child and Julian was the "little boy a-wooing."

Julian's parents suggested that the crying indicated a need
for psychoanalytical help, and his analyst recommended Ralph
Jacoby, a young Freudian whom Judith began seeing every other
afternoon.

Much of November and December of 1948 was spent preparing the Wooster Street space. The tiny basement could only accommodate thirty seats at most, and since it could never conform
to the fire code, it could never be licensed. Kreymborg gave them
a list of names as possible subscribers, and they were encouraged by the initial response from Robert Edmond Jones and the
poet Babette Deutsch. With a two-hundred-dollar investment,
they planned to begin with a medieval morality play—Williams's
play had too many characters. "Chamber drama," Paul Goodman
called it when they visited for dinner. Goodman read to them
from *Faustina,* a play he had just completed about the wife of Marcus Aurelius that drew on the *Meditations.*

Despite weeks of preparation, designing a set, and interviewing actors the Wooster Street project foundered before it ever really began. When Judith tried to place a call for actors in the *Daily News*, she was informed that her notice sounded more like a lure for a brothel or the white slave trade than for a play, and the paper refused to print it.

Julian had not been enthusiastic about the cramped basement, and he was distracted by the demands of his classes. Disillusioned, unhappy with her domestic arrangements, Judith gave in and abandoned the Wooster Street project. She informed Ezra Pound, writing to him at St. Elizabeth's in Washington, D.C., where he was confined, that the theatre had been shut down, suspected of being a front for a brothel. "How else can one run a seeryous teeyater in N.Y.?" Pound scrawled on a postcard in his backwoods burlesque orthography.

While Pound's card seemed an appropriate comment on the Wooster Street fiasco, it could not relieve Judith's unhappiness. Neither did the psychoanalysis with Dr. Jacoby. What he claimed as progress, she saw only as haphazard inconsequential confession. Though it seemed congratulatory to spend a few hours a week talking about herself, it was like talking to the gray wallpaper or the frazzled carpet in Jacoby's room, because his presence was a silent one.

Miserable, anxious to change her situation, Judith found some comfort in Paul Goodman. One afternoon, she audited his class at NYU. With Julian, she had been reading Goodman's essays in *Art and Social Nature*, intrigued by his concept of "drawing the line," taking a stand on some moral point beyond which an individual could no longer be coerced by the superior power of the state. The "line" was a basis of libertarian principle, Goodman explained over another dinner at his Chelsea loft. Goodman and his wife, Sally, were warm and accepting Judith observed, and the permissiveness they preached was evident in the freedom they gave to their infant son, Matthew Ready, even giving him a little beer when he reached for it. As a moralist, Goodman could be exasperating but usually in a tonic manner, and his insistence was tempered by humility, a sense of anguish over the world's disasters, and a recognition of his own involvement in the mess humans were making on the planet.

As a belated wedding gift and as a way to brighten Judith's outlook, Mabel and Irving Beck agreed to pay for a honeymoon trip to Mexico. Out of the windows of the train to New Orleans, Judith was only able to focus on the poverty of the shabby, weathered Negro shacks. In New Orleans, they saw Olivier in a filmed version of *Hamlet* and an awful local attempt to perform *Macbeth*. They walked around the French Quarter and went to a nightclub, but the whole area looked more like a stage set than anything real.

Mexico City was overwhelming because of its poverty: the barefoot beggar boys, the peasants selling religious articles, a man without arms weaving baskets with his toes. Judith proposed that their projected theatre should attempt to relate to such people, not just to the middle-class patrons who could afford to purchase seats. Repelled by the luxury of their hotel, she speculated that Julian was "too eager to see the good," and it was her implicit expectation that what they would see in Mexico would open his eyes.

In Taxco, the silver town south of Mexico City, Judith argued that primitive conditions were unimproved by the government as a means of attracting tourists. A blind beggar boy, with suppurating sores in place of eyes, stopped them, begging for alms, and Judith screamed in revulsion. For Julian, the lesson in their honeymoon was hard and bitter: the blind beggar boy became an epiphany, moving him closer to Judith's position that assisting the impoverished untouchables of the world had to become the real object of their work in the theatre. For years, they would remember the blind beggar boy as a symbol of what it was they wanted to change about the world.

ll
Experiments

11. Anarchists and Babies

For Judith, living with the Becks meant becoming a "prisoner of family life." In the spring of 1949, seven months advanced in pregnancy, she found it impossible to tolerate the sounds of Mabel and her friends playing mah-jongg, and Irving playing cards with his friends. Judith found herself living with a domineering mother-in-law who saw Julian as a sort of prince.

Dr. Jacoby's bland evaluation that she was rebelling seemed to lack profundity, but she admitted that without rebellion, she would only feel impotent. Julian suggested moving into the studio when the child was born, but that meant living in a fire hazard, three flights up, without heat.

As if to shut out such pressing concerns, they escaped almost every night to the theatre, opera, or film. Broadway theatre was as dull as "anonymous messages received during sleep," Julian observed. In New Haven with Piscator, they saw a mediocre production of *Faust* and, under the Manhattan Bridge, the Peking opera, whose staging would have a profound influence on The Living Theatre. Judith read J. B. Rhine on telepathic communication and Pound's "Pisan Cantos" as annotated by Julian. Pound, she reflected, like Wilde, was the poet imprisoned to learn pity and discover his humanity.

A distant relation of the Becks, who happened to live across the street on Ninety-ninth and West End Avenue, moved out of a seven-room apartment. With cartons, like gypsies in the night, Judith and Julian occupied the space knowing they lacked a landlord's permission. Two days later, they were chilled by Winston Churchill's Iron Curtain speech.

In his final weeks at City College, Julian reluctantly went to work for his father. When he was informed that he was one credit shy of graduation—because he had characteristically registered for certain English electives without the necessary prerequisites—he refused to complete his degree on some vague, undefined anarchistic principle. It was less a case of "drawing the line" than youthful rebellion, but there was little his parents could do about it. And even though one of his paintings was accepted in a group show at the Laurel Gallery, he felt vanquished by school and work.

Under anesthesia, on 17 May, Judith delivered a tiny son whom they named Garrick. Judith thought the name had a noble theatrical ring, but her mother detested it. Weeping in the hospital, she said it sounded too Irish. As soon as she left the hospital, Judith discontinued her analysis with Jacoby, who had been unable to help her. In their final session, he had explained that her neurosis related to her feelings about her mother. Rosel's reaction to her pregnancy had been that it was a disgrace, enough to provoke threats of suicide, and Rosel's inability to accept her grandson's name was yet another sign of irreconcilable generational differences.

Garrick looked like her father, Judith concluded, and she spent the summer caring for him. While she was glad to hear that they would be able to keep the apartment, this was balanced by the fact that Mabel could come to visit her grandson daily. Judith spent all her time with her new son, working on poems and reading. She read *Paradise Lost, To the Lighthouse,* André Gide's account of traveling in the Congo, Lewis Mumford on utopia, and began to lose herself in the vast sumptuousness of Proust. Two writers who particularly impressed her were Joseph Campbell, who in his *Hero with a Thousand Faces* argued that all action was ultimately illusory, a notion that stung the activist side of her, and James Agee, whose personal history of southern sharecroppers, *Let Us Now Praise Famous Men,* was tremendously moving, reminding her of the poverty she had seen from the train going to Mexico and that political reality could be presented aesthetically.

Mabel Beck gave them an eight-millimeter camera to record Garrick's first movements, but Julian was more interested in the camera as a way to learn how to make a film. He could hardly bear working for his father, and the inventory of motorcycle parts seemed meaningless. Using packing cartons from Beck Distributing as tables, and with Rosel's torn lace curtains on the windows, they had a small gathering with Pierre Garai, who seemed all selfish ambition to Judith, and one of Julian's professors who read from *Finnegans Wake* to demonstrate its unintelligibility. Always rebellious, Julian read from Tennyson to prove the same point.

As a lesson in coherence, in Robert Motherwell's Eighth Street loft, they saw an anarchist group without stage or facilities perform Paul Goodman's *Faustina* in stifling summer heat to a packed house. Another evening, Bill Simmons visited to show off a sailor lover. Loud, dressed in expensive clothes, boorishly laughing at his own jokes, Simmons seemed to Judith a man of unfulfilled potentials, so full of himself that no one else counted in his company.

Simmons was so flamboyantly gay that he reminded Judith of the alternative path her husband had been counseled to overcome. Julian had completed his analysis with Dr. Arkin but was still touchy and unsettled on the question of gay life. At a party at the Goodmans, with Harold Norse, whom Julian had known in Provincetown, and the poet Edouard Roditi, much of the talk was about homosexuality. Judith observed that her husband frequently seized her hand during the evening, perhaps as a way of denying this other part of his sexuality.

Judith resumed making the rounds of theatrical producers that fall, leaving her son with her mother, a fact that—along with her unwillingness to cook—she hid from Mabel. Looking for work as an actress was a wearying procedure that for three years had resulted in only rudeness and rejection. She had not performed since the Cherry Lane and felt constrained, contemplating the difficulty of a life in the theatre while Garrick was so young.

Expressing disappointment with his painting, Julian gave up his studio in November, intending to use one of the rooms in the apartment instead. With Judith, he attended Motherwell's opening at the Sam Kootz Gallery, a series of collages that seemed like "brilliant flashes." A few days later, they heard Cummings read at the 92nd Street YMHA. Harold Norse was at the reading and so was another poet, Claude Fredericks, whose gentle manner imbued him with a mystical air.

Fredericks was a friend of Bill Simmons's, whom Julian had met in 1944. He had graduated from Harvard and met Anaïs Nin; with Nin's printing press, Fredericks learned how to set type and produce elegant books. He divided his time between New York and Vermont, and ran the Banyan Press, a very small publishing house that specialized in finely wrought handprinted books. Julian invited Norse, Fredericks, and another writer named Walter McElroy, whose translation of Tristran Corbière had been published by Banyan, to his house after the reading. The talk ran to anarchism—a friend had renounced his citizenship and destroyed his passport—which they interpreted as an anarchist act.

The subject of anarchism was important to them, and on another night, Julian and Judith went to a talk by Paul Goodman on anarchist and pacifist morality. Goodman de-emphasized the traditional association of violence and disorder with anarchism, which had originated in the late nineteenth-century history of political assassination and bombing in Europe. In the United States, in 1892, Henry Clay Frick, manager of Andrew Carnegie's steel operations, had almost been assassinated by Alexander Berkman, consort of the notorious Emma Goldman, and President McKinley had been murdered by a self-proclaimed anarchist in 1901.

A salvationist expression of romantic individualism, anarchism was a nineteenth-century reaction to the concentrated powers of the centralizing state, such as the oppression of the czars in Russia. Goodman understood there was no longer any place for the extremist terrorism of Bakunin, who in Russia had represented the destructive edge of anarchism and led to its sinister reputation. Goodman spoke more about an ideal, as in the Russian Prince Kropotkin's notions of mutual aid and the voluntary association of self-reliant, self-supporting communities. For Goodman, the real focal point of anarchism was a respect for the autonomy of all individuals. Goodman denied the Hobbesian principle that war and competition are the natural condition, and Adam Smith's contention that most people try to improve their own place in the world rather than care about the world itself. Order does not depend on punitive laws administered by a repressive hierarchy, and society has no inherent need for an oppressed underclass doomed to suffer. Unlike Darwin's notion of survival of the fittest or Mill's utilitarianism, which essentially were nineteenth-century attempts to rationalize the inequities of wealth and power, Goodman's advocacy of an egalitarian ethic had great appeal for Judith and Julian.

Congenial, always extending himself, Goodman was becoming a good friend of Judith and Julian's. As a spokesman for a nonviolent, pacifist anarchism, Goodman offered a theoretical and philosophical guide for future action. He also tried to help in more pragmatic ways. When Julian began investigating the feasibility of building a Quonset hut to house their yet unborn theatre, Goodman introduced him to his brother, Percival, an eminent architect. Julian and Percival met with a number of city officials but soon realized that building a new structure required much more money than occupying one that was extant and only needed renovation, so the matter was dropped.

Judith had been receiving the anarchist newsletter *Resistance* for seven years. There, in the fall of 1949, she read an essay by Emile Armand on the idea of a moneyless society that convinced her that anarchism was an appropriate attitude in a time when the power of the state seemed more threatening than ever. Earlier in the summer, when on Centre Street to get a learner's permit to drive a car, she saw a group of demonstrators in front of a courthouse denouncing the trial of eleven leading American Communists. Impulsively, she entered the courthouse and watched the proceedings, realizing that what was really on trial was the freedom to disagree with one's own government.

In one sense, her anarchism was reactive, a rejection of the folly of her refugee mother's blind trust in the American system. More subtly, it countered the settled state of marriage. In the matter of anarchism, as in the matter of forming a theatre, she moved Julian in the direction she felt was necessary. Julian was prepared to accept the turn toward anarchism, because of the economic injustices he had witnessed on the trip to Mexico the previous winter. But by choosing anarchism, Beck and Malina made themselves marginal in America.

12. Broken Love

There was no sudden decision to wave the black flag of anarchism or to proselytize Kropotkin's theories. Instead, Judith and Julian plunged into the cultural life of the city. During the winter of 1950, Judith read a magazine article describing the "New Bohemia," and thought it was decadent and possibly poisonous to be part of it even though it seemed like the frivolous part of Judith's constituency. At a party for Anaïs Nin, a pampered princess of 1930s Parisian bohemia, she listened to Alfred Kreymborg talk endlessly about himself. Paul Goodman was also at the party, optimistic about the future possibilities of The Living Theatre.

That winter, Judith read two plays that she found appropriate for her future theatre: Gertrude Stein's reworking of the Faust myth and its story of overreaching human ambition, *Doctor Faustus Lights the Lights;* and Claude Fredericks's *The Idiot King,* about a just ruler who suffers defeat. Fredericks knew the photographer Carl van Vechten who controlled the rights to Stein's play and offered to approach him.

Pursuing possible theatre locations, Julian sought relief from the boredom of real estate agents with painters. Judith and Julian went to the van Gogh show at the Metropolitan Museum and to a Baziotes opening. A few weeks later, Baziotes and his wife Ethel came over for a vegetarian meal, and to talk about painting and a moneyless society. Short, wiry, a former boxer, Baziotes was charming and sociable. His family had been financially ruined during the Depression, and he had sold newspapers, shined shoes, and stood guard for bootleggers. His naivete was a good match for Julian's optimism, and Judith found him easy to like. A country girl dressed in city clothes, Ethel was forthright, unpretentious, and even easier to like.

At Mark Rothko's opening at the Betty Parsons Gallery, Julian asked Rothko whether he would design for their theatre. Swaying with drink, Rothko replied that he felt too limited by theatre, but Robert Motherwell, standing next to him, expressed interest. Julian spoke to him again at Barnett Newman's opening at Betty Parsons. Full of a quiet, unostentatious enthusiasm, Motherwell visited the Becks' new apartment, immediately grasped the poetic and experimental ambitions of The Living Theatre, and was sympathetic.

Julian felt an affinity with Motherwell who believed that painters who did not express an ethical consciousness were only decorators. The *New York Times* had announced the development of the hydrogen bomb—for Julian it was the "Hell Bomb"—and the news sent tremors of despair and fear through the artistic community. Judith decided the bomb was a sign of a "planetary forest fire" that artists would have to confront, resist, and extinguish no matter how unequal the odds. Paul Goodman, Claude Fredericks, and Walter McElroy visited, discussing ways to work against the war consciousness, but private words seemed limited in their effectiveness. At Piscator's Dramatic Workshop, Judith and Julian saw a shattering antiwar play, *There Is No End,* but that would only reach a few hundred people, most with a predisposition against war anyway.

Political concerns could seem pressing, even overwhelming,

and they had the power to make art seem like mere distraction. Near the end of January, Judith and Julian attended the Broadway opening of T. S. Eliot's *Cocktail Party,* running into Tennessee Williams in the lobby. Eliot's play impressed them, combining verse drama with a principle of social utility they wanted to emulate. In February, they heard Dylan Thomas read at the 92nd Street YMHA in his oratorical, deeply moving voice, which they considered a theatrical experience, and then saw a performance of *Tosca* and a balletic version of W. H. Auden's *Age of Anxiety,* a poem about the inability of people to transcend their shells, to help each other in a time of paralysis.

The Auden poem appealed to Judith because she felt it had some application to her marriage. Auden had disparaged homosexuals who married "with separate latch-keys" to disguise their essential needs, and this was certainly not what Judith desired. She and Julian had become emotional and tense. She was experiencing periods of deep depression that Julian referred to as "the Eumenides," and they had stopped making love. Judith felt oppressed by her fear of the bomb—when Julian brought home the issue of *Life* magazine describing its possibilities, she threw it out of a window—by the lack of any prospects in the theatre, and by what she considered domestic burdens, compounded by caring for Garrick.

After a night of Garrick's incessant crying, at 5 A.M. in their kitchen, Julian exploded in a fit of temper and burned Judith's forehead with a cigarette, leaving a slight scar. Their "broken love" left Judith with the lonely realization that genuine merging, even for lovers or mates, was rare and transient. In the weeks after the fight, Julian seemed more distant and unknowable. Almost as a compensatory gesture, he stumbled down a flight of stairs at work and tore a tendon so badly he had to spend a week in bed.

In the beginning of April, while Julian was painting, Judith attended her first anarchist meeting, a talk on the subject "Is an Optimistic View of Human Nature Laughable?" organized by *Resistance*. The meeting was held in a small downtown loft on

Broadway between Eleventh and Twelfth streets, and rented by a group of Spanish anarchists known as the SIA, the Sociedad Internacionale Anarquista. Tables were made of boards resting on carpenter's horses, on which were piled stacks of books and pamphlets; there was a kettle heating on an old wood stove and a large, plaster bust of a comrade martyred in the Spanish Civil War.

A year earlier, Judith had noticed that anarchists seemed slovenly, irresponsible, and selfish. Now she noticed the grim cheer of career anarchists who did not seem particularly idealistic. They used "pacifism as a tactic," and she wondered as well whether they were anarchists to rationalize personal psychopathic conditions. Despite such reservations, she was drawn to a disaffiliated quality in the group, a lonely courage that somehow seemed to confirm a view she had first understood reading Gide: that humans could act without the constraints of accepted morality.

Julian began attending the meetings of the anarchist circle at the end of April. His painting at the Laurel Gallery show had been sold. Although he had only received seventy-five dollars for it, he was encouraged by the sale. At a party, he had a long talk with Anaïs Nin about keeping journals. Nin was a still unrecognized writer who had been Henry Miller's mistress in Paris in the early 1930s, and who had helped him spiritually and financially while he was writing *Tropic of Cancer*. For years, she had been publishing her own obscure short stories, and the lack of recognition she had received drew Julian toward her. Nin seemed hesitant, shy, and insecure, Julian thought, perhaps misinterpreting her mannered coquettishness as reticence. Nin had been keeping her unpublished journals for two decades, in Paris and in New York, and though Julian spoke of his wife's journals, he wanted to begin his own.

Journals could be therapeutic, and Judith often used hers to weather the bouts of depression that made her mourn for the "spent light" of the world. In better spirits, she could paint the walls of the apartment, read a biography of Gandhi, or another of

Thoreau, or continue with Proust, though even his meticulously over-refined sensibility could seem morbid at times. One of the poems she wrote that spring was called "Odious Climates," which was indirectly related to Joseph McCarthy's public hearings in New York investigating Owen Lattimore and Communists in the State Department.

Even more odious, from Judith and Julian's point of view, was the news in the summer of 1950 that conflict had begun in Korea, a war in which thousands of Americans would be killed during the following three years. Truman alleged that he had entered the war to prevent another world conflict, and at first the war was popular in America. The country was at a military, economic, and perhaps moral peak of power in 1950, but support for the war would decline as losses soared.

Fundamentally, Julian thought, the American public was as unconcerned as "people playing bingo in a bomb shelter." In a movie theatre, watching newsreel footage of young men in troop trains, Julian stood up shouting "You are crazy to let them make you kill and destroy and not protest!"

Realizing that some independent action was warranted, Julian and Judith bought sheets of gummed labels on which they printed denunciations of the war to be pasted on lampposts, mailboxes, and in subway stations. Brief, provocative—"Answer War Gandhi's Way," "Don't Let Politics Lead You to War," "War Is Hell, Resist It!"—the labels anticipated the challenges of the 1960s. On a rainy summer morning, long before the sun rose, they began pasting hundreds of labels, and they continued the activity on succeeding mornings.

When Julian discovered an order at Beck Distributing for batteries to be shipped to Korea, he quit his job, even though his parents regarded this act as sheer insanity. He informed his parents that he planned to leave the city because of fears of nuclear annihilation, and they volunteered to pay his rent if he stayed in New York City. Mabel and Irving were still intent on keeping Julian as their little prince. The offer was tempting because it would enable Julian to continue painting without having to work, and it was accepted though Judith argued the money was tainted by the war.

Furtively, all summer, late at night or very early in the morning, Judith and Julian pasted their antiwar labels. Once, they were berated by a policeman who informed them that such activity was un-American. The road the country was taking, Judith realized, could only lead to great difficulty and hardship, and possibly even to tragedy.

13. Séances and Mumbo Jumbo

As a way to relieve the tensions caused by the Korean war—one source was Julian's fear of being again called by the draft board—Julian and Judith began to indulge in a form of homemade spiritualism. They had been reading L. Ron Hubbard's *Dianetics,* and the work of the Duke university parapsychologist J. B. Rhine on telepathy and psychic communication.

Harold Norse claimed to know how to invoke spirits. He lived in a railroad flat on Thirty-eighth Street and Third Avenue with Dick Stryker, who had spent the Second World War in a jail cell as a conscientious objector. Just below them was Claude Fredericks's friend Walter McElroy, who was elegant, like a precise schoolmaster, and slightly "satanic." Judith had a crush on him although McElroy lived with his lover, Glynn Collins, an ebullient painter who had once been married to the poet Muriel Rukeyser. Another participant in this newly formed psychic circle was a seventeen-year-old, strikingly handsome actor named Robin Prising, who wanted most of all to communicate with his idol, Isadora Duncan. Affable, helpful with Garrick, Prising began by sleeping at the Becks' and eventually became part of their household.

The first séances occurred during the summer of 1950. Both Judith and Julian were skeptical about the existence of disembodied beings, though Julian as an agnostic preferred not to rule out any possibility. The procedure was to touch fingers on Norse's Gothic black table until it rocked as a signal of the spirit's presence. At the first attempt, they sat for almost an hour before there was any movement. When there was a response to their questions, the answers seemed vague and indeterminate. Judith believed that the table moved when one of the participants jostled it, and interpreted this as an unconscious expression of the particular participant and not the sign that a spirit was speaking. Norse, however, interpreted the spirit's advice that war was imminent and that it would be best to flee from New York City. Judith stated that this was on all their minds: what they feared most was that the United States would use nuclear weapons in China, provoking massive Soviet retaliation.

One night, Norse brought Michael Fraenkel to the Beck's apartment for a séance. A tiny, pale man with a staccato delivery, Fraenkel had spent the 1930s in Paris. In 1931, he had acted as a mentor to Henry Miller, telling Miller to write the way he spoke, which resulted in the stylistic breakthrough of *Tropic of Cancer*. Judith quickly realized that Fraenkel had a gift for stirring people and altering their lives. As a practical rationalist, Fraenkel scoffed at the séances, suggesting that they were only a form of narcissistic inaction. As an anarchist, he maintained a strategy of resistance to what he termed "the system" at any opportunity. He had bought a farmhouse and some land in Indiana, and proposed that Judith, Julian, Norse, Stryker, McElroy, Collins, and Robin Prising join him in establishing an anarchist commune.

For several weeks, the nascent communards debated the prospects of growing vegetables in Indiana until, early in the fall, Fraenkel abruptly announced that he was sailing back to Europe. Walter McElroy and Glynn Collins also left New York, sailing on a freighter to England.

An American force had invaded the west coast of North Korea from the sea, intensifying the tensions. Both Judith and

Julian plunged into work as a response to the war. Julian was painting every day. He had also assumed the care of Garrick and most of the domestic concerns of the household. Preparing a speech from Djuna Barnes's densely experimental novel *Nightwood,* Judith was making the rounds of producers' offices, hoping to audition for television. Her choice of material was characteristically inappropriate, revealing a certain self-defeating tendency. Like Judith's other choices of material, Barnes was much too obscure, elliptical, esoteric, and poetic for television producers, so Judith got no work.

Judith and Julian regularly attended the anarchist meetings at the SIA hall during the summer and fall of 1950. In the middle of November, they were asked to deliver a talk about pacifism and what they called the moneyless revolution, but they were greeted with challenges and doubts. The anarchists, Judith concluded, felt revolution was now impossible, and all their efforts were devoted to challenging authority. They were too concerned with breaking down the existing order to imagine a better one.

The rebuttal by the anarchists was disturbing, especially for Judith who was worried because there seemed to be no place in the theatre for her. She had translated a play from German for Piscator, but at his Dramatic Workshop in November, he had refused to consider her for the role of Lady Macbeth, arguing that she was too small.

At the end of the month, she began seeing an ad hoc therapist who used the techniques of dianetics, hypnotizing his patients to focus on crucial life passages. In overdecorated rooms with a lavish Oriental flavor, Judith was encouraged to consider the traumatic moments of her conception, her father's death, and Harald Brixel's departure while her therapist held her hand. He suspected that Julian was having an affair with Robin Prising, and guessed that Judith and Julian were no longer lovers and that Judith was suffering from a sexual void.

Brash, authoritarian, aggressive, the therapist began to flirt with Judith, making her uncomfortable. Manipulative and domineering, he soon recruited Harold Norse and Dick Stryker as patients, and convinced them that they were unsuited for each other. Judith wondered how much of this therapy was "mumbo-jumbo" and how much the simple unburdening of one's difficulties, but after a month, the therapist began to represent to her a "dictatorship of the psychiatrist," and she terminated her sessions. Although the analysis seemed weird, it had "galvanized her," helping her to overcome her terror of being ridiculed and encouraging her to assert herself as an artist.

Underlying the séances and dianetic analysis, her pervasive concern during the summer and fall of 1950 was the progress of the Korean conflict. The Chinese were supplying the North Koreans with manpower, and the Americans could not seem to win on the ground, compounding her fear that the military would resort to nuclear strikes. Harold Norse bought a sixty-acre farm near Canterbury, Connecticut, about forty miles from Hartford, and invited Judith and Julian to build their own cottage on his property. Julian bought a 1935 Ford for the trip to Canterbury on the street for fifty dollars and called it "the Pardoner."

With Garrick, they drove Norse—who did not drive—up to Canterbury on Christmas Eve. The old heap had difficulty accelerating, and its brakes barely functioned. Unpainted, sitting on a knoll off a dirt road, without electricity, the house was surrounded by woods, a forest of oak, pine, maple, and apple trees. Wrapped in overcoats and blankets, the Becks slept on a cold floor for two nights, ate sandwiches and drank coffee, and trudged the snowy fields. They had fled to Canterbury more like Boccaccio's refugees escaping the plague than Chaucer's pilgrims; but Judith knew that she could not really spend her life in so isolated a place and that perilous as the city might seem, it would draw her back.

14. The New Musicians

Judith and Julian were home with a few friends on New Year's Eve. Harold Norse, wearing a Japanese kimono, performed an Oriental dance with Judith in a Persian skirt, Balinese earrings, and a silver tulle veil. They saw it as an overture, an invitation to the muses. Judith reminded herself in a diary entry that "the future is a dream to which I cling." The dream was their emerging theatre. Richard Gerson, one of Julian's friends from Horace Mann, had rented the Cherry Lane to showcase his play about Alexander the Great, *The Thirteenth God*. He asked Judith to direct it and play Alexander's wife, and Julian to design the production. No one, including the actors, would get paid, but the performances would become a sort of trial run for The Living Theatre.

January, February, and March of 1951 were spent in preparation. Julian went to the Metropolitan Museum of Art to research costumes. Actors and actresses (one of them Geraldine Page, who would play a prostitute) auditioned in their living room full of bamboo poles to which sketches were attached.

The play opened late in March and ran for three weeks. Gerson had refused to allow any cuts, so the play was hurt by its excessive length. It was compromised, as well, by snickering innuendos and homosexual jokes. Audiences were quite small—Judith noticed Kreymborg on the third night—and there was no critical notice. The world was more concerned with the news that President Truman afraid that General Douglas MacArthur might carry the war over into Chinese territory, had recalled him. Nevertheless, the experience for Judith was elating. She wondered, in a naive and self-congratulatory moment, whether the effort was comparable to that of the great modernists who had gathered together in London and Paris to inspire each other in the early part of the century.

The most tantalizing aspect of the play for Judith had been the opportunity to meet Lou Harrison. A big, rosy-cheeked, flamboyant, forty-three-year-old westerner, Harrison was a composer who also painted and wrote poems. Erudite, scholarly—he had studied with Schönberg and Virgil Thompson—and also a pacifist, he was perversely attractive to Judith. Poised, demonic at times, he would listen to music while inhaling the fragrance of a yellow rose, always supremely conscious of his effect on others. Judith saw him as a man with a sudden smile that would vanish just as she was ready to return it—perhaps because he was moody, changeable, and unsure of the extent to which he was attracted to her. Judith knew that Harrison was suffering a prolonged nervous breakdown and that he was involved with one of Merce Cunningham's dancers, a man named Remy Charlip. She spent one drunken night in his room on Prince Street, listening to him play the piano and making love to him, which helped her realize that Harrison inspired love more than he was able to return it.

Harrison declared that he was leaving New York at the end of June to teach at Black Mountain, a community of artists who under the aegis of poet Charles Olson ran an experimental college in the foothills of North Carolina that had become a mecca for the avant-garde. Before his departure, Judith and Julian attended a dance concert in which he was performing. Jean Erdman was dancing to sounds made by camel bells, glasses, a gourd drum, pebbles, and a bamboo pole, an unusual collocation, perhaps, but indicative of a new music. After the performance, Harrison introduced Judith and Julian to John Cage and Merce Cunningham, who would become stalwart allies of The Living Theatre.

Harrison also introduced Judith to Joseph Campbell, Erdman's husband, whose *Hero with a Thousand Faces* had already impressed her. Surrounding the circumstances of her marriage to

Julian was the panoply of artists who were becoming part of their circle. Unformulated as a principle, perhaps, but psychologically motivating for Judith was the notion that she could be both muse and lover to many of the great men she would meet in her life. She began reading Robert Graves's *White Goddess*—a book Harrison had recommended—hoping it might create more common ground with Campbell, whom she wanted to meet again.

Judith's conception of herself as a muse-goddess may seem excessively romantic. Some may choose to see it as a rationalization for promiscuity. Feminists may remember that a century ago, ambitious women like Alma Mahler searched for great men to serve in the spirit of Nietzsche's remark that "man is made for war, woman for the recreation of the warrior," and may condemn Judith's stance as retrograde and old-fashioned.

If the handsome Campbell radiated health, another man she met that spring was a case in counterpoint. In April, Harold Norse brought Judith and Julian to a book party at the Gotham Book Mart, a literary bookstore incongruously located in the heart of the diamond district. By this time, Julian felt that Norse had become pretentious and egocentric to the point of solipsism, but Norse was a pale version of his friend Chester Kallman, whose book of poems was being celebrated. Tall, stooped, pouting, with blond hair awry, a chalky pallor, and dark circles of dissipation around his eyes, Kallman had been painted when he was ten by the Mexican muralist Siqueiros and obviously had never gotten over it. He boasted about a libretto, *The Rake's Progress,* that he was completing with W. H. Auden for the composer Stravinsky.

Kallman seemed to be on the road to success and fame. No matter how obnoxious he seemed, he was protected by the doting patronage of Auden, who was willing to continually suffer Kallman's promiscuity. Judith understood that her dream of The Living Theatre was still unrealizable, and all she could absurdly mention was a bit part she had played a week earlier on a Molly Goldberg television serial. Norse had helped place five of her poems in a little magazine, *Voices,* but next to the crowing Kallman her achievement seemed a minuscule matter indeed.

However, the important work had already begun, and Judith's plan was to now utilize her living room as her theatre. Paul Goodman had described the Wooster Street location as "chamber theater," and an actor named Julian Sawyer had performed Eliot's *Cocktail Party* as a monologue before a dozen enthralled friends in their living room.

Harold Norse was encouraging, quoting Yeats in an essay called "Instead of a Theatre" where the Irish poet imagined an "ancient theatre made by unrolling a carpet or marking out a place with a stick, or setting a screen against a wall." Judith knew that she and Julian belonged to an underground artistic network whose center was in New York, and her hope was that these artists would form the core audience for her theatre. Although there had been much floundering and delay, a long interuterine period, she reminded herself of the biological fact that the longer the gestation, the higher that organism would be on the evolutionary scale.

One of the artists Judith wanted to attract to her chamber theatre was John Cage, whom she had seen playing piano with his elbows early in May and then conducting a piece for twelve radios. Forty-eight years old, mercurial but soft-spoken, Cage was a genuine innovator who had introduced chance elements into his work as a principle of musical composition. Cage argued that harmony, the unifying structural principle of classical music, had been replaced by the variable time lengths of Anton Webern and Erik Satie. Contemporary music was simply sound without any hierarchy. Squealing auto brakes, for example, were as valid a source for musical composition as the violin, and the musical revolution Cage suggested would come to incorporate street sounds.

Judith met Cage again in the middle of May at a downtown art show. Rebelling against the uptown galleries, artists were beginning to show work in whitewashed quarters on Ninth Street, and these artists, Judith realized, could become her constituency. Cage told her how he had come to New York in 1943 to stay with Peggy Guggenheim, who abruptly rejected him when she discovered he was planning to give a concert at the

Museum of Modern Art instead of Art of This Century. Guggenheim's rejection of Cage, similar to her treatment of Julian, had
a sexual motivation, and this was another link between Cage
and the Becks.

15. The Saintliness of the Beaten

Despite the excitement of meeting artists such as John
Cage, Judith was impatient since her theatre had not yet
emerged—not in her living room or anywhere else. She was
debilitated by anemia and felt "dumb as a pantomime" in her
inaction. She would be twenty-five in June but felt she had not yet
accomplished anything significant.

In the late spring and summer of 1951, she began to spend
lots of nighttime in the San Remo, a Village bar frequented by
writers and artists. In New York City, bars were like Parisian cafés
or public squares in Europe, places where artists and intellectuals could congregate and discuss issues of the moment—though
Judith was well aware that bars could also become "blind alleys
in the maze where dreams die." The denizens of the Village
bars—the San Remo on Bleecker Street, the White Horse where
Dylan Thomas drank when he was in New York, the Cedar Bar
favored by Pollock and the abstract expressionist painters, or the
Minetta Tavern on MacDougal Street—were what Jack Kerouac
would call "the subterraneans." They were pursuing, as Norman
Mailer put it rather romantically in a seminal essay called "The
White Negro," "the saintliness of the beaten"; and the flagrant
self-destructiveness of drinking every night until four in the morning was one perverse expression of their total contempt for the
cautious pragmatism of the middle class.

The San Remo had a pressed-tin ceiling, black and white tiles on its floor, wooden booths and a restaurant in the back, a long bar, and a jukebox that played Verdi and Donizetti. Run by tough Italians who used to walk around with baseball bats—Milton Klonsky named them the Bleecker Street Goths in an article in *Commentary*—the bar was what Harold Norse called a bohemian ghetto for jazz musicians such as Miles Davis, and analytical intellectuals and writers such as James Baldwin, Anatole Broyard, Allen Ginsberg, Gregory Corso, or Paul Goodman (who came but did not drink). The Village then was an oasis in the puritan desert of America, Norse asserted, and the atmosphere of the Remo was loose enough for those wanting to escape their cold-water flats to meet and mingle. A noisy, brassy bar, the Remo was a place where surprising events could occur at any moment, Judith observed. When the essayist Seymour Krim brought a psychiatrist friend to the San Remo, she demanded to leave because it reminded her of the admissions ward at Bellevue Hospital.

Many of those who came there were unknowns and could not even afford to drink, but poverty, as Seymour Krim observed, was romantic in the early 1950s; and some writers like Krim would revel in it. Mary McCarthy popularized the Remo in a condescending article in the *New York Post,* complaining that its patrons pretended to be artistic while accomplishing little, a description that somehow contributed to the notion that those who imbibed at the Remo were consigned to an underground that the responsible world could never take seriously.

In the middle of one August night at the Remo, Judith and Julian met Maxwell Bodenheim, a legendary representative of 1920s and 1930s bohemia. Gaunt, shabby, his glazed eyes making him seem bludgeoned by alcohol, Bodenheim would always trade a poem for a shot of gin. The son of a German-Jewish whiskey salesman, he had once been a flamboyant figure notorious for his scandalous overtures to women, and several of the women who had become involved with him had threatened or committed suicide. Bodenheim had deserted the army during the First World War and had been sent to Leavenworth. After his release, he participated in the Chicago Renaissance, publishing his poems in *Poetry* and *The Little Review.* He left Chicago and lived with Alfred Kreymborg in the Village. But, at the age of fifty-eight, dissipated from drink and a life on park benches, selling his poems on street corners for the previous twenty years, he was an artifact of the Jazz Age he had once satirized in his novel, *Naked on Roller Skates.*

With a sardonic, bitter edge to his voice, Bodenheim introduced himself to Judith and Julian as an idiotic poet and then lurched off. They knew him by the photograph that hung over the bar, and what they admired about him was his absolute refusal to submit to the system. In bars, Bodenheim would proclaim that he had a "malady of the soul," but to Judith and Julian, it seemed symptomatic of a more universal illness. The ravaged, spectral wreck of bohemia had been Eugene O'Neill's friend, and some of his plays had been performed by the Provincetown Players. His appearance in the Remo had been so fugitive and sudden that he seemed like a gasp from the past, a mysterious omen, or an annunciation from the underground.

Meeting Bodenheim was both scary and propitious as Judith and Julian finally began to move toward the realization of their theatre. Julian had inherited six thousand dollars from Leon Goldrich, a favorite uncle who had no children; and Julian decided to use all of it to launch The Living Theatre. Through Leo Shull, former owner of the now defunct Genius Incorporated, Julian rented the Cherry Lane for nine hundred dollars a month.

Too eager to wait until the Cherry Lane was available, Judith and Julian spent the summer of 1951 preparing to use their living room as their theatre. The program was to be *Crying Backstage,* a brief farce by Paul Goodman; *Ladies Voices,* a three-minute interlude by Gertrude Stein that was basically a funny conversation between two women about a third who was represented by a dressmaker's dummy; and a Lorca dialogue from the play *If Five Years Pass* between a young man played by Julian and a manikin played by Judith. The program would end with two linked didactic early Brecht plays called *He Who Says Yes* and *He Who Says No* about a boy faced with the quandary of sacrificing his life for a moral position. In these Brecht plays, Remy Charlip, a dancer with Merce Cunningham, would play the boy, Judith would play the boy's mother, and Julian, the teacher.

Julian could talk of nothing else but his preparations. Scavenging wood at night, he constructed primitive sets. With ink and crayon, he fashioned personal invitations. There would only be twenty people at each performance: ten seated on a bench, the others on cushions in front of them. John Cage and Merce Cunningham came, and Carl van Vechten, who had permitted them to do the Stein, came as well. Near the end of August, there was only a week of performances, the actors practically in the laps of their very select audience. It would never again seem so difficult to act on a stage, Judith thought, where the lights and the distance from the audience were like a protective barrier.

The Cherry Lane was available around Christmas. Judith and Julian had decided to stage Paul Goodman's *Faustina,* a play by the anarchist poet Kenneth Rexroth called *Beyond the Mountains* that had three roles for Judith, and Stein's *Doctor Faustus Lights the Lights* which Judith would direct. Julian would design all the productions.

At the end of September, they visited Cage and Cunningham who had expressed an interest in sharing a place that could be used for concerts and dance recitals. Gracious, unassuming, the two men lived in a large white room, bare except for matting, a marble slab on the floor for a table and long strips of foam rubber on the walls for seating. The environment reflected their minimalist aesthetic. Cage proposed to stage a piece by Satie that consisted of eight hundred and forty repetitions of a one-minute composition. He advised them not to rely on newspaper advertising but to use instead men with placards on tall stilts and others with drums. The suggestion may have been impractical, but it emphasized a turn to older methods of gathering a crowd, more ritualized and personal perhaps, and also paradoxically repudiating mass technology.

In October, they began searching for a choreographer for

Rexroth's play, and a printer for tickets and announcements. They also visited Eric Bentley. Only thirty-five but already a prodigy in the theatre, Bentley was an Englishman, an Oxford graduate who had studied acting with John Gielgud and received a doctorate from Yale. He had taught at Black Mountain and at UCLA, where he met Brecht and translated several of his plays into English. Judith found that Bentley was intimidating, though she was encouraged when he suggested he might want to direct a play.

The stress of trying to build her own theatre had left Judith unhappy and alienated. On her birthday the previous June, she had given some of her poems to Paul Goodman, knowing that he would be less interested in any aesthetic dimension than in what they revealed psychologically. He complained that the poems suffered from a lack of distance and reflected a guilt that prevented her from realizing her own potential as an actress. Goodman offered to counsel her with a few free sessions. In November, after she had passed out from drinking in the San Remo, she resolved to resume seeing Goodman, who wanted to see her three times a week.

Forty-years-old, Goodman was a poet, novelist, playwright, essayist, and libertarian philosopher with a very small audience. He was not unhappy about the size of his following, pointing out that any libertarian becomes an influence merely by existing. He was also not a Marxist because he felt Marxism only led to the coercive state, not the fraternal socialism he desired. As an undergraduate at City College, he had read Freud but was dissatisfied with the message of adjustment to the system that he heard in Freudian followers like Erich Fromm or Karen Horney.

Twice married, he had children but was aggressively promiscuous. Boyish, playful, impudent, and insubordinate, he subscribed to a posture of complete openness. At a Christmas party a year earlier, Judith had been offended when Goodman publicly embraced several young male acolytes who revered him as a Socratic master. Goodman asserted his homosexuality had been the reason for the loss of three teaching positions.

An iconoclast, Goodman had a tremendous need for attention. He had been rejected from the army during the Second World War and was the first of the New York intellectuals to read Wilhelm Reich's *The Function of the Orgasm* and *The Mass Psychology of Fascism.* He began writing about Reich who, unlike any other psychiatrist, believed in changing social rules rather than adapting to them. Existing norms, Reich argued, were grounded on a systematic sexual repression that led to social pathology and even to cancer.

In 1946, Goodman went into Reichian therapy—a series of physical exercises rather than talking—with Alexander Lowen. Rejecting the Freudian view that civilization required sublimation, Lowen was an early Reichian who believed that sexual gratification could lead to creative productivity. Goodman wrote *Communitas,* a radical history of community planning with his brother Percival, and a number of other books that did not sell many copies. Ambivalent about his own calling as a writer, he made an impact on New York intellectual life when he wrote *Gestalt Therapy* (1951) from the notes of Fritz and Lore Perls, two German Jews who had practiced psychoanalysis in South Africa during the war. Goodman spent two years in therapy with Lore Perls and began treating patients himself, an extension, he claimed, of counseling his friends.

As a therapist, Goodman's purpose was never to condemn neurotic behavior, but to ascertain and relieve the guilt causing it. As Judith soon learned, he had an unusual capacity for accepting frailty and loving his patient. His therapy was Reichian insofar as it was based on physical exercises that might alleviate tension and break down inhibition, but it was also political. As an anarchist, he believed that in most human affairs more harm than good resulted from central authority or coercion. His touchstone, with quite defining implications for Judith, was that ideas should involve "acts and words for which persons are in fact thrown in jail."

People were swamped by the awful conditions of modern life, he argued, and so conditioned by them that they could never imagine alternatives. Goodman was most concerned by what he regarded as a collapse of public ethics and the delinquency of youth who were rebelling against unlivable communities in which a third of the population was poorly housed, poorly fed, and practically outcast. Cynicism and indifference resulted from an economy based on waste and war in which work became meaningless. The exclusive value was money, obsolescence was planned, and needs invented by advertising. In the 1950s, housing developments and interstate highways were accelerating urban sprawl, and shopping malls sprouted in cornfields. Mass marketing was touted as a science, and television would carry its insidious appeal to buy and consume. For Goodman, American life had become a kind of lie, a resurgent affluence that seemed incompatible with an extensive poverty.

Some of Goodman's ideas seemed crackpot, especially because he stressed sexual permissiveness not only for adults but for children as well. He was often seen as brilliant but perverse. His book *Communitas* begins with the debatable anti-Malthusian assertion that the world has an "immense surplus productivity" far beyond what is necessary to provide subsistence for all its inhabitants. Such an argument is based on an equitable distribution of resources that has only been a utopian dream, though it would have had great appeal to Judith and Julian.

Goodman saw art as a means of creating community value, not as an end in itself, and in this matter, Judith and Julian, as students of Piscator, would have been in accord. When Judith noted that Goodman could be condescending, however, she touched a chord she would discover more fully in her analysis. With an unexpected patriarchical attitude, Goodman believed women did not really need useful work, because they could have children.

16. The Gypsy Path

One of the cardinal priorities of The Living Theatre, as Malina and Beck envisaged it from its inception, was to encourage poetic theatre. From the start, this implied a sacrifice of the more conventional aspects of realistic drama for the sake of language. The first Cherry Lane production, *Doctor Faustus Lights the Lights,* was clearly in this poetic tradition. Language, Gertrude Stein's hypnotically reiterative and circular use of it, was a central feature of the play as is evident in Doctor Faustus's opening chant on the subject of hidden knowledge: "I knew it I knew it the electric lights they told me so no dog can know no boy can know I cannot know they cannot know the electric lights they told me so I would not know."

A version of the Faust myth written originally as an opera libretto in 1938, Stein's play seemed maddeningly dense and obtuse to the few reviewers who saw it. In the play, Faustus's beloved Marguerite has died and is in hell. Faustus encounters Mephisto and asks how he can join her. Mephisto tells him he must kill, so Faustus kills a dog and murders a little boy. These acts so change Faustus that when he reaches Marguerite, she can no longer recognize him or relate to him.

The Faust myth is a modern archetype, Julian believed, and he wrote to Donald Gallup, a Yale librarian and Pound's bibliographer, with questions about Stein's use of the earlier plays by Marlowe and Goethe. Julian felt Stein was the best playwright of the twentieth century, though he must have realized that her unusual innovativeness limited her audience. The play was produced for the coterie of underground artists who could appreciate it despite its murky labyrinthine mood and who would understand the importance of Faustus's tragic choice for knowledge and power as the principle underlying Western development since the Renaissance.

One member of the audience was William Carlos Williams, who sent a long letter full of praise. He acknowledged that the "entrancing" performance was far above the level of commercial theatre and existed as the "first really serious, really cleanly written, produced and acted play" that he had seen in a long time. Characteristically enthusiastic, Williams was also hoping The Living Theatre would do his own *Many Loves,* but he had felt an unusual vibrancy in the production to which he was responding. Actually, the Stein play might have become a hit, and it played to full houses during its two-week run.

If the Stein play was a risky proposition for a new theatrical company, Kenneth Rexroth's *Beyond the Mountains* was even riskier. No one in theatre was as experimental as Stein, but at least her reputation and the fact that her plays were so rarely performed might help draw an audience. Rexroth's reputation as an irreverent California poet, a classicist and an expert on Oriental poetry, was much more local. Irascible, highly opinionated, mercilessly satiric, and utterly bohemian, Rexroth would intimidate most people with his encyclopedic knowledge. Rexroth was also a libertarian who had organized weekly anarchist meetings in San Francisco in the late 1940s, paralleling on the opposite coast the SIA meetings that Judith and Julian attended, which had made them sympathetic to his play from the outset.

In *Beyond the Mountains,* Rexroth had written a stiff verse adaptation of the *Oresteia.* Unfortunately, no part of Rexroth's goatish personality was reflected in the impersonality of his play. Julian, however, wanted to direct it, even though the play had little to do with the more pragmatic concerns of any contemporary audience. He was drawn to the play because he saw in it parallels between the fall of Greek civilization and modern disintegration, as represented by the horde of Huns who crowd the stage in the last part of the play. And there were three roles that Judith wanted—Iphigenia, Phaedra, and Berenike. In several parts, the play was exceedingly long, running over three hours. To his credit, Rexroth advised it would be folly to play all the parts on the same night, correctly predicting that any audience would be "worn out halfway through."

Beyond the Mountains was slow, ritualized, hieratic, a sort of frozen sleepwalk through the classical period. William Carlos Williams had reviewed the published version of the play in the *New York Times*, praising the contrast of the play's colloquial tone with its tragic circumstances but admitting the play was much more suited to print than performance. John Cage, Merce Cunningham, and Harold Norse (who had also reviewed the published version and called it archaic, melodramatic, and pretentious)—all advised against doing the play. The choreographer, the Japanese dancer Teiko, applied the sparse, stark tradition of No to Rexroth's play, resulting in a highly stylized effect that might have seemed portentous to the audience—if there had been any real audience to speak of. The play was merely a collection of beautiful moments—actors draped in black and gold squares of cloth tied with ropes—Julian later realized, with more concern for its form than with any potential emotional truth. Vernon Rice, the critic who reviewed the play in the *New York Post*, had no idea of what it was about. The play was a fiasco, and even though the actors were unpaid, it lost twenty-six hundred dollars.

The worst loss, however, was personal. On the last night of 1951, in the opening scene of the play, as the stage gradually lightened, Judith playing Phaedra was carried onstage in a palanquin as she agonized over her love for her stepson, Hippolytus. After Judith spoke the line "Someday they may discover the moon's held in its orbit / by the menstruation of women," a woman who played the oboe in the orchestra pit began to laugh uncontrollably. The laughter spread, and Judith completely lost control, discarded her veil, and fled the stage.

In a daze, she went to Harald Brixel's old apartment on Hud-

son and Tenth streets. Weeping in the hallway, she was overheard by a sculptor who invited her to share some green tea. In
his small bedroom, he spoke about yoga and Buddhism, and later
they made love. Shortly before midnight, she left for the San
Remo, where she was consoled by a soulful-eyed dancer with a
sad, sympathetic manner named Philip Smith.

On New Year's Day, Julian informed Judith that the cast had
decided not to perform with her again. The incident had been an
extreme form of "breaking," the fear triggered by facing a live audience with a part that might not seem completely convincing.
That night, there was no scheduled performance of the play. John
Cage had been in the ticket booth all day selling tickets to a concert of his music performed by the pianist David Tudor. Unlike
the tiny audiences for *Beyond the Mountains,* the Cage event was a
sellout, with people even seated onstage. At a party afterward at
the home of composer Morton Feldman, two Harvard poets, John
Ashbery and Frank O'Hara, were particularly sympathetic to Judith, though whatever chivalry they managed could hardly compensate for the defeat she felt she had suffered.

Judith spent most of the nights of January 1952 in the San
Remo, which by then she was calling the "San Remote" or the
"Sans Remorse." Philip Smith, Frank O'Hara, and John Ashbery
were often there—all good conversationalists with an interest in
theatre. Daffy, insouciant, mixing the ordinary and the ultraso-
phisticated, full of levity and excitement, O'Hara was a particular
source of comfort. As a harbinger of the future more than a ghost
of the past, Bodenheim appeared in a vindictive mood one night
with a story and photograph in *Time* about his arrest a few nights
earlier for sleeping on the subway.

Much of the time, Judith felt nervous and on edge, and she
had various altercations with Julian, Dick Stryker, and Paul Goodman, who all ended up striking her. Sometimes, Judith represented a kind of defiance that angered peaceful men to the point
where they would lose control.

Rehearsals had begun for Goodman's play *Faustina* in a
mood of discouragement, and when its production was post-

poned, Goodman showed his anger during therapeutic sessions. Instead of *Faustina,* Julian and Judith had decided to produce what Eric Bentley advised them to call "An Evening of Bohemian Theater." The program would begin with Stein's *Ladies Voices;* proceed to T. S. Eliot's *Sweeney Agonistes,* which Judith soon found funereal and somnambulistic; and the major event of the evening would be a surrealist farce by Picasso, *Desire Trapped by the Tail,* about cold, hungry artist lovers who resist the Germans in occupied Paris. Even though its plot was influenced by Stein and complicated by a cubist breakup of language, Julian was drawn to the play because it stressed the power of love to overcome all difficulties.

In February, one of the actresses in *Desire,* Seraphina Hovhaness, introduced Judith to her husband, Alan, a composer who agreed to give a benefit concert on one of their Monday special events nights with Paul Goodman reading homoerotic poems. An American of Armenian heritage, Hovhaness was influenced by an ancient, pre-Christian musical heritage, and his compositions were haunting and magical, Julian thought. On another Monday night, Dylan Thomas read his poems with his oratorical grandeur.

Julian exhibited a selection of his paintings in the lobby of the theatre, and it seemed to him as if the dream of making The Living Theatre a free community of artists and friends was in the process of being realized. He wrote to his friend Robin Prising, who had moved to England, that he was trying to foster a weltanschauung among artists and that New York had become "the most creative place in the world now," comparable to ancient Babylon or Alexandria.

The energy of the theatre was spilling over into their private lives. One night, Seraphina and Alan Hovhaness invited Judith, Julian, and a group of the other actors to their place in the Village, which was decorated with astrological drawings. Naked, Judith sat in Alan Hovhaness's zinc-lined orgone box and felt a Reichian rush of heat and excitement.

The obligations of rehearsals, performances, and theatre administration became so demanding that both Judith and Julian began sleeping in the theatre. Irving Beck had been supporting them for two years, paying their rent, giving them an evening meal, and caring for Garrick. Irving was disappointed with his son and began to resent the expense, but Mabel defended Julian. Irving's disapproval caused tension in his home, with frequent contradictions and quarreling, which Julian and Judith avoided by staying downtown.

Judith had begun an ambivalent liaison with Philip Smith, each seeking more of a refuge than a love affair. Charming, pliant, and always gracious, Smith wanted someone to take over his life, to give him direction. Judith and Julian had tacitly agreed to allow each other the freedom to have lovers, though Smith became more the object of compassion than an active lover. Julian, for his part, provided no objections to the principle of Judith's having lovers. Fearing most the entrapments of middle-class existence, Julian understood that lovers could be a route to liberation but still did not have the courage to find them himself.

Julian was spending much of his time with Frances Clarke, one of the actresses in *Desire*. Ethereal but warm, a woman with thick black hair that fell to her waist, she was, to Julian, startlingly beautiful, and soon she was sleeping in the Cherry Lane as well. With Frances, Julian was adventurously romantic, perhaps because they were only pretending at love. There was an air of strained tolerance and circus hilarity among Judith, Philip Smith, Julian, and Frances Clarke, as if the farcical elements of the Picasso play were determining the nature of their relationships and encounters.

Even though he had only thirty-five dollars to spend, Julian had brilliantly designed the Picasso play. There was a curtain made of tatters of colored cloth, and the play featured scenes with poets John Ashbery and Frank O'Hara as Picasso's "Bow-wows" in dog costumes simulating buggery, which had considerable appeal for parts of the audience in 1952. For the first time, there was consistently enough of an audience to begin paying actors, and there was money to set aside for the Roman frescoes Julian was designing for *Faustina*.

Irrepressible, cheerful, and optimistic, Julian worked on the preparations for the play during March. Every afternoon, Goodman appeared, often walking to the Cherry Lane with Judith and conducting their analytic session as they walked. She was troubled by her voice, still subject to fits of nervous laughter that would occur in *Ladies Voices* whenever her concentration lapsed. Goodman said it reflected her hostility toward her audience.

Judith persuaded Goodman to give some of her time to Philip Smith, saying that she would switch to group sessions. By April, Philip, Frances, and a young man with almond-shaped eyes whom Judith had picked up in the San Remo to satisfy Philip, were all domiciled at the West End Avenue apartment. "It was easy to find lovers," Judith observed wistfully, but "difficult to love." The young man eventually stole the receipts from the cash box at the Cherry Lane one night and absconded. Philip had been seduced by Paul Goodman, and though Julian was deeply interested in Frances, Judith was confident that she remained connected to Julian by "our child and our theatre," which would continue to swing between them "like skip ropes held by playmates." And the "tenuous swinging connection is always love," Judith concluded.

Rehearsals for *Faustina* began in late April, complicated by the affair between Goodman and Philip Smith who would make love in a dressing room while Judith and the other actors would wait onstage. Smith, who had taken the role of a soldier in the play, was supposed to be assisting Judith with the direction, so his disappearances were aggravating. The incestuousness was compounded when Goodman canceled a therapeutic session with Judith, claiming he had to prepare for a departure to Black Mountain when he was actually with Smith. "I lie in bed at night beside my lover who is not my lover," Judith confided in her *Diary*. She had not made love with Julian for four years although he was more faithful in his care for Garrick and their theatre than any of her lovers.

The issue of faith seemed crucial to Judith who was trying to direct a play in which the actors had little faith. Goodman's Reichian play told the story of the wife of Marcus Aurelius, emperor of Rome, who falls in love with Galba, a gladiator. To assuage Faustina's jealousy, Galba is sacrificed in a ritual ceremony of horror, and she is bathed in his blood. At the end of the play, in perhaps its least stylized or gothic moment, the Roman scenery collapses, representing the fall of that civilization. Faustina crosses a bare stage and admits that the actors have enacted a brutal murder, and suggests that if the audience were worthy, it would have "leaped on the stage and stopped the action."

Julie Bovasso, whom Judith and Julian had seen in a play at City College, was unable to say this. Judith thought her reluctance seemed part of the problem of contemporary theatre, the pretense that the audience did not exist and could be safely ignored. To be fair, however, only an anarchist audience could have responded as Goodman's script suggested it should, and theatre as we know it would have very little future in such circumstances. Later, Julian admitted that the speech was insulting, and could only rile and affront an audience. But the speech was clearly central to the direction The Living Theatre would take, and by the late 1960s, such appeals to rouse the audience to direct action would be frequent.

Faustina opened at the end of May to mediocre notices. Some critics saw that Julian's design, his use of collage, his wire sets using aluminum foil, scraps of cloth, rope curtains, plastic sheeting and plaster panels combined with sand and bits of broken glass were much more effective than either the writing or the acting. After a few performances, Bovasso left the cast, unhappy with the pressure caused by her inability to give her final speech, which had been spoken by another member of the cast. There were additional problems with anxious creditors, particularly Con Edison, the utility company, which threatened to extinguish the lights. To relieve mounting tension, Judith shattered a dressing room mirror, and then fought bitterly with Julian who went to his mother-in-law's house for a couple of days.

The "humiliating agony" of *Faustina,* to use Julian's description, compounded by its lack of audience support, lasted until the middle of June. A few blocks away, at the Circle in the Square theatre, Tennessee Williams's *Summer and Smoke* had become a hit with Geraldine Page, putting off-Broadway on the theatrical map.

That summer, Judith and Julian collaborated on a translation of Alfred Jarry's absurdist fantasy *Ubu Roi,* a "madhouse tornado farce" Judith called it, a spectacular and fluid arrangement in twenty-three brief scenes depicting the illusion of power. Designing the sets with brown wrapping paper because it was the least expensive material he could imagine, Julian fashioned over a hundred costumes out of rags by splattering paint on them in Jackson Pollock's manner, which was time-consuming labor. Shoeless, dirty, Julian assumed he appeared relaxed; but Judith thought he was a mess and wondered whether she would be able to follow Julian if he chose a gypsy path.

Although she kept her shoes on, always conscious of her small stature, she seemed to be on such a path already, eating many free meals in a soup place on Second Avenue owned by a benevolent lover of theatre. Studying Japanese and calligraphy, she was using the I Ching, the Chinese "Book of Changes," which could advise on the future if one was sensitive enough to decipher its often elliptical replies. She had been introduced to the I Ching by John Cage one night in the San Remo. On another night, she met a ribald and raunchy photographer named Weegee, who specialized in photographing dead gangsters for the *Daily News.* Weegee persuaded her to accompany him to his shabby studio behind the main police station on Centre Street.

Along with *Ubu Roi,* the staging for *The Heroes* was being planned. In Ashbery's surreal play, the voyaging Ulysses, returning from the Trojan Wars, encounters Circe, the ultimate temptress with the power to turn men into swine. Set in the Hamptons, colloquial in language but affected in the precious manner of Wilde and Cocteau, Ashbery's work offered a number of outrageous allusions to homosexual love. Looking old-fashioned in a white suit, Julian would play Theseus, though Judith thought he brought to the role many of his faults as an actor—a histrionic affectation, a monotonous tone, and an overdrawn casualness.

At the chess tables in Washington Square Park late one night, working on the *Ubu Roi* translation, Judith and Julian saw Jackson MacLow, a poet they had met among the anarchists in the SIA hall. While MacLow was eager to act in *The Heroes* and agreed to compose its musical score, his participation emphasized the degree to which chance governed Judith and Julian's choices.

They had been introduced to hashish for the first time at the end of June, and they were also smoking marijuana. Judith liked the ritual delicacy of passing the thin cigarette that would diminish until it burned the lips and seared the fingers. At first, she felt anxious because of its illegality, even though its effects seemed much less ravaging than those of alcohol. Her initial fear was not so much an anarchist's reaction as that of the rabbi's daughter who remembered Tolstoy's warning in his journals against the use of wine or tobacco because it would only weaken him.

Ubu Roi and *The Heroes* opened on 5 August to an enthusiastic audience. Though some jeered at the homosexual innuendos in Ashbery's play, the final ovation was so clamorous and there was such general commotion that the curtain collapsed. After three performances, the Cherry Lane was closed by a fire department inspector, but not before he was chased down the ironically named Commerce Street by Judith brandishing a bamboo spear. Her rage was shared by the company, which had hardly slept for weeks, living on bread and peanut butter, and for lack of money going without cigarettes or coffee.

The Fire Department had declared that Julian's sets were hazardously flammable. Both Judith and Julian were convinced that the department's action had been instigated by Kenneth Carroad, who had assumed control of the Cherry Lane early in July. Genteel and quite wealthy, Carroad owned lots of Village property, which in the 1950s was inhabited by working class tenants, many of them employed as longshoremen on nearby docks that were still active. Seeking gentrification, Carroad considered The Living Theatre actors "the wrong element." According to Julian, he "loathed our barefoot and barechested bohemian theatre." Neither Julian or Judith, in their private journal excoriations of their persecuting landlord, mention what must have frightened him most—the fact that they and some of their actors were using the theatre as a living space, a place for eating, sleeping, and loving. This was beyond outrage, beyond *épater le bourgeois,* and it pointed clearly to the gypsy path. The expulsion from the Cherry Lane, just at the time when it looked as if they had a hit, was not quite an expulsion from Eden; but it presaged the conflicts with authority that would become the very subject matter of the plays they would stage in the future.

17. Unspeakable Cries

The end of the Cherry Lane was crushing. The entire six thousand dollars that Julian had inherited—a considerable amount of money then—had been dissipated on props, costumes, and rent, and Julian still owed money to friends. He wrote one of his creditors, Robin Prising in England, that he refused to seek work only to be "broken by the system . . . in the obvious potboiler job." What was an obvious choice, of course, was to accept a job with his father, but his brother, Franklin, had already been "beaten incapable" by the family business, which his father wanted Julian to continue. To Robin, Julian confessed that he lacked the requisite organizational talent, although it would seem that administering a theatre company requires similar skills.

They ate one meal with Julian's parents, another with Judith's mother, and scraped by. Mabel Beck found Judith an afternoon job posing in a white outfit as a nurse for a pediatrician. Lost without the theatre, Judith was desperate and resumed her sessions with Paul Goodman, feeling more like a disciple than a patient. The time with Goodman had become more of a learning and teaching experience than a conventional psychoanalysis, and the course of study was Judith's psyche.

Goodman told Judith about the startling events that had transpired at Black Mountain during the summer. Cage, Lou Harrison, Remy Charlip, and Goodman had all tried to persuade Judith and Julian to come to Black Mountain, but at that point they had already rented the Cherry Lane. They had wanted to extend the boundaries of poetic and experimental theatre while at the Cherry Lane, and to some extent, they had succeeded; but the really giant step had been taken by Cage.

Early in July 1952, Cage performed a series of his sonatas and interludes in a large tent. Charlip had printed programs on tiny pieces of toilet paper and placed these programs on a table next to the entrance. Also on the table was a large bowl of tobacco. During the concert, the audience was invited to roll cigarettes with this tobacco, using their programs as cigarette papers. The concept exemplified the extremely improvisational spirit of Black Mountain, a community in touch with some of the most advanced ideas in the arts and sciences, from Dada to Zen Buddhism and gestalt therapy to Alfred Jarry, Reich, and Artaud (Artaud's works were being translated into English by M. C. Richards, the college registrar). Charles Olson, the college rector, had been conducting a class in verse and theatre, and was interested in No, in Yeats's poetic plays, and Pound's version of Sophocles' *Trachinae*. Teachers like Olson and Richards were advocating a theatre that was not a part of literature but an alchemical art with its own language and practices, closer to magic and ritual than reporting. Instead of dramatic organization and planned control, they wanted hysteria and Reichian release.

Near the end of the summer, Cage conceived a theatre piece where each performer was assigned a time bracket determined by chance in which to enact a particular activity. There were no specific assignments, so each "actor" would have to devise a part. There was no rehearsal, no script, no costumes. The painter Robert Rauschenberg draped an all-white painting from the dining hall rafters, and Franz Kline hung a large black and white painting. From a ladder, Cage read a lecture on Zen, then the Bill of Rights and the Declaration Of Independence. Richards and Olson were speaking from other ladders while Merce Cunningham danced around all the ladders to music provided by Rauschenberg playing Edith Piaf at double speed on a windup phonograph. All this occurred simultaneously while films were projected. The result was what would be called the first "happening," a fluid and unpredictable event. Its origin arose from the nonliterary and nonnarrative bias of the Bauhaus in Germany in the 1920s, which envisaged the stage as a laboratory for experiment, and introduced the new lighting technologies and sounds that had influenced Piscator. While Goodman's reports of Cage's accomplishments at Black Mountain fascinated Judith, they were also a bit depressing in light of the failure at the Cherry Lane. The happening would only enter popular culture a decade later exercising enormous influence on all art, including the presentations of The Living Theatre in the 1960s.

On the ninth anniversary of their 14 September meeting, Julian took Judith to see Cocteau's *Blood of a Poet* for the sixth time. Cocteau was a reminder that they had met in the glory of innovative art. He represented a new fusion of drama, film, and poetry that had consistent appeal for them. Julian thought the film was a "visual poem" and planned to make his own film about love.

Later that fall, they would encounter another reminder of their first meeting: William Marchant who seemed entirely unchanged in nine years, like a Dorian Gray with a porcelain soul. Marchant claimed he was taking the same drug Stalin used to ensure youthfulness. Marchant was writing plays, but Julian thought he had become a superficial dilettante and could not believe that Marchant had once been a close friend.

Refusing to allow himself to become downhearted over the loss of the Cherry Lane, Julian threw himself into the study of German and into reading—Elizabethan drama, Robert Browning's *Sordello* and *The Ring and the Book,* and Edith Sitwell's poems. He was painting prodigiously, he informed Robin Prising, but he still lacked the confidence even to sign most of his paintings and troubled by his lack of progress, destroyed fifty canvases he found inferior. Since he was so literary, so cerebral, others found it all the more difficult to accept him as a painter. He also resented artists' dependence on galleries and typically wanted to eliminate the dealers, who were enriched by a "constricting system which relies on commerce for success." Such attitudes, publicly espoused, would not get him very far in the art world.

On the dresser mirror he shared with Judith was a photograph of Gandhi and a few lines taken from an Auden poem: "the lie of Authority / whose buildings grope the sky / there is no such thing as the State . . . ." The Auden lines were a reminder of their anarchist credo and that now Judith and Julian wished to perform his *The Age of Anxiety* in their living room as a continuation of their notion of a poet's theatre.

Early in November, Dwight D. Eisenhower assumed what Julian called the "vile function of the state," graduating from the presidency of Columbia University to that of the country. The Becks resumed their anarchist contacts, meeting on alternate Wednesdays in their apartment. On election eve, Judith and Julian went to Jackson Pollock's opening at the Sidney Janis Gallery. Julian had attended such events for years but still felt like an outsider, unaccepted and unwanted. Later that night, in the San Remo, Julian saw John Gielgud talking to John Ashbery. Gielgud was thin, impeccable, unapproachable, Julian thought, realizing how disturbed he always was by celebrity, ashamed of his own desires for glory.

In the middle of November, they saw Jean-Louis Barrault's troupe in a version of Kafka's *Trial*. Barrault had been an associate of Artaud's but unlike Artaud could not manage to make his play sufficiently agonizing to move an audience to action: to make them "go out and destroy the outer law and the inner chains, the state's yoke and the spirit's harness," as Judith would put it. Unmoving and intellectual as she found Barrault's company, it was a catalyst, helping Judith define what she wanted in the theatre.

Barrault lacked what Judith called the "unspeakable cry" for which she would reach in her work, particularly in the 1960s. This cry was an echo of her father's attempt to let the world know what was happening to the Jews in Europe, and it would always be an essentially unpopular message.

A few weeks before Christmas, Julian found a temporary position demonstrating a toy fish that did stunts in a tank at Macy's. Mindless mime, this work kept him occupied on the most superficial level. Evenings, he rehearsed *The Age of Anxiety* with Judith and four other actors. Known as the "court poet of the left," Auden had lived in Berlin during the Weimar period after graduating from Oxford and had been influenced by Brecht's plays. He had emigrated to the United States in 1935. First a Freudian and then a Marxist, he was sympathetic to the working classes, although his depictions of them reflected an intellectual voyeurism.

The Age of Anxiety, which received a Pulitzer Prize in 1948, was a dramatic poem that Auden called a baroque eclogue, in which four Americans meet in a New York bar and explore their recollections of the war, and their fears and hopes for the future. Allegorically, each of Auden's characters represents a distinct faculty—thought, emotion, intuition, sensation. The play is slow going, burdened by its language as the characters speak in long soliloquies that are essentially undramatic. Extremely elegant and polished, though moralistic, many of the speeches were quite unbelievable, far too refined and literate, and completely without the authenticity of the barroom felt in the plays of O'Neill or Tennessee Williams. For Judith and Julian, still shocked by their loss of the Cherry Lane, Auden was a sort of soporific, a poet writing for the theatre with all the correct liberal opinions, but hardly voicing the "unspeakable cry" Judith sought.

A more visible representative of that spirit, perhaps, was Jack Kerouac, who came to their annual New Year's Eve party. Kerouac had already published *The Town and the City,* his first novel, and had written *On the Road,* which no one seemed eager to publish, a fact that had filled him with despair. Later, he would put all his fiction in the category of the "unspeakable visions of the individual." Kerouac arrived with marijuana and his friends, poet Allen Ginsberg, novelist John Clellon Holmes, and a record producer named Jerry Newman. Julian found his former classmate endearing though only half-cultured. Handsome, sardonic, a free-flowing heroic spirit, Judith thought, Kerouac soon became raucous and incoherent. In the morning, Newman took them in a cab to his studio to hear North African music. They listened with difficulty because Kerouac was shouting obscenities while encouraging the group to share a bottle of Sandeman port.

Judith and Julian were particularly social beings although Julian often felt a gaping awkwardness in groups and believed his wife learned more from people while he was more dependent on books.

In the middle of January, they attended a Jean Erdman dance concert conducted by Lou Harrison, who earned his living accompanying dancers as well as working as a music critic. Back in New York, he had received a Guggenheim Fellowship. After the performance, he invited Judith and Julian to a party at Jean Erdman's place in the Village.

The Waverly Place flat was tiny and crowded with dancers. Julian thought Erdman's dancing had been sloppy and awkward, and a chat with Harrison convinced him that the composer was hysterical and anxious. Julian spent much of the evening discussing film with Maya Deren, a striking, high-strung but ebullient woman with a broad, tense face surrounded by ringlets of red hair. He had met her in the White Horse the evening Dylan Thomas had read at the Cherry Lane. The daughter of a Russian psychiatrist, Deren was both a film maker and a writer. She had lived in Haiti and filmed voodoo ceremonies, which she described in *Divine Horsemen,* a book that had just been published.

Judith spent most of her evening in the cramped kitchen with Joseph Campbell, Erdman's husband, helping with the preparations and drinks while he discoursed on Hindu sculpture, the beauty of Sanskrit, and witchcraft. When Judith confessed her unrequited infatuation with Harrison, Campbell advised using black magic, even though he admitted it would not succeed unless first used for evil purposes.

Tall, charming, fastidiously groomed, and radiating health, Campbell was drawn to creative women, and he had helped Maya Deren with *Divine Horsemen* and to find a publisher for the book. Although Judith in her projected role as muse to great men would easily have been drawn into a closer relationship, Campbell only wanted platonic friendships with the women he met. Judith would continue to pursue him, though in many ways he was a foil since he was conservative, did not endorse any form of political activism, and could not accept any art that used aesthetic elements for a political message.

18. In Praise of Love

At the end of January 1953, Julian found work typing catalogue cards for the New York Public Library at a salary of fifty dollars a week. An obscure hole, an invisible occupation, it was a way to put bread on the table.

He had been reading Stanislavsky's *An Actor Prepares,* painting and drawing as usual but aware that he was overreaching for effects, and felt forced and uncomfortable with oils. In addition, he sensed that in some subtle way, Judith was discontented by his painting. He took his son to see the art in the Fifty-seventh Street galleries, guilty about times he had flared in anger when Garrick wanted to go out to play after school while he was intent on completing a drawing or poem. Complaining in his journal that artists were judged by their characters before their creations, he admitted that his was lacking. When a friend arranged for him to leave five paintings with Leo Castelli for a group show, Julian was convinced they would be rejected, as indeed they were.

More disturbing for Julian, however, were the investigative hearings of Senator Joseph McCarthy and the House of Un-American Activities Committee, which he felt bound to listen to on the radio. McCarthy had been hounding the novelist Howard Fast, who had admitted he was a Communist. Relentlessly, the paradigm of rude intolerance and prejudice, McCarthy insisted that Fast identify others. It was a "monstrous, horrifying, vile and disgusting" procedure, Julian thought, that made him want to get out of the house and away from the radio.

Still rehearsing *The Age of Anxiety,* at a production of *Love's Labors Lost,* they spoke with Eric Bentley and noticed Chester Kallman leading an exhausted Auden. A week later, they were in Hoboken with Cage, Cunningham, and Paul Goodman watching experimental films to the mournful music of Hudson River foghorns. The evening led to an invitation for Julian to play a bartender in a scene set in a Brooklyn waterfront gay bar, which was shot at the end of February by a drunken Maya Deren.

On the sidelines, Judith watched with Paul Goodman, who was working on his novel *The Empire City* and wanted to integrate some of what he saw. Judith was now seeing him in group sessions, although she felt manipulated by the psychodramas he wanted his group patients to enact, which would perhaps be used as material for his novel.

Goodman had decided that Judith's main problem was that she sought love where it could not be found while neglecting it where it was. Her psychic affliction, he had concluded, was in large part a function of an oversimplified division of the world into matters of good and evil, devils and angels. Practically, as an exemplification of Goodman's observation, Judith found herself in court over the permissions rights for the *Ubu Roi* translation that she had done with Julian. Arming herself with a copy of Kafka's *Diaries,* she found herself standing before a judge allegorically named Chimera. The judicial process was based on humiliation, Julian observed, with the court ordered to rise, sit, and remove hats at the convenience of authority.

In April, Judith and Julian were relying on Dexedrine for late-night rehearsals of *The Age of Anxiety* and working on a production for Madame Piscator, who had assumed direction of the Dramatic Workshop when Piscator returned to Europe. The tension of overwork contributed to another explosion of Julian's "ugly and wicked temper," a fight, and talk of separation. Julian felt frustrated by his inability to physically express his love for Judith, and he berated himself for acting like an uninterested partner.

The conflict was in part caused by Julian's unhappiness with the fact that friends were always staying over or moving in. While Julian saw the presence of such guests as a test of his ability to give without receiving anything in return, the test itself could be hard to bear if repeated often enough. Robin Prising had brought his lover, Alex Burdett, from England, and they had been in the apartment for weeks, dispossessed finally by Judith's mother whose breast cancer had metastasized.

Judith had been seeing a morose and disapproving man who owned a hi-fi shop on Eighth Street, but he was just a convenient sexual stop after the San Remo. In the disorientation caused by her mother's illness, taking her to Mount Sinai Hospital for radiation treatments, Judith fell in love.

One night in early April, she saw the writer James Agee in the Remo talking to Frank O'Hara. Immediately struck by his presence, she decided to seek him out as a lover. Two weeks later, Julian reported having had a friendly talk in the San Remo with Agee whom he had originally met at one of Peggy Guggenheim's parties.

In the middle of May, in the San Remo where Judith always expected the marvelous might occur, she spoke with Agee about writing and an individual's responsibility for war. During the Second World War, Agee had been a conscientious objector. Before the war, he had worked for *Fortune,* which had sent him to Alabama with the photographer Walker Evans to write about the fate of itinerant sharecroppers.

Agee had felt compromised by the fact that he had been prying for *Fortune,* which he saw as a symbol of the corruption that kept the farm workers impoverished. The book he wrote, *Let Us Now Praise Famous Men,* was burdened by its mannered rhetoric and a preachy tendency to melodrama, but it revealed a tremendous compassion that made it required reading for those on the left. Agee extended his audience as film critic for the *Nation* and in 1951, had written the screenplay for John Huston's *African Queen,* the classic film starring Humphrey Bogart and Katharine Hepburn.

Tall, still slim at forty-three, with a full head of dark hair, a resonant voice, and a southern accent, Agee wore old suits, chain-smoked, and drank a quart of whiskey every night. Witty, articulate, he presented a vigorous facade, except for the warning signs of his rotting front teeth. As a precautionary measure, he slept with a bottle of nitroglycerin tablets near his bed because he had suffered two serious heart attacks while working on *The African Queen.* Married for the third time, he was living with his wife, Mia, and their children, the marriage strained by numerous infidelities. When he met Judith, he was writing a screenplay on the life of Gauguin and was at work on *A Death in the Family,* a novel about his father's early death in an automobile accident, for which he would receive a posthumous Pulitzer Prize.

Waiting to see Agee at the Remo, Judith spoke with Chester Kallman; Harold Norse, whose first book of poems, *The Undersea Mountain* had been published; and Allen Ginsberg, who inscribed a poem, "The Shrouded Stranger," into her notebook. Regularly, at around three in the morning, Agee would come into the bar for a nightcap, and he and Judith would return to the little red house on King Street in the south Village where he lived, five minutes from the Remo.

Before seeing Agee, Judith had worked in the pediatric office all afternoon and helped Julian in the evenings. He had been fired from the public library for consistent lateness caused by the

Auden rehearsals and was designing a version of Edna St. Vincent
Millay's pacifist play, *Aria da Capo,* for the Dramatic Workshop.
On heavy doses of Dexedrine, he worked for sixty-six consecutive
hours without sleeping, completing his stage set ten minutes
before opening curtain. This terrific outburst of energy was itself
a sign of disorganization, and it would become a continuing pattern for Julian.

Together, they saw Tennessee Williams's *Camino Real,* Sean
O'Casey's *Plough and the Stars,* a de Kooning show where Julian
pointed to the places where the painter had allowed narrative elements to compromise his abstraction for the sake of audience,
and a Motherwell show at the Sam Kootz Gallery, which Julian
denounced as too commercial.

Early in June, Judith and Julian had a joint birthday party
that ended at 7 A.M. on the banks of the Hudson, where Paul Goodman, Allen Ginsberg, Jackson MacLow, Philip Smith, and his
lover, Lester Schwartz, bathed their feet. Julian was unrelieved by
the festivities. At twenty-eight, he was unemployed and being
helped by his parents. He was unsuccessful as a painter, and no
magazine had accepted a poem after four years of submissions.
Like Paul Goodman, he was an outsider, secretly ashamed of his
intellect because it prevented the acceptance by others that he
craved. Balding quickly, he felt he was being eaten away by time.
Sexually, he was a "suicide," languishing in knots of frigidity and
abstinence. His various artistic activities—painting, designing,
writing, and acting—were motivated to attract Judith, who he
thought was insufficiently interested in him. These were strategies to prevent a boredom that Judith saw as an attempt to block
pain.

All personal neuroses or the concerns of art were put aside,
however, at the horror they felt at the electrocution of Julius and
Ethel Rosenberg near the end of June. Convicted of passing crucial atomic secrets to the Russians, the Rosenbergs represented
an ugly apex of anti-Communist hysteria that ravaged the lives of
artists and intellectuals in the 1950s. Their execution was a collective trauma for the left, comparable only to the execution of

the anarchists Sacco and Vanzetti in the 1920s; the novelist E. L. Doctorow has tried to understand the historical conditions leading to it in *The Book of Daniel:*

> Many historians have noted an interesting phenomenon in American life in the years immediately after a war. In the councils of government fierce partisanship replaces the necessary political coalitions of wartime. In the greater area of social relations—business, labor, the community—violence rises, fear and recrimination dominate public discussion, passion prevails over reason. Many historians have noted this phenomenon. It is attributed to the continuance beyond the end of the war of the war hysteria. Unfortunately, the necessary emotional fever for fighting a war cannot be turned off like a water faucet. Enemies must continue to be found. The mind and heart cannot be demobilized as quickly as the platoon. On the contrary, like a fiery furnace at white heat, it takes a considerable time to cool.

A number of American artists would be stunned by the execution. The poet Sylvia Plath, for example, then working as an assistant editor at *Mademoiselle* in New York, reported in her journal that she broke out in hives at the exact moment she thought the Rosenbergs had been killed; the next day, she would begin her novel, *The Bell Jar,* "wondering what it would be like, being burned alive all along your nerves."

On the day after the execution, at two in the morning, Judith and Julian took the subway to a Brooklyn funeral home. Staggering, awed, among American flags and a praying rabbi, they passed the Rosenbergs' bodies, lying in adjoining coffins and dressed in white like bride and groom, an unexpected look of composure on their faces.

The next day, Julian took Garrick to the Museum of Natural History, where he jotted down a remark of Theodore Roosevelt's inscribed on the walls: "If I had a choice between righteousness and peace, I would choose righteousness." The remark seemed indicative of the threatening bellicosity in America that characterized the era and made life seem all the more precarious.

Still emotionally shocked by the Rosenberg execution, Julian began working as a shoe salesman in a department store on Fourteenth Street. The humbling art of fitting shoes was one way of avoiding Judith, who was returning at seven in the morning from Agee's. Something about his presence made her buoyant, though it was clear that Agee had established certain boundaries, and his daughters represented a family he did not want to lose. He did not permit Judith the illusion of romantic, irresponsible love, though he admitted that sex could lead to love.

Much of the lovers' time together that July was spent in discussion—each of them was extremely opinionated—and some of it, reading to each other. When Judith read her poems, Agee reciprocated with his. He serenaded her with Beethoven, which he played on his piano, and read her all of his short novel about adolescence, *The Morning After,* and from his progressing screenplay on Gauguin, the romantic who had abandoned family and culture for the sake of primitive adventure.

In bed, Agee was powerful, and sometimes he made Judith feel like a mouse being played with by a giant. Though Agee would not call it love, and Judith knew he had other lovers during the summer of 1953, she still invested his every movement—the way his face would shift from tenderness to scorn, his labored breathing at night—with significance. She liked the way he served the morning coffee in a kitchen that faced a ruined statue of the Virgin, a constant reminder for Agee of his Roman Catholic childhood. Every time she left him, she was afraid it had been their final meeting: that he would leave to make a film somewhere or possibly die from his heart condition. When she saw him acting the town drunk in his film version of Stephen Crane's "The Bride Comes to Yellow Sky," she wondered why he had to squander his talent but was still tremendously excited by his image on the screen.

Still buried in the department store selling shoes, Julian was reading Dante and Krishnamurti, searching for a new loft to resume the theatre, and was now only painting sporadically. He was struggling to complete a long poem that he called "Heroiad." Cutting it down to size seemed difficult, though it helped him to see the extent to which his writing was hurt by a prophetic tone of blame, a didactic declamatory quality that often seemed turgid.

One night in July, Judith and Julian were visited by the photographer Weegee who was making a documentary film on Coney Island. Dirty, disheveled, lecherous, with a perpetual cigar in his mouth, Weegee was a grotesque Ubu-like figure, an absurd clown, who like Bodenheim blindly followed his instincts, convinced of his genius. Characteristically, Weegee wanted them to pose nude for him, and his brazen casualness about the request impressed Julian.

During the summer, Julian was also trying to complete a film of *Ladies Voices,* which he found an excruciatingly laborious process. For advice on the film, he met Maya Deren at the Blue Mill Tavern, just outside of the Cherry Lane. All in black, looking like a cinematic witch, Deren was animated, outlandish yet languorous at the same time. She warned that sloppiness or impatience would ruin any film and then took him to her apartment—reeking of cats and painted blue like a novelty shop in Port-au-Prince—to show him her voodoo sculptures.

Another night in early August, he spoke with Agee at the Remo about film, and Agee told him about his friendship with Chaplin, who had always been one of Julian's heroes. Curiously, Julian felt relieved by the affair, knowing that he had been unable to give Judith "the heart of his love." But a few nights later, when he accompanied Judith and a few other friends to Agee's place just before Agee left with his wife, Mia, for a few weeks in the country, Julian felt impotent and jealous.

19. Circling the Moon

The dark void Judith felt upon Agee's departure was relieved by two events: Agee returned at the end of September, and with Julian, she rented the top floor of a three-story wooden building on One Hundredth Street and Broadway, just a few blocks from their West End Avenue apartment.

The landlord, who was suspicious about their plans for a theatre, owned a fruit and vegetable business on the ground floor. He had reason to be apprehensive. The loft was unlicensed by the Department of Buildings for the sort of assembly any theatre required; it had only one exit; and as a wooden structure, the building could never satisfy the fire codes. Characteristically, Julian's blithe anarchism disregarded the dangers though consequences were inevitable.

Previously, the loft had been occupied by a beauty parlor. To disguise the floral wallpaper, Julian used brown wrapping paper and painted the ceilings black. He began to forage in abandoned buildings on Amsterdam Avenue, retrieving the old wooden floorboards for lumber to construct sets, a prospect Judith no longer found romantic.

Work on the loft made Julian consistently late for his job, and once again he was fired. He had been hired during a strike—though at first unaware of it, he was working as a scab—and he was dismissed when it was settled. He found a free-lance position in the "pink chic" world of window dressing. Run by well-groomed homosexuals who "preened their windows," the work was at least related to set design though its scale was smaller. De Kooning had been a window dresser during the Depression, Duchamp had done windows, and Dalí had decorated them for Bonwit Teller in 1939. In any event, Julian understood that he needed to work to help support his family as well as his theatre and any theatrical effort was a means of engaging Judith.

The emphasis on the affair with Agee had shifted because of the prospect of the new theatre, and the work made Judith less available. One night near the end of October, he asked her to meet him. Instead of waiting at the Remo, she went to the White Horse. Some people were at a table arguing about Trotsky with a tall, lanky young man with broom-straw hair, a boyish grin, and a Missouri twang. After a long commentary on Ukrainian anarchism, the young man, whose name was Michael Harrington, persuaded Judith to leave with him. Coincidentally, he lived in a room just below Harald Brixel's old room on West Tenth and Hudson streets. Two hours later, she confessed that she had to leave to meet James Agee. Scandalized and offended, Harrington, who knew Agee, was innocently convinced that the writer would never deceive his wife.

On the night Judith had met Harrington and later saw Agee, Dylan Thomas was at the White Horse, drinking heavily. He was in New York to rehearse his radio drama *Under Milk Wood* for a performance at the 92nd Street YMHA. Judith and Julian had heard him desultorily talking on a dull panel on film with Maya Deren and playwright Arthur Miller on 28 October. Ten days later, they heard that he had died. In a furious fit, Judith crashed her hand through a glass pane, realizing too late that he was the "flower among us, the drunken sweet singer, screaming like a child and penning like a prophet."

Troubled by Thomas's death, Agee began to ration himself to five drinks a day. He told Judith about his difficulties with women, who "circled him like the moon," and she understood that he was now too conflicted, confused, and fearful to continue the affair—"too torn for me to lean on."

She had needed him as an escape, partly from her situation

with Julian, partly because in the fall of 1953, fifteen people were sharing their apartment, including her ailing mother. One of their housemates, Nina Gitana (a pseudonym for "gypsy girl") who had been part of the company at the Cherry Lane, had become disoriented, talking incoherently about Nietzsche, dancing and singing, and punning incessantly. Madness, Judith observed, was "a breaking down of hierarchies."

The real signal that the affair with Agee was changing occurred at a party that Judith and Julian had at the end of November to which they invited Agee, who brought Mia, his wife, a tall, stern, beautiful woman. Judith felt intimidated by Mia and unable to communicate with her. Agee and his wife spent the evening improvising film scenarios with Lore and Fritz Perls. Watching Agee, Judith saw how he must have felt vicariously fulfilled by the "prehistoric manliness" he had drawn for Bogart in *The African Queen.*

A version of that coarse machismo was evident in another of the guests that evening, who would impinge greatly on both Judith's and Julian's lives. Very handsome, Lester Schwartz was a gruff thirty-year-old man who worked in the Brooklyn shipyards. Feigning stupidity and despising anything intellectual, he was actually quite brilliant. Early in the evening, he began flirting with Julian, accusing him of wearing a mask of joy to cover a soul in sorrow and informing Julian that he had the reputation of unhappy celibacy. Lester had heard this from his lover, Philip Smith, who passed out that evening from an excess of alcohol and had to be put to bed.

Much later, after most of the guests had left, Lester—who had an incorrigible appetite for seduction—began flirting with Judith. Finally, Lester, Julian, and Judith—after having made passes at each other all night—went to sleep in the same bed as Philip Smith. Except for Lester, these were all people with certain reservations, who were trying as best they could to create an open sexual community without quite knowing how, to some extent suffering the curse of a "perpetually ardent" generation as the poet Frank O'Hara would put it in his poem "For the Chinese New

Year." The evening may have ended on a note of farce and without any sexual consummation, but it was a seed of the much broader sexual sharing that they would experiment with in the future.

In the winter of 1953, rehearsals of *The Age of Anxiety* continued. Julian dressed windows during the day and built a stage in the loft in the evenings. Depending on Dexedrine, he only slept three or four hours a night. One morning, depleted and hung over, he imagined his body stiffening with age, his teeth decayed, the corners of his mouth turning down, his rapidly thinning hair gone.

Most of the time, however, he felt energetic and enthusiastic. With Judith, he saw Broadway productions of *Richard III* and *Coriolanus,* Geraldine Page in Gide's *Immoralist,* and on Broadway, Jane Bowles's *In the Summerhouse,* which they agreed had been written according to a rigid formula. They saw Ian Hugo's films, Merce Cunningham dance, and heard a mass by Lou Harrison with the composer at a rosewood piano singing ecstatically, and a concert of Alan Hovhaness's music. When they saw Jean Erdman dance, they again found her work lacked vitality. At a party at her apartment afterward, Judith remarked that Joseph Campbell looked like a movie star.

While the affair with Agee had abated, it had not entirely terminated. One night at a party at the Perlses', Fritz cornered Judith in his bedroom, demanding to know whether she experienced orgasms. Perls was trying to flirt, but the incident seems typical of a sort of reckless inquiry common among New York intellectuals and artists in the 1950s. Whatever had terrified the general culture into silence, they could brazenly admit. Absolutely nothing was private or sacred, and every fugitive fantasy was available for discussion or analysis. Agee arrived at the party after two in the morning, and shared a cab west with Judith and Julian at dawn.

He had agreed to record the role of the radio announcer in *The Age of Anxiety.* A few days after he did the recording, Judith visited his Cornelia Street work studio, making love while in the fireplace old reviews of his work provided heat and light. On another night, he complained of being too old for her. They were still meeting for talks that would last through the night, and he was reading to her installments of *A Death in the Family* as he wrote them, dropping pages filled with his tiny, round pencil marks on the floor like a radio actor.

At the same time, she was being pursued by Alan Hovhaness. Meeting him for tea or lunch, she found his mood was restrained and mystical, and he told her on one occasion how the spirit of Prokofiev spoke to him through candles during a performance of *Romeo and Juliet.* Hovhaness traveled frequently, and in letters, he became more ardent, declaring his love with "my life's fire burning at the center with burning mouth." These rapturous declarations, full of longing and adoration, would continue. He wrote that he carried her picture with him, that he wished to serve her, that she was the apex of his life. For Hovhaness, she was a goddess whose mind had all the "brilliance and nobility of the sun."

20. The Broadway Loft

Work on the new loft was so demanding that Judith and Julian did not even pause to celebrate the New Year. The winter of 1954 was full of disconcerting signs of violence. Although an armistice had been signed in Korea, the anger, as Julian argued, had karmically come home.

In group sessions, Judith found Paul Goodman insulting and antagonistic. Around the corner from the loft, the police found boxes of ammunition in a place where, supposedly, cardboard boxes were being assembled. Their friend Frank O'Hara was shot in the thigh by a robber.

Most horrifying of all, early in February, Maxwell Bodenheim and his third wife, Ruth, were stabbed and shot to death by a man named Harold Weinberg in the hallway of a Third Avenue rooming house. Both attracted and repelled by Weinberg who was half her age, Ruth Bodenheim had been flirting with him. At his trial, he proclaimed that he should be rewarded for having killed two Communists.

By the end of February, the stage was completed and covered with a patchwork of old carpeting Julian had salvaged. Early in March, the oddly assorted chairs that Julian had retrieved from abandoned lots and mended were lacquered black, and a curtain was made of Julian's *Ubu* costumes. *The Age of Anxiety* opened on 21 March with admission by donation placed in a tambourine near the entrance.

Judith had been worried about further episodes of "breaking." Feeling some constriction high in her chest, she saw a hypnotist, after which her lines were delivered unimpeded. At first, the loft was packed, especially on weekends, with enthusiastic audiences and friends—Joseph Campbell, Alan Hovhaness, Paul Goodman, Fritz and Lore Perls—but on later nights, they had to face the despair of tiny audiences. Julian rationalized such disappointments by arguing that recognition was no longer his aim, just the theatre work itself, which he began calling "the revolution."

As a revolutionary act or at least as an extension of the open community of artists they envisaged, Judith and Julian began inviting the audiences to the West End Avenue apartment after performances. *The Age of Anxiety* ran through April, closing with a celebratory party at John Ashbery's apartment, though Judith resented the presence there of all the artists who had not attended the play.

Although *The Age of Anxiety* was an extended dramatic poem, a fulfillment of their original intention to present poetic drama, Julian knew that the play was old-fashioned as theatre and whatever he and Judith wanted to say as directors was as yet undiscovered. Strindberg's *Ghost Sonata,* their next production, was another transitional choice, like Chekhov's or Ibsen's plays the work of a nineteenth-century sensibility straining toward the future but not fully part of it.

Subtitled a chamber play, *The Ghost Sonata* exposed the illusions and false values buttressing a rotting social structure by relating how a young idealist rises above the hypocrisy of the privileged class. Julian's set was a burned-out forest, and his Salvation Army costumes were decorated with hyacinths, appropriate symbols for the innocence of the young idealist. He had been designing displays for a department store in Brooklyn, work that he found pathetic and useless, the erection of painted curlicues to sell merchandise. Like so many millions doing work they did not want to do, he felt full of despair.

When *The Ghost Sonata* opened in June, he had not slept for four nights. He was hallucinating, and cracks in the wall became witches and frogs. This vision of what he called in his journal "alternate mind," intensified by Dexedrine and marijuana, gave him a glimpse of the second sight attributed to madness.

In a state of creative arousal after the opening of the play, Judith and Julian met in their own bedroom for a night of lust, a rare moment for Julian that left him temporarily swimming with passion. But the sexual circumstances of their lives had already formed patterns that were hard to change.

All during the rehearsal period, Julian had courted Irma Hurley, who played the dying daughter in the play. Walking alone in Riverside Park at night, they had long conversations together. Julian thought Irma seemed lonely and in need of affection like some heroine in a play by Tennessee Williams. Similar to his pursuit of Frances Clarke, whose wedding Julian had attended a year earlier, Julian's relationship with Irma Hurley was an exercise in artificial passion, an affected attempt to gauge the extent to which he could be attracted to women.

Judith had become involved with one of the actors she was directing, Tobi Edelman, who had the role of the idealistic student. Prior to the opening, she made love to him on the stage set. As an actor, Tobi posed constantly. He was either excessively sincere or obviously clowning, a silly mask shellacked to his face, Julian thought, but Judith idolized him.

When the play closed at the end of June, after several weeks of dwindling audiences, Julian borrowed his father's car to drive Tobi, Judith, and her mother to Washington, D.C., for a tour of museums and monuments. As in some tale by Gertrude Stein or André Gide, Julian realized he was drawn to his wife's lover. Since Tobi was willing to accept him, they all formed a strange triangle escorted by the ailing Rosel Malina. From one point of view, this alliance was another outgrowth of the dream of a community of artists; in a more sinister, psychological sense, it represented another competition using the powers of attraction and love.

Julian returned to New York to his job in the Brooklyn department store. Judith had received another role in "The Goldbergs," this time playing the pregnant niece of Molly Goldberg, a role she felt was lifeless. When the filming was completed, Julian took Judith to Sardi's. The movie star Franchot Tone, for Julian a reminder of the lure of commercialism, was seated at the next table.

By the middle of July, both Judith and Julian felt they needed to escape the sweltering heat of the city. In Washington, Tobi had left them to direct a production of *Much Ado about Nothing* in Annapolis. Julian felt abandoned by someone who he decided had a lack of genuine commitment to their relationship and to the theatre he was building. At the same time that he yearned for Tobi, he was full of a sense of his own guilt and embarrassment.

Julian's parents were traveling in Europe, and he could use their car. They drove north through Maine and then to the lonely, severe wilderness of the Gaspé Peninsula in Canada. Julian was working on another dense long poem. With Judith, he began to work on a translation of Racine's *Phaedra,* and Judith worked on a libretto for an opera on the life of Buddha, on which Alan Hovhaness wanted to collaborate. Each full of creative energy, Judith and Julian joined as lovers again.

21. A Death in the Family

In September, Judith finally left the pediatric office she so despised, and Julian resumed his work designing windows with the perennial complaint that there was not enough time left to write or paint. He was able to read Kafka's *Castle* and James's plays, which only showed him how a great novelist could botch drama. To his journal, he confided that he felt like Celia in Eliot's *Cocktail Party,* searching for an alien life pattern in which he could never fit and despising himself in the process.

Even stage design seemed like a dubious accomplishment, but for Jean Cocteau's *Orphée,* he planned to simulate a Greek village. Tobi had returned from Annapolis, prepared to take the role of Orpheus. Nina, sound again after a summer in Provincetown, would play Eurydice, Judith would play Death, and Julian and Philip Smith were to be angels.

Opening in the beginning of October, the play ran for six weeks to audiences that seemed respectful but discouragingly small and unresponsive. Wallace Fowlie, Julian's Yale professor, attended, as did the baroness de Rothschild, but not as many of the friends who had supported previous productions. One exception was James Agee, who showed up for the final performance and told Judith that no matter how long the intervals between their meetings, he would never grow cold or distant.

Judith and Tobi had resumed their relationship. Their involvement seemed wildly passionate to Julian, who believed that the lovers might have run off were they less concerned with his welfare. At the same time, Julian berated himself for his cautious restraint with Tobi, his inability to announce his own desires. By the middle of October, Judith's infatuation seemed to ebb, in part because she found Tobi's Orpheus pompous and too Shakespearean. It made her suspect shallowness and insincerity. But Tobi's reluctance to continue the relationship prevented Judith from functioning, leading her to episodes of self-destructive dramatization that Julian thought only marked a subconscious desire not to act.

To free herself of Tobi, Judith spent an evening with Lester Schwartz in a Village hotel and then made love with him on another night on the loft stage in front of Orpheus' villa surrounded by Julian's nine sculpted muses. She thought Lester was too vigorous a lover, too ardent and unsettling, but he helped alleviate the sense of loss she felt for Tobi.

But if Tobi was no longer a lover, he was still very much a collaborator, directing Claude Fredericks's *Idiot King* in Piscator's epic style, with rehearsals beginning in November. A sober allegorical morality play about a pacifist king played by Julian, the play lacked a defined line of action. Julian realized the central problem posed by the play was the danger of combining the spiritual and the worldly, but despite its seriousness, its language was imitative, affected, and repetitious. Like *Beyond the Mountains,* it would fail to find an audience, and a number of performances were canceled in December because no one except the actors had appeared. Playing a nun, Judith was frequently afflicted with her "breaking" problem. *Beyond the Mountains* had failed due to inexperience, but *The Idiot King* was a flawed play.

Lamely, *The Idiot King* ran through the first week in January when Julian began preparations for Pirandello's *Tonight We Improvise.* Judith was still working on the libretto for Hovhaness. She attended a concert of one of his choral works at Carnegie Hall, sharing a box with Martha Graham. A week later, with Julian, she saw Clifford Odets's *Flowering Peach,* with Hovhaness conducting the music he had composed for it. The production was mediocre, Julian thought, but during an intermission, he exchanged a few words with Tennessee Williams, who was, as usual, indifferent to any notion of drama other than his own.

Julian had a similar experience with the arrogance of narcissism when he took Judith to an opening for Dalí on Fifty-seventh Street. Looking like some caricature of a surrealist artist, Dalí was swollen with his accomplishment. Judith noted that he was now quite unpopular with the avant-garde, who felt Dalí was only interested in manipulating an audience for money.

Most of January and February of 1955 was devoted to rehearsals of the Pirandello play, a period marked by a frequent use of hashish by Judith and Julian. As usual, Julian had the pressures of attending to the hundreds of tiny details of sets and costuming that had to be resolved before any opening. At the last moment, he had to dry an abstract painting made by Jackson MacLow for the stage floor with electric heaters.

Opening in early March, *Tonight We Improvise* was greeted by a spirited audience. Irving Beck was so carried away by the provocations of a heckling actor that he hit him with his umbrella. The critic Lionel Abel, John Cage, and Merce Cunningham were all full of praise, and Fritz Perls spoke about possibly backing the play in a larger theatre. Julian felt the production succeeded because he had so carefully followed Pirandello's intentions.

A playwright of the age of relativity, Pirandello wrote plays that were epistemological probings of the subjectivity of truth. His masterpiece, *Six Characters in Search of an Author,* had been written in 1920 at the start of Pirandello's attempt to test the reality of the stage as a medium. Although *Tonight We Improvise* was written a decade later, after Pirandello had done his best work, it applied and to an extent clarified his concern with role-playing that was not particular to the stage but a part of the psychology of everyday existence.

The experimental trigger of *Tonight We Improvise* is its prologue when the beginning of the performance is disrupted by an offstage commotion that confuses and annoys the audience. The problem is that the actors have decided they can no longer accept their lines or their roles, and they tell the director, played by Julian, that they want the power to shape their speeches as they see fit. In an interlude, the actors mingle with the audience, expressing their dissatisfaction with the preordained structure of the play. This attempt to suggest the autonomy of the actors as creative principals would become a central feature of the work of The Living Theatre in the 1960s, and what seemed a revolutionary departure to many in their audiences was actually a notion that began with Pirandello.

In *Tonight We Improvise,* Pirandello's reaching for spontaneity may have been an idea with more weight than his dramatic situation could support. In the play, an Italian named Palmiro and his shrewish, dominating wife guard their four daughters, who are being courted by four aviators. The daughter with the most prominent part, Mommina, was played by Judith, and her suitor, by Tobi.

In love with a cabaret singer who spurns him, Palmiro is stabbed in a barroom brawl but refuses to die, much to the consternation of the director. Then the other actors quit, refusing to continue as mere marionettes of author or director, in effect resuming the conflict of the prologue. Stressing Pirandello's inconclusiveness, his unbalancing sense of the paradoxical, the play might seem cerebral, a drawing room comedy whose humor depends more on an incipient sense of anarchy onstage than on a language that turns on itself. But audiences responded to the dispute between the actors and the director in the late winter of 1955 as they had to no previous production The Living Theatre had attempted, and every night, extra chairs had to be brought in to accommodate the overflow crowd.

The success of the Pirandello play continued through March, despite the absence of advertising, reviews, or tickets since audiences were still solicited for donations. Judith had discontinued her private meetings with Paul Goodman and only attended group meetings intermittently. She had been outraged when, in a joint session with Julian, Goodman had flatly declared that a woman could not be an artist because her primary concern was with her body. At the same time, he was pressuring her to stage *The Young Disciple,* another of his plays.

In the spring of 1955, Julian felt particularly overworked. He was revising the translation of Racine's *Phaedra* with Judith, which began rehearsals under Tobi's direction in March. At Columbia University, Julian studied illustrations to help with the Louis XIV style he needed for the costuming. Still occupied on some level with his paintings, he left a group of them at the Stable Gallery and was told to bring new work in six months. When he showed the work to Betty Parsons, she declared it was too decorative—a criticism that Julian interpreted as meant for the eye alone.

At the same time, he was revising a long poem, "The Isle of the Dead." Writing and painting no longer seemed as invigorating as work in the theatre, and he only seemed to come alive on the four nights the loft was open to the public. Secretly tempted by glory, he felt as if he had broken wings. Almost thirty, he was "wounded by ambition" and stunned by all that he had not yet achieved.

Julian's sense of the fragility of life was emphasized by the shocking news in the middle of May that James Agee had died at the age of forty-five of a coronary occlusion in a taxi. He had been trying to finish *A Death in the Family,* troubled by painful attacks of angina, and had been taking nitroglycerin and chloral hydrate, a sedative. Judith was crushed, perhaps as much for the talent that had been lost as for the love they had shared. Agee had once explained that they were not in love, a condition the world associated with a pain they were civilized enough to avoid. Now, however, Judith was left with only the memory and pain.

Phaedra opened two weeks after Agee's death, and Judith had plunged into its preparation. Racine's seventeenth-century version of a play by Euripides, the action revolved around Phaedra's lustful passion for her stepson, Hippolytus. In red velvet and gold lamé, Judith identified with the "struggle for control over relentless passion" that the role required—in some sense, all the men she had slept with outside her marriage, including Agee, were versions of Hippolytus.

Julian covered his stage with a white velour, and the walls were illuminated from behind to create just the glow he wanted for his costumes, but still they seemed stylized to the point of precious affectation to him, pretty poses for actors who failed to soar. What the play required was a fabulous display of passion, Julian observed, but Tobi's sterile, shallow, and pedantic direction put Judith in a straitjacket. For Judith, the result was a return of her "breaking," and one night, she blanked out on her lines for one terrible endless minute, unable to remember who she was.

22. Halls of Bedlam

Early in June 1955, Julian returned to what he regarded as the sheer torture of Beck Distributing. With Judith, he had ingested peyote, and experienced the overwhelming pleasures and terrors of a simulated schizophrenia. After the intensity of the trip and the enormous relief he felt afterward, he could no longer face the false extensions of show windows. He knew his father would accept any level of performance, and if organizing the distribution of automobile parts meant he would have less energy for The Living Theatre, he expected that Tobi's contribution would compensate.

In the middle of the month, however, Tobi suddenly announced that he was leaving New York to return to his directing position in Annapolis. As far as Judith and Julian were concerned, he was abandoning *Phaedra* and them permanently.

The jolt of Tobi's decision would turn out to only be a minor tremor in the light of what would follow. Julian had asked Jackson MacLow whether he wanted to take a small role in *Phaedra* even though Julian found he had become grumpy and bitter, suffocated by his own bohemianism. When MacLow called to express his interest in the role, he spoke to Judith and added that he was on his way to City Hall to join a group from the Catholic Worker to protest against the State Defense Emergency Act, which mandated taking shelter during air raid drills.

The Catholic Worker had been started by Dorothy Day in 1933. Anticapitalist as well as anti-Communist, it was composed mostly of pacifist and anarchist volunteers who worked without pay and helped maintain a newspaper and a national system of homeless shelters and communal farms. Believing in direct action and hostile to war in any of its forms, they chose to oppose the state in the Quaker tradition of nonviolent resistance and had been chastised by the Roman Catholic hierarchy in New York for advising young men not to register for the draft in 1948.

In a white lace dress, Judith took the subway to City Hall Park, where she saw MacLow parading with a placard protesting the resumption of nuclear testing. One of the other demonstrators, a thin, angular man missing several teeth, Ammon Hennacy had wavy gray hair and wore a red bandanna across his forehead. He had seen *The Idiot King* and began talking to Judith. As a young boy working on his grandfather's farm in Ohio, Hennacy had driven the pioneer labor leader Mother Jones in a horse and buggy to a miner's meeting in West Virginia. He spent the First World War in a penitentiary in Atlanta because he was a conscientious objector, where he met and studied anarchist philosophy with Alexander Berkman, interned for his attempted assassination of Henry Clay Frick.

Hennacy introduced Judith to Dorothy Day, who immediately impressed her. Fifty-eight years old, she had thick white hair braided tightly around her head, high cheekbones, and slanting eyes. She wore a Hopi cross, and had an air of indomitable resolution and contained anger. Her father and her three brothers had all been newspapermen, and she had been a journalist as well. As a young woman, she wrote round-robin verses with Maxwell Bodenheim, and she was so often seen drinking with Eugene O'Neill in a Village bar called the Hell-Hole that she was reputed to be his lover. During the Depression, she had been moved by Kropotkin's *Memoirs of a Revolutionist,* which was being serialized in the *Atlantic Monthly,* and was determined to do something to relieve human suffering.

Day and her followers believed that there could be no genuine security in the event of nuclear attack and that the current civil defense program only created a false sense of security while preparing for the eventuality of a catastrophic war. Warned that they would be arrested if they remained in the park when the sirens sounded, Judith and the demonstrators were bussed to a police precinct and arraigned. The seventeen men and eleven women were separated and placed in cells. Judith had brought Saint-Simon's memoir of the corruption of Louis XIV's court, which she was reading for the performance of *Phaedra* she was scheduled to give that night, but she was unable to concentrate.

After a few hours in the Tombs, the demonstrators were brought before Judge Louis Kaplan. In the court, Judith was able to speak with Julian and noticed Michael Harrington, who was affiliated with the Catholic Worker and whose pale face reminded her of Agee's.

The judge picked her out of the group immediately. Several of the demonstrators were laughing when Ammon Hennacy's name was mispronounced, and Judith offered as an explanation the fact they they were all giddy with hunger. The judge then asked her where she lived, and how long she had lived there. Flustered by the second part of the question, she turned to Julian, who reminded her it was six years. Loudly, the judge said he had asked the question of Judith, not Julian. When Judith told him not to shout at her, the judge asked whether she had ever been in a mental institution as if any protest was, from the viewpoint of the state, insane. Quietly summoning all the accumulated rage she felt for authority, she retorted, "No, have you?"

It was not the most tactful reply. The judge immediately committed her to Bellevue for a psychiatric examination. Pandemonium ensued when Julian rose in protest, shouting "No!" and Judith scrambled on a table, eluding the grasp of two policemen. Momentarily, however, both were seized and carried aloft, struggling, and out of the courtroom by police. The court was cleared, the riot squad summoned, and in the confusion, Julian avoided arrest.

In the Criminal Psychiatric Observation Ward at Bellevue, Judith received a perfunctory physical examination, an open, beltless smock, slippers, a tin cup of milk, and a wet jam sandwich. The next day, she met a number of women on the ward, some hardened by years of institutional life. One of these women, the informal boss of the ward, attempted unsuccessfully to molest her that night. Judith was interviewed by a woman psychiatrist who had seen the Becks' production of the Picasso play and who asked her to explain Julian's paintings, which had been displayed in the lobby of the Cherry Lane. The psychiatrist told Judith she would have to remain for a period of ten days but then would surely be released.

In the afternoon, she was allowed to see Julian for fifteen minutes behind bars and a heavy mesh screening. Distraught, exhausted, he told her that Paul Goodman had helped him reach an important staff doctor. Later in the evening, she was able to see the doctor for a brief interview. Brusque, annoyed, he announced that she could be released the following morning, 17 June. Julian had paid five hundred dollars to a lawyer, a former judge himself, to assist in the release. Alan Hovhaness put up another five hundred dollars for bail.

Out on bail and therefore not really free, Judith could not return to the dry classicism of *Phaedra*. Suspending the production, Judith and Julian drove to New England. In Newport, they visited Mrs. Cornelius Vanderbilt's home. The queen of American righteousness and manners had lived in a seventy-room marble mansion, paid for by the riders of the New York Central railroad, Julian reflected. That night, they slept in the woods, bathed in a brook, and ate berries for breakfast. Meeting Alan Hovhaness in Tanglewood, Judith heard his Easter Cantata. She then went to Stratford, Connecticut, to see *The Tempest* and rejoin Julian; together they visited Garrick at camp.

The combination of the peyote he had taken in June and Julian's terror at Judith's incarceration in Bellevue seems to have broken down certain of his inhibiting barriers. Earlier that spring, Julian had complained in his journal that he was sexless and shied from sexual encounters because he felt inadequate. Paul Goodman had admonished him for not seeking a male consort. Celibacy, Julian concluded, had only produced a fear of feeling. He blamed himself for not making more of the opportunity that Tobi had presented. In August 1955, he began spending time in gay bars for what he termed "nights of pleasure," not searching for sexual contact but not refusing it if it developed. At this point, his journals changed. Unlike Judith's, which were available for anyone to read in the West End Avenue apartment, Julian's were secret, and no one except Judith even knew he kept them. Now they became much less elaborate, more selective, more like workbooks, with only occasional journal entries, so he would not have to describe homosexual encounters.

Early in August, on the tenth anniversary of the bombing of Hiroshima, Julian and Judith distributed leaflets with members of the War Resisters League in front of the Empire State Building, and later downtown near Wall Street. Ammon Hennacy, on a tenday fast of atonement for Hiroshima, picketed the IRS office nearby, and Judith joined him with her own sign.

Back at work for his father, Julian spent his evenings casting for Paul Goodman's *Young Disciple*. He wanted Merce Cunningham, who had agreed to do the choreography, to play the master, but Merce recommended a young dancer named Paul Taylor for the role, a part eventually taken by Philip Smith. With Philip, Judith began dancing classes with Eric Hawkins, which she interrupted to play a forty-year-old woman on the Molly Goldberg television serial. The role was banal but observing the fierce, obsessive Gertrude Berg who played Molly made the experience valuable.

Work on *The Young Disciple* was helped by contributions from several friends, in particular Hovhaness. He had been sending Judith daily letters of praise, calling her his "ideal of courage, beauty and intelligence," his "heaven on earth." For the role of the disciple, Julian had found an untutored, raw, innocent young man named Hooper Dunbar. Although he was ultimately disappointing because he so quickly transformed himself into a *prima donna,* Dunbar provided an early example of Beck's notion that the most genuine performances came from those with the least formal training and affectation. This grew from Piscator's belief that excessive training could cripple an actor and would lead to considerable criticism and charges of amateurism from the critical establishment.

In September, with Dunbar and his friend Soren Agenoux, a pale young man who had followed the progress of The Living Theatre since *Tonight We Improvise,* Judith and Julian attended Paul Goodman's birthday party. With *The Young Disciple,* Julian sought only to please Goodman, though he was no longer sure Goodman even liked him. Everyone at the party seemed intent on influencing each other's affections, and Goodman was particularly attentive to Dunbar. Judith observed that Lester Schwartz, who was again staying in the West End Avenue apartment, continued to be affectionate and loving and Nina Gitana, who was still in the apartment, was disoriented and mad.

Julian resumed his painting. Soren Agenoux had brought Albert Urban, owner of the Ganymede Gallery, to see Julian's work, and he agreed to give him a one-man show in November. Hoping to dispel the notion that he was a dilettante, Julian began a series of new paintings, painting over some of his old oils. At the same time, he was at work on a group of movable panels and painted collages made of corrugated cardboard for the set of *The Young Disciple.*

Julian was also rereading Ezra Pound's translation of Sophocles' *Trachinae,* which he planned to direct after Goodman's play. When Judith wrote to Pound in St. Elizabeth's, informing him of their intention and asking about his health, Pound replied that he was not well, "but yu can do nowt about that. Taint yr fault" in his bizarre shorthand. Pound was the most extreme example of the artist as outsider, so both Julian and Judith could identify with him. That was more important to them than his politics or, for that matter, that of Cocteau or Pirandello, who had melted his Nobel medal down for Mussolini.

A very free interpretation of the Gospel according to St. Mark, *The Young Disciple* was a fulfillment of Goodman's own Socratic fantasy, his belief that he could advise youth on how to live in a disintegrating universe. The play opened on 12 October 1955 to minuscule audiences. Julian felt The Living Theatre had been hurt by a reputation for being too arty. Even more disturbing was the news that cast members had been questioned by local police on the street approaching the loft, asking about their obscene production.

On a freezing, wet afternoon in the middle of November, while Judith and Lester were making love on the cold stage floor, a licensing inspector from the Department of Buildings appeared with an order to close the loft on the grounds that its occupancy was for a maximum of eighteen people, including the actors. While Julian admitted that they had violated "every law there was to break" as far as the building code was concerned, he realized the closure might be a proverbial blessing in disguise. With *The Idiot King* and now a second impoverished effort by Goodman, he had chosen to advance his idea of an artistic community at the expense of his theatre.

Three days after the closing of the loft, Julian had his show at the Ganymede Gallery. By then he was disconsolate. Very few people came to the reception, which, though convivial enough, seemed tepid. Stuart Preston, an art critic at the *New York Times,* dismissed his painting as "florid and mushy." At the end of November, when Julian attended the fifteen-year Jackson Pollock retrospective at Sidney Janis, he noted in his journals that in comparison, his own painting was puny, timid, and unsensational.

23. Naughty Bliss

In her *Diary*, Judith admitted that what she wanted most was "la gloire," that only recognized accomplishment would fulfill her ambitions. She had begun teaching acting privately, which was certainly no route to glory but did keep her connected to her craft. Her dream of her own theatre had again collapsed, her mother was again seriously ill in the winter and spring of 1956, Garrick had chicken pox, and they had too little money because of debts incurred for the loft, but she was not depressed because of the passion she was experiencing with Lester.

While she knew ecstasy was ephemeral, she felt it would help her overcome the loss of the loft, even though any relationship with Lester was problematic, since he was drinking excessively and was also involved with Julian, sexually as well as emotionally. Still working in the shipyards, a binge drinker with a rough, belligerent, anti-intellectual persona, Lester liked to disparage art and the mission of The Living Theatre. Able to earn money and willing to spend it on the expenses of Julian's household, Lester became a sort of surrogate husband, and Judith immediately began complaining that he only wanted to domesticate her, to turn her into the drab, obedient wife. Curiously, Lester was jealous—of Judith's attentions to her mother and the consequent migraines, and of her diaries, which he encouraged her to discontinue and burn.

She resumed work on the libretto for Hovhaness and her classes with Eric Hawkins, but she had gradually weaned herself away from Goodman's group. He was still angry over the failure of his play. When Judith complained to her *Diary* about how hard she always worked for everything she hoped to achieve, she remembered Goodman's observation that busyness was often a vain effort to avoid confronting oneself.

In the spring, she began reading Sacher-Masoch's *Die Liebe des Platon,* a love story of two men, one of whom is disguised as a woman, a mixture of prudery and prurience, which she began to translate from German. With Julian, she saw Orson Welles in a wheelchair at the opening of a revival of *A Streetcar Named Desire* featuring an aging, fatigued Tallulah Bankhead as Blanche Dubois, her grating voice often verging on incomprehensibility. In a restaurant afterward, Williams came over to greet Julian, who compared Bankhead to a matador in a bullring. Five minutes later, Williams was back at their table, quoting the remark as if he had conceived it himself.

Almost every night was spent at the theatre, though most of what they saw was mediocre. At a panel on myth and the unconscious in film, they met Joseph Campbell and Maya Deren, who spoke about Haiti. Frequently, they attended social gatherings, though often without real enthusiasm.

The only person Judith admitted caring about was John Cage, "mad and unquenchable" with his "hearty, heartless grin." With Julian, she visited Cage in Stoney Point in the Hudson Valley. Cage lived in a small hill community of houses built of stone, plywood, corrugated metal, and glass, influenced by Shakerism, anarchist theory, and some of Goodman's ideas. Julian thought Cage was the "chain breaker among the shackled who love the sound of their chains." Cage collected wild mushrooms, which Julian interpreted as a tribute to his reliance on chance as much as to his exquisite taste. He introduced them to Paul Williams, an independently wealthy architect who had studied with Buckminster Fuller and lived at Black Mountain, helping to support it with money. Williams wanted to help find a new location that Cage and Cunningham could share with The Living Theatre.

In July, Julian and Judith drove to Cape Hatteras in North

Carolina to share a cabin on the beach with Lester. There they sunbathed and walked the beaches for miles, astonished at the many ruined, derelict ships they saw offshore. Evenings, they read aloud to each other, read silently, played cards, and continued their ménage à trois.

Julian admitted that he was "inundated with love," though the situation presented its impossible and absurd aspects. Both a lover and the object of a subtle competition, Lester represented the secret salvation of bohemian freedom. Even if it was a competition in which Julian knew he was fated to lose, it contributed a creative edge to the marriage. As mason, welder, and builder, Lester was an emissary from the real world, one of Walt Whitman's working-class toughs with little tolerance for precious distinctions or idealistic notions, and he kept them grounded in pragmatic circumstance. As long as Lester stayed with them, Julian knew he could never follow his parents' middle-class path to acquisitive comfort. Judith thought she could somehow become closer to Julian through the virile surrogacy of Lester. They could all live together in a kind of "naughty bliss," Julian thought, enjoying the "danger of being discovered"—ostensibly by his parents. With Lester around, Julian felt relieved of his sexual responsibility to Judith that had not been fulfilled, he knew, by her "fleeting romances" and felt free to pursue his own clandestine engagements. To Julian, his permissiveness did not seem shocking, though he realized it was unusual.

By the middle of August, Julian saw Lester more as a comrade than a lover. He had been dismayed to learn from Frank O'Hara, while in the sculpture garden of the Museum of Modern Art, that a completely intoxicated Jackson Pollock had crashed his car and killed himself. A leader and the "virtuous daredevil" of the new American painting was gone, and it seemed a testament to the brevity of life.

Another even more pressing reminder was Judith's mother, moaning and crying, poisoned by the pain of her disease. Berating those around her, she seemed to need others to share in her suffering. Judith found her mother's pain intolerable. To protect himself, Julian found that he too had to cut himself off from an awareness of her pain. Near her end, Rosel was moved to Harlem Hospital.

As a reprieve, Judith and Julian drove to Vermont to spend some time with Claude Fredericks. Bland, slightly depressed but quite serene, spending each day in a clockless repose, without anxiety or hurry, Fredericks lived in a white house with a sparse, clean atmosphere. There were very few images on the walls and throughout the house, even in the bathroom, an absence of personal articles. Fredericks had renounced city life and seemed to live without ambition or desire. He was a foil for Julian and Judith: if their apartment seemed like a crowded passageway for friends, visitors, and lovers, Fredericks's ordered house was a retreat, a pure oasis, though his life did seem isolated and detached from social issues.

The city was the place of temptations and connections. In the fall, Judith had a bit part in a film about Jimmy Walker, the colorful mayor of New York during Prohibition. She was on-screen for two minutes as a long-haired Village intellectual in *Bachelor Party* and, more fugitively, as an extra in Elia Kazan's *Face in the Crowd.* With Julian, she saw Julie Bovasso in Michel de Ghelderode's *Escurial* and Ionesco's *Lesson* in a small downtown theatre that displayed two of Julian's paintings in its lobby.

Judith and Julian were still searching for a new location for The Living Theatre. The manager of the Cherry Lane told Julian that Pirandello was certain death at the box office and that he would have to approve any play that they wanted to stage. Off-Broadway had become, Julian realized, as commercial as Broadway, and finding a location would be difficult. A theatre on Sullivan Street in the Village was available (*The Fantasticks* would play there) but too expensive. Fritz Perls spoke of spending ten thousand dollars for a building that once housed a notorious nightclub, but he had spoken before without acting.

Looking for potential backers, Julian and Judith went to a poetry reading at an East Side mansion. In a Louis XV white and gold room with an enormous chandelier that must have held a hundred bulbs, they heard a fat lady in a blue strapless gown declaim her bathetic verse. "Love is a toreador," she cried, "waving the cape of desire." Julian knew her poetry was awful, but it helped him to see how much of his own, in particular the "Heroiad," was too ornate, wrought too ostentatiously.

Every day, Judith and Julian visited Rosel in the hospital, where her condition had deteriorated. She was getting morphine for pain, and she had an infection in her cheek that would not heal. In the middle of October, they entered her room and were shocked to discover her dead. Although her death was not unexpected, Judith was stunned with the realization that so much of what she had tried to do as an actress had been for her mother—a way, vicarious as it may have been, to please her father. Julian arranged for a simple service read by a German rabbi, Naphtali Carlebach, who had been Max Malina's teacher in Berlin. There was no eulogy, no flowers, no music, and Julian covered the pine coffin with dirt.

Judith and Julian observed a week of traditional mourning at home. Near the end of November, Judith entered a hospital herself for elective surgery. For years, she had thought of having her nose reshaped by a plastic surgeon. Irving Beck had told Julian that she could have become a great actress if she had been more conventionally good-looking. As a teenager, she knew that though she was not beautiful, she might be perceived that way, and changing her nose would be a step in that direction.

Just before Rosel Malina entered Harlem Hospital, she had given Julian a sum of twenty-five hundred dollars, the scrimped savings of a woman who had spent sixteen years as a widow on welfare. Judith decided she would use $500 of the money to reshape her nose. Julian was present during the operation—he had wanted to use all the money for the new theatre, and as this was a related step, he could appreciate the droll, middle-class implications of Judith's choice.

24. Celebrations

A year of multiple deaths, 1956 had seen the loss of Agee, Pollock, Rosel, and the loft. In December, Judith and Julian invited Joseph Campbell and Jean Erdman for dinner, and spoke about the symbolism of dreams. Christmas week began with a party at Percival Goodman's small brownstone on lower Fifth Avenue, where Judith and Julian were able to mend their friendship with Paul Goodman. A few nights later, they were at a party at Maya Deren's where Campbell, Eric Hawkins, the art critic Clement Greenberg, and others were entertained by Deren on her voodoo drums. At their own New Year's Eve party, Julian wore his Spanish vest with its gold embroidery and Judith a wide, sweeping white gown purchased at Bonwit Teller rather than the Salvation Army. Maya Deren, again, banged on her drums and danced as if possessed.

A few weeks later, they were still partying, back at Maya Deren's where Tennessee Williams appeared carrying a one-day-old kitten. In the middle of January 1957, they saw Merce Cunningham dance at the Brooklyn Academy of Music to John Cage's music. At a party afterward, Cunningham and Cage laughed all night like "two mischievous kids who had succeeded in some tremendous boyish escapade."

That sort of puckishness delighted Judith, and she visited Joseph Campbell, who shared the same playfulness. She was still working on the libretto for Hovhaness's opera on the life of Siddhartha Gautama, and Campbell began showing her photographs of the erotic statuary at Borobudur. Listening to Japanese No music as it grew dark, they caressed and embraced each other, but Campbell turned contrite. Judith knew that he was bound to his wife by an old-fashioned sense of loyalty. Judith's immediate sexual needs were still met by Lester, though she shared her deepest emotions with Julian, who was again courting her with plans for a new theatre. "My devotion to the theater is a means of making love to Judith," he confessed in his journal.

Intent on raising money for the new theatre, Judith and Julian had a series of dinner parties. The first of these, in February, included Alan Hovhaness; Eric Hawkins; Eric Bentley, whose production of Brecht's *Good Woman of Setzuan* they had just seen; Anaïs Nin and her husband Ian Hugo; Maya Deren; and Julie Bovasso, who now had a theatre of her own she was willing to rent. Julian proposed another run of Cocteau's *Orphée* with Bovasso playing Eurydice, but negotiations collapsed when she refused to work under Judith's direction again.

At a reception at Joseph Campbell's after another Jean Erdman dance concert, Judith stayed in the tiny kitchen again listening to Campbell field questions on mythology, the Cabala, and the Tibetan Book of the Dead. The poet Meyer Kupferman approached Julian, proposing that he and Judith design and direct two operas Kupferman had written, a project that would occupy much of the spring.

Julian was ambivalent about the librettos and his own role as a stage designer. Reading Lester another long poem he was writing—"How to Lament," prompted by Rosel's death—Julian became more aware than ever of his own hyperbole, his tendency to overelaborate, to "gild the lily" by substituting lush detail for substance. He related such deficiencies to his own stage design, reflecting that he had not received sufficient respect from his fellow artists because set design was considered an inferior art. He admitted that his obsessive concern with stage sets could easily transform him into a frivolous "roi-soleil." In the presence of other artists, he was handicapped by his overabundant admiration, which they sometimes regarded as flattery. But those artists were a crucial element in the community The Living Theatre had been trying to establish. The result was that after ten years of struggle, their theatre had still not found a permanent place and had achieved little success or financial support. "Our taste is simply not popular," Julian reflected.

Nothing, however, prevented Julian from working on Kupferman's opera or from going to the theatre. In April, Judith and Julian saw productions they liked of *The Duchess of Malfi* and *Long Day's Journey into Night,* and a preview of Tennessee Williams's *Orpheus Descending,* which Julian believed was Williams's finest effort. When the critics decided the play was too complex, Julian defended it as "unsurpassed" social writing in a letter published by the *New York Times,* worrying, however, that people in the theatre would think he was trying to curry favor with Williams.

Judith had been taking classes in Shakespearean acting with Fanny Bradshaw, and in the middle of April, after attending a lecture on Stanislavsky, she and Julian ran into William Marchant— the man who had introduced them—at Jim Downey's, an actor's bar on Eighth Avenue. Marchant had written the popular Broadway comedy *The Desk Set,* and Julian saw him as a sort of alter ego, a commercial, flashy version of himself.

Reading the "Rock Drill" section of *The Cantos,* Julian noted that he had been reading Pound for a decade, admiring him even as the poem became more incomprehensible. *The Cantos* were the great long poem of the age, Julian believed, and his cerebral nature fed on such difficult works as those of Gertrude Stein or Joyce in his later period. He was also reading William Carlos Williams's long poem *Paterson,* which he felt lacked greatness but which he wanted to read because he was still hoping to produce *Many Loves.* For the Williams play, a location was essential, but after seeing dozens of lofts and theatres, even revisiting the long defunct Genius Incorporated in the St. James Hotel as a possibility, they found nothing. The only bit of encouraging news was a letter from Jean Cocteau allowing them to use his drawing of Orpheus with oak leaf laurels as their signet: "Je suis votre ami et j'accepte tout ce qui peut vous faire de plaisir et vous rendre service."

Most of May was spent rehearsing the operas, which by then Julian thoroughly loathed. With Judith, he visited Cage in Stoney Point, where they made strawberry jam and gathered mint, wild watercress, and asparagus for dinner. Feeling a surge of confidence in his own writing, he gave Cage a group of poems to set to music.

He had left Beck Distributing on civil terms with his father, who finally understood that Julian's heart would never be in the auto parts business. Feeling like an idiot in a vacuum, he began making the rounds of theatrical offices with Judith.

Lester was now contributing most of his salary to the household, caring for Garrick in the evenings, wanting to belong to a family. His need for constant sexual gratification, however, began to weary Judith, and the affair started to pall. The trouble with sensuality, Julian observed, was that after reaching a certain peak, it could become tiresome; and satiety occurred when all possibilities had been explored.

Julian and Judith saw Marchant again in May. The film version of *The Desk Set* had been released, starring Spencer Tracy and Katharine Hepburn, and Marchant was completing a play on the life of Clarence Darrow. Over dinner at Downey's, with Ben Gazzara and Maureen Stapleton drunk at the next table, he read to them from his new play, *Counsel for the Defense,* which was scheduled to open on Broadway in the fall. Name-dropping celebrity after celebrity, Marchant quoted Hollywood producers as if they represented the highest degree of intellectual achievement and argued that he had no faith in "art."

Marchant was attracted to glamour and power, but for Julian, he existed as a prototype of phony success. Marchant's success was galling, especially in view of the fact that The Living Theatre did not even have its own space. But that would soon change. On a stifling day in the middle of June, Judith visited Alan Hovhaness for lunch. She read to him from Robert Graves the stories of Zagreus's frenzy, Poseidon, and Dionysus. Hovhaness played the piano, claiming to be possessed by what he called a blue Japanese flame, a spirit who was dictating his creativity.

Later that afternoon, the gods brought fortune. With Judith, Julian, Cunningham, and Paul Williams, John Cage drove from "columned loft to aerie garage" in his Volkswagen bus, smiling despite the traffic and the fact that their search was now in its fourth month. Finally, they found an abandoned building, formerly a department store, on Fourteenth Street and Sixth Avenue, which Williams declared would be suitable for sharing as a theatre and dance space. This venue would become the home of The Living Theatre and the scene of its greatest American success.

III
Accomplishments

25. Prison

Though Judith and Julian had found what they considered to be a suitable site, they knew that they would need negotiations, lawyers, and then a long process of renovation before their new theatre could begin to function.

Early in July, they visited Garrick at camp. With Lester, they drove north, camping at night, through Maine and Nova Scotia to a town called Pugwash, where there was a conference on nuclear war. As a result of Rosel's long illness, they had let their anarchist-pacifist activities lapse. When they returned to the city, they resolved to join the annual Catholic Worker protest against the State Defense Emergency Act.

On 12 July, a clear bright day, they walked from Dorothy Day's shelter on Chrystie Street on the lower East Side to Sarah Delano Roosevelt park on Houston Street. When the air-raid sirens sounded, Judith, Julian, Dorothy Day, and a group of two other women and five men were arrested, booked, and brought before a judge who angrily sentenced them to thirty days in jail after Ammon Hennacy argued that the group had acted in penance for Hiroshima.

At first, Julian was sent to a prison on Hart Island, where he slept in a dormitory for a hundred men rather than in a cell. For the first time in his life, he was treated as a chattel, ordered to strip for delousing, given a gray uniform, and required to shovel human excrement that was being converted to fertilizer.

As prisoner number 58601, Judith was sent to the Women's House of Detention at Eighth Street and Greenwich Avenue in the

Village. After a shower, she was searched rectally and vaginally for drugs. With Dorothy Day, she was placed in a narrow, airless, six-by-nine-foot, roach-infested, cement cell that had originally been designed for a single inmate. It contained a sink, a toilet, a tin table and shelf, and two small cots, one under the other. Standing on the lid of the toilet, Judith could manage to see Eighth Street and at night the sweeping searchlight from the top of the Empire State Building through a one-inch opening of a small window encrusted with dirt and painted over.

Judith was assigned to mop floors and polish banisters. After her work detail, Judith would return to her cell, where she would try to read Tolstoy. Reading was difficult because of heat that reached ninety-eight degrees, the dimness, and the constant noise of clanging cell gates, the shouted obscenities of prisoners, and the television in the recreation room always set at a high volume—the "trumpet of Babylon," Julian called it in one of his letters.

Prison was becoming a turning point for Judith largely because of the model of integrity and dignity she saw in Dorothy Day. She related to the most hardened prisoners with a kind of simple sanctity that was never sanctimonious and always helpful as the women on the ward brought her their problems. When they cursed as they expressed themselves, she reproved them and went on, offering suggestions. Sometimes, Day read prayers aloud in her cell, which helped Judith to see that she did not have to abandon her own Judaism for the sake of her politics. For Judith, Day represented a crucial link between ethical and spiritual ideals, and political activism, and exemplified how to combine them in ordinary life.

Every evening, prisoners were allowed access to the roof, which was protected by a six-foot wall and covered with mesh. According to Dorothy Day, this was an area where many prisoners exchanged sexual favors. Standing on a bench, Judith could see where E. E. Cummings lived on Patchin Place, Joseph Campbell's Waverly Place apartment, The New School, and the broken windows of the abandoned Hecht's Department Store on Fourteenth Street, which she hoped would one day contain her theatre.

One afternoon, she was visited by Lester, who was inebriated. On another, she heard a dry lecture by Eleanor Roosevelt, the dowager of liberalism, compensating for the guilt of her privileged birth with words on integration and her trip to the Middle East. The talk was poorly attended, but those who heard it were rewarded with ice cream. The entire episode seemed ironic because Judith had been jailed for protesting in a park named for Mrs. Roosevelt's late mother-in-law, and the addicted prostitutes who formed the prison majority had never imagined taking a trip to Jerusalem.

In the third week of July, during an unbearable heat wave, she received a letter from Julian who had been transferred to the Tombs, a maximum security jail in lower Manhattan. Sparrows built nests in the window grill and flew freely in his cell, Julian observed. He had no view of the sky and no roof access, and the omnipresent indoor twilight made him feel forgotten, a subjugated automaton. Working every day as a dishwasher, sometimes for up to thirteen hours at a stretch, he found the real problem was monotony. Prisoner number 483326 reported that he had never been more touched or satisfied by any act in his life than by the resistance that had caused him to be jailed, even though he suffered from terrible bouts of loneliness. Civil disobedience could only succeed in the absence of vanity. It was the opposite of acting onstage, where the actor expected applause and roses. Prison life was based on the humiliation and intimidation of the prisoners, people who were regarded as the dregs of society and for whom Julian, the perennial romantic, expressed considerable admiration. They possessed an unusual degree of altruism, he felt, however restricted their conditions.

Released on 5 August, Julian admitted the experience had shaken his foundations and changed his bearings. In Hart Island, he had boasted to a fellow inmate, ornamenting his career in the theatre with a success that he knew had eluded him. The boast was idle, but it made him promise himself never to lie again. He knew there could be no more self-aggrandizement, though the danger he would have to avoid would be self-righteousness and sanctimoniousness.

If anything, the prison experience moved Julian closer to Judith's and Paul Goodman's view of the 1950s as a period of insidious betrayal, a moment in American history when traditional ideals had been traded for affluence. The Eisenhower era was dominated by constant pressures for conformity and agreement; thinking seemed regimented, alternatives discredited, and dissidence was regarded as deviance. During the 1950s, an obsessive fear of a Communist menace had been exaggerated into a mania by Joseph McCarthy, the scowling senator from Wisconsin with a flair for manipulating the media. The result was loyalty oaths, jingoistic patriotism, and something called un-Americanism. The supposed external Communist threat became a convenient excuse to ignore pressing domestic concerns like poverty and racism, and it enabled big business to join with government in subtle ways. Business emphasized advertising and public relations, and the initial consequence of such a strategy was that the quality of a product was sacrificed to its packaging.

By the middle of the 1950s, the economy became inextricably and addictively tied to the manufacture and export of military hardware and sophisticated weapons systems. The presence of nuclear weapons—which the American public was taught was essential for its safety—created a pervasive fear, a psychic powerlessness. No wonder that in the 1950s, a generation became dependent on tranquilizers, and developed the ability to repress feelings and to shut out reality whenever it seemed inconvenient. In 1959, the top instrumental recording was called "Sleepwalk," a perfect characterization of a somnambulistic decade.

Prison hardened Judith and Julian. They would become even more vocal in their opposition to an age of apathy and abundance, both on- and offstage. Early on the morning after their release, feeling like "little crusaders," Julian reflected, they picketed the Women's House of Detention. After a lunch with Dorothy Day, who had been interviewed by John Wingate for his television program, "Nightbeat," they joined a Catholic Worker contingent at the Russian embassy on Sixty-eighth Street, wearing mourning bands on Hiroshima Day to protest nuclear testing.

26. Cage's Drums

In the middle of August, attempting to recover from the shock of prison, Judith, Julian, and Lester drove to Claude Fredericks's house in Pawlet, Vermont. Living at the end of a dirt road, surrounded by the lush farmland and stunning vistas of the Mettowee Valley, Fredericks had set up his printing press in one of his rooms and was teaching at Bennington College.

In this ambiance of grace and tranquility, every object in the house seemed chosen to please the senses. Breakfast on a grassy, terraced knoll in front of the house was like "breakfast in heaven," Julian observed. For those staying with Fredericks—working in his huge vegetable garden, reading Joseph Campbell's *Hero with a Thousand Faces,* playing croquet on the lawn—life seemed an effortless glide to sunset with, Julian felt, "no impulse to go against the grain which is smooth."

This unreal rhythm continued for a week until Judith told Julian that Lester had the fantasy of having a child with her. Julian was terribly upset, immediately tortured by a jealousy he knew he should transcend but could not. Furthermore, he was convinced that Lester's motive was more possessive and manipulative than loving and that Lester could one day abandon the child to Julian's care. Julian's reaction was hardly surprising. Even if, as a homosexual, he aspired to a sexual identity that was apart from Judith's, they did have a son in common. Garrick had just been bar mitzvahed, and Julian had attended his first Jewish high holiday services since his childhood; and if Judith and Julian saw themselves as part of an extended family rather than a nuclear unit, the extension just did not go as far as Lester's fantasy.

Back in Manhattan, Julian realized how he and Judith had grown together like entwining rivers, each serving the other as both prop and goad. Julian understood that another man's intention to father his wife's child was so threatening and throttling because Julian was still trying to overcome his own sexual inhibitions, still caught in the skin of his own old conditioning.

Lester's proposal, whatever the motive, was still consonant with a thawing of the repression of the frozen fifties and was an incipient ingredient of the new sort of artistic communalism The Living Theatre would eventually propose. The new spirit that might make such a proposal feasible was evident, Julian thought, in another "Nightbeat" television program in the middle of September featuring Jack Kerouac, who had been Julian's classmate at Horace Mann.

With the success of *On the Road,* Kerouac was in the process of becoming a media darling. His replies to John Wingate's pedestrian and belittling questions seemed like the thrusts of a Zen master. *Beat* stood for *beatific,* he asserted, and what he wanted most was to see God's face. When Wingate wanted to know about Kerouac's politics, he answered that he believed in nonviolence, noninterference, and that he never voted.

It was the most persuasive demonstration of anarchism Julian had ever seen. For the first time, he thought, he had glimpsed the character of his generation and its groping for ethical values, a search arising from the despair generated by the Second World War. Though Kerouac could seem confused and uncertain, he was still an "emblem of hope."

If Kerouac seemed poised on the brink of success at the age of thirty-five, Julian felt far from having achieved anything. He faced the almost unbearable prospect of working in the packaging room for his father who would pay him the most money for the least amount of his time. His mother, in the past his strongest support, told him he was crazy to have protested and gone to jail. His immediate circumstances were strained. Lester was still contributing some money to the household and Judith was reluctant to abandon him. Lester's contributions were sporadic and uncertain as he spent his money on alcohol and remained drunk most of the time.

Julian had resumed painting, at the end of September completing a large abstraction he called *The Judgment of Paris*. Instead of the lyric and gaudy mythological worlds he had previously explored, he was now trying to capture his dreams and fantasies, painting in a "subconscious world I have never seen." He had seen a show of the Chilean painter Matta. Its decorative emphasis, and its dependence on aesthetic charm made Julian see that art should be in a state of imbalance and imperfection, like life itself. Painting still left him dissatisfied, a sign of his vacillation, his tendency to want to explore possibilities in too many directions simultaneously—poetry, painting, theatre—without fulfilling any of them.

In October, negotiations for the new theatre on Fourteenth Street began in an atmosphere of unusual excitement. "Burdened by failure," Julian wanted to make his theatre "big" with the kind of "fat applause that Broadway gives." Its purpose would be to stage plays that would not be performed elsewhere, to allow the voice of the poet to be heard in the theatre, and to defy all the compromises of Mammon and the critics representing the standards and values of a dissatisfied society.

One of those critics was Eric Bentley, whom Judith and Julian visited for tea in his white study overlooking Riverside Drive. Julian believed Bentley was one of the best of the critics, although limited by his Marxist perspective. Sitting under a large poster of the Berliner Ensemble, famous for their Brecht productions, Bentley was flattering and encouraging.

In the middle of November, Julian signed a lease for the new theatre, aware that he would need thousands of dollars to renovate the former department store so that it could function as a theatre. He was gratified to the point of tears when his mother pledged the first thousand.

Almost as soon as the legal papers had been signed, Paul Goodman visited the new space, bringing along a potential donor. Goodman did not even inquire about Judith and Julian's experiences in prison but instead began pressuring them to produce another one of his plays.

The visit seemed premature and opportunistic, but it forced Judith and Julian to think about what sort of play could make the strongest statement in their new theatre. To this end, they visited Anaïs Nin, who had once objected to their doing Eliot's *Sweeney Agonistes* but now had few ideas of what to do and only wanted to talk about the problems of keeping a diary.

There were also a series of meetings with Paul Williams, the architect who had originally shown Julian and Judith the Fourteenth Street space. Williams had inherited a large sum of money, some of which he wanted to use for good purposes, and he had offered to draw the plans for the renovation.

The first step toward the realization of the artistic community that Julian wanted his theatre to encompass was taken by Merce Cunningham, who had decided to use the fourth floor of the new theatre as a dance recital and rehearsal space. Early in December, with John Cage's assistance, he moved some of his backdrops into the space. Cage brought with him a variety of percussion instruments—he owned more than three hundred of them at that time—which he donated to the theatre. Julian thought there was a distance about Cage that prevented intimacy and the fullest communication, but he felt Cage's gift was a real sign of the artistic support that would be crucial to the success of The Living Theatre.

27. Pledging the Temple

Judith and Julian celebrated the New Year of 1958 with a giant New Year's Eve party attended by over two hundred guests, half of them uninvited. The raucous hilarity left Julian depleted, even though the painter Larry Rivers had complimented him, encouraging him to show his work more frequently. Actually, Clement Greenberg had praised Julian's work and persuaded the dealer André Emmerich to see his work, though nothing would come of the visit. One of Julian's collages was in a group show at the Great Jones Gallery featuring the work of Jasper Johns, Franz Kline, Robert Rauschenberg, and Robert Motherwell. He had also been asked to review a book on the theatre designer Robert Edmund Jones for *Art News*.

Estimating that twenty thousand dollars was necessary to renovate the Fourteenth Street location, Judith and Julian sent hundreds of appeals to prospective donors, but they only received seven hundred dollars in January.

Julian thought that Hazel McKinley, one of Peggy Guggenheim's sisters, would donate money or lead them to other contributors. Plump, dowdy, a dyed blonde in her mid-fifties who fancied hats clustered with pink roses, she organized a cocktail party and invited twenty young men but was more interested in seducing one of them than in raising any money. There was another cocktail fund-raiser organized by John Preston, an unassuming man who belonged to the Social Register. His brother, Stuart Preston, was the art critic for the *New York Times* who had disparaged Julian's painting and who snubbed him at the party.

In another effort to get backing, they had lunch with Oscar Serlin, the producer of a Broadway play called *Life with Father.* They met him in Louis XIV, an elegant French restaurant in Rockefeller Center decorated with huge chandeliers and a grand staircase, where Serlin ate so frequently the waiter would bring him his food without an order. Brash, boastful, Serlin acknowledged that he could not see beyond Broadway, and Rodgers and Hammerstein's musicals were the salvation of American theatre. When Judith and Julian tried to describe their intentions, he hardly seemed to be listening but remarked that it was dangerous to be what he called "arty-farty." For Judith, it was another experience in "pledging the temple in the marketplace."

Fund-raising was a sort of game for Julian; Judith was more discouraged by the inevitable rejections. She cried frequently and had periods of deep gloom. The quest for her own theatre that had so bound her to Julian was also, she realized, a way of making him suffer, and she confided to her *Diary,* "How cruelly I make him fail in trying to make me happy."

To relieve the gloom caused by the prospect of insufficient funds, the tension before the mail arrived, and the disappointment afterward, they plunged into the life of the city. They were impressed by Dalí's immense thirteen-foot-high "Santiago el grande," which depicted Saint James on a rearing white horse. They met John Cage and Merce Cunningham at Philip Guston's opening at the Sidney Janis Gallery and saw a Robert Edmund Jones exhibit at the Whitney Museum.

At the jazz club the Five Spot, where they heard Kenneth Koch read poems to jazz, Frank O'Hara told them that he wanted to act in their productions and given the right roles, he could become an American Peter Lorre. When Larry Rivers also expressed an interest in acting, they felt the artistic community was responding to their idea of a new theatre. Afterward, they went to a party for Kenneth Rexroth. Speaking in a hip argot, Rexroth was gruffly warm and played them a tape of his own jazz poetry.

Pursuing other forms of knowledge, they listened to Eric Gutkind lecturing on the joyfulness of man. A friend of Rabbi

Malina's, Gutkind was a peer of German intellectuals such as Walter Benjamin and had studied anthropology with J. J. Bachofen in Berlin. He had emigrated to the United States in 1933 and taught at The New School, and had written the books *The Absolute Collective* and *Choose Life,* in which he argued that God was not dead as Nietzsche had claimed, only absent as Kafka implied. A small man who spoke in a heavily accented voice, always repeating key words, Gutkind argued that the final conflict would occur over the money system. The crumbling superstructure of civilization is beginning to rock, Gutkind warned in a message that had particular appeal for Julian, though the real crisis of our times is its sense of hopeless exhaustion.

There were kinkier distractions as well. Lester had left the household in a row on Christmas Eve and returned with Philip Smith for a reconciliation dinner. Later, Lester, acting like James Cagney, brought them to a club in Harlem called Artie's Pad, a dimly lit tenement apartment where a small group smoked marijuana, listened to jazz, and lounged about partially nude storing what Julian referred to as "orgone energy." Some of the orgones were released when two women made public love, surrendering to each other with joy and unmistakable pleasure. The party ended quite suddenly, however, when the police arrived.

The entanglement with Lester was not quite finished, and Judith persisted in the illusion their ménage could succeed. Julian, aware that the relationship was crippled by Lester's lust and his resentment of Judith's commitment to theatre, waited for the next inevitable explosion, which occurred in a violent scene in the middle of March.

Using Judith's tears as an excuse, Julian demanded that Lester leave, and he moved into a rooming house on Broadway with a door that didn't quite close, paper-thin walls, a window on an air shaft, and curious neighbors. The room was only a block away, close enough for Judith to visit whenever she was inclined.

Lester's departure left Julian and Judith with enough money to pay the April rent for their apartment and twelve dollars for everything else. Julian earned a few dollars by erecting a wall of randomly illuminated black and white wine cases for the dancer James Waring, and only compliments for appearing on a panel on architecture at Columbia University, but the overwhelming problem was how to raise the rent for the theatre.

Pleading for money, they visited a wealthy young socialite named Penelope Potter who, gazing at her grand view of the East River, blandly informed them that they would have to apply for tax-exempt status before she could donate. Several weeks later, she would bring them to her lawyer's office, but the immediate problem of how to pay the theatre rent was resolved by a generous sixteen-hundred-dollar contribution from Irving Beck.

Relieved for the moment from pressing financial needs and waiting for Paul Williams's renovation plans to be approved by the city agencies, Julian and Judith resumed their calender of social and cultural events. They attended a Rauschenberg opening at Leo Castelli's elegant East Side apartment. The work was giddy and mercurial, Judith observed; in comparison, Julian's paintings were like cries of distress, desperate and terrifying.

One such cry of distress was raised in a peace march down Broadway, at which Julian carried a Walk for Peace sign. Adlai Stevenson, in the 1956 presidential campaign, had suggested that the Russians wanted to suspend nuclear testing, but Eisenhower adamantly refused to consider ending the tests. Begun by a group of Philadelphia pacifists, the demonstration of seven hundred marchers was small, but it was the first of its kind. Singing, wearing olive arm bands, the marchers, most of whom were young, walked to a granite wall outside the United Nations that had the biblical prophecy "and they shall beat their swords into ploughshares" engraved on it. The atmosphere of vitality at such events, Judith observed, was similar to the high energy flow she often felt in successful theatre collaboration.

Two other events in early April contributed to maintaining this energy. One was Judith's discovery of a poem with a torrential rhythm and an epic sweep that she realized was of "vast significance." Allen Ginsberg's "Howl" was a "scream of anguish and beatific love," which she read aloud to Julian driving in the spring snow. Like Judith, Julian was able to immediately identify with the poem and to accept it as the poem that best spoke for his generation.

In the same week, a young man named Jack Gelber brought them the script of a play he called *The Connection*. As soon as they read the play, Julian and Judith decided to do it. About a group of drug addicts waiting, like Samuel Beckett's tramps, for their fix, their unadorned street speech contrapuntal to a jazz group playing on stage, the play was unusual and had considerable power. Essentially a play without plot or conflict, and therefore unlike the dramatic play now so difficult to believe that audiences could no longer suspend their disbelief, *The Connection* was related to the jazz poetry of Kerouac, Ginsberg, and Rexroth. Tremendously excited by the unfeigning realism of a play that broke through fictional pretense, extending Pirandello's intentions in *Tonight We Improvise,* Judith read the play to Lester, who responded to it enormously because of its raw, unliterary flavor. Now they had a new theatre and the play that later would help to redefine American drama.

28. *Communitas*

In the spring of 1958, Judith and Julian received the Lola D'Annunzio Award given by the *Village Voice* for their decade-long contribution to the off-Broadway movement. Judith's good mood was sustained by Lester, even though there were still battles with him because he wished to return to the apartment and kept appearing in the evenings with mysterious sums of money. One night, he took Judith back to Artie's Pad in Harlem where, after smoking some marijuana and examining photographs of an orgy, they made love.

Together with Julian, but sometimes with Lester joining, they went to a series of parties in April. In the poet LeRoi Jones's loft, there was a party for Jones's magazine *Yugen,* which was attended by women in jeans without make-up, the space illuminated entirely by candles since the power had been cut off by the electric company. At a party for Paul Goodman in Hoboken, with Goodman glowing with the news that his novel *The Empire City* had been selected by a book club, Julian met Barney Rosset, the intelligent, hip publisher of Grove Press. There was a party at Maya Deren's apartment, during which Deren danced with her eyes drawn tight in anger, hair frizzily wild, looking like a gypsy in her embroidered clothing, and another in Anaïs Nin's apartment, where M. C. Richards spoke to Julian about the importance of Antonin Artaud's *Theatre and Its Double,* which she had almost completed translating. Richards also praised James Agee's *Death in the Family,* which had been posthumously published and was about to receive the Pulitzer Prize. John Cage and Robert Rauschenberg were at Nin's party and at a dance concert, sitting next to Judith, Julian, and Jasper Johns, a few nights later.

Such stimulating encounters were less important to Judith and Julian than a lecture by the philosopher and theologian Martin Buber that they attended at a Unitarian church at the end of April. They had been reading Buber for some time, and Judith had entered his remark "Eternity beats against me in the flame of the lived moment" in her *Diary.* Eighty years old, a short man with a large head, a warm, genial face framed by a trimmed white beard, Buber spoke in a soft voice, without notes, on his dedication to peace between Jews and Arabs in Israel.

As far as the theatre was concerned, a major source of worry was whether Paul Williams's plans would be approved. Extremely handsome and especially genial, Williams was spontaneous and quick to accept suggestions. Primarily due to his interest in Merce Cunningham, he volunteered to subsidize most of the renovation costs himself early in May. Irving Beck guaranteed the theatre rent for four months, and Lester's Bronx working-class parents loaned them a thousand dollars. Near the end of May, the Department of Buildings officially approved Williams's plans so that the actual work could soon begin.

Before that occurred, Julian and Judith brought their son, Garrick, and Lester to College Park, Maryland, where they met Jackson MacLow, and Paul Williams and his wife, Vera, at a Quaker meeting house. There they heard Michael Harrington give an angry talk on how 8 percent of the world's population consumed half its wealth. From College Park, they joined a peace march to the White House in Washington, D.C., passing Ammon Hennacy in front of the Atomic Energy Commission, where he was in the fourth day of a forty-day fast. Eisenhower should have appeared in the robes of Oedipus outside the White House, Judith thought, but he was playing golf. For Julian, it was a moment of apocalyptic anxieties. France was in upheaval because of the Algerian revolution, and the United States was arming for "monstrous wars."

Most of the world was "blind and bruised," Julian declared in his journal, and at the age of thirty-three, he had been diagnosed as having colitis, which he understood was psychosomatic in origin and probably caused by the strain of soliciting prospective theatre patrons. The cure was in work, Julian realized, but everything depended on the character of that work. With Judith, he had attended another of Eric Gutkind's lectures, this one on the idea of the Israeli kibbutz. Privacy was only a bourgeois prejudice in the kibbutz, where there were no locks, no keys, no private property. Much of the work on the new theatre was to be accomplished in such a spirit.

Given their resources, a lot of the work had to be done by volunteer labor, with a sense of what Paul Goodman called *communitas*. Julian would open the theatre at ten in the morning and only close it after a communal meal at eleven at night. In ninety-degree July heat, Julian, Lester, and a group of others including Claude Fredericks's former lover Jimmy Spicer began removing the partitions of the former Hecht's Department Store, and demolishing sixteen-inch-thick brick walls for a backstage door and a main entrance door. The tiles had to be removed from what would become the lobby floor, and the floor itself was treated with muriatic acid. Paint was stripped from walls with a gasoline torch; windows had to be scraped and cleaned; broken marble steps had to be replaced; and rubble stored in cardboard boxes was disposed of all over the city.

One day, the men formed a chain gang passing eight hundred gypsum blocks; another, 225 bags of sand weighing ninety pounds each were passed. Bags of cement had to be hauled, and one day in August, Judith estimated that 3,400 bricks had to be carried in. One hundred and sixty chairs from the old Orpheum movie house on Eighth Street and Second Avenue had been donated. Judith and Vera Williams scraped these and painted them in gray and lavender pastels, reupholstering the seats with striped awning fabric and drawing oversized circus numbers on the seat backs in bright magenta or orange.

The lobby demanded special attention as it included a brass-piped fountain running as in a public square. Its walls were exposed brick as in a courtyard, its columns painted orange, its floor gold, and its ceiling was sky blue. The stage had to be built of fireproof wood; bathrooms and actors' dressing rooms had to be constructed; and the entire theatre was to be painted in alternate stripes of glossy and flat black paint with a black ceiling as if each member of the audience were inside an old-fashioned folding Kodak with its narrowing perspective. All the work had to be done with the tension of frequent inspections by various city agencies.

In the middle of the work, Paul Goodman would stop in for lunch or a chat. Mabel Beck visited with the news that she and Irving had decided to pledge another three thousand dollars for the renovation work as a tenth wedding anniversary gift for Judith and Julian. In August, M. C. Richards left the galleys of her translation of Artaud's *Theatre and Its Double,* and a month later, Paul Goodman gave Julian the galleys of his *Nation* review of Artaud's book. Julian was drawn to Artaud, recognizing immediately how instrumental Artaud's radical approach to theatre could be.

The Theatre and Its Double had an irresistible appeal for Julian because of Artaud's premise that the plague (rather than bacchanal or divine rout as Nietzsche speculates in *The Birth of Tragedy*) was a primal source of the sense of spectacle. For Artaud, the plague acted as a "scourge," routing morality and destroying the social order. The delirium of the plague state was powerful enough to activate the latent anarchy in all people, to move them to demonstrate with extreme gestures. Theatre, as well, could induce extreme gestures, particularly by imposing a mode of suffering or cruelty on the audience.

In *The Bacchae,* Euripides had dramatized the idea that a community could become demoniacally possessed, but according to Artaud, such a possibility had been rationalized away by the modern world. The most potent form of theatre was analagous to the plague state: "I wanted a theatre that would be like a shock treatment, that would galvanize, shock people into feeling," Artaud had proclaimed. Pure, desperate, primal, such a theatre found its insight in a recognition rooted in its own pain, and unlike the Greeks who worked progressively to gain insight into that pain (catharsis), Artaud used his insight into pain as a disordering point of departure. Artaud's theatre was visceral, an experience of the body, of guts and trembling rather than the mind, a test of the capacities of the nervous system. Julian and Judith were one of the first in American theatre to recognize the importance of Artaud, although it would take a few years for the impact to register in The Living Theatre productions.

Some of the visitors to the theatre during the renovation were, in an Artaudian sense, harrowing. One was Carl Solomon, whose bizarre escapades—such as jumping ship at sixteen in France to go to Paris and see Artaud reciting poems—figured largely in Allen Ginsberg's poem "Howl." Tall, gaunt, with a soulful face but stammering and embarrassed, Solomon said he had walked and hitchhiked to Manhattan from Pilgrim State Hospital, a mental institution forty-five miles out on Long Island, where he had been incarcerated and given repeated shock treatment for four years. Unkempt, ill at ease, Solomon asked if he could work as a stagehand. Incapable of any concentrated effort beyond moving chairs, terrified that someone would call the police, Solomon slept in the theatre one night and disappeared.

A refugee from the state and the system, a Tiresian figure, Solomon symbolized an igniting quality that Judith and Julian wanted to achieve. And like Solomon, they had to suffer certain indignities like getting fingerprinted as part of the procedure to obtain their theatre license and public assembly permit. The fingerprinting process must have grated on the anarchist sensibility and made Judith aware that "everything in our lives is always somehow illegitimate, and therefore alive, changing, moving, actual."

29. A Poet's Theatre

In the fall of 1958, Julian was completing the final details of the renovation and dealing with city electrical, plumbing, and fire inspectors, as well as designing another wall for James Waring's dancers. He was also casting and rehearsing William Carlos Williams's *Many Loves,* a play he had been working on with Judith for years. Feeling considerable pressure, some of it financial since the theatre had only eighty-five dollars left in its account, Julian had been taking Dexedrine for weeks. His commitment to staging the play remained firm, for Williams was a major American poet, and one goal of The Living Theatre was to encourage poets to write for the theatre.

Many Loves had been written in 1940, inspired in part by

Noël Coward and based on one of many cases of unorthodox sexuality Williams had witnessed as a medical intern in the old French Hospital in Manhattan. The play is comprised of three completely unrelated love stories, each one featuring a struggle of some sort and stressing a failure of communication between the sexes. These encounters are observed in what Williams termed a verse "counterplay." Peter, an older man, the suave and elegant backer of the plays, is in love with Hubert, the director, who in turn is planning to marry the leading lady (played by Judith Malina) who plays the three women in the various sequences.

Although the play was almost twenty years old, it had only been performed by an amateur theatrical group in Williams's hometown of Paterson, New Jersey. Williams had declared the belief that no serious drama could be produced in his time because there was no audience for it, but his play had special appeal for Julian. Hubert, the director, wants to revolutionize theatre, "to write for the stage such verse as has never been written heretofore." And the poetry, he asserts, "should be the audience itself," transported to a "world it never knew." Peter, more pragmatic, reminds the younger, idealistic director that audiences are hardly the stuff out of which poetry is made but instead are the bored middle class with the money to pay for tickets, seeking entertainment exclusively. Perennial but fundamental to theatre, such a conflict was exactly what The Living Theatre sought to resolve.

Opening on 13 January 1959, Judith feared that Brooks Atkinson, known as the "Butcher of Broadway," the influential critic for the *New York Times* would not respond to the harsh lack of sentiment in her portrayal of the three women, but apparently the audience liked her because she received eleven curtain calls. Julian had noticed Atkinson rushing out before the end of the play to make his deadline, but his review was respectful, praising Judith's expressiveness and the originality of Williams's form without fully approving of the play.

The review was read aloud at a party arranged by Lester in

his room uptown. Paul Williams; Allen Ginsberg, who kneeled in homage at Julian's feet; an inebriated Jack Kerouac with Garrick Beck riding on his back; Kerouac speaking to poet Gregory Corso in surrealist non sequiturs; Paul Goodman; Jackson MacLow; and a dozen others—all crowded into the room and on the bed drinking champagne, sharing a sense of wild joy and victory.

Two weeks after the opening of *Many Loves,* The Living Theatre hosted the first of a long series of poetry readings and special events. To an overflowing crowd photographed by Henri Cartier-Bresson, Paul Goodman read a series of short sonnets, and Allen Ginsberg read "Kaddish," a long, shattering poem about his mother's insanity. Goodman had previously expressed his jealousy of the younger poet's future fame, and Ginsberg's powerful dramatic presentation overshadowed Goodman's more cultivated and self-conscious poems, emphasizing a certain generational difference between the poets. Julian, who had sometimes felt a distance with Goodman, felt no such barrier with Ginsberg. Early in February, he spent a night "gallivanting" with Ginsberg and Gregory Corso in Village bars, Ginsberg quoting freely from Shelley's poems.

Many Loves continued its run in February and March. Henry Hewes wrote a favorable piece on the play in the *Saturday Review of Literature,* which helped to enlarge its audience. Eric Bentley came and praised the play, and so did Madame Piscator. A baroness appeared in a Rolls-Royce bearing a bottle of Canadian Club, asking to be considered for a future role.

Williams himself attended a matinee. Debilitated by a series of strokes, he sighed repeatedly, telling Paul Goodman, who sat with him, that he did not have long to live. After the performance, he told Judith that though he had not fully trusted her at first, he was now sure she was an actress.

In the spring of 1959, Julian worked on an article on avant-garde drama for the *New York Times,* in which he formulated a credo for his theatre:

If we want to revolutionize the theatre it is because we have faith in a modest mystical awareness we have of things that could happen in the theatre, things no one has yet imagined, things that could happen in the theatre and in life as well. It is like a dream of things to come, a dream we have all dreamed but cannot quite remember.

To enlarge the artistic community Julian sought, they presented poetry readings by Edward Dahlberg, Josephine Herbst, Kenneth Patchen accompanied by the jazz bassist Charlie Mingus, Frank O'Hara, and Gregory Corso. The O'Hara and Corso reading was characteristic of a kind of raw, disreputable energy that became associated with The Living Theatre, and it almost caused a riot. The difficulty began when Gregory Corso started commenting loudly on O'Hara's reading, causing O'Hara to leave the stage in tears. When Corso read, he was heckled by the painter Willem de Kooning who was a friend of O'Hara's. One of the poems Corso tried to read was "Marriage," perhaps his best-known poem, but as he read it, he interspersed comments about how he had stolen one of Jack Kerouac's girlfriends. As it happened, Kerouac, red faced and drunk, was slumped in a stupor under the reader's table, and he began goading Corso to the point where Corso could no longer read. Many members of the audience were drinking and jeering throughout, and when Kerouac began to read from a set of galleys he had pulled out of his shapeless, gray overcoat, he was unable to continue.

The poetry readings were a step toward Julian's notion of artistic community, and even if the Corso reading looked more like a misstep, it was lively and it brought people to the theatre. In April and May, there was a lecture by the designer Frederick Kiesler, Paul Goodman talked about censorship in the theatre, Eric Bentley spoke on melodrama, M. C. Richards on Artaud, and there were talks by Maya Deren, Joseph Campbell, and Eric Hawkins. Audiences for *Many Loves* were diminishing, but people continued to come even though Judith feared the performances had become mechanical and flat.

During the spring, Julian had been directing and rehearsing another play by Paul Goodman, *The Cave at Machpelah,* based on the biblical story of Abraham and his sacrifice of Isaac. Like

Buber, Goodman was interested in the roots of Arab-Jewish brotherhood. Machpelah is the genealogical source for the Jewish as well as the Arab peoples, the site where Adam, Eve, Abraham, and Sarah were supposedly buried.

A young actor named Joseph Chaikin was in the play, and he later complained that though the play was rehearsed for ten weeks, "everything kept going wrong technically—with the company, with the building; there was the threat of bankruptcy, and we kept being stopped, and the production kept being delayed."

Judith, playing Sarah in a gray wig, felt stiff and uncomfortable in her role, a feeling that was aggravated when the air-conditioning failed to function. One of the concepts of Goodman's play was the Jews' problem with idolatry, since they are permitted to worship no image, idol, or fetish. Goodman had been working on his three-act verse drama for twenty years, perhaps for too long. The play was too moralistic, and the actors, Julian felt, were inadequate in the face of the play's complexity. The critics agreed, unanimously deploring a play that was more philosophical than theatrical. "Now we have the inconvenience of a flop," Julian declared, and the play closed after a run of seven performances in July.

30. Jazz

All during the spring of 1959, while Julian had been rehearsing the actors in Goodman's play, Judith worked with Jack Gelber, the twenty-seven-year-old author of *The Connection.* A "sweet, intelligent bohemian," with dark blond hair, as Judith characterized him in her *Diary,* Gelber came from the South

Side of Chicago where his father and grandfather had been sheet-metal workers. After attending the University of Illinois, he worked in the shipyards in San Francisco where he met Kenneth Rexroth. He had gotten involved with a group of addicts, and then he moved to New York. The police burst into his rented lower East Side room when he was making cocoa, suspecting him of preparing heroin. Arrested, he spent several weeks in the Tombs, three days of that time sharing a cell with a murderer, until he was released. He found a job as a clerk at the United Nations but, after writing *The Connection* on unemployment insurance, was supported by his pregnant wife who worked as a secretary.

The Connection is a "jazz play" depicting what critic Jerry Tallmer called the "deep freeze of detumescence and utter hopelessness" of a group of heroin addicts waiting for a middleman or "connection" to bring their drug. Such a subject was unusual in the creamy mayonnaise of the 1950s. The point of view taken by Judith and Julian was also unusual. "We had to show," Julian has explained, "that these, the dregs of society as they were regarded, were human, capable of deep and touching feelings and speech, worthy of our interest and respect; we had to show that we were all in need of a fix, and that what the addicts had come to was not the result of an indigenous personality evil, but was symptomatic of the errors of the whole world."

Instead of presenting the action as a staged performance, Gelber followed Pirandello's route, and invented a producer and writer—both caricatured as "squares" utterly removed from the world they are trying to exploit—who are using actual addicts as subjects of a filmed documentary.

However, from the start, the addicts (like the characters in *Tonight We Improvise*) refuse their roles, murmuring together conspiratorially, awkwardly staring at the audience, and offering, quite gratuitously, abrupt, discontinuous confessions explaining their attraction for their life-style. Sometimes, they are filmed by two cameramen with glaring floodlights, forcing them, as the *New Yorker* critic Donald Malcolm observed, into the grimacing smiles of a toothpaste commercial. During the entire first act, the addicts tortuously complain, anxious, irritable, waiting in Leach's room for the connection. Leach, another sort of middleman who gets his commission by allowing the other addicts to use his room, is afflicted with a horrible boil on his neck. The pace is agonizingly slow, time becomes a heavy weight, the "terrible languor" that critic Harold Clurman observed was so functional a part of the movement of the play.

Against Julian's surrealist background mural of two Egyptian pyramids in a desert, surrounded by palm trees, a turquoise sky, and a winged Magritte eye, the bare stage is illuminated by a naked green light bulb. Off to one side is a jazz quartet comprised of pianist Freddie Redd who composed the music, alto saxophonist Jackie McLean, drummer Larry Ritchie, and bassist Mike Mattos. Periodically, as the addicts whine or snarl, the musicians enliven the pace by jamming. The jazz is never ornamental or programmatic but organic and dynamic, a force on its own, and the musicians interact with the actors.

This is a crucial principle of the play. "When I perform the sax I remain who I am; I don't transfer my whole being into becoming another fictional person," Jackie McLean has stated. The musicians, untrained as actors, were unaffected, and this encouraged the actors to avoid roles or posturing. This would become a permanent feature of the acting in The Living Theatre.

Jack Gelber, Judith observed, was particularly helpful in casting for the play, shrewd, canny, both subtle and enigmatic in his choices. Garry Goodrow, a friend of Gelber's, an actor who had been a saxophonist, was recruited to play Ernie, one of the addicts. Goodrow knew Freddie Redd, who, along with Jackie McLean, had played with the great original bebop saxophonist Charlie Parker. His wife had been impressed by a young actor named Warren Finnerty in a play in Chicago, and when she encountered Finnerty in the Cedar Bar in Manhattan, she introduced him to Gelber, who decided to use him as Leach.

While both Goodrow and Finnerty would become pivotal actors for The Living Theatre for several years, the musicians were less reliable. They were all available to play for low off-Broadway wages because they were each unable to obtain cabaret licenses in New York because of legal problems with heroin, and one of them overdosed—though not fatally—in the bathroom during a performance. Sometimes, a musician passed out during perform- ance or disappeared during rehearsals because of drugs. The drug ambiance, of course, was a violation of the public safety proviso of the theatre license, and it became the risky edge Julian and Judith accepted. Paradoxically, however, the drug ambience helped to foster a sense of family and community not convention- ally associated with drugs.

Lester had become involved with a sentimental, whining woman who had six children, a charitable heart, and an appe- tite for psychodrama. Feeling deserted, Judith "defected," as she put it, with one of the musicians though this was a tempo- rary liaison. Julian approved of his wife's love affairs. Now he was ready to become more actively homosexual. In search of "exotic" pleasures at night, aware of his baldness and his sunken eyes, he seemed a little ridiculous to himself. The sexual demarcations of his marriage were all part of a "confused, mixed-up life," he concluded. "Judith has more demons than anyone I have ever known," Julian confided in his journals, and sex with Lester and others was a way of both manifesting and expelling those demons.

Such "demons" may have affected members of the cast as well, a number of whom experimented with heroin during the run of the play. The painter Larry Rivers, who would later perform in plays by Frank O'Hara and Kenneth Koch at The Living Theatre, has reported that "there was real heroin in the capsules handed out to the anxious actors waiting onstage, some of whom shot up in front of the audience." One premise of the addicts in *The Con- nection* is that the outside world—the "straight" world—is equally addicted to getting and spending, and at the end of the play, one of the actors declares that "everything that's illegal is illegal because it makes more money for people that way." While the middle class might want to vicariously understand the perils of addiction, they would hardly be expected to accept the radical perspective such an argument implies.

The New York critics were no exception, and they universally denounced the play. The *New York Times* assigned it to a second-string reviewer who said the play was "nothing more than a farrago of dirt, small-time philosophy, empty talk and extended runs of 'cool' music." Judith Crist of the *Herald Tribune* found the play "completely tasteless" and without merit. Jim O'Connor in the *Journal-American* wrote that he had seen a "depressing, disgusting play."

The one exception was Jerry Tallmer in the *Village Voice* who found the play "extremely theatrical," praised the jazz and the realism of the actors, and compared Gelber's play—despite its "self-consciousness and over-obviousness"—to *The Iceman Cometh* and *Waiting for Godot.* Tallmer's review alerted his downtown Village constituency to see the struggling play. Dismayed at debts that had quickly risen to over $25,000, Julian moaned to his journal, "not again a theatre of poverty."

His father's gift of another five hundred dollars allowed him to stave off a few of the most pressing creditors, and he was encouraged by a letter in the *Village Voice* by novelist Norman Mailer calling the play "dangerous, true, artful and alive." This would be followed by a letter by Allen Ginsberg, who attacked the daily critics and defended the play as a "miracle of local consciousness." Ginsberg persuaded the influential British critic Kenneth Tynan to see the play. Tynan liked its stark,, unsensational, and unsentimental tone, and he declared it the most exciting American drama he had seen since the war.

Robert Brustein, a young critic writing his first review, understood the significance of the play as a "brilliant occasion," a theatrical event "produced by people who had somehow managed in this one play to break down barriers between what was going on onstage and what was going on in life." An equally enthusiastic piece was written by drama critic Henry Hewes in the *Saturday Review of Literature* entitled "Miracle on Fourteenth Street." Hewes called *The Connection* "the most original piece of new American playwriting in a long, long time."

31. A Dream of Transformation

At the point that *The Connection* was produced, off-Broadway had suddenly blossomed in full flower, and *Show Business* reported that seventy theatres were functioning there as opposed to only thirty on Broadway. In the fall of 1959, besides *The Connection,* an enterprising theatregoer could choose between such works of serious drama as Ibsen's *Enemy of the People,* Thornton Wilder's *Our Town,* an adaptation of Robert Penn Warren's *All the King's Men,* Synge's *Deirdre of the Sorrows,* and Tennessee Williams's *Orpheus Descending.*

While audiences for *The Connection* were beginning to improve, the theatre was three months in arrears with the rent. Julian felt burdened and took more Dexedrine to lighten his load. Judith was rehearsing *Tonight We Improvise,* in a new translation by Claude Fredericks, to be performed in repertory with *Many Loves* and *The Connection,* but Julian felt everything else was on his shoulders, from manning the box office to janitorial duties. Fearing his creditors, he found it more and more difficult to answer the telephone.

On 14 September, his parents' fortieth wedding anniversary and the date sixteen years earlier that Julian and Judith had met, they all drank Moët 1943. Irving gave Julian a gift of seven hundred dollars, and Julian noted that he put the "bourgeois money to bohemian use" in his theatre. Ammon Hennacy and Julian's War Resister friends had received six-month sentences for trespassing on a missile testing ground in Omaha, and Julian regretted his necessary absence, wishing he could have taken his stand with them "against the mutilating power of our time."

He was suffering from insomnia that was only aggravated by cocaine use. He had stopped painting and writing poems because the theatre was all-consuming, but at the same time, Julian admitted in his journal that it was also ephemeral. In October, Lawrence Ferlinghetti, in a lumberjack shirt, read from his book of poems, *A Coney Island of the Mind.* Anaïs Nin read her dense, labyrinthine stories a week later, and her husband, Ian Hugo, showed four of his experimental films.

Tonight We Improvise opened on 6 November 1959 to mixed reviews. While Jerry Tallmer in the *Village Voice* and Robert Brustein in the *New Republic* liked it, Brooks Atkinson in the *New York Times* was disturbed by the rebellion of the actors in the third act when they try to free themselves from the tyranny of director and script. Julian concluded that Atkinson could not understand the play's Joycean dimension, Pirandello's drive for spontaneity and autonomy, and his attempt to engage the audience; but Atkinson was probably disturbed by the staged heckling provided by Jackson MacLow and actor Garry Goodrow.

The good news was that *The Connection* was becoming a *succès de scandale* and a Village cause célèbre. *Time* reported that playwright Lillian Hellman said it was "the only play I've been able to sit through for years." Tennessee Williams was so excited that he left his seat, and paced back and forth at the rear of the house during the entire performance.

A long procession of the celebrated came to see and applaud: Leonard Bernstein; John Gielgud; Anita Loos; Celeste Holm; Lauren Bacall, whom Judith had known at Genius Incorporated; the director John Huston; Salvador Dalí in a gold-brocaded vest with ruby buttons and holding a silver-headed cane; United Nations Secretary Dag Hammarskjöld; and the publisher Bennett Cerf. Anna Kross, the commissioner of prisons, asked the cast to perform for a group of prison officials at an opening of Narcotics Anonymous. Grove Press decided to publish the play; Kenneth Tynan's sister-in-law, Shirley Clarke, wanted to film it; and scenes were shown on Charles Kurault's "Eye on New York" television program on CBS.

Although audiences were now strong for *The Connection* and the theatre was almost breaking even, it was also now $30,000 in debt. Con Edison threatened to cut off power, and Julian was summoned to court because of a violation of the administrative code—a failure to report taxes. To raise money, Julian and Judith had dinner with a wealthy socialite who practically fell off her overstuffed chair when she learned they had been to jail. In the middle of January, they had a cocktail party for three hundred potential donors celebrating the first year of their theatre's existence.

The problems with the audience—the "wild beast" Julian calls them in his journal—continued in *Tonight We Improvise* with a recurrence of rude remarks and fistfights in the audience. Musing over John Cage's remark that "the problem is that of giving people freedom without their becoming foolish," Julian realized the audience could present a crucial, unresolvable dilemma in the future.

The dissension in the audience was reflected in a cast that was not ready to handle the "wild beast" of an audience. They were not yet a real company, Julian reflected, but all strangers to each other, insufficiently connected to support each other's weaknesses. In his journal, he entered a declaration of what he hoped his company could become:

> I dream of a theatre company, of a company of actors that would stop imitating, but that would by creating a full view of the audience move that audience in such a way and imbue that audience with ideas and feeling that transformation and genuine transcendence can be achieved. None of the actors know what I'm talking about.

For the first time, Julian had really formulated the goal of The Living Theatre, a program that would take years to fulfill.

32. Mammon's Revenge

In the interim, there was a theatre to fill. In January 1960, The Living Theatre sponsored presentations of one-act plays by Paul Goodman, Frank O'Hara, Kenneth Koch, as well as a Beckett evening. John Cage read his one-minute Zen parables for three hours, manipulating five tape recorders while David Tudor played the piano.

Julian was particularly driven at this time, taking speed, and smoking marijuana and hashish. With Judith, he spoke at the Artist's Club on Eighth Street, the home of the abstract expressionists, predicting that the next development in theatre would be audience participation. At the Museum of Modern Art, he saw new work by Jasper Johns and Robert Rauschenberg but felt strangely disconnected from it, no longer able to relate to the painting, perhaps because he had stopped painting himself.

He felt a similar distance on a quick trip to a museum in Philadelphia where he had gone to speak on the radio and lecture—looking like a "harried genius," Judith noted—to a few hundred ladies in a synagogue in Wyncote. A suburb ten miles out of Philadelphia, Wyncote had been a restricted town when Ezra Pound was raised there at the beginning of the century with no Catholics or Jews allowed. Now Julian was planning to produce *Women of Trachis,* Pound's version of Sophocles' *Trachinae,* along with Jackson MacLow's chance play *The Marrying Maiden.*

With enough money coming in to keep the creditors at bay, Julian felt he could take time off to see some friends. One night, with Judith, he went to see Tennessee Williams's *Sweet Bird of Youth* with Geraldine Page. Another night, he shared some "oriental delight" with Allen Ginsberg and his lover Peter Orlovsky. Ginsberg had pictures of Baudelaire and Verlaine taped to his refrigerator, and he showed them blades of grass he had collected at Shelley's grave. In any conversation, Ginsberg listened with the same intensity that he listened to poetry, Judith observed.

One afternoon, Judith and Julian watched their friend John Cage performing on "I've Got a Secret," an inane television program. With a Waring blender full of ice cubes in front of him, a vase with roses, a grand piano with five radios on it, and a bath full of water, Cage began wildly striking the piano, watering the roses, drinking a soda, lowering a ringing gong into the bath, and then pushing the radios off the piano. It was outrageous and absurd, Julian thought.

Another absurdity occurred when Julian was asked—along with Helen Hayes, Franchot Tone, and Margaret Truman—in the middle of March to sit on a dais at an occasion honoring Brooks Atkinson, who was leaving his position as chief drama critic of the *New York Times*. Atkinson was the "courier of the bourgeois standard," a champion of fools, liars, sentimentalists, simpletons, and mediocrity, as far as Julian was concerned. The fake gilt of the afternoon confirmed Julian's understanding that he wanted, as Artaud had suggested, to be a man who made creative events happen, rather than merely an off-Broadway producer.

"Make It New," Pound had written, and the spring was spent rehearsing for *Women of Trachis* and MacLow's play. Some of the drawings Julian had done for various stage sets were being displayed at an art gallery—along with work by Frederick Kiesler, pastels by Kenneth Rexroth, and John Cage's scores—but the gallery scene no longer appealed to Julian. Although he knew that theatre work was also inadequate to fulfill all his energies, he was more excited by it than ever.

Tonight We Improvise ended its run in May after 107 performances. It had been the repertory plan to stage two or three different plays every week. To fill the gap, Julian and Judith organized a series of weekly readings of Greek drama. *The Connection* was still drawing well, and it received two off-Broadway Obie awards from the *Village Voice.* Gelber was given one for best play and Warren Finnerty the other for best actor.

Though Julian said he always felt he had done something wrong when he got an award, these awards were needed to offset the ghastly reviews that both *Women of Trachis* and *The Marrying Maiden* received in late June. Even Jerry Tallmer, who had been so staunch a supporter in the *Village Voice,* admitted the program was an "absurd and pathetic failure." The critics deplored Pound's lively vernacular interpretation of Sophocles' play, using it, Julian thought, as a way to batter Pound's revolutionary genius. There could be no new life without new speech, he had read in Eric Gutkind's *Choose Life,* and that Pound had provided.

None of the critics appreciated the randomness of MacLow's play or the cutup score that John Cage had composed for it. In the *Times,* Brooks Atkinson called it "a play composed of gibberish." The "gibberish" was a use of the vocabulary of the I Ching, a Chinese classic by Confucius, intended for "random" techniques of interpretation.

Too abstract for the New York critics and perhaps too self-consciously avant-garde, *The Marrying Maiden* was poorly received, which caused further dissension in the cast, who wanted to abandon it. The actors were only interested in success, Julian thought, believing that he had led them down a path of folly. When Julian asked them for more community and argued that they could begin to take more responsibility for decisions, some of them replied that he was only trying to shift his burdens. With some cast members demanding their salaries, with other creditors threatening to call the marshals, the success of *The Connection* seemed transient and insubstantial.

Gelber, furthermore, had changed after receiving his Obie. He began to haggle over money, and he showed signs of arrogance. For Julian, Gelber and the actors had become conspirators in what he often called "Mammon's revenge." The theatre was a monster of sorts that devoured money with insatiable appetite.

This pointed to a central dilemma for Julian: no matter how, as an anarchist, he despised money as a medium and its accumulation, he knew theatre was utterly dependent on it.

At the end of July, feeling the need to escape the city, Judith and Julian visited their son, Garrick, in a Connecticut camp. Garrick had been spending much of his time with his grandparents, in effect raised by them since the renovation of the Fourteenth Street theatre, but he had performed in *Many Loves* and was usually in the theatre at night. From Garrick's camp, after visiting Yale and Hawthorne's House of the Seven Gables in Salem, Massachusetts, Julian and Judith took a Greyhound bus to Calais, Vermont, ten miles from the Canadian border, to stay with their old friend Nina Gitana who had retreated from the theatre and the life of the city, and was now studying with a Sikh master and living in a cave.

Grim and taciturn, Julian read Shakespeare's history plays, Simone Weil's notebooks, Pound's "Thrones," the poetry of John Ashbery, and Ginsberg's "Kaddish," which moved him because of its spiritual yearning and agony, and its "great love for everything." Judith read Brecht's bloodcurdling *In the Jungle of the Cities,* his *Man Is Man,* and some Ouspensky, and together they took long walks in the woods and climbed hills. Vermont was a place for healing and Julian, whose colitis had gotten worse, fantasized about asking his father to help him buy a place where he could live on the land.

With the entire country occupied by the coming presidential race between Nixon and Kennedy, Julian with Judith and Paul Goodman drove to New London, Connecticut, early in August to participate in a training for nonviolent protest against the building of Polaris submarines. After a week of workshops and a reunion with poet Ed Sanders, who had often been in the Fourteenth Street theatre and had mimeographed copies of *Fuck You: A Magazine of the Arts* there, they picked Garrick up at his camp and took him to Washington, D.C., for a promised trip. At the National Archives, they saw the Declaration of Independence and the Bill of Rights. At the Jefferson Memorial, they took particular delight in Jefferson's words, inscribed on Vermont marble, to the effect that countries needed a revolution every twenty years. From the Jefferson Memorial, they sent Ezra Pound a postcard with Jefferson's rigid, haughty portrait.

33. Europe

Word of *The Connection* had reached Europe, and The Living Theatre was asked to participate in the next Théâtre des Nations festival in Paris in June 1961. This was the most prestigious gathering of international theatre, so it was a highly desirable invitation even though Julian had no idea of how to pay for the company to go. *The Connection* was still drawing well, but the theatre's debt had grown to $35,000. During the summer, both Brendan Behan and Langston Hughes—one night after having dinner with Fidel Castro—had seen the play. *The Connection* now had a new actor named Martin Sheen, a young man with a blank expression who nevertheless seemed able to light up the stage with his presence.

On two Monday nights in the fall of 1960, The Living Theatre presented a group of three one-act plays by William Butler Yeats. The reviewer for the *Times* found the evening audacious but first-rate and singled out Martin Sheen's performance. In the weeks before the Kennedy-Nixon presidential election, Kenneth Koch's parody of the political process and *The Connection,* with Larry Rivers playing Lyndon Johnson and Allen Ginsberg his friend, was staged.

After a performance of the Koch play, Julian accompanied Ginsberg and Peter Orlovsky to the Cedar Bar, where they spoke till four in the morning about sex and psychoanalysis. Although he had flirted with love with a young Dutchman, Julian had held back from any full engagement. Sex with men filled him with a sense of intolerable waste, he confessed in his journal, yet, at the same time, he was beginning to feel "a quivering lust for men that rises like a fire."

Through the fall, Julian was again terribly worried about money, having an insufficient amount to appease either his landlord or the IRS. Julian had agreed to make estimated payments of $150 a month to the IRS. The Living Theatre had applied for and received nonprofit status so that donations from patrons and sponsors could be tax deductible, but they were still charging, though not responsible for, the tax on admissions.

The constant money crisis, frequent appearances in various courts—once for a failure to pay New York City taxes—and the pressure of rehearsals of Brecht's *In the Jungle of the Cities* "demolished" Julian. He was using cocaine and marijuana and was desperately unable to sleep. His eyes were always glassy, surrounded by dark, sunken rings. For days, designing his set in paint-covered clothes, he would eat only peanut butter-and-jam sandwiches at his desk at the theatre. A number of the other actors in the company seemed to be experimenting recklessly with drugs. Julian joined Jim Spicer, who had been running the box office, in a night of heroin and got horribly ill.

The hard drugs had their obviously deleterious side, but marijuana and hashish may also have contributed to a new rehearsal atmosphere that Judith had created, based more on collaboration than telling the actors what she wanted, allowing the actors to design their own movements and encouraging members of the company to incorporate their own ideas. The director, Julian noted, "was resigning from his authoritative position."

Opening a few days before Christmas, the play seemed to baffle the daily reviewers. A play about money and the corruption it causes, it focuses on an extended metaphysical battle between Shlink, a Malayan lumber dealer, and Garga, a young American. The action moves swiftly in eleven short scenes mostly set in the

Chinatown slums of Chicago. As a Marxist, Brecht maintained that issues like food and money were more important to drama than the old issues of love and power. An early play, written when Brecht was only twenty-five, its message—a suggestion of future clashes between East and West—seemed less important than the way it was staged, presented, and designed by Judith and Julian, and audience response was strong.

By the middle of February, Julian was playing Shlink and concerned with raising an estimated $40,000 to bring the company of thirty-three actors and technicians to Paris for the Théâtre des Nations. In March, accompanied by Congressman John Lindsay, Judith and Julian went to Washington to try to get State Department assistance. A nattily dressed State Department official, dangling a cigarette holder, refused to help on the grounds that many congressmen would object to the plays about drug addiction and homosexuality in the repertory, as well as the fact that one of the plays had been written by a Communist.

Judith and Julian returned to plead with Pierre Salinger, President Kennedy's press secretary, who was more sympathetic and warm. Since Salinger's office was next door to Kennedy's in the White House, every few minutes a buzzer would ring, and he would enter the Oval Office. Finally, he telephoned the United States Information Agency to request a reevaluation but then admitted that there was no budget available, and nothing further was heard from Washington.

Howard Taubman wrote a piece in the *New York Times* encouraging support for the trip to Paris, but Julian was only able to raise six thousand dollars. Then a gesture from the artistic community he had for so long envisaged changed the picture. Larry Rivers suggested that a group of artists could donate paintings, drawings, and manuscripts that would be auctioned off in his studio. Allen Ginsberg immediately offered the manuscript of "Kaddish," and this was followed by the donation of a group of drawings by Elaine and Willem de Kooning, and oils by Franz Kline, Helen Frankenthaler, Jim Dine, Robert Rauschenberg, Jasper Johns, and others. Sardi's supplied champagne for the crowd of over three hundred people who paid to attend. The event was like a Fellini grotesque, Julian remembered, and Parke Bernet sold fifty-five works, raising $17,000.

Julian, Judith, and the cast and musicians of *The Connection* boarded a French ship appropriately named *La Liberté* at the end of May. For Julian, France was a place where artists were honored. It represented freedom, a world less limited by the shackles of bourgeois prejudice where he would be able to free his own inhibitions and release his own creative powers. His friend Maya Deren, who threw an opening night party for *In the Jungle of the Cities,* had urged him to write plays for the company himself.

That idea had great appeal because Julian was unhappy with himself. In the Cedar Bar, a few nights before the departure, he had heard someone refer to him as a thinker, not an artist. He was about to celebrate his thirty-sixth birthday, and he felt his belly beginning to swell and could see his chest hair graying. To temper his discontent and change his mood, he took mescaline with others in the company and spent a night on the deck of *La Liberté* watching the stars. The next morning, he began reading Wittgenstein, and went back to Ginsberg's "Howl" and "Kaddish," the kind of poems he had tried to write without succeeding. Ginsberg's relentless frenzy and hyperbole was somehow magnified into an ecstasy he had never reached, although he felt a kinship with the poet's messianic ambitions.

In Paris in June, Judith and Julian met Claude Planson, the director of the Théâtre des Nations. Shrewd, humane, a man who had spent six years in the prisons of five countries because of his activism, he was someone they could respect and admire. Judith told Planson that what interested her most was politics which attempted to alleviate human suffering. Performing *The Connection, In the Jungle of the Cities,* and *Many Loves,* the company won the Grand Prix of the Théâtre des Nations, and the Paris Theatre Critics Circle awarded the entire company its medal for best acting.

From Paris, they took a train to Rome, where Judith and Julian, seated in medieval chairs like potentates under a Fragonard ceiling, presided at a press conference with forty journalists.

It was their first real taste of the enormous interest Europeans would manifest in their work for decades to come. To the tremendous acclaim of audiences of a thousand and fifteen hundred people during the summer of 1961, they played in Milan, Frankfurt, Berlin, Zagreb, Belgrade, and then Athens.

34. Militants

In the fall of 1961, Judith and Julian returned to New York to the disquieting news that the Russians had decided to resume nuclear testing and the United States was considering the resumption of atmospheric testing. Judith picketed the Soviet embassy and with Julian conceived of the General Strike for Peace. The idea was Gandhian. It presumed that everyone would stop their ordinary activities, whether that meant driving a tractor or working in a defense plant, to assemble and demonstrate for peace. Although the notion might have seemed quixotic to someone like Henry Kissinger, it marked a milestone in the American peace movement.

The tactic of the general strike had been imagined as a "social myth," with its consequent unifying power, by the French syndicalist George Sorel. Europeans, particularly the French, had the historical precedent of successful general strikes and a tradition of radical unionism. However, except for the IWW, there was no radical union movement in the United States; and there had never been a general strike that took hold in more than one city in the United States. In September, Judith and Julian sent an organizational letter to some thirty groups, among them the Committee for Sane Nuclear Policy and the War Resisters League; established an action committee that included Paul Goodman, Elaine de Kooning, and Jackson MacLow in New York; and began planning their radical assembly for the end of January.

The voyage to Europe had succeeded in loosening Julian's inhibitions to the extent that he could work politically on such a scale, and it also released a sexuality that he had restrained during the 1950s—"I am becoming a woman," he admitted in his journal. Giving in to the "sodomic yen" had improved his health, and his colitis finally began to dissipate. At the same time, Jack Gelber observed a "palpable spirituality" about Julian that was reflected by the painter Alice Neel who did his portrait, emphasizing a calm, ascetic, anchoritish, and almost prayerful manner.

Early in October, Judith and Julian were stunned by the news that their friend Maya Deren had died of a cerebral hemorrhage, an event that made Julian aware of how he had abused and scorned his own body. The company had begun rehearsing *The Apple,* a new play by Jack Gelber—a play that Judith was more enthusiastic about than Julian—and preparing to reopen *Many Loves* at the end of the month.

They were for the moment more caught up with the idea of the General Strike, and Julian was particularly buoyed by a letter from Bertrand Russell recognizing the "exceedingly great step" of the idea, the "immense work" involved, and offering to sponsor it in England. The theatre became the headquarters for the General Strike, and Julian had telephones installed and bought a mimeograph machine for the rehearsal room.

Judith tried to persuade a meeting of Actors Equity to lend support. When Judith asked the Equity members to consider striking, the actor and singer Theodore Bikel seized the microphone and said she could not ask for a strike. The meeting broke up in mayhem when another red-faced member protested that Judith was management and therefore could not ask Actor's Equity to consider a strike vote.

The Apple, its title a jazz term for New York City but also an allusion to the object of Eve's temptation, opened in December. The theatre became a cabaret where a Chinese woman, a black cook played by James Earl Jones, a Jewish con man, a spastic, a nihilist, and a Pirandello-like drunken heckler witness the death of a stranger, and then, in a lurid communal nightmare with animal masks, imagine his journey after death according to the Tibetan Book of the Dead. Steeped in a mood of cold terror, the play was full of ferocious scenes: a mad dentist drugging his patient and drilling away to "The Flight of the Bumble Bee," and people turning into huge black ants. It was also playing the edge of revulsion—insults, jibes, loathsome anti-Semitic, anti-black and anti-Oriental remarks.

The reviewers were respectful, if uncommitted. While Gelber's play would not duplicate the continuing success of *The Connection* for The Living Theatre and left the theatre "tottering like a maniac on a cliff," it was, in its way, a demonstration of Julian's position that any theatre had to be allowed the "privilege of failure" if it even hoped to break new ground.

A week after the opening of *The Apple,* Julian and Judith received a letter by Martin Buber from Jerusalem. Man's common life depends on good will and responsible accord, Buber had stated in his book *Good and Evil,* and although he shared the feelings that had led to the idea for a general strike, he could not believe there was any possibility of its success. Furthermore, he added, "I dread the enormous despair that must be the consequence of the inevitable failure."

The General Strike had been publicized by articles in the *Village Voice,* by Judith on an all-night radio program, and by Brooks Atkinson in the *New York Times,* now working occasionally as a cultural reporter. When $5,700 was raised for a full-page advertisement by the New York Committee, the *Times* refused to print it, arguing it could be a threat to public safety. In a driving rainstorm, Judith, Julian, and eighteen others picketed the newspaper, and then began distributing the advertisement announcing the times and places of the seven days of protest by hand as a broadside.

From the beginning, Judith and Julian saw the General Strike as a theatrical activity. On 29 January 1962, the General Strike was initiated with a march down Fifth Avenue from the Plaza Hotel to Washington Square Park, where Julian addressed some 350 demonstrators carrying placards. For the next few days, there were torchlight processions, speeches, picketing in front of the New York office of the Atomic Energy Commission, and a rally in front of the United Nations, where Adlai Stevenson, American ambassador to the United Nations, refused to meet with a delegation. Torch-bearing runners maintained twenty-four hour vigils at a half-dozen locations in the city, despite below-freezing temperatures. There was a sit-down demonstration at a display of fallout shelters at Grand Central Station, and over a hundred people picketed at the New York Stock Exchange. At the Soviet Mission to the United Nations, Julian, Judith and journalist Arthur Sainer spent an hour with L. A. Gouliev, the Russian first secretary, expressing their concern over Soviet inability to stop the arms race. The folksinger Pete Seeger sang "We Shall Overcome," and the then-unknown Bob Dylan sang "Blowing in the Wind" for the first time at a strike benefit at the Village Gate. Thousands of strike leaflets had been distributed, a thousand of them sent up in balloons at Battery Park. Similar demonstrations occurred in Boston, San Francisco, Mexico City, and European cities.

The few hundred demonstrators—mostly artists and young people, many bearded, according to the *New York Times* reporter—were only a beginning. The marchers, though they could not have known it at the time, were on the road to the great peace march on Washington of 1968, along with groups like the Women's Strike for Peace and the Congress of Racial Equality.

At the end of February, Kennedy announced the resumption of atmospheric testing. Julian was already in mourning because his father had died earlier in the month from a heart attack while playing poker. When the first hydrogen bomb was exploded, Judith and Julian were at a midnight vigil at Times Square.

On Saturday afternoon, 3 March, Judith and Julian participated in another rally at Times Square organized by the Women's Strike for Peace. On this occasion, several thousand people had appeared, lining the sidewalks from Forty-third to

Forty-eighth streets. The Tactical Forces Division of the police, the so-called riot squad, was prepared to maintain order and keep traffic flowing, fielding 150 officers. On Forty-sixth Street and Father Duffy Square, an island separating Broadway and Seventh Avenue, during a half-hour silent vigil at the end of the demonstration, a man named Richard Kern fell down to provoke a scene, and was immediately beaten and kicked by police. Judith and two other members of The Living Theatre company, Bill Shari and Joseph Chaikin, sat down to shield Kern. They were immediately attacked by police with nightsticks and forced into a paddy wagon.

Julian, standing on the sidelines, saw that Judith's head had been beaten. Outraged, he began screaming, "Shame! Shame!" Suddenly, his head was seized and twisted by a policeman, and he felt blows on his head and stomach. Blood began to pour out of his mouth and nose. Mounted police charged down Seventh Avenue while the foot patrolmen continued to strike Julian, puncturing his left lung and injuring several ribs.

35. A Mad Gambler

While being booked and released by the police, Judith saw Julian on television, on a respirator with his head bandaged. Julian was hospitalized in Bellevue, from which he sent a telegram to Governor Nelson Rockefeller. The patrician scion of an oil fortune was hardly likely to be impressed by Julian's appeal, particularly since he had sponsored a bill requiring universal fallout shelters and had set up his own company to produce them. The scientist Linus Pauling estimated that by 1962 the American government had stored a million megatons of explosive capacity and this figure was scheduled to double each year. No wonder Julian and others in the fledgling peace movement felt that the imminence of nuclear disaster was only encouraged by testing. The real tragedy, as the poet Thomas Merton observed, was that most people could not understand the kind of "witness" in which Julian had participated: in "their blind craving for undisturbed security, they feel that agitation for peace is somehow threatening to them."

In Bellevue, Julian was in a forgiving mood, reading Merton's essay "Red or Dead," Tolstoy's "The Only Commandment," and the anarchist Prince Kropotkin's "Mutual Aid." He left Bellevue after a week to find his theatre close to financial collapse. The company had been again invited to tour in Europe, but no contracts had been signed.

In the next few weeks, Julian went on a marathon personal fund-raising mission and received enough money (including a Brandeis University Creative Arts Award) to pay passage for twenty-seven company members on the *Queen Elizabeth,* with enough money left over for just a week of food and lodging in Paris. On departure day, there was a late-spring snowstorm in Manhattan, and all transportation was paralyzed. Julian managed to hire ambulances, sirens wailing, to transport some members of the cast to the dock. It was a spectacular mode of departure, Julian realized, appropriate enough for a voyage undertaken by a vain, mad gambler, he admitted in his journal.

At the Théâtre des Nations, in May 1962, The Living Theatre performed *The Apple.* The *New York Times* reported that the French audiences seemed particularly charmed by the way the actors gregariously mingled with the audience before and during the performance. This mingling, a Pirandellian extension, was to become a trademark of The Living Theatre. Touring twenty-two cities in France, Belgium, Holland, Switzerland, Germany, Spain, and Italy, The Living Theatre established a crucial base for future operations. Julian was becoming adept at dealing with state-sponsored theatres and commercial managers. Whenever the company performed, Judith sought out the company of other anarchists to set up a local General Strike committee. Eating, sleeping, and traveling together on the road made the troupe begin to feel like an entity. As Joseph Chaikin observed, they lacked "neat edges" and they were not conventionally pretty, but "in Europe they have taken us under their wing."

On May Day in Paris, Julian had written "disobey as much as you can; everything needs alteration" in his journal. It was a dangerous anarchist credo, the sign of a subtle shift in his ability to take risks, and it would inform many of his future actions. In Baltimore on 4 July, with Judith, several other members of the company, and almost four hundred demonstrators, most of them clergymen, he was booked in a courthouse for integrating an amusement park in what was then called a "freedom ride." Back in New York, throughout the summer of 1962, Julian and Judith prepared for a second General Strike, and the company began rehearsing Brecht's *Man Is Man*.

Described by Brecht as a comic play, *Man Is Man* presents the bizarre transformation of Galy Gay, an Irish day laborer, into a human fighting machine. Set in a burlesque India of 1925, the guileless Gay innocently leaves one morning to purchase some fish for his wife, and is tricked by three British soldiers and the seductive widow Begbick into becoming a ferociously aggressive soldier.

"A person is what people want him to be," declares Galy Gay, the eternal victim in Brecht's sardonic play. A dupe in a corrupt world, Gay is used to demonstrate Brecht's belief that there is no justice in the world, though it often occurs incidentally or accidentally, sometimes through error or subterfuge. Written in 1924 and revised considerably over two decades of fascism and war, *Man Is Man* stressed that human will is weak and malleable, and predicted that government would be able to one day "with ease, turn a man into whatever you please." Believing that ultimate reality depended on sociological and political roots and power was a function of expediency, not morality, Brecht was intent on investigating brainwashing and the harsh persuasions of militarism. To relieve an emphasis on ideology that Brecht realized could cause an audience to lose interest, the play was staged in a stark version of Piscator's epic style.

When the play opened in September, the New York critics were respectful, but they found the play too didactic, repetitious, tedious, and overlong. Also, audiences were limited by the rival production of Eric Bentley's translation of the same play.

Man Is Man, with its emphasis on the loony fanaticisms of the military mind, was timely because the propagandistic bellicosities of the cold war had suddenly heated to a boiling point. An American spy plane returned with evidence that the Soviets had deployed two dozen nuclear missiles in Cuba. At the end of October, another American spy plane flying over Cuba was downed by a surface-to-air missile. The confrontation caused unprecedented tensions and fears of Armageddon.

Early in November, along with civil rights activist Bayard Rustin and peace activist A. J. Muste, Julian told an overflowing crowd at the Greenwich Village Peace Center about plans for the second General Strike. On 5 November, leading a procession of demonstrators, Judith and Julian walked from Columbus Circle to the tip of Manhattan to protest in front of the headquarters of the First Army. At Brooklyn College, eighty students stood silently and refused to take shelter during a mandatory civil defense drill. On Election Day, strikers picketed at polling places with signs declaring DON'T VOTE FOR COLD WAR CANDIDATES! Other pickets demonstrated in front of the New York Stock Exchange and the offices of the National Association of Manufacturers, Standard Oil, Boeing Aircraft, General Motors, General Electric, and Union Carbide. These demonstrations occurred—even though the New York police had banned all demonstrations in midtown—and were part of a pervasive turbulence in the country caused by the fear of nuclear holocaust and civil rights agitation.

Political priorities seemed to be at a fever pitch, and people were taking strongly defined positions. Judith received a curt note from Joseph Campbell demanding that his name be removed from The Living Theatre's mailing list "as I am entirely out of sympathy with your cause."

While the second General Strike was smaller and grimmer

than the first, its supporters were no less determined. Julian spoke at the War Resisters League on what artists could do to resist war, and he used The Living Theatre as a prime illustration of the sort of things that could be done. Its future, however, seemed uncertain to him, particularly because he had been served with a State Supreme Court judgment for $6,800 in back rent. From April through August, the company had been in Europe and then busy with the rehearsals for *Man Is Man.* If the debt was not settled, the theatre's tangible assets—office furniture, lighting equipment, the air-conditioning—were to be placed on auction by the city sheriff, and a notice to that effect was placed in *Variety.*

The auction was preempted by another auction. Once again the New York artistic community rallied to The Living Theatre's cause. Julian made two fifteen-minute appeals on radio station WBAI. Alice Neel donated some oils; so did Julian; someone came up with a drawing by Tchelitchew; and someone else, a lithograph by Toulouse-Lautrec. Berenice Abbott and Richard Avedon volunteered some photographs; Weegee offered a group of shots of Dalí; and Helen Leavit, of children playing. Paul Goodman donated two notebooks; Kenneth Koch, the manuscript of a play; Kenneth Patchen contributed a set of silk-screened poems; Jack Micheline gave some poems and drawings; and there were manuscripts by Kay Boyle and Ben Hecht, whose daughter Jenny had joined the troupe. Once again, dangling on its furthermost edge, the theatre was rescued.

Judith with her parents, Rosel and Rabbi Max Malina.

Julian, seated, with his parents and brother, Franklin.

Julian in 1947 (photograph by Bill Simmons).

Julian hanging a poster for *Beyond the Mountains* at the Cherry Lane Theatre, December 1951 (Living Theatre Archives).

Judith and Julian on the set of *Beyond the Mountains*, 30 December 1951 (Living Theatre Archives).

Judith, Julian, and their son, Garrick, in Bryant Park on 4 April 1958.

Judith and Julian in poet John Ashbery's *Heroes,* 19 July 1952 (Living Theatre Archives).

Grove *Diaries* cover (photograph by Helen Brill).

Scene from *The Connection:* Lou MacKenzie as Cowboy, Martin Sheen as Ernie on the floor, Helen Ray as Sister Salvation (photograph by Leroy MacLucas, Living Theatre Archives).

Warren Finnerty as Leach in the second act of *The Connection* (Living Theatre Archives).

Ezra Pound's *Women of Trachis,* 1960. From left to right: Cynthia Robinson, Martin Sheen, Judith Malina in wig (Living Theatre Archives).

Julian and Judith on Sixth Avenue in front of the billboard for *Many Loves* (Living Theatre Archives).

Judith and Julian conversing with William Carlos Williams after a performance of *Many Loves,* February 1959 (Living Theatre Archives).

Scene from *The Brig* (Living Theatre Archives).

Bill Shari and Julian Beck in *The Maids* (photograph by Gianfranco Mantegna).

Mary Mary, Bill Shari, and Julian on *The Brig* set in the Odéon in Paris, 27 June 1966 (Living Theatre Archives).

Judith and Julian in a performance of *Antigone,* 1968 (photograph by Gianfranco Mantegna).

Jenny Hecht (Living Theatre Archives).

Set of *Frankenstein* (Living Theatre Archives).

36. The Fluorescent Tunnel

In January 1963, in the middle of a particularly severe and snowy winter, Judith and Julian received a play called *The Brig* about the brutal incarceration of American marines who had committed some infraction of the military code. Subtitled "A Concept for Theatre or Film," the work was less a play in the conventional sense than a structure with which Judith and Julian could experiment.

The Brig seemed to Julian like a "brilliant connection," a kind of "hideous fluorescent tunnel" between the middle-class conditioning of a past he wanted to abandon and a future he was beginning to imagine. Immediately, Julian decided that *The Brig* should become the next presentation of The Living Theatre and Judith was to direct it.

Its author, Kenneth Brown, was a bartender who read Camus, a Brooklyn "street kid with a rose in his mouth," as he has characterized himself. His first attempt at dramatic writing, his forty-page script had been written three years earlier. He had casually given it to a friend who had passed it along to a happening artist named Al Hansen, who, in turn, eventually passed it along to Julian.

Brown had been in the marines for three years, from 1954 to 1957, stationed in an encampment at the base of Fujiyama in Japan, a place of remarkable natural beauty. While a marine, Brown had an opportunity to discover "manhood": a bizarre combination of war-games, long forced marches, whorehouses filled with Asian women, marathon drinking bouts, and all-night poker games.

Such distractions as wine and women may have been necessary for him to cope with the extreme marine discipline, but when Brown returned from leave four hours late one night, he discovered that he had been declared AWOL. He was confined in the marine brig for thirty days. After his release, he went to sick bay, where he found a former fellow prisoner in a straitjacket. At that point, he decided to write down what he had experienced.

Notorious in the Marine Corps, the Fujiyama brig was a wood barracks with a dormitory of thirty bunk beds enclosed within an iron grating. Prisoners had their heads shaved and were absolutely forbidden to speak to each other no matter what the circumstances. In fact, any speech was carefully controlled. When a prisoner needed to address a guard, a rigid protocol was employed: "Sir, prisoner number . . . requests permission to speak, Sir." Prisoners were frequently punched in the stomach, and constantly insulted and belittled by guards called "maggots." The program employed depersonalization, anonymity, and isolation as methods of control.

Every millisecond and millimeter of the marine brig was about control, and space was one measurement of it. The floor was sectioned off by painted white lines, and permission was needed to cross any white line. If permission was granted, all movement had to occur at a running pace or at least a trot. If any guard was the least unhappy with the prisoner's speed of execution or his attitude, he could harass him by ordering a strip search. The prisoner then would have to undress and hand his clothes to the guard piece by piece for inspection.

The action of The Brig was simple, repetitive, and hellish. Its emphatic point was that sane prisoners had been conditioned to behave like madmen. Implicitly, it suggested that the world was a prison. Brown showed the progress of a day from sunrise to bedtime, arranging the action in a series of dehumanizing episodes where the excruciatingly boring routine of the prisoners was interrupted by the torture imposed by guards.

The first act opens with the intimidation of a new prisoner. The others wash hurriedly; there is a gymnastic session in an open area, then a cigarette break where prisoners are expected to inhale and exhale on command. A guard is accidentally touched by a prisoner, and he hits him hard in the stomach. There is a general search. In the second act, there is a feverish cleanup and an inspection; more prisoners are punched in the stomachs; they are forced to sing the "Marine Hymn"; and one of them collapses with a nervous breakdown.

The military choreography that Brown had re-created had a powerful documentary quality, and its threatening edge of menace, manipulation, and torture made it an appropriate illustration of Artaud's ideas on the theatre of cruelty. The prisoners in *The Brig* were so spiritually defiled and beaten that they were always in danger of snapping, losing all mental control, and breaking down like the prisoner at the end of the play. Artaud maintained, arguing from his own painful experience of mental institutions and electric shock, that the only way to break out of our imprisoning conditioning and to escape the power of the authoritarian state was by rejecting society's madness at whatever cost. For Artaud, the state of madness was analogous to the medieval plague, which presented the basis for an ideal dramatic situation because reason—which he saw as the ultimate, Aristotelian, Western delusion that could only rationalize our mess—would no longer prevail. Furthermore, he suggested that all theatre should reach for such a condition. He wanted a theatre so violent that no one who saw it would ever be able to tolerate violence again.

The critic Susan Sontag has argued that the history of contemporary theatre should be divided into the periods before and after Artaud's influence. Artaud's appeal lay in the vehemence of his denunciations and the violence of his vituperative rhetoric in an age of silence. In accord with Artaud's notion of the outcry, a penetrating scream of protest, Judith directed her actors to stick to the required Marine Corps gestures, inhibited movements suggesting pain. The actors would seem like Artaud's inquisitional victims being burned at the stake, so intent on delivering their urgently apocalyptical message that they continue to signal through the flames while being consumed by the fire. Artaud's scream was suggested by the unusually high noise level of *The Brig,* which caused audiences to complain. Such complaints were appreciated, Julian said, because the high noise level was part of the affliction the audience was expected to feel—"the reverberations of sound in steel and concrete jails."

In order to get the actors to fully feel the sadistic terms of their confinement, Judith required them to read *The Guidebook for Marines,* "the acme of the venerable line of study manuals designed to teach men to kill and function in battle situations." This became the handbook for rehearsals, and in the lobby of the theatre, the actors were relentlessly drilled in the precise calculations of the military. They learned how to march and chant in meter, to pitch the voice with the proper tone of insubordination, to crawl, to take measured steps, to turn corners squarely, to slash with a bayonet. Kenneth Brown demonstrated how to make the beds, how to fold the uniforms, how to swab the floors, how to frisk and be frisked.

At the outset, Judith realized that the free and easy spirit of spontaneous invention that had previously characterized the company during rehearsals could only work in contrast to the mood of absolute tyranny that she wanted to suggest with *The Brig.* She scheduled long rehearsals, usually lasting seven hours. In addition, she formulated a set of unusually strict rehearsal rules, forbidding any lateness, conversation, joking, or eating in the theatre, with smoking restricted to a particular area. Lapses would be penalized by work details.

Such rules helped to enforce an unprecedented discipline for the actors. If the tension of the rehearsals became too great, any actor at any moment could "cry for mercy," and the cast took a five-minute break. Roles were switched frequently, so that a guard one day could experience the humiliation of being a prisoner the next. More than in any previous production of The Living Theatre, Judith required that each particular of the play be "examined with care and we talked without limit until we were all agreed on the meaning of each element." These discussions were the beginning of the consensual spirit that began to govern the group and unify it.

An important communal bonding ritual was marijuana, which was freely smoked by Julian, Judith, and most of the cast. Another was politics, which was why *The Brig* had been chosen in the first place: to dramatize the excesses of authority buttressing an unjust system. Early in February, after rehearsals had begun, the actors were invited to a meeting of the General Strike for Peace that was being held in the theatre and that would be addressed by Paul Goodman. A day later, as one of the special programs The Living Theatre would frequently organize, they saw a series of peace films, including one on fallout shelters, another demonstrating the impact of a one-hundred megaton bomb on New York City, and Eisenstein's *Strike*.

The combination of rehearsing *The Brig* and General Strike activities affected even the apolitical members of the troupe. Joseph Chaikin recalled that he started getting involved in political demonstrations, getting arrested and jailed: "I began to feel that the political aspect of the Living Theatre, which had looked so ridiculous, was very necessary. And the fact that it *was* ridiculous didn't make it any less necessary."

For the first time, actors were beginning to understand that the theatre Julian and Judith were forming was not merely a matter of a role in a given play but a repertory company that was ongoing, and had a particular social and political agenda. One of the new members who had joined because of the General Strike was a tiny blonde named Jenny Hecht, whose father, Ben Hecht, was a dramatist and novelist who had been an outstanding figure in the Chicago Renaissance after World War I. A free-spirited Shelleyan revolutionary capable of soul-searching honesty, Jenny Hecht had acted in Hollywood and on Broadway, although she had the reputation of being difficult and demanding.

Another new figure was Steven Ben Israel, who had started with a small role in *Man Is Man* and replaced Joseph Chaikin in the role of Galy Gay when Chaikin developed heart problems. Born in

Brooklyn, he was a self-taught jazz drummer working as a stand-up comic in the coffeehouses of Greenwich Village—the Gaslight, the Café Wha, the Bitter End, the Café à Go Go. He had also acted in *The Threepenny Opera* during the last six months of its run. Influenced by comedians like Lenny Bruce, Mort Sahl, and Jonathan Winters, he had done an imitation of Lord Buckley, another monologuist he admired at the Village Gate benefit for the first General Strike, came to see *The Connection,* and was astounded by it.

In February, Judith and Julian brought some of their actors to a rally in Washington Square, where a group of young men, including the poet Ed Sanders, publicly burned their draft cards. Such acts were fraught with terror given the retaliatory power of the state. President Kennedy was sending "advisers" to South Vietnam, and the mood of the American public was decidedly hawkish as expressed in such influential organs of opinion as the *New York Times* and the *Washington Post.* Paul Goodman, whose son would refuse to even register, proclaimed to Judith that they would all be arrested for "pot and perversion." The event was so harrowing that Judith dreamed of being executed by a firing squad that night.

Throughout the winter and spring of 1963, the company continued to rehearse *The Brig* and prepare for another General Strike in May. Rehearsals became so intense and money to pay actors so scarce that a number of them began living in the dressing rooms with wives or girlfriends. The front door of the building was never locked, people were wandering in and out at all times, and a number of transient friends of the company began sleeping on the five double cots that formed part of the stage set.

On 8 May, a warm sunny day, Judith, Julian, and their small band of activists assembled at Columbus Circle to hear civil rights leader Bayard Rustin address them. Marching to Times Square, thirty-five of them—surrounded by one hundred policemen, fifty on horseback—were permitted to stand in Father Duffy Square in a silent vigil. In the afternoon, fifty demonstrators picketed the Atomic Energy Commission. That evening, at a rally at the Community Church, A. J. Muste, Paul Goodman, Julian, and Judith spoke; and Bob Dylan sang. Judith and Julian had unsuccessfully attempted once again to persuade Actors Equity to support them. The third General Strike was the smallest and shortest, and one reason was that *The Brig* was scheduled to open on 15 May.

Separated from the action by Julian's barbed-wire fencing that replaced the conventional curtain, the critics generally did not know what to make of *The Brig*. In the *New York Post*, Richard Watts wondered whether what he saw could be called a play and decided that whatever it was, its naturalism bored him. In the *Times*, Howard Taubman would call *The Brig* a play only by the loosest definitions and dismissed it as a "painful evening," though he suggested that the marines should be investigated. Walter Kerr in the *Herald Tribune* called it mindless, and, on the whole, far too self-evident and self-conscious. Only Michael Smith in the *Village Voice* was able to treat the play with respect, although he opened his piece with the recognition that *The Brig* was not a play in the conventional sense but, like Cage's music, an example of art "making it new."

The Brig received the same initially hostile reception as *The Connection,* but now the financial circumstances of the theatre were more desperate and political circumstances more polarized. As a reaction to the civil rights and peace movements, right-wing groups all over the country were pressuring to have books removed from libraries. A week after *The Brig* opened, an off-Broadway satirical revue called "The Establishment" was forced to remove a sketch showing the Crucifixion from its repertoire. A few weeks later, copies of the June *Evergreen Review* were confiscated by New York City police because of a series of erotic photographs that had been taken underwater with bubbles blurring the images.

In June, Julian was unable to placate Con Edison, the utility company, with a back payment, so performances of *The Brig* had to be canceled. Julian and Judith went to a memorial service for the Rosenbergs, who had been electrocuted with Con Edison's power, and sat in at Con Edison. Julian managed to get some emergency assistance, and the theatre was reopened. In July, Judith and Julian marched in front of the West Street jail, a federal penitentiary, protesting the fact that a friend had received a six-year sentence for boarding an atomic submarine. In August, Judith sat on a sidewalk in Greenwich Village for two days reading Martin Buber—who had organized the opposition to an Israeli nuclear program—in front of the Atomic Energy Commission.

Performances of *The Brig* continued through the summer, its audiences boosted by a three-page spread in *Life* in August. After the performances, Julian started something he called the "Phantom Cabaret," a revue featuring the comic Hugh Romney (later known as "Wavy Gravy"), the blind poet Moondog, and an unknown singer named Tiny Tim. *The Brig* was so demanding of the actors—at least one of them had a genuine breakdown because of the stress of the play—that the repertory system had been abandoned, but *The Brig* was bringing in enough money that the theatre showed a small profit.

But The Living Theatre again had accumulated five thousand dollars of debt to its landlord, a real estate firm whose lawyers served Julian with an eviction notice on 17 October. The next morning, a Thursday, three IRS agents with a seizure kit occupied the theatre, declaring it government property in lieu of $28,435 in back taxes, and informed the actors that they were trespassing. It looked like the final curtain.

37. *The Brig* Bust

J ulian immediately arranged a press conference that was attended by all the daily newspapers. In a melancholy mood, wearing jeans, a work shirt and sandals, he pointed out that since it first occupied the Fourteenth Street location, The Living Theatre had been harassed by warrants, court cases, sheriff's notices, and daily calls from creditors. They have been our alarm clock, he explained, admitting ruefully that Mammon would not disintegrate just because a theatre seating 162 people said it should.

Now 85 percent of his time was devoted to fund-raising, and the $150,000 he had managed to raise over the years had sent the company to Europe twice but had not balanced a loss of $500 a week. The IRS claimed that The Living Theatre owed $23,000, plus an additional $5,000 in penalties. Another $3,500 was owed to New York State, as well as smaller sums for insurance and the services of a theatrical advertising agency. None of the large foundations had been willing to assist—the Ford Foundation refusing because the actors were insufficiently paid. The Living Theatre had paid over $75,000 in taxes, always filing, and only filing delinquently when they could not even afford an accountant. Withholding taxes from actors' salaries were not paid to the government, Julian claimed, because there was barely enough money to pay the actors their insufficient wages.

Julian noted that he had had a "running dialogue" with the IRS for years. They regularly examined the books of The Living

Theatre and received a weekly sum of one hundred dollars as a sign of their "intent to pay." He was not sure precisely whether someone in the IRS office panicked on learning of the landlord's eviction notice or "whether something more sinister was happening." He pleaded with the agents to let the theatre remain open through the weekend so that he could at least pay his actors something to tide them over, but they adamantly refused, padlocked the box office, and individually labeled all the equipment on the three floors of the theatre.

On Thursday night, 17 October, Julian, Judith, and a dozen members of the cast stayed in Julian's second-floor office, which had windows on Sixth Avenue, while the IRS agents waited in the lobby. The police declared that the building was quarantined, which meant that there could be no entry. Supplies and food delivered by neighborhood restaurants was passed up with ropes and baskets. Outside, a group of picketers began chanting "Help Save The Living Theatre," marching with signs declaring CULTURAL ATROCITY!, UNJUST SEIZURE! and ART BEFORE TAXES. Reporters and television crews arrived.

The next day, Friday, 18 October, the actors remained inside the theatre, periodically chanting "Help!" from windows while police and chanting pickets remained outside. When IRS agents attempted to move Julian's personal files, he sat on the stairs blocking them. The agents claimed they were only following their orders, which Judith told them was unacceptable as an excuse after Adolf Eichmann. On the street, with a megaphone and a tape recorder, drama critic and director Richard Schechner conducted a public interview with Judith, who answered from the sill of the second-story window.

That night, the IRS agents left the building, warning that none of the seals or locks could be tampered with. At two in the morning, suffering from an abscessed tooth that made him look as if he had a walnut in his cheek, Julian left the building with Judith, leaving a few of the others behind to protect the premises.

On Saturday, Julian decided that there would be a final performance of *The Brig*. Most of the company believed that the IRS seizure had just been a pretext and that actually The Living Theatre was being harassed for daring to perform a play offensive to the Marine Corps. They had staged Brown's play as a symbolic protest in the first place, and although the company felt an immense sense of loss because of the IRS seizure, they experienced an element of liberation as well.

At three in the afternoon, Julian went to a window and announced to an assembled crowd below that there would be a free performance of *The Brig* that night. In the theatre, he found that two doors to the auditorium were not sealed. All the tagged property in the auditorium and onstage was moved.

By late afternoon, the crowd had grown, and the police had set up barricades. In a scene reminiscent of the Paris Commune of 1871, ladders were leaned against the building, the police pulling the ladders away while people were still climbing them. Two actors with Marine Corps training led about a hundred people up a fire escape and over the roof of an adjoining building.

Kenneth Brown had called all the newspapers, and reporters, who were able to pass freely through the barricades, swarmed in. When the IRS agents removed the fuses from the stage switchboard, the lights of the television cameras were used to illuminate the stage. *The Brig* was then performed as an anarchist direct action, an act of civil disobedience, Julian asserted, for the freedom to create, uninhibited by the state and its money system.

After the performance, an IRS official asked the audience to disperse, and most of them went outside to join pickets chanting "We Shall Overcome!" Julian was asked to leave, but he replied that he and the cast would remain and they intended to offer two more performances on Sunday. When Julian, Judith, fourteen members of the all-male cast, and nine female friends stoically locked themselves into the stage brig, they were arrested, placed in paddy wagons, and brought to the Women's House of Detention and the Federal House of Detention on West Street. Later, in a poem, Judith declared that she had locked herself in *The Brig* set because—paraphrasing Thoreau—that was the only "honorable place for an honorable woman" in a dishonorable society.

On Sunday, hired moving men came to the theatre and carted everything away, including the barbed-wire set of *The Brig.* Late that afternoon, Federal District Judge Edward Weinfeld ordered the actors and their friends fingerprinted and photographed and released them from jail on their own recognizance, setting bail for Judith and Julian, and charging them with impeding federal officers in the performance of their duty.

Company spirits remained high, and there were regular meetings in the Becks' apartment. There was some promising news. Irving Maidman, a real estate developer who owned five theatres in the Times Square area, offered one of them to The Living Theatre for a continuation of *The Brig.* A Los Angeles production was begun. Oscar Lewenstein, a wealthy British producer, asked Julian to bring his company to London to perform *The Brig.*

Some company members began living with Judith and Julian. Others were housed in a Bowery loft owned by Jim Tiroff, a gifted graphic artist who had joined the company. A visionary and an adventurer constantly seeking bizarre thrills, Tiroff and his girlfriend were nudists who cavorted publicly and sought to foster an orgiastic atmosphere. Another group of company members lived in a big house on Long Island. This group was experimenting with LSD. There was Indian music, frequent yoga practice, and a lot of reading of books such as the I Ching, *The Psychedelic Experience,* and *The Search for the Miraculous.*

Judith had fallen in love with Carl Einhorn, one of the cast members, a curly red-headed, handsome young man fifteen years her junior, who had originally appeared fresh out of Alfred College to work on the General Strike in 1961. In an early notebook, he had written that he came from nowhere, belonged nowhere, and was still engaged in a "life of attempted flight." At the same time, he was a fervent and enthusiastic poet, bold, full of revolutionary aspiration and heroic gestures. He could also be arrogant, with an Adonis attitude that demanded admiration for his acts, which may have been a subtle form of compensation for his lack of self-confidence.

On 22 November, eating breakfast in a diner, Judith and Carl were stunned to hear on a radio turned high for everyone to hear that President Kennedy had been assassinated in Dallas. That news plunged the country into despair.

38. Demeaning the Court

Near the end of January 1964, in a dingy, drafty room painted a dull green, the color of the brig walls, Julian addressed a grand jury for an hour. "O my America, you have goofed again!" Judith entered into her *Diaries,* as she and Julian were presented with an eleven-count felony indictment for impeding federal officers in the performance of their duties and the administration of the Internal Revenue Code. The trial was scheduled for May.

Judith and Julian spent February and March in Europe, arranging for bookings of *The Brig,* which the company was performing under the banner of "Exile Productions" in Irving Maidman's Midway Theatre in Times Square. At first, Maidman had offered his theatre rent free, but then he decided on a rent that could not be paid with the level of audience support the play received. On the night of the final performance, film maker Jonas Mekas saw the play and decided to film it. Although the theatre was padlocked, the set was still intact and unmoved. The actors and the camera crew sneaked in through a sidewalk coal chute and filmed through the night. It was a surreptitious bit of anarchism for the cause of art, a sort of preview of the way the company would treat the rules of any establishment throughout the 1960s.

Back in New York City in April, Judith and Julian attended the trial of comedian Lenny Bruce on obscenity charges, both because they felt a sense of kinship with him, and because they had decided to represent themselves in their own trial and wanted to familiarize themselves with the intricacies of court procedure.

Julian told a reporter for the *New York Times* that he was shocked and surprised that the grand jury had been unable to differentiate "between the devotion of artists to their art and criminal acts." As a demonstration of that devotion, when their trial began in May in the federal courthouse on Foley Square, Judith and Julian decided to use the courtroom as a theatre for a surrealist spectacle. In a moment of rage, arguing over the propriety of having a probation officer visit them at home, Judith had put her foot through a glass doorpane, and as a result, Julian decided to carry her—costumed in a black Portia robe—everywhere: up the grand marble steps and into the courtroom, to the bathroom and to the witness chair.

The prosecutor charged that Julian had unlawfully entered Judith's sealed dressing room and taken props, costumes, and a sewing machine; that he had used a sealed mimeograph machine with an IRS label on it to prepare a press release; and that he had lowered a ladder and harangued the crowd, shouting "Storm the barricades!" from a window. Such a cry would have violated his nonviolent principles, Julian disingenuously claimed. The sewing machine was borrowed from Mabel Beck, and he had entered Judith's dressing room to retrieve her Tampax. In support of this, incongruously, he summoned the aged Rabbi Carlebach, who had been Rabbi Malina's teacher and had buried Rosel, who now seriously testified in his long, white caftan that according to Judaic law, a husband had to insure his wife's cleanliness during her period.

As company members and witnesses were presented to the court, Judith insisted on using their first names, with the judge reprimanding her every time she did it. Judge Edmund Palmieri, who had been the military governor of Italy after the war, kept taking Judith and Julian into his chambers to admonish them. Usually soft-spoken and known for his fairness, he was furious that his court was being used as a theatre, and that Judith and Julian had recruited the New York press, who recognized a good show.

Members of the company and their friends were in the court-room causing numerous disturbances: Steven Ben Israel led a chant in court while the judge screamed for silence; and Jenny Hecht was dragged from the court by her feet. At various times during the trial, Judith and Julian were arrested by municipal police for chanting in the courtroom, and throughout the procedure, they played with the prosecutor's attempt to restrict them to legal procedures.

Once, during lunch when Judith was being photographed by Fred McDarrah of the *Village Voice* on the grand, spacious marble steps outside the courthouse, a policeman, perhaps perversely, issued her a citation for obstructing public passage. Henry Howard, one of the company, then tried to make a citizen's arrest of the policeman, and he was put into a police car. The vehicle was immediately surrounded by members of the cast and their friends, who sat in front of the car and would not let it move. The prosecutor, Peter Leisure, was terrified by this incident, screaming that if any member of the jury saw what had happened out of the window, the entire trial—which lasted thirteen days—would have to start again.

In a poem, Judith fantasized performing fellatio on the prosecutor—an indication of the absurdity of the trial. In another long poem later published in *Evergreen Review,* she complained of the boring courtroom with the "wrong men in charge," the judge's robes hiding his nakedness. "I suggest that everybody take all their clothes off," she cheerfully announces in the poem, and if she gets cold, she can make mad love to the IRS agents.

In short, Judith and Julian insisted on remaining outrageously impossible even though they had been warned that they could face a thirty-five-year sentence for inciting a riot and income tax evasion. Their argument, they claimed, was with the rigidity of the law. Throughout the trial, Judge Palmieri refused to rule on the central question of whether passive resistance was obstructive, saying that was a matter for another court to decide. In his instructions to the jury, however, he argued that no individual can be permitted to challenge any law on the basis of his own moral convictions.

At the end of the trial, when the prosecutor requested that the jury find the defendants guilty on the eleven counts, Judith, after each count, repeated quietly but firmly, "Innocent!" When the judge demanded that Judith stop acting like an infant, Judith said apologetically that she had a moral duty to correct the prosecutor each time he said "guilty," thereby demonstrating the resistance to authority that she was advocating. "I can assert my innocence at any time in my life," she said, "and you cannot stop me! The only way you could stop me is by cutting out my tongue!" As far as the Court was concerned, the coup de grace was delivered by Julian who, in his final summation, argued it had been his "moral obligation to demean the majesty of the court."

The "grey and grim" jury of one woman and eleven men—a stockbroker, a salesman, an engineer, several accountants and teachers, a man in the nut business, and a sports editor at *Time*—found Judith and Julian guilty on seven counts. Early in June, the company was fined $2,500. Judge Palmieri ruled that Judith and Julian were "misguided but sincere people who were unable to adjust to living in a complex society." For contempt of court, Julian was sentenced to serve sixty days; Judith, thirty; and both were placed on probation for five years. Since they had engagements booked in Europe, Judith and Julian were permitted to leave the country with the company, pending appeal.

IV
Exile

39. *Mysteries*

Just before Judge Palmieri passed sentence, Judith entreated him, with her arms uplifted in front of the court, pronouncing that he was about to "murder" The Living Theatre. On 4 July, she ran an advertisement in the *Guardian* stating that she was selling 1,500 books and most of her worldly possessions.

A week later, she was with Julian on a German ship. "We know we are not travellers, but refugees," she wrote in her *Diary*. Though this sentiment may seem melodramatic, it was an important aspect of the way she saw herself. When her father was dying of leukemia, he had warned her that her country might some day betray her, and she fully felt that time had arrived.

In August, they were in Paris, Amsterdam, and Berlin, arranging for bookings of *The Brig*. One night, without money for a hotel, they slept in Potsdammer Platz and woke to the questions of police. The German people were methodical, but mercurial and mercenary, Judith observed, and there were liberties in West Germany unavailable in East Germany. When they wished to perform *The Brig* in East Berlin, Helene Weigel, Brecht's widow and the head of the Berliner Ensemble, told them it would never be permitted.

The company began rehearsing *The Brig* that August in London. Money was very limited, and there was grumbling. One actor left because he found a better offer; another received an urgent message from home; Warren Finnerty's wife was threatening to leave him, and he had to return.

The play opened early in September at the Mermaid Theatre

where swans would gather at curtain time, glowing white on the black surface of the dirty Thames. Although reviews were mixed and some critics were appalled, audiences at the Mermaid were good, and there were two performances a day. Laurence Olivier saw the final performance of *The Brig* standing just offstage, shifting uneasily from foot to foot.

The English had difficulties with the loose anarchism of some of the company members. Mark Duffy, another company member, had stolen a motorcycle to get to the airport in New York after having been released from Bellevue. In London, he stole a car and was arrested for seducing a minor. To outwit customs officials looking for drugs, Jim Tiroff and a few others had flown to England wearing clerical collars and black suits, registered as ministers in the Universal Life Church, a mail-order outfit with neither parishes nor seminaries. A sly joke at the expense of authority, the act demonstrated as well a flirtation on the part of some company members with the dangerous edges of acceptable behavior, which they would continually transgress.

Three weeks into the run of the play, Bernard Miles, who owned the Mermaid, a distinguished former actor who had romanticized The Living Theatre, declared that he was going to break the six-week contract. When the actors picketed in front of the theatre, he agreed to pay them for the last three weeks as long as they left England.

A few days before their departure, as an ironic tribute to the cold, phlegmatic British people, Judith planted a batch of marijuana seeds behind Hogarth's statue in Leicester Square. Then, Judith and Julian visited Kenneth Tynan for dinner in his home off Berkeley Square. Tynan was doing a piece on The Living Theatre for *Playboy.* Suave, friendly, he seemed too much the doctrinaire Marxist who found it difficult to understand that Julian could have told the entire company to meet in Paris at two in the afternoon in a week on the steps of the church of Saint-Germain-des-Prés.

In Paris, Judith was full of new energy, planning to stage Jean Genet's *Balcony* and his *Maids.* In exchange for a benefit evening of performance, Julian had arranged for the company to receive free rehearsal space in the American Center on the boulevard Raspail. During the month of October, in this space, the company collectively created a work called *Mysteries* and *Smaller Pieces,* which represented a complete departure from what Julian called the theatre of intellect.

Artaud, in an essay called "No More Masterpieces," had declared that the classic theatre of the past was moribund and the writers of other eras had little to say to the present conditions of peril. In his essay "The Theatre and Culture," which Julian used in the program note for *The Connection,* Artaud called for a breakthrough of language to re-create the theatre. In 1958, when she was reading Artaud, Judith had "dreamed of a stage on which Mysteries are recalled out of the oblivion of pre-classical times." These "mysteries" were practiced at Eleusis, outside Athens. There, a cult worshiping the goddess Demeter incorporated secret sexual rituals, stylized into dance, gesture, and invocation, one of the beginnings of drama as we know it. In his essay "Storming the Barricades," Julian acknowledged his interest in Judith's dream, trying to imagine ways

> to aid the audience to become once more what it was destined to be when the first dramas formed themselves on the threshing floor: a congregation led by priests, a choral ecstasy of reading and response, dance, seeking transcendence, a way out and up, the vertical thrust, seeking a state of awareness that surpasses mere conscious being and brings you closer to God.

Mysteries would become one of The Living Theatre's most popular European productions, and it clearly depended on a new understanding of the potentials of theatrical presentation and represented an enormous breakthrough in form. "Pierce the shell" and "Break down the walls," Julian had declared in his essay "Storming the Barricades," and these goals applied to life as well as theatre. Art, he wrote, was not an end but a means of communicating, and since the IRS seizure of the Fourteenth Street theatre, he had decided to make his message one that stressed social action.

Divided into nine distinct "ritual games," each one lasting from five to fifteen minutes, *Mysteries* was an experiment in what Judith called nonfictional acting, in which actors played themselves, not characters in roles. There was no set, and the action occurred on a bare stage. There were also no costumes, and actors wore whatever they happened to be wearing on that day.

The play began with a single actor standing at attention in the center of the stage for six minutes. This ploy was pure provocation. By expecting that some audience response would begin the play, The Living Theatre was signaling its priorities. But the deeper purpose of the play—despite aesthetic overtures such as an Indian raga, and the use of incense and meditation—was Artaudian politics, demonstrated in the final scene, "The Plague."

Inspired by Artaud's description of a great plague that devastated Marseilles early in the eighteenth century, the scene lasts for half an hour. Moving about, the actors gradually become aware of the symptoms of the plague. Some actors clutch their bodies—sputtering, blubbering, groaning, gasping—writhing on the ground. Overcome by fear and panic, the actors drop to the floor; others roll off the stage and lurch into the audience. In tears, salivating, staggering, shuddering, actors grasp the arms of the aisle seats, doubling over at the feet of audience members. Like medieval doctors during the plague crisis, six of the actors rise and arrange the dead in a pyramid onstage.

The first performance of *Mysteries* in Paris lasted for over three hours. It ended with a scene called "Free Jazz," performed by Dutch poet Simon Vinkenoog, during which he crawled into a grand piano, playing it from the inside. At one point, a member of the audience began to pile the seats into a mountain, which he then scaled. Once on top, he began to give the Nazi salute, screaming obscenities repeatedly. Such behavior was way beyond the parameters Pirandello had envisaged when he tried to engage the audience. The "wild beast" Julian had encountered

in the audiences of *Tonight We Improvise* was ready to roar his
rage.

   Through the rest of the fall, the company continued to perform *Mysteries* in Berlin, Metz, Heidelberg—in the courtyard of a
twelfth-century castle built by King Otto—and Antwerp. In Brussels, about fifty members of the audience began to die with the
actors in the plague scene. In Trieste, *Mysteries* was banned after
one performance because an actor appeared nude in one of the
tableaux vivants for three seconds and because the audience refused to leave the theatre despite orders by the police. In Vienna,
in the elegant Theatre An Der Wien, the fire department forced
the curtain when a group of Viennese acting students began to
die onstage during the plague scene, and future performances
were banned. In Rome—at the tail end of *la dolce vita* with money
and glamour all over—there was general pandemonium during
the plague scene. With *Mysteries,* the company had collectively
merged to create a work that profoundly shocked and moved
audiences all over Europe. It was clearly the beginning of a new
stage in the life of The Living Theatre.

40. Heist-sur-Mer

One of the Europeans who had responded to Judith and
Julian's appeals for support during the General Strike in
1961 was a Dutch aristocrat named Baron Allard. Known as the
"Red Baron," Allard was a pacifist who had converted the queen
of Holland to a leftist perspective. He owned a summer camp in
the little town of Heist-sur-Mer on the Belgian coast, which he
used as a center for antiwar activities, and he agreed to let the

members of The Living Theatre live in it during the winter of 1964–65.

Judith and Julian had received a telegram from the American embassy in Brussels to "surrender immediately." They had lost their appeal of Judge Palmieri's decision because their lawyer had failed to appear for a hearing. Early in December, they sailed back on the SS *United States* to serve their prison terms, while the twenty-five members of the company and their three small children installed themselves in a primitive old farmhouse on the Red Baron's property.

In the Passaic County Jail, in Paterson, New Jersey, Judith spent a "month of silence" in a room without windows that had seven thin mattresses on metal beds, seven shelves, perpetual fluorescent lighting, and sixty-eight hexagonal bars through which she could just slip her hand. Two of her cellmates had been charged with knifing their husbands; one had killed her baby; a woman from Colombia was charged with illegal entry; another had forged checks; and an older woman insisted she was there to investigate prison conditions.

Sometimes, she was able to work on her plan to direct *The Maids,* but mostly she worked on her translation of *Antigone.* Sophocles' classic version of one woman's defiance of the state's monolithic power had been translated by Brecht. Judith had brought the original play, Hölderlin's German version from which Brecht had worked, Brecht's version, and Greek and English dictionaries—a tiny, anomalous library that she stacked under her metal prison cot.

Judith was only allowed to leave this cell when, guarded by matrons in blue, she was assigned to mop floors. There was no other exercise. The only other activity was sewing mattresses and patching uniforms. At one point, she refused to work on the repair of a torn American flag, risking the loss of her flimsy mattress by telling the matron that the flag symbolized a system that had thrown her out of her country and prevented her from working in her craft.

As soon as she was released, she visited Julian, who was incarcerated in the federal correctional center in Danbury, Connecticut, where Judith's cousin—Jerome Malino, who had married them—was chaplain. After the visit, in a cabin "as chaste as a cell," she sailed back to Heist.

Characteristically, Julian had an optimistic view of life in prison. Although he was confined to an ugly, barred room, he had some access to books, lectures, and movies. In jail, he wrote his friend Karl Bissinger that he could get close to his companions with an understanding and affection that never occurred in other situations. They spoke, he felt, with a real, honest quality often missing from the theatre. He was thinking all the time about how freedom and honesty could be dramatically portrayed, and working on notes for a production of Jean Genet's *Maids*.

While Judith and Julian were serving their sentences, the company was rehearsing Genet's play and working on *Mysteries* in Heist under conditions of great duress. The winter of 1965 was terribly cold, and the farmhouse faced the sea, whose damp, salty presence touched everything. The first floor of the old farmhouse was heated by a few tiny potbelly stoves. The sleeping area upstairs, a dormitory space, had no source of heat. It got so cold that the outhouse malfunctioned and the outside pump froze. Water had to be obtained on a daily basis from a town fire department truck. There was no hot water at all, and the available water had to be rationed carefully. The stoves used coal and covered everything with a sooty, inescapable film.

Stanislavsky had once suggested that his actors form a monastic community in the country, but what transpired at Heist could hardly have satisfied his expectations. The farmhouse was a few kilometers out of Heist, a gray, silent town surrounded by flat fields, and when members of the company would come in for supplies, they were called the gang from "Bonanza"—an American television western—because the men were bearded and so bedraggled, and the women wore long dresses and tinkling jewelry. There was very little money, and Nona Howard began organizing communal vegetarian meals.

Although water and money were in short supply, the nascent community was stocked with drugs. A supply of hashish and kif had been brought back from Morocco by one of the communards. In addition to this, there was LSD, mescaline, magic mushrooms, and morning glory seeds to compensate for, or complement, the deprivation many of the members felt. The drug use was part of a process of deconditioning—a way to separate themselves from values that depended on competition in the money system—as well as a form of bonding. The communal spirit was intensified by the struggle to obtain food, prepare it, and keep as warm as possible.

A number of the actors were reading Artaud, who spoke of the need for strong actors chosen less for their skill than for a kind of "vital sincerity." This sincerity, or sense of commitment, was an identifying concern of each member of the group at Heist, most of whom saw the trip to Europe as a way of breaking with a meaningless anomie. As Henry Howard put it, his earlier life had been "too smooth. Too pat. My life was like an automat—you put your money in and get your thing. I had my college degree. I was married to a beautiful girl, but it was like nothing was *happening.* I said to myself 'Is this it? Is this all there is?' "

Heist had helped forge a subtle tribalism that would enable the group to cohere despite the inevitable differences that ensue in any group. As one of its members, Luke Theodore, observed, "I thought the work was to find out about myself, but in Heist I saw that it was to find out about other people. I never had time to think about myself. I learned not to be selfish by learning about other people. Whenever I think about myself, the work goes right out the window."

Judith returned to Heist in the beginning of February to lead her "horde, her cult, her troupe of wandering actors" to Brussels and Amsterdam, and then to Berlin to perform *The Brig* and *Mysteries* for two weeks. Julian joined the company in Rome where Judith feared the company was suddenly treated with such respect that "we are becoming statues."

Rufus Collins, who had not gone to Heist, rejoined the company in Rome, amazed by the new spirit he sensed and aware that "an entirely different" group had emerged. Collins introduced Judith and Julian to Mary Krapf—a young American with defined cheekbones and burning eyes that made her look like a female version of Artaud. Krapf—who would become known as Mary Mary—had just been released from a Rome jail on a fabricated drug charge. When she saw *Mysteries,* she felt an immediate affinity for the company and was asked to join.

Unaffected, full of the "vital sincerity" Artaud maintained was such an essential prerequisite, Mary Mary fit into the new acting style Julian advocated. "When you leave jail, you don't leave altogether," Julian noted in his "Thoughts on Theatre from Jail." The experience left the prisoner with an indelible urge for freedom of speech as well as of the body. Life was very dramatic, he argued; it did not need to be faked by the tricks imposed by stage designers. Prison was the place where he had heard "real speech," not the false elocution of the Broadway actor seemingly intent on impressing a nonexistent royalty. Broadway and Hollywood inculcated a false tone and insincere mannerisms. The actors of The Living Theatre, even when they were awkward and untutored, would defy conventions by refusing to pose as anything but what they actually were.

This was a tall order, and the company took it on the road, traveling in three used Volkswagen buses. Through the spring, they performed *The Brig* eight times and *Mysteries* twenty times in Rome, Naples, and Florence. In Trieste, during "The Plague" scene, the police panicked when actors began touching members of the audience. When police stopped the performance, the audience refused to leave. The police headquarters was located next door to the theatre, and the chief of police threatened a general arrest. In the end, the entire company was arrested.

In the beginning of May, film director John Huston, who had seen *The Connection,* used the company as the inhabitants of Sodom in his film *The Bible.* By the middle of May, they were back in Berlin performing *Mysteries* at the Akademie der Kunste. In July, they premiered Genet's *Maids* in Berlin and went south to Munich for two weeks, where they were when Lyndon Johnson signed the Voting Rights Act on 6 August in Washington. A week later, the Watts riots erupted in Los Angeles.

The insurrectionary anger of Genet made sense in the light of such catastrophic events as Watts. In the tradition of Dostoyevski, Genet was an anarchist who rejected all forms of social discipline. The son of a prostitute, he had spent his youth in reformatories, where he was sexually brutalized. He was imprisoned as a repeat offender for burglary during the Second World War. While in prison, he wrote *The Maids* and began a correspondence with Artaud, who was then interned in a madhouse at Rodez. After the war, both Jean Cocteau and Jean-Paul Sartre championed his caricaturing, expressionist plays, so clearly designed to shock audiences by playing on their racial, religious, and political prejudices. Genet was an arch rebel, a gob of spit in the eye of the middle-class public. Since The Living Theatre came to Europe with the reputation of being beleaguered exiles persecuted by American puritanism, their decision to perform Genet was entirely consonant with their rebellious image.

The Maids is based on a famous case of two sisters raised in a convent who were placed in a bourgeois household. Submissive, they tolerated insults and abuse. One day, they seized their employers, a mother and her daughter, and brutally murdered them. Genet's play reinvented this sensationalist story with an emphasis on the paradoxical love the underclass feels for their persecutors. The sisters, in love with their employer, impersonate her and spend much of their time playing in her dressing room, sometimes primping in her clothes, sometimes pretending to strangle her. One of them has anonymously denounced Madame's lover, who has been sent to prison. The sisters try to poison Madame's tea, but she rushes off to rejoin her lover when she hears of his release. One sister, wearing Madame's white robe, takes the tea and drinks it herself, committing suicide on her employer's bed.

In the penitentiary in Danbury, Julian had carefully designed every element of his set, which would be "simple, classical, austere," he wrote to Judith, yet chic and glittering with the right sadomasochistic edge for Genet. Madame's boudoir would be or-

ganized by a semicircle of white velvet–draped pillars surrounded by white pocelain vases of gladioli and mimosa. Madame
should wear a black, ribbed, heavy taffeta suit trimmed with fur
cuffs and a large diamond spray pin on her lapel. The sisters
would wear shiny satin black maid's uniforms with white cuffs
and collars, and black, highly polished laced shoes. Fulfilling
Genet's intention, all the female characters would be played by
males.

The Maids was a brilliantly bizarre parody of the drawing
room comedy written with the serious purpose of questioning
the class structure and the assumptions of power and privilege.
With a small cast and a set limited in scope to a single room, it
was eminently portable, a convenient play to stage in the new
repertory The Living Theatre was formulating, one that had
moved from the Fourteenth Street location to a more international stage.

41. *Frankenstein*

In spring 1965, mostly while traveling, the members of the
company began to devise a production epic in intention
and nonlinear in scale, a spectacle like Wagner's *Götterdäm-
merung* that could totally immerse an audience and involve all its
senses. In a letter to the director of the Venice Biennale, an international forum for the arts that had offered to finance part of the
production and to premiere it, Julian outlined his idea:

The production which we planned which I would most highly
recommend for a Venice premiere is the version of *Franken-*

stein which we have been planning for over a year. This production, based loosely on the Frankenstein concept of Mary Shelley, would be created in much the same manner as our production of *The Mysteries* which has recently had such success in Brussels, Amsterdam and Rome. This means that there is no text for the play. The action, the words, the effects will all be created by the company working together with the techniques we have developed amongst ourselves. We plan it as an elaborate spectacle with many visual, musical and mechanical effects, but without a set text. The theme—the attempt to create life in order to create servants for man, the attempt to eliminate the strugglesome aspect of work in this world, and the tragic effects of this kind of thinking—seems to us particularly appropriate for this phase of man's development.

I know that it must be unusual that a theatre propose doing at Venice a work without a set text, but then it is my hope that you will be excited, as we are, at the prospect of a work in the tradition of Artaud's concept of a non-literary theatre which, through ritual, horror and spectacle might become an even more valid theatrical event than much of the wordy Theatre of Ideas which has dominated our stages for so long.

In April 1965, in the enormous living room of a villa in Velletri, a village in the Alban hills south of Rome, where the company was temporarily housed, there were long talks about violence in society, its reflection in horror films like Murnau's *Nosferatu,* Mary Shelley's *Frankenstein,* and the capacity of science to turn humans to evil. One model the company studied and discussed was Artaud's outline scenario "The Conquest of Mexico," which stressed the sensory impact of cries, groans, apparitions, brilliant lighting effects, and the use of masks and surprising objects. Julian took notes on these discussions and began making preliminary set drawings.

From Rome, the company moved to Berlin. For several

weeks, members of the company found friends to put them up or slept in theatre lobbies. Finally, the Berlin senate gave them free accommodations for a month on the outskirts of the city, near the Berlin Wall. In Spandau—the dungeon-like prison accommodating one prisoner, Rudolf Hess—the company lived communally, and the discussions resumed, mounting in intensity and lasting for six or seven hours each day. The word *community,* Julian maintained, grew out of communication, and by creating their next play together, by talking it out almost as a form of group therapy, the group might achieve an unprecedented binding and unification. The process of collective creation depended on a sensitivity and heightened attentiveness, magnified by the use of LSD by various members of the company. The purpose of the group interaction was to increase a mutual consciousness that could then be formulated in a drama. To reach an audience, the actors first had to learn—and it was a lesson in elementary anarchism—how to communicate with each other without being hurtful or competitive, even though they were conditioned to competitive behavior. Ultimately, and this was the test of Artaud's "vital sincerity," they had to become, as Judith put it, "worthy of our ideas."

Not all of the actors were prepared for so arduously intellectual an initiation into the new theatre. A third of the twenty-five Americans who had spent the winter in Heist-sur-Mer had departed, some unhappy about the scanty spending allowance of a dollar fifty a day; others, by the demands of the incessant travel and collective creation. Those who had left had been replaced by Europeans, so the company was becoming internationalized even though it retained its uniquely American character. Peter Hartman, who had helped manage business affairs and was working on the music for *Frankenstein,* commented on the difficulties caused by collective creation:

> There had to be a general agreement about every given aspect of the production before it could go on to the next step. And because the ability and intellectual capacity and educa-

tion of the company was not all at the same level, the struggle to realize any basic point in the production was monumental. The roundtable discussion technique exhausted my patience and physical strength. I found it extremely difficult to wait and wait, and wait and wait.

As the money from the Venice Biennale was received in installments, the set for *Frankenstein* had to be built slowly, more or less as the play evolved in the actors' imaginations. Julian's set was a cubist space and would have a clear influence on later productions like Philip Glass's *Einstein on the Beach*. A thirty-foot-high iron grid of wooden platforms and steel piping, the space was divided into fifteen connected cubicles on three levels. Using Mary Shelley's novel and the various *Frankenstein* films as a springboard, The Living Theatre wove fragments of the familiar tale through three acts and over three hours of ritual, myth, nightmares, and legends of ancient science and contemporary civilization.

While *Mysteries* had begun with six minutes of silence, *Frankenstein* opened with a full half-hour of silence, during which the actors try to make a woman at center stage levitate. The levitation fails, and she is thrust into a coffin and carried into the audience in a funeral procession as an emblem of death. When one of the actors shouts "No!" he is hung from a noose. Others are executed in an electric chair and a gas chamber; by guillotine, firing squad, and crucifixion—all screaming in various cubicles. These corpses provide the body parts Dr. Frankenstein will assemble for his creature. With the help of the ghosts of Paracelsus, Freud, and the cybernetician Norbert Weiner, who advises using electricity, the creature is assembled, the body of the monster created by seventeen actors silhouetted against a backdrop.

An eccentric, extravagant indictment of civilization tinged with sadomasochism, the play presents a nightmarish allegory of human domination of others. The final act, which takes place in a prison, is characteristic of a quality of spasmodic, expressionist spectacle in the play. The actors search the audience with flashlights for other actors, whom they arrest. Dr. Frankenstein is one of those apprehended. When the prisoners revolt, Dr. Frankenstein starts a fire to divert the guards. Screaming in panic, the prisoners assemble to form the giant, twenty-foot Frankenstein monster who, a flashlight in one hand, a net in the other, lurches threateningly toward the audience, the symbol of civilization menacing itself.

The company rehearsed *Frankenstein* during the summer of 1965 while performing *The Brig* seven times, *The Maids* nineteen times, and *Mysteries* seven times in Berlin and Munich. The real work had become *Frankenstein,* which Julian called "the communal effort of a group of people shipwrecked, drowning, and trying to save one another." A "leap into the abyss of our own helplessness," *Frankenstein* was an attempt to cut what Julian called the "evil madness" of the world that was in all human hearts and to "hang it up in the public square which is our theatre."

According to Peter Hartman, they were less interested in suggesting a hallucinatory vision than immediately involving an audience in that vision. The consequences of such an approach were immediate and drastic. At the end of September 1965, they presented *Frankenstein* in Venice at the Biennale. There were problems with the lighting technology and the apprehensions of Dr. Wladimiro Dorigo, the director of the Biennale, who was nervous about the unconventional play. Just before the opening at the Teatro La Perla on Lido, Julian spit at him in a quarrel. Immediately after the performance, Julian was informed by police that the company was banned from Italy. No explanations were offered—but members of the company assumed that the ban had more to do with what had happened in Trieste when Jim Tiroff appeared nude for a few seconds in the tableau vivant scene in *Mysteries*—and the caravan of three dilapidated Volkswagen buses was escorted to the Austrian border.

42. Beggars and Stepchildren

Although the expulsion from Italy was baffling and frightening, and it made Judith feel like a fugitive, no one in the company was intimidated. Brecht said that he changed his shoes less often than his country, Judith ironically noted in her *Diaries,* and the company spent the fall of 1965 in Germany and Austria, performing *The Brig, Mysteries,* and *The Maids* but unwilling to schedule another *Frankenstein* until they could develop its third act.

One incident at the end of November seems to characterize the way Julian influenced the company in a general hardening toward the system, a withdrawal from a politics that he saw as dependent on warfare and armament. In a performance of *Mysteries* in Vienna, an informant for the American Federal Bureau of Investigation observed that Julian appeared onstage alone and said in German, "No more war in Vietnam! Free the Blacks! Make peace now! No more war!" What was unusual about this were not the sentiments, but the fact that the informant alleged Julian repeated each of them some sixty to eight times. While a cold warrior might have found such proclamations seditious or threatening enough to include in a report, it indicated the degree of alienation that united the company. Like Dostoyevski's underground man, the company could feel inspired and empowered by the release of such feelings, even as they realized they would have to live in a condition of permanent exile more psychological than geographical.

In December, the company toured the Scandinavian countries, playing *Mysteries* in Copenhagen, in a theatre with a gilded ceiling ornamented by circling wild geese. It was a design the company could identify with as they seemed inexorably to circle Europe, a theatre of diaspora on what seemed a perpetual peregrination.

By the end of January 1966, they were back in Italy performing *The Brig* ten times in Bologna. *Mysteries* was staged another twenty times in Milan, Venice, and Genoa, where, Judith observed, the American Sixth Fleet "filled the water with bombs." From Genoa, the company sailed to Sicily to perform *Mysteries* another five times.

In April, performing in Sarajevo, the company saw the film *The Bride of Frankenstein.* A few weeks later, they were back in the disintegrating jewel of Venice, where Judith and Julian heard the old master, Ezra Pound, break his famous silence to speak a few words about Dante. When they sought him out afterward in the gardens of the Accademia as the young Americans who had produced his *Women of Trachis,* Pound gently seized Judith by the shoulders and lifted her off the ground, gazing deeply into her eyes and never saying a word. Judith was wearing a black tulip because she had just heard of the death of her teacher, Piscator. "He never knew how I trembled before him," she confided to her *Diaries,* thinking of Piscator, "or how all my work is in his honor."

Judith was working on a novel called *Lies* and her translation of *Antigone,* and reading Paul Goodman's *Growing up Absurd,* his most successful book. Julian was wondering how to transform a spectator into a revolutionary and how to best depict warfare on stage in connection with *Antigone.* He was constantly preoccupied with strategies for the company's survival, a rotation of bookings at theatre festivals and large theatres with free places to stay and rehearse in between. In addition, there were always the emergencies, an actor arrested in a Milan bar that spring for disrobing when intoxicated, which caused a flurry of telephone calls to lawyers.

At the same time that he attended to the daily comforts of

his nomadic tribe of twenty-five actors, their lovers, children, and friends, he had to organize the continuing collective process of working on *Frankenstein* and meliorate the political discussions occupying the troupe. While Julian was overtly for "sowing the seeds of divine discontent," his position was based on the axiom of nonviolent pacifism, which was not shared by everyone in the company. Carl Einhorn, for example, argued that nonviolent approaches to political change were the sentimental luxury of those who had never really been oppressed.

The impasse made Judith uneasy as her relationship with Carl was faltering over such political questions, and the jealousy caused by his sexual dishonesty and his liaisons with other women in the company. The conflict remained unresolved and left Judith with a recurrence of migraines so severe that she gripped the top of her head in fear that her skull was rising. Carl was now twenty-five and Judith, forty, so the age disparity seemed even greater than it had five years earlier; but the real problem was political. At company meetings, Carl spoke of "the enemy" with a grimness that made Judith remember Brecht's comment that whoever speaks of enemies is already the enemy.

In May 1966, Julian found accommodations for the company in the town of Reggio Emilia, half an hour outside Bologna, so that they could continue to work on *Frankenstein*. The company was now inventing the tradition of "free theatre" in which theatre was completely improvised. At that point, life in Italy was extremely chaotic with trains, mail, and telephone services interrupted by strikes. Julian was having difficulty getting work permits from Rome for scheduled performances because Italian officials claimed The Living Theatre was in Italy more for the sake of political agitation than theatre.

On 30 May, the company was invited by *Sipario,* an Italian theatre magazine, to offer an evening of "free theatre" at the Countess Borlotti's Palazzo Durini in Milan. Julian's practice—the one thing about business he said he learned from his father—was to insist the company be paid their one thousand dollar fee in advance of the event.

Based on the proposition that *anything* one did was perfect, a proposition derived from John Cage, the evening infuriated the audience. The company formed a compact circle in its center and remained absolutely silent for a long time. Eventually, the state Julian usually called "creative disorder" broke out. Members of the audience, mostly wealthy youths from the upper classes, poked at the actors, shouted insults, and tried to embrace them. Many members of the audience were outraged and angry, breaking some lights and defacing murals with shaving cream. The Countess Borlotti was slapped and she summoned the police, so the actors left. Accused of failing to perform, Judith replied that their purpose had been to pose a fundamental question: What is a theatrical event? The evening only added to The Living Theatre's scandalous reputation.

At the end of June, the company boarded its Volkswagen buses to drive to Paris where they were to perform *Mysteries* and *The Brig* under the ornate chandeliers of the Odéon. To sustain its realism, *The Brig* required short hair at a historical moment when long hair for men had become a sort of honor badge that the male members of the company wanted to display. At first, the actors had tried disguising their long hair with hair nets, and it became more and more difficult for Judith to cut each actor's hair.

After the company performed *The Brig*, Artaud's friend the actor Jean-Louis Barrault translated for Julian and Judith at a large press conference. Self-effacing and modest, Barrault praised *The Brig* as the legacy of Artaud, but *Mysteries* made him feel, he confessed, like a man driving a car while watching a wheel come off and proceed on its own.

Another wheel was Jerzy Grotowski, the earnest, young director of the Polish Theatre Laboratory, whom they met at the end of June and whose state-subsidized actors seemed as inspired as the members of The Living Theatre, though their reach and scope—perhaps because they only played to an audience in Wroclaw of forty each night—were more limited.

The members of The Living Theatre were closer to the radical edge of social change. They felt kinship with the wild and naive young Provos in Amsterdam, who were often arrested in violent and nonviolent protests. From New York, they heard news of street theatre, parades, student demonstrations, and widespread use of LSD. In *Time,* they read that the American embassy in Calcutta had been burned and that the civilian population of Hanoi had been evacuated because of American bombing. The portents of discontent were all over the walls of the Sorbonne: spray-painted signs reading ANARCHISME and YANKEE NAZIS, notices of peace marches, protests against the war in Vietnam, an American flag with skulls and dollar signs in place of stars.

In July, the company drove through the Alps, returning to Reggio Emilia to continue working on *Frankenstein* and to spend the hot nights under mosquito netting. At the end of the month, after packing the sets of *The Brig* and *Frankenstein,* the company boarded their old, beaten-up buses for a long drive along the Mediterranean coast to Cassis in Provence. There, they were met by poet Taylor Mead and film maker Jonas Mekas, and quartered in unfinished buildings meant for French Algerians. In the nagging wind of the mistral—reputed to drive people mad—surrounded by stone-pocked hills, they performed *Mysteries* under the sky in a stone amphitheatre built by Jerome Hill, their host, the black sheep of an American railroad family, who had given the company $20,000 to help pay for their 1962 European tour. Taylor Mead found the performance "communal to the point of sameness." He was irritated by the frequency with which Julian kept repeating "End the war in Vietnam!" and began shouting "A bas les intellectuals!" and "Vive la guerre de Vietnam!" in response.

Under a full moon, near the sea, they did an extravagant five-hour version of *Frankenstein.* The local newspapers parodied the company, maligning them with implications of drug use, but the curious audiences still came. As usual, there were supporters as well as unsympathetic observers, one of whom filled a hubcap with gunpowder and left it under one of the buses. Fused and detonated, it fortunately did little damage but existed as an ominous sort of warning.

The organizers of the festival at Cassis permitted the company to stay on for an additional three weeks, and in the middle of August, with the mistral wind bending the trees and one of the buses leaking oil because of a faulty piston, they drove to Berlin. As always, there was the paranoia of the border guards, intensified by the bravado of the troupe. Judith wore a peace button, and Julian had a photograph of Gandhi in his wallet. Housed in a decayed theatrical pensione, rehearsing in the Akademie der Kunste, the group discussed every scene of *Antigone*. A new member, an iron-willed German girl who had studied classical theatre in Salzburg named Petra Vogt, made valuable corrections to Judith's translation.

In East Berlin, the company saw the famous Berliner Ensemble, led by Helene Weigel, doing *Coriolanus,* a play where a strong leader usurps power. At the Volksbuhne, Piscator's theatre in the 1920s, Judith saw an exhibition of his designs and reminded an interviewer that Piscator had predicted that America would eventually turn fascist. When, a few days later, Judith met with Madame Piscator, she heard of the difficulty in finding a burial spot for Piscator. Berlin never loved him, Madame Piscator sighed, so it was no wonder that even in death he could not find a corner.

Like "beggars and stepchildren," playing to small audiences because all their work had already been seen in Berlin and so short of money they were thrown out of their pensione, the company performed *The Brig* for ten days in September and then began *Frankenstein.* Most of the actors were ill with the flu, moving in a delirium of redemptive agony. The play was still changing, *Village Voice* critic Michael Smith observed, the staging and the set being continuously refined and further elaborated, but the form was complex and the play, obscure and difficult to follow. With *Frankenstein,* the company had shifted from a theatre of character to one that relied on archetypes. The play was so different from anything he had ever seen before, Smith decided audiences had to learn how to see it. And if the play was a failure, if it seemed too long, at times boring or repetitive, "by definition experiment required the freedom to fail."

From Berlin, the company drove to Venice at the end of October to perform *The Maids* in the ornate, crystal-chandeliered, red-carpeted but unheated Teatro del Ridotto. The rainy, chilly afternoons were spent rehearsing *Antigone,* which had to be ready for a German television production that would give them enough money to get through the winter.

In the beginning of November, they were in the mountain city of Trento. Surrounded by rolls of barbed wire and military police, they performed "Street Songs"—with slogans like "Abolish the State," "Open All Jails," "Make Love, Not War"—from *Mysteries* for university students who had been protesting for eleven days against restrictions. The students showed Judith a book about the Berkeley Free Speech Movement, which they regarded as a sort of bible. This was a forerunner of the European student protest movement, and one of the students who had asked the company to Trento was Renato Curcio, who would later help found the Red Brigades. A week later, they were playing *The Maids* in Turin, waiting an entire day, like the junkies in *The Connection,* for money to pay their hotel bills.

On 7 November, Judith and Julian were in Brussels, dismayed that parts of the *Frankenstein* set had arrived smashed. One bus was stalled in the Alps; the other had four flats in France. The company spent a week performing *Frankenstein* in Brussels to enthusiastic, overflowing crowds and proceeded to Amsterdam's Doelenzaal Theatre, where the Nazis had once rounded up Dutch actors for deportation during the war. Judith and Julian met with Simon Vinkenoog, the Dutch poet who had organized the Provos. From their dressing room windows, they could see ducks in the canal; inside the theatre, audiences for *The Maids* were small but receptive.

Money was still scarce although audiences improved when the company began performing *Mysteries.* Using Amsterdam as a base, the company made forays to perform in the Dutch and German countryside, but these were hardly pastoral retreats as Judith recalled: "without sleep and barely enough money to eat, harassed by landlords; traveling, waiting, freezing in unheated theatres, stiff and aching from sleeping while sitting upright in the bus, afflicted with sinuses, bronchitis, upset stomachs, vomiting."

In the beginning of January, they were again in Berlin to film *Antigone* for German television. Driving south to Munich through the Ruhr, the landscape seemed nightmarish with omnipresent smokestacks and air that smelled of oil and sulphur. Entering Munich, one of the buses was stopped by police demanding to see papers. When the driver, photographer Gianfranco Mantegna, could not produce them quickly enough, the police tried to remove him from the bus. Henry Howard, Rufus Collins, and Jimmy Anderson sat in front of the door. The police drew their pistols and placed them along the sides of the seated actors' heads, and Bill Shari began shouting "Hitler!" Immediately, the bus was invaded by a dozen leather-clad police who began to strike everyone with clubs.

The police attack challenged Judith's pacifism, leaving her "amazed at one's own capacity for violence, and by not acting on it, knowing it even better." The Munich police chief agreed to drop charges provided that no member of the company pressed any, but he threatened that The Living Theatre might be expelled and the company prevented from future engagements in Germany.

Judith felt from every quarter—even in their hotel—an angry hostility disguised by the "sweet whipped cream" of Bavarian coyness. The *Suddeutsche Zeitung* declared in a front-page editorial that they were provocateurs. The most overt manifestation of the endemic hostility was the Munich fire department's disapproval of the electrical system for *Frankenstein,* which had to be performed under very modified conditions.

43. A Deaf Man Answers Unasked Questions

All through the winter and spring of 1967, The Living Theatre continued to perform on the road in Germany and Switzerland. In Geneva, performances of *Mysteries* were sold out, and the visit was extended. In Berlin, Günter Grass came to a performance of *The Brig*—where the men now had their long hair encased in hair nets.

Judith was still working on *Antigone.* Her health had been adversely affected by the pressure of completing the translation and the difficulties of travel. Any two chairs could provide a bed for her, she noted in her *Diary,* because she was so small and slept curled up; and if there were no chairs, she could sleep on the floor; but such ad hoc arrangements took their toll. Complaining of a heaviness in her breasts and frequent nausea, she saw doctors who dismissed her as merely suffering from nerves. Finally, after Julian brought a bottle of her urine to a drugstore, she learned she was pregnant. At the age of forty, Judith had thought she was past the age of childbearing, and now she had to play the role of the virgin Antigone while struggling through the physical discomforts of pregnancy.

Unfinished and still unready, *Antigone* opened in Krefeld, Germany, with Judith playing the title role, and Julian, that of the cruel tyrannical Creon. In this tragedy, Creon has begun the war against Argos to loot its iron mines and ordered that Polynices,

Antigone's brother, be left as carrion for vultures on the field of battle. For the Greeks, to lie unburied meant perpetual restlessness in death and was a source of great family shame. Antigone, in an act of defiant civil disobedience, buries her brother with dust she collects. This causes the tragic conflict of the play, which for Judith was an illustration of Paul Goodman's lesson of "drawing the line": the moment when one's moral principles no longer can be compromised by any fear of the overwhelming physical power of the state.

Judith's verse translation was based on Brecht's version of the lofty translation the German Romantic poet Friedrich Hölderlin had done of Sophocles' play. Brecht's version begins with a prologue in which two sisters emerge from an air-raid shelter after the Second World War to find their brother, tortured and dead, hanging from a butcher's hook. Judith replaced this scene with the murder of Polynices in the laps of the audience. On a bare stage, without light changes, the actors wore their own clothes. Instead of props, the actors used their bodies, four of Elders of Thebes becoming Creon's throne, and another four, the prison walls enclosing Antigone.

Using his famous "alienation" effect that was supposed to distance the actor and the audience from the myth, Brecht had had a stage manager read a poem describing exactly what would occur before each event. In Judith's version, the actors recited these lines in the language of whatever host country they were in to make sure the audience would understand the implicit warning of the play—if a culture uses violence against its enemies, it will also use it against its own citizens.

Early in March, the company performed *Antigone* in Kiel—Judith's birthplace. Judith was full of mixed emotions about returning to Kiel, and when she visited the old theatre in which she had first lived with her parents, all she found was a playing field with pussy willows at its edges. When a maid saw two male company members embracing in a room, the innkeeper threatened to notify police and demanded that the entire company leave immediately, chasing them down the street.

221

In April, in a baroque music box of a theatre with heckling stagehands in the town of L'Aquila in the Apennines, ill and weak, her voice rasping, she was Antigone again. It was difficult to play in Italian and to believe in the role of the virgin Antigone with something moving inside her swelling belly. Exhausted after the performance, in a freezing hotel room illuminated only by candles, she learned that she was in *Harper's Bazaar*'s "One Hundred American Women of Accomplishment" issue, although she was still on probation in her own country.

In Rome, Judith suddenly felt she was being treated like a celebrated actress. With Julian, she had lunch with the writer Alberto Moravia, who offered hashish after the pasta. She met Anna Magnani backstage after a performance of *Antigone.* Judith and Julian were interviewed on Italian television and by Leonard Lyons, the *New York Post* columnist.

The Italian director Pier Paolo Pasolini invited Judith and Julian to dinner. Pasolini was a radical critic of bourgeois culture, a poet, novelist, and film maker whose outspoken Marxism and homosexuality caused frequent confrontation with legal authorities. He particularly admired Julian's rendition of the maid who impersonates her mistress in *The Maids,* a play initially banned in Rome. Pasolini wanted Julian to fly to Morocco for four days to play Tiresias in his version of *Oedipus,* which Julian was eager to do because the company was always short of money.

At the end of April, Julian returned from Casablanca ill and sunburned, full of stories about dying Frenchmen in a colonial hotel. As a director, Pasolini was possessed by his conception, able to identify with his spectators while seeing through the eye of the camera. The film had been shot in the desert beyond the Atlas Mountains, and Julian had been fitted with contact lenses to simulate Tiresias's blindness. The lenses, combined with the intense sun and sand, had almost succeeded in actually blinding him.

In May, back in Rome, several of the actors—women wearing bracelets and rings, some of the men in earrings—were carrying musical instruments in the streets, where they were stopped by police and questioned. Brought to police headquarters, they were asked to wait while telephone calls to various parts of Italy were made to determine whether there were any outstanding charges against them. They were playing *Mysteries,* and the theatre owner, a Tunisian Jew, brought Julian into the toilet to tell him the company could no longer announce political slogans like "Basta con la polizia" or "Basta con gli stati" in his theatre, an injunction Julian ignored.

Europe suddenly seemed less of a refuge. Initially, European intellectuals had greeted them as a "kind of saintly group of theatrical geniuses" as Peter Hartman once put it. However, some intellectuals soon became disillusioned by newspaper scandals, the reputation for drug use, and the establishment's misapprehension that they were socially irresponsible anarchists who demonstrated little respect for law. Such opposition, however, helped to bring members of the company together and made them more determined.

At the end of May, performing in front of the haughty stares of the Florentine burghers, Julian spent his forty-second birthday visiting Savonarola's convent cell, bare except for a sketch of the burning of the monk. The adjoining cells were decorated with Fra Angelico's paintings, which caused Julian to muse that "art was not enough" to prevent a man from being burned alive. The violent potential of the world seemed particularly evident because war had erupted in the Middle East, oil supplies to the West had stopped, and Tel Aviv and Cairo were being bombed.

In June and July, the company had engagements in Paris, where they performed *Mysteries* and *The Brig* in long hair, much to Julian's consternation for he felt the play's realism had been sacrificed. As a group, the company saw *Marat/Sade,* Peter Brook's brilliant spectacle about the French revolution, which deepened their debate about the imminence and probability of renewed revolutionary ferment.

When the company traveled to Normandy, Judith remained in Paris reading *War and Peace.* Garrick, who was attending Reed College in Oregon, visited, declaring that under no conditions would he accept being drafted and that he would go to prison before he would go to Vietnam.

On 19 July, Judith gave birth to a tiny daughter who was named Isha—Hebrew for "woman"—Manna, the bread from heaven that fell on the wandering Israelites. A week later—while Judith remained in Paris with her new daughter in an incubator—Julian was in Rome playing a dying cardinal in *Agonia,* a film by Bernardo Bertolucci. One night, on the roof of a small hotel, he spoke with members of the Polish Theatre Laboratory about the differences between The Living Theatre's communal creation and Grotowski's more authoritarian control. For Grotowski, The Living Theatre was too spontaneous, though he saw how each company reflected surrounding political and social circumstances.

In the beginning of September, Judith took her newborn daughter in a reed basket on the train to Belgrade. From Belgrade, the company of thirty-two actors and eight children traveled by train and ferry to Wales and Dublin. In October, they were in Belgium, and in November, they performed *Antigone* and other plays in Franco's Spain. In December, they performed *Mysteries* at Nanterre in France, and a little-known radical student named Daniel Cohn-Bendit participated. In *Time,* in an article called "Anarchists of the Anti-Word," a writer pointed out that The Living Theatre was probably "the only repertory group in the world operating on a pay-as-you-go basis and without subsidy."

All through the fall of 1967, in *Time* and in newspapers, they read of marches to the Pentagon guarded by paratroopers and mass demonstrations against the war. In New York, 264 demonstrators were arrested, including Allen Ginsberg and Dr. Benjamin Spock, at an antiwar rally in early December. "Modern history," Judith read in her Tolstoy, was like "a deaf man who answers questions no one asks," and the planet seemed to have spun into a strange gyration making change possible.

44. *Paradise Now*

In a characteristically brilliant act of persuasion, Julian convinced the owner of Club Méditerranée to allow the troupe to use the Villagio Magico in Cefalù, Sicily, a resort that accommodated fifteen hundred tourists at a time in summer but was vacant in winter. The estate, landscaped to look like an African jungle with giant cacti and straw huts, faced the city across the bay of Cefalù, with sprawling beaches, rocky cliffs, and a square turreted watchtower that suggested danger and romance. The city itself, connected to Villagio Magico by a concrete sea walk, was dwarfed by a gigantic mountain looming above it, topped by a sloping plateau. The entire effect was overwhelming.

Installing themselves in February 1968 in a dilapidated wooden palazzo and in several straw huts with thatched roofs that they decorated with bright scarves, beads, and posters, the company met to plan matters of sanitation, cooking, supplies, and finances. Their primary objective was the creation of an event they would call *Paradise Now* which would become the defining experience of The Living Theatre.

At first, the company assembled in a large, yellow room in the old palazzo for long discussions on the idea of paradise; its biblical and other mythological manifestations; more recent romantic and utopian conceptions; texts such as the I Ching, the Tibetan Book of the Dead, and the Cabala; philosophers such as Rousseau; and psychiatrists such as Wilhelm Reich and R. D. Laing.

At the same time, the group worked on meditation, yoga, and daily exercises devised to heighten sensitivity and expressiveness. For example, an actor would limply lie on a mat intoning a particular sound that best characterized his or her self while others would touch his or her skull, breasts, and belly. As the intoning continued toward a trance state, others would breathe on the temples. Finally, they would lift the body.

Although Julian and Judith had declared to a *Time* reporter that their intention as directors—in an anarchist echo of *The Communist Manifesto*—was to "wither away," they provided much of the ideological framework used during the evolution of the play. At Cefalù, Julian wrote an essay called "Theatre and Revolution" in which he asserted that "a money-oriented, cold, amoral, power-crazed society" required a "feelingless violence" to maintain the status quo. The search for feeling was a revolutionary contradiction to the feelingless torpor that was the price paid for order and civilization, for slavery and the authoritarian state. To discover the feeling, the first step was Artaud's declaration that the texts had to be burned, that the theatre of intellect had to be abandoned, that the actor would have to find feeling through inner resources.

For *Paradise Now,* Julian wanted to devise a form that could allow the release of spontaneous creative forces which could transform audiences and society. Activating the audience was a key. In Pirandello, and in *Many Loves* and *The Connection,* improvisation had been written into the plays to the extent that spectators imagined that what they were seeing was being invented on the spot by the actors. But, as Julian would argue in *The Life of the Theatre,* "you could not be free if you are contained within a fiction."

Instead of an enactment that could be repeated night after night, Julian declared he wanted the act itself, primary and unrepeatable. The act would project a revolutionary situation and lay the groundwork for anarchist action cells which would begin the work of revolution. The premise of the first scene was that the human condition was that we are temporarily excluded from the gates of Paradise, prevented from entering by the frustrating and controlling prohibitions of the authoritarian state, which in the next scenes would be overcome.

Early in March, after daily, prolonged discussions, Judith and Julian sequestered themselves inside one of the huts for a week, emerging with an arcane map of eight levels of revolutionary action necessary to achieve liberation. Each level included a ritual, an action, and a vision—among them, the loss of Eden, the resurrection of the American Indian—the last of which was performed by the audience. These levels were then organized according to Martin Buber's explanation of the Hasidic concept of rungs on a ladder—the rite of I and Thou, the rite of the Mysterious Voyage, the rite of prayer—leading to heaven or permanent revolution.

After three months at Cefalù, the company had defined the play. If there was a choice of what to clarify, Julian had posited, he would always choose whatever led to political clarity, and by "political," he maintained, he meant "leading to action." At the same time, *Paradise Now* was conceived as an alternative to the increasingly frenzied opposition to the war in Vietnam.

Paradise Now begins with "The Rite of Guerrilla Theatre" and a quality of provocation that informs the entire event. When the audience is seated, they are approached by actors speaking—first softly, then with rising intensity to the point of a prolonged scream—the following propositions: "I am not allowed to travel without a passport"; "I don't know how to stop the wars"; "You can't live without money"; "I am not allowed to smoke marijuana"; "I am not allowed to take my clothes off." Addressing one spectator after another, the actor enacts a frustration with social restrictions curtailing liberty.

Though such exhortation was regarded by some members of the audience as accusation, The Living Theatre wanted to create a revolutionary consciousness in which an audience does not merely or passively observe but enacts its destiny. Utterly unlike conventional drama which sustains and develops a thesis, *Paradise Now* presents a series of tableaux intended to induce a state of psychic and emotional rebellion against conditioning, in which concepts are reiterated and collide, moving toward an idealistically conceived resolution. While the company premise was a rejection of the audience's negativity, the actors knew that they would try to use whatever response emerged.

Instead of the conflict-resolution patterns of conventional drama, each rung of the play becomes more physically challenging for the audience. The fourth rung, for example, begins with "The Rite of Universal Intercourse." In a pile of practically naked figures on the stage floor, the actors making a low humming sound caress each other, undulating and embracing. In *The Birth of Tragedy,* the German philosopher Nietzsche had conjectured that the origin of drama could be found in the orgies of the pre-Doric Greeks when, three to four thousand years ago, they were still nomadic sheepherders. This part of the play suggests the volatile energies that had given birth to theatre in the first place.

Sexual repression, Julian argued, is the basis of most violence, and the theatre, as Artaud envisaged it, was created as one outlet for these repressions. Spectators are invited to speak out about sexual taboos, to undress, and to join the "body pile," a gathering onstage of actors and audience groping for each other.

Several hours later, depending on the quality of audience participation, the final rung begins with "The Rite of I and Thou." In this action inspired by the Tibetan Book of the Dead, the actors die, are reborn, and form the Tree of Knowledge. The rebirth is another way of announcing that no revolution can occur without a parallel transformation of the individual. The actors encourage the spectators to taste the fruit of the tree with no prospect of divine retribution. Carrying spectators on their shoulders, actors lead the audience out into the street in a mood of jubilation, beginning the quest for Paradise. As they exit, they recite: "The theatre is in the street. The street belongs to the people. Free the theatre. Free the street. Begin."

Only if "the audience leaves the theatre to start the revolution," Julian wrote in his essay "Theatre and Revolution," can we be successful. After four or five hours of the unprecedented spectacle, the end of *Paradise Now* was regarded as incendiary provocation by authorities. Usually, the exiting actors, still in various states of undress, were met by the police who tried to stop them from streaming into the city.

45. The Events of May

P *aradise Now* had been conceived in an atmosphere of a worldwide rebellion largely initiated by young people. The Free Speech Movement at Berkeley, which had begun in 1964, became a continuing forum for the questioning of American goals in Vietnam, and opposition to the war was a vehicle for criticizing American society. European radicals saw the war against Vietnam as representative of an American attempt "to dictate to the rest of the world," as French radical Daniel Cohn-Bendit put it, while the European socialist bureaucracies stood by.

In 1967, there had been unrest in universities in Milan, Turin, Barcelona, Madrid, and Berlin. In the fall of 1967, ten thousand students at Nanterre, a suburban extension of the Sorbonne, demonstrated because of overcrowding and the lack of library facilities. On 22 March 1968, after four students from Nanterre were arrested for hurling concrete blocks through the Paris office of American Express in an anti–Vietnam War protest, two hundred students led by Daniel Cohn-Bendit took over the administration building.

A short, pudgy, redheaded anarchist, the son of a German Jew who had escaped Hitler, Cohn-Bendit was a sociology student at Nanterre who attacked authoritarianism, hierarchy, and repression. Known as Danny the Red, he argued that the business community disregarded workers and the university was a kind of factory producing technicians for industry. Lectures were canceled, and the police surrounded the campus while students debated the prospects for change in the main courtyard of the university. The agitation at Nanterre became a semipermanent feature of life at the school, with students boycotting examinations and calling for reform of the psychology and sociology disciplines.

In the United States, there were similar disturbances in many universities. In March, President Lyndon Johnson, shocked by the success of the North Vietnamese in the winter Tet offensive, declared that he would not run for reelection. On 4 April, the civil rights leader Martin Luther King, Jr., was assassinated, causing riots in over a hundred American cities, among them Washington, D.C., which was shrouded in a pall of smoke.

In West Germany, student uprisings resumed after the attempted assassination of Rudi Dutschke, a leftist student leader. Disturbances continued in Franco's Spain, in Rome where the university system was paralyzed, and in Poland and Brazil. The most extensive protests, however, were in France, where World War II hero General Charles de Gaulle, at the age of seventy-seven, had been in power for a decade.

Just before the arrival of the French tourists, early in May, The Living Theatre left Cefalù, worried that several of its members had come down with hepatitis. Crossing the Tyrrhenian Sea, they saw the Parisian students rioting on Italian television. They had assembled to discuss the boycotting of examinations. Essentially unchanged since Napoléon had reopened the Sorbonne in 1808 after the French Revolution, most of the instruction consisted of professors reading old lectures in large, unheated halls. Before the students could even act on anything, the feared CRS—Compagnies républicaines de securité, the paramilitary special forces—intervened, aggressively carting many students off to jail. French police, as the American novelist James Jones who lived in Paris observed, were trained to be brutal and made American police look like a "high school football squad."

The French had a tradition of popular resistance to oppressive authority. They had erected barricades in Paris in 1789 during their revolution, in 1848, and in 1871 during the Paris Commune. In May 1968, the students began overturning and then burning cars in the Latin Quarter, and uprooting the paving stones to throw at police. The chairs, tables, and awnings of Paris's cafés were used as barricades. The CRS responded with clubs and tear gas.

What had begun as a student protest against the constrictions of a smothering university system quickly escalated into a national crisis and a call for the removal of de Gaulle. Workers were told by union leaders that if the students could challenge repressive hierarchical structures in the university, they could apply similar methods in their factories. As former Premier Pierre Mendès-France put it, the conflict "dramatized the determination of millions of Frenchmen no longer to be considered impotent subjects in a harsh, inhumane, conservative society."

The extensive police violence moved the unions to side with the Sorbonne students, and they called a general strike for 13 May 1968. From the outset, this action was planned as a symbolic show of support. Judith and Julian, driving through France with the company, saw the General Strike as the beginning of the new revolutionary consciousness they were trying to dramatize in *Paradise Now*.

On 12 May, they reached Paris to try to arrange a television contract to film a series of street plays, what they called "guerrilla theatre." These negotiations were unsuccessful. Instead, Judith and Julian, passing through corridors of police vans, went to the Sorbonne to work with the students. With red flags draped on the walls, the place was teeming with excitement and crowded with wild-eyed, exhausted students with long hair.

Although the Right Bank of Paris seemed orderly on 13 June, four million unionized Frenchmen out of a work force of some twenty million went out on strike. Another eight million workers stayed away from their jobs. Workers occupied factories and offices. In Nantes, an aircraft plant was seized. A Renault transmission plant was occupied by five thousand workers in Brittany, and another Renault plant outside Paris was seized.

In Paris, there were nightly battles between police and students in the Latin Quarter. The tear gas was so thick that infants living three floors above the street were said to be affected. There was no gas or garbage collection in the city, electricity services were disrupted, and public transportation was paralyzed.

One of the first leaflets issued by the students at the Sorbonne was Artaud's letter to the chancellors of European universities in which he asserted that Europe had slowly "mummified itself under the chains" of its frontiers, factories, law courts, and universities. Artaud had always maintained that gradualist political action was useless.

With a group of artists at daily meetings at the Sorbonne planning the occupation of the Eiffel Tower, the Folies Bergère, or the Louvre, Julian convinced the committee that the Odéon Théâtre de France, one of the glories of French architecture located near the Latin Quarter and directed by Jean-Louis Barrault who had been Artaud's friend and disciple, was a more strategic choice. The Odéon had been known as an antibourgeois theatre that had staged the work of Beckett, Ionesco, and Genet.

On 16 May, Julian and Judith led the insurrectionary crowd of insurgent students, workers, and actors singing the "Internationale" and waving black anarchist flags. This throng managed to transform the venerable building into what Julian called "a place of live theatre in which anyone could become an actor." The entire theatre became a stage for twenty-four hour periods of confrontation and debate in which anyone could freely participate. Barrault spoke, appealing for the safety of the theatre. Ionesco and many of the leading artists of Paris appeared. Daniel Cohn-Bendit declared that theatre had to become a "major instrument of combat against the bourgeois."

In an atmosphere of tremendous ferment and intensity, reminiscent of the French Revolution in which citizens of all classes seized power and determined the fate of the state, students and workers spoke, and were answered by others. Julian believed that what he saw at the Odéon provided the "greatest theatre I've ever seen." As in *Paradise Now,* the "architecture of elitism and separatism," the "barriers between art and life" that only falsified conventional theatre, had been broken, and the result had brought "theatre into the street and the street into the theatre."

For the most part, French intellectuals were too amazed at what had transpired to participate fully. Raymond Aron warned that the upheaval involved more risks than hopes. Sartre addressed the students at the Sorbonne and interviewed Cohn-Bendit for *Le Nouvel Observateur.* Maurice Merleau-Ponty, one of the intellectuals associated with Sartre's magazine *Les Temps Modernes,* argued that true humanism was able to reconcile the virtuous goal of a classless society with the use of terror to facilitate that goal. From Judith and Julian's viewpoint, this argument for violence could only strengthen the forces of containment and reaction.

De Gaulle, using a favorite delaying tactic, called for a national referendum for change. There were mass demonstrations supporting him in Paris and others in opposition. Students marched chanting "Elections are treason." Garbage in Paris was piled ten feet high in certain quarters; traffic signals did not work; twenty thousand had rioted at the Gare de Lyon; and people were hoarding supplies. The graffiti on the Sorbonne walls included Bakunin's motto: "The urge to destroy is a creative urge." The students were now calling themselves the *enragés,* and on the night of 24 May, they stormed the Bourse, the national stock market.

At the end of May, the troupe settled in the Vieille Ecole Frederick Mistral, an old high school in Avignon in the south of France, where they were scheduled to premiere *Paradise Now* at the famous theater festival begun by Jean Vilard. Although they were being paid poorly, part of the deal Julian arranged included three months of accommodations in the old school and the construction of a large wooden platform in the spacious courtyard to be used as a rehearsal area.

Ironically, the previous inhabitants of the Lycée Mistral had been the CRS, but early in June, over a hundred of the *enragés* moved in—sleeping in the dormitories of the school or in sleeping bags on the crowded platform—trying to push The Living Theatre into all kinds of violent political action. The *enragés* continued their marathon discussions about Marxism, Leninism, Maoism, anarchism, and the question of violence or nonviolence. Some of the *enragés* had weapons—much to Judith's particular horror—and some of them represented a lunatic fringe that might be expected at such gatherings. As in the Odéon, the students seemed intoxicated by the endless talking.

The very freedom exhibited by the *enragés* at the Lycée Mistral outraged some of the citizens of Avignon and coincided with the June electoral campaign. Jean-Pierre Roux, a Gaullist candidate for the National House of Deputies, accused the local Socialist mayor of having imported a group of "ragged fanatics" and their "amusements for the mentally sick."

When de Gaulle promised wage increases, the labor unions shifted their allegiances, and many workers in the coal, gas, and auto industries started returning to their jobs. Although the students were still occupying their universities, and there would be further rioting in Paris on the nights of 10 and 11 June, the press began writing about normalization. Banks and stores were opening; telephone service had resumed; and trains were running.

News of striking workers was replaced by media shock at the assassination of Robert Kennedy on 5 June. The mood of the students was, however, still incendiary. When Julian addressed students occupying the University of Marseilles a few days after the Kennedy assassination, he was heckled by Maoists and nihilists who waved a large black placard in front of his face as he tried to speak. Though this may have been frustrating, Julian knew it was a typical expression of the mood of the moment, the complexity of countercurrents among the revolutionaries.

In the middle of June, CRS troops repossessed the Sorbonne and the Odéon, ending the students' one-month occupation. The "psychodrama of pseudo-revolution," as critic Raymond Aron put it, was over.

As the national election campaign reached its climax, de Gaulle implied that if he lost, France would be run from Moscow. He blamed all social disorders on the left and used the student movement as his scapegoat. The French—who are said to have their hearts on the left and their wallets on the right—reelected him by a landslide at the end of June.

In the middle of July, a local, long-haired communal group known as the Théâtre Chêne Noir was prohibited by the Avignon police from staging a play. At a demonstration in support of the Chêne Noir, in the Place de la République in Avignon, a large force of helmeted CRS attacked with clubs, arresting everyone on the street. In support of the Chêne Noir, The Living Theatre played *Antigone* with the French group sitting cross-legged on the stage, their mouths sealed with tape painted the colors of the French flag.

"Theatre is the Wooden Horse by which we can take the town," Julian later wrote in *The Life of the Theatre*. The company performed *Mysteries, Antigone,* and *Paradise Now* in the hope that the incipient violence at Avignon might be calmed. But on several nights when they did perform, the Lycée Mistral was threatened by belligerent marauders who threw stones and broke windows, practically creating a state of siege.

There were three explosive performances of *Paradise Now* at the Palais de Papes, where the troupe was heckled by right-wing Gaullists who on several occasions threw pails of water at actors. As always, the members of the company regarded the hecklers as part of the show, proving the point that society needed to change. The daily *Le Méridional*—taking the standard approach of right-wing newspapers that anything American was synonymous with "without culture"—expressed its shock and dismay at the barbarism of the performers who were compromising the tradition of the Avignon Festival. At the same time, the *enragés* in the audience greeted *Paradise Now* with a spirit of jubilation, and the second performance ended at two in the morning with two hundred spectators marching and chanting on the streets with Le Living, as the group is called by the French.

Julian announced that the company would perform in the streets without charge. The troupe had long been considering a commitment to only playing in the streets. In New York, Richard Schechner had organized "guerrilla theatre" groups, and Peter Schumann had used the streets for his Bread and Puppet Theatre. When Julian assembled the troupe on a square in Champfleury, the workers' quarter of Avignon, they were prevented from performing *Mysteries* by seventy-five helmeted police. Using a clash in the streets between right-wing and left-wing youth as a pretext but actually worried about the possibility of street demonstrations after *Paradise Now,* Mayor Henri Duffaut issued a decree forbidding any further performances of *Paradise Now.*

Julian then issued a long statement explaining that The Living Theatre would withdraw from the Avignon Festival because it could not perform a play about liberty in an atmosphere of censorship. As a sign of mourning, some members of the company dyed the sheets loaned to them by Avignon black and returned them to the mayor's office. The conflict in Avignon was characteristic, Judith realized: "If a life style or an artistic tendency has any intrinsic power, it will, I think, put itself in a position where it won't be accepted. If it can be contained, then its value is not revolutionary."

46. Naked in New Haven

Avignon was no exception to a European experience that had been consistently unpredictable. One day, they were praised and the next, reviled. One night, they might dine in an elegant palace; the next night, there might not be enough bread and cheese to go around in a third-class rooming house.

Under an August full moon, in the garden of Voltaire's house in Geneva, the company worked on *Paradise Now.* When they offered it in the Palais des Sports, a huge arena accommodating fifteen hundred spectators, many of the solid Swiss burghers in the first-night audience walked out while others stayed to cheer.

There were plans for returning to the United States. Reading about the Democratic National Convention in Chicago, where police battled young demonstrators protesting the war in Vietnam, made some of them paranoid. Jenny Hecht, for example, feared they would all be arrested or killed in America; but Saul Gottlieb, who had worked with The Living Theatre in New York, had scheduled a cross-country tour under the auspices of a group called the Radical Theatre Repertory.

At the end of August, the company of thirty-four actors and their children sailed to New York on the *Aurelia,* an Italian cruise ship bringing American students home after a summer abroad. In exchange for a performance of *Mysteries,* Julian had arranged for a reduced rate. The ship's captain offered Julian a Campari in his cabin, reporting that he had heard that company members were liable to copulate in the corridors like wild animals. "I like things square," he observed. Julian replied that he preferred "things circular" and reassured the captain that the company members were more inhibited than their reputation suggested.

All during the voyage, members of the company participated in student forums on politics, on the presidential election race between Richard Nixon and Hubert Humphrey, on Senator Eugene McCarthy's more progressive challenge, on student power, and on nonviolence. When Julian led a forum on anarchism, Judith observed the students wanted to be thought of as radical but were actually afraid. The *Aurelia* entered New York harbor flying a subtle sign of anarchism—Judith's black kerchief which hung from a rigging in the center of the ship unnoticed by any of the crew.

At a press conference outside of the customs area, a reporter warned Judith that America was not ready for The Living Theatre. A policeman told Jenny Hecht the group—in its flowers, beads, and lace and feathered finery—should be in padded cells. Lawyers gave the actors a detailed set of legal instructions in the event of police questioning or arrest. It was the time of "choosing of the sides," Judith reflected, a moment of unprecedented polarization when groups like the Black Panthers and the Weathermen were provoking insurrection with violence.

It was in such a tense atmosphere that The Living Theatre began its tour with a two-week run of *Mysteries, Frankenstein, Antigone,* and *Paradise Now* at Yale University in New Haven where they had been invited by Robert Brustein, now dean of the Yale School of Drama.

At first the atmosphere seemed warm. Yale, in its Gothic quaintness and quiet tastefulness, seemed removed from revolutionary questions, cloistered, manicured, and genteel. Brustein had hired Kenneth Brown as the resident playwright at Yale, so Judith and Julian felt they had a friend who could help garner support. Brown found Julian lean and haggard, craggy and almost skeletal, his bald scalp contrasting with the aureole of long, graying hair starting at the lower limits of a receded hairline. The company as well seemed transformed by the images of both Judith and Julian. The women were confident, effusive, and proud; the men seemed reverent and almost monastic.

Mysteries opened in the middle of September. Joining in the "Plague" scene in increasing numbers, the students participated with a totality that had been missing in Europe where the young people had been more self-consciously political but somehow more reserved. One of these students, a young man named Hanon Reznikov, left the theatre disturbed by what he felt was sloganeering and formlessness, although he was immediately taken by Judith. The always traditional Yale community was jolted, some arguing that the play was amateurish and others proclaiming it a juggernaut, the most powerful theatre they had ever witnessed.

In an ambivalent review in the New Haven *Register,* a critic admitted the play had provided a "jagged, exhilarating, nauseating and commanding night in the theatre. It is a kind of creative hysteria." *Time*'s reviewer praised the stagecraft and body language of the group which permitted "the world to break through the fourth wall." What the reviewer found less admirable was that The Living Theatre seemed to become the mirror image of what it claimed to oppose. Its silences were aggressive, the play was latent with violence, "the cast drilled to such impersonal military precision that it most resembles a company of Green Berets." While the analogy of long-haired actors to marines seems implausible, the *Time* reviewer had noticed an emotional contradiction that was implicit in Artaud as well—the benevolent man who can become so enraged in his prose indictment of civilization that he approaches a kind of verbal violence.

There were others who were troubled by contradictions as well. Robert Brustein found that the group acted as a sort of cult espousing revolution, the resultant rabid energy having helped them cohere for so long. The consequences, he imagined, were not quite as real as The Living Theatre pretended because revolutionary talk could only be a kind of theatrics, a romantic rhetoric, since he believed "revolution is simply impossible in a mass state."

Besides the romanticism and the ideology masquerading under the guise of anarchism, Brustein felt the actors were particularly manipulative, preventing the expression of freedom whenever the point of view was different from theirs. When a female student launched into a passionate denunciation of The Living Theatre during their performance of *Antigone,* she was "hustled offstage by a group of performers who embraced her into silence—unbuttoning her blouse, feeling her legs, and shutting her mouth with theirs."

Eric Bentley commented that the actors were able to burn money in a symbolic protest onstage but then would appeal to the wealthy for support. While the group affected a revolutionary context, at the same time, they tended to talk down to the audience "as if we're all squares, as if we're all afraid of sex, for instance, and they're not."

Near the end of September, Judith was invited to speak at the Yale Divinity School, where she admitted that she had no illusions that a theatre alone could stop the war in Vietnam, but "I have complete faith in the ability of the theatre to destroy the values that caused the war, and eventually destroy the culture that has created those values."

After performing *Antigone* and *Frankenstein* before receptive audiences larger than the capacity of the six-hundred-seat auditorium at Yale, on the pleasantly warm evening of Thursday, 26 September, *Paradise Now*—in what was only its seventh performance—opened to another overflow audience including celebrities like the film maker Bernardo Bertolucci. Lots of people in the company as well as in the audience were on LSD. Eric Bentley had commented that the impulse of The Living Theatre was orgiastic, and during the "Rite of Universal Intercourse," when the actors in bikinis and G-strings began to grapple in a communal embrace, they were joined by almost two hundred spectators, many of whom were partially or totally disrobed. Most of these were still naked when, at the end of the play, the actors and several hundred members of the audience streamed out of the theatre, Judith mounted on the shoulders of a Yale student named Tom Walker who would later join the company.

On Chapel Street, a few blocks from the theatre, she saw a wiry, sandy-haired sixteen-year-old named Windy Simons lying on the street with only a red handkerchief around his genitals. Windy was doubled over, for he had been maced by police. Julian, wearing only his G-string, was in a police paddy wagon with another member of the company, and Judith, who asked to accompany her husband, was arrested as well. A bearded poet named Ira Cohen, who like many in the audience had been enthralled by the performance under the influence of LSD, demanded to be arrested. Cohen was wearing a colorful sari, and when the policeman pointed out he was dressed, Cohen immediately threatened to disrobe and was placed in the wagon also.

Altogether, five spectators and five members of the company—Julian, Judith, Jenny Hecht, Nona Howard, and Pierre Davis—spent the night in cells charged with indecent exposure, breaching the peace, and resisting arrest. After a courtroom arraignment, the judge ordered a test for venereal disease because of the indecent exposure charge, and agreed to release the actors so that they could perform again that evening as scheduled, provided there was no street processional ending.

On the evening of the second American performance of *Paradise Now,* there was almost a riot in the Yale Theatre. Members of the audience were furious because seat reservations could not be honored as several hundred students without tickets had rushed the gates despite the fact that policemen surrounded the theatre. Although too many people wanted to see the play, some members of the Yale community felt that the issues had been oversimplified and that it was intellectually dishonest to project an unreal freedom. So Wagnerian a theatre as *Paradise Now* depended on an "emotional swamping of the audience," Robert Brustein observed, admitting to Judith that he had hated the play and that in the face of excessive freedom people might swerve to fascism. Eric Bentley felt The Living Theatre was trying to shame the audience because they were middle class, and acknowledged that he might not know how to live his life, but the actors were the "last people from whom I could reasonably take advice or accept help."

The intensity of the performance was continued the next day when Judith met with students at the Yale Divinity School to learn that formerly lethargic students had been activated and, in some cases, radicalized. Other members of the company met with a contingent of local Black Panthers who harassed Rufus Collins, one of the black members of the troupe, as an apostate and proselytized for revolutionary violence, claiming that nonviolence died with Martin Luther King, Jr. Julian's reply was that violence itself was counterrevolutionary, the very condition that caused reaction to any change, but there was little possibility that any of the Panthers could have appreciated so Gandhian a position at that time.

For Judith, the experience at Yale confirmed the difficulty and exhilaration of the revolutionary path which meant "constantly trying to find an unwobbling pivot in a very wobbly situation." Despite the spirit of mayhem that had been aroused at Yale, surely as an expression of his congenital optimism or a sort of abstracted serenity that shielded him from harassment, Julian remarked to a reporter for the *New York Times* that the company was "breaking down the barriers that exist between art and life, barriers that keep men outside the gates of paradise."

47. Religion and Rigidity in New York

In October, The Living Theatre was scheduled for a three-week engagement at the Brooklyn Academy of Music. *Frankenstein* opened on 2 October with forty policemen in the theatre and three squad cars parked outside. Audiences were large and, for the most part, enthusiastically receptive, even if the New York critics were characteristically unsympathetic. The most favorable piece appeared in *Newsweek* where the reviewer discerned an "authenticity of impulse" and the "mad purity of heart" with which to carry it off. The Living Theatre, the reviewer said at the end of the piece, was "the most coherent, concentrated and radically effective company in the world."

At a party onstage after the opening, Judith danced with Allen Ginsberg, who told her about the anguish of the Chicago convention and the mantras he used to calm police. Backstage before the next performance, he practiced chanting with members of the company and discussed ways to prevent despair from turning into hatred.

Frankenstein poses the unanswerable question of how to resolve or end human suffering; and still in search of answers, Judith and Julian spent an afternoon at The New School listening to

Mary Mary and Paulo Augusto in the House of Love in a *favela* in São Paulo, Brazil, 23 December 1970 (Living Theatre Archives).

Judith and Julian in the DOPS prison, July 1971 (Living Theatre Archives).

Male members of the company in the Colonia Penal in Minas Gerais, 10 July 1971 (Living Theatre Archives).

Julian and Judith in a scene from *Seven Meditations* (Living Theatre Archives).

Hanon Reznikov and Steven Ben Israel in the *Strike Support Oratorium* in New York, 1974 (Living Theatre Archives).

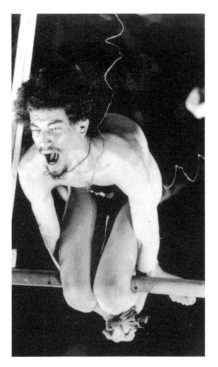

Ivanildo Silvino Araujo in the "Parrot's Perch" demonstrating torture in Brazil in *Seven Meditations* (Living Theatre Archives).

Julian, carrying Isha, with Bob Dylan at the Chilean Refugees Benefit at the Felt Forum in New York, 9 May 1974 (photograph by Bob Gruen).

The Money Tower in Homestead, Pennsylvania, 1975 (photograph by Judith Malina).

Isha, Garrick, Judith, and
Julian in Nantes, 1982
(Living Theatre Archives).

Living Theatre company
before leaving Nantes
(Living Theatre Archives).

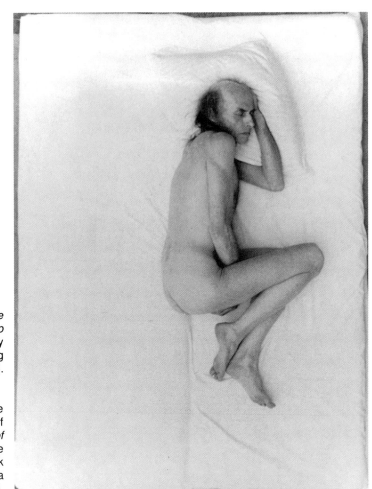

Julian asleep in *The Archeology of Sleep* (photograph by Bernd Uhlig, Living Theatre Archives).

The last bow at the final performance of *The Archeology of Sleep* at the Joyce Theatre in New York (photograph by Ira Cohen).

Francis Ford Coppola, Julian, and Ira Cohen
after the opening of *The Cotton Club*
(photograph by Ira Landgarten).

Judith and Julian (photograph by Ira Cohen).

Allen Ginsberg with Judith and Julian
(photograph by Ira Cohen).

Judith and Hanon
Reznikov (photograph by
Carol Wallit, Living
Theatre Archives).

John Tytell and Judith at
the National Arts Club
after the premiere of
Household Saints,
8 September 1993
(photograph by Mellon).

the Indian philosopher Krishnamurti. Thin, elegant, perfectly poised, conspicuously well-groomed yet with a face suggesting great suffering, Krishnamurti argued that suffering could be transcended by diminishing attachment to self. Though his language and presentation were beautiful, Judith was unconvinced, believing that the alleviation of suffering depended on engaging the self with society.

After two performances of *Frankenstein,* Judith, Julian, and several other members of the company returned to a New Haven courtroom to face the indecent exposure charges. Technically, Judith and Julian were still on probation in the fourth year of their suspended sentence for the IRS seizure of the Fourteenth Street theatre. Idealistic but at the same time pragmatic, they knew they could neither evade nor postpone judicial process. Charges against Jenny Hecht, Nona Howard, and Pierre Devis were immediately dismissed because the arresting officer could not identify them. Julian, in the state of Confucian calm that Brustein decided was a spiritual expression, dressed in a black T-shirt, black jeans, and sandals, explained that his loincloth was his costume and his use of it on the street was valid as an extension of the play. Robert Brustein and playwright Jules Feiffer testified, and at the end of what Judith regarded as a "wasteful day," she and Ira Cohen were each ironically fined a hundred dollars for interfering with an officer even though they had both volunteered to be arrested.

There was a performance of *Frankenstein* at the Brooklyn Academy that night and others through the week. As if that were not enough to occupy them, Richard Avedon photographed the company, some of them in the nude, and there were more formal sessions with *Newsweek* and then with *Saturday Evening Post* photographers. To add to the intense media exposure, Elenore Lester's very long and detailed magazine article appeared in the Sunday, 13 October, *New York Times,* and CBS interviewed Judith and Julian, filming the "Brig Dollar" and "Plague" scenes in *Mysteries.*

The negative establishment reviews of The Living Theatre were predictable. Jack Kroll in *Newsweek* recognized immediately that traditional critical standards would not work. When *Mysteries* opened, Dan Sullivan, the reviewer at the *New York Times,* was full of praise for the company's "extraordinary physical discipline." He noted that they worked more like a dance company than any company he knew of but faulted them for self-indulgence. The Living Theatre had become a family "with a mission to change the world" and, like most families, could not afford to be objective about themselves. Their work, Sullivan asserted, was less like theatre than a religious revival.

Clive Barnes, in his *New York Times* review of *Paradise Now,* extended the religious analogy, comparing the length of the four-and-half-hour performance—even longer than *Parsifal,* he complained—to a drawn-out church service. The tedium, he noted, was momentarily relieved when drama critic and director Richard Schechner stripped completely in his seat. Schechner's nudity was part of a revolution that "led to nowhere," drama critic Richard Gilman asserted, the expression of a naivete that was more an act of self-love than anything else. Fundamentally, the company's purpose was to "castigate the bourgeoisie," Gilman asserted, with a hatred and fury that Gilman thought approached dementia.

To the extent that one participates in *Paradise Now,* Robert Pasoli observed in a piece called "To Intervene in Life" in the *Village Voice,* "one engages in a ritual enactment of the revolution," which may have explained the presence onstage of Abbie Hoffman, who several weeks earlier had floated real money from the balcony of the New York Stock Exchange, or Paul Krassner, editor of the *Realist,* one of the crucial counterculture publications.

The "ritual enactment of revolution," which Pasoli recognized as a key principle of the play, afforded the beneficial possibilities of release as well as an extremely dangerous potential. The "wild beast" in the audience that Julian had discerned years earlier when doing Pirandello's *Tonight We Improvise* could now assume more monstrous proportions. In "The Rite of Universal Intercourse," early in *Paradise Now,* on the crowded stage, Judith was grabbed by a group of short-haired young men who "hurt me beyond my capacity to either yield or resist." While at least a hundred oblivious people surrounded her, she was held down and assaulted by one of them until another member of the company rescued her.

The religious analogy, the priestly function of theatre, Pasoli argued in his *Village Voice* essay, was a sort of red herring, a disguised dismissal of most critics' fears of being personally touched or moved to action. One critic who had been moved was Ross Wetzsteon of the *Village Voice* who admitted he had been exhausted as well as replenished by the urgency of The Living Theatre and ultimately nourished by their vision of possibility. What some of the other critics saw as aggressiveness, he asserted, was intensity; their harangues could be seen as supplications for change. Julian Beck's aim, Robert Pasoli had pointed out in his piece, was more modest than transcendence or religious transfiguration and was stated very bluntly in the Brooklyn Academy program: "If we can reduce the amount of aggression in one person, or change one person from being more rigid to less rigid, then the effort is worth the while."

The whole question of rigidity was tested one evening in the Fillmore East on Second Avenue when The Living Theatre performed the first scene of *Paradise Now* at a benefit for the legal defense fund for Columbia University SDS (Students for a Democratic Society) students who faced prison in connection with a strike conducted the previous spring. A radical lower East Side group known as the Up Against the Wall Motherfuckers occupied the stage during the performance, demanding that Bill Graham, the owner of the Fillmore East, restore his policy of a free night for the community. If he refused, they threatened, they would burn the theatre down. Julian spent hours negotiating onstage with Graham—the moralist trying to convince the businessman who organized entertainment for the counterculture. Graham finally agreed to the demands—though he would never actually honor the agreement.

All during the Brooklyn run, Judith and Julian were brimming with revolutionary fervor. At the Washington Square

Church, they spoke about revolution and anarchy. On WBAI, the progressive radio station, Judith and Julian were interviewed by *Village Voice* editor Ross Wetzsteon while station officials worried about the fact that they were all smoking marijuana during the interview. There was less smoke when Merv Griffin interviewed them about their politics between two nightclub acts for Channel 5 television.

At the end of October, the company left New York in a large bus—followed by two smaller Volkswagen buses and an old green schoolbus purchased by Bill Shari for himself, his wife, Dorothy, and their three children—to give two performances at the State University at Stony Brook on Long Island. The students, Judith reflected, seemed to misconstrue revolution as the right to smoke dope while listening to loud music. From Stony Brook, the company drove to Orient Point at the end of Long Island; a ferry then conveyed the caravan to New London, Connecticut. From there, the company drove to Boston and the real beginning of the American tour. They were on the road again for a six-month expedition during which they would perform over a hundred times, mostly to capacity audiences, in every part of the country except the South.

48. A Revolution Disguised as a Theatre

In Cambridge, Massachusetts, The Living Theatre was scheduled to give ten performances during the first week of November at the futuristic Kresge Auditorium at MIT which at that moment had become an agitated hive of protest. It was the week before the presidential election and the final campaign speeches of Richard Nixon, Hubert Humphrey, and George Wallace. A soldier had deserted and the MIT students—most of them planning to go into technological research—were giving him sanctuary. Hundreds of students were seated on blankets in the auditorium lobby and outside. Occasionally, some of them would sing choruses of "We Shall Overcome." Others were circulating petitions or making speeches against the war in Vietnam. A few particularly nervous students with walkie-talkies were prepared to give advance warning of any appearance by the police or federal agents.

The Boston newspaper critics did not like *Frankenstein, Antigone,* or *Mysteries,* and they seemed particularly offended by *Paradise Now.* On the night of the presidential election, an MIT professor came on the stage overcrowded with several hundred students during *Paradise Now* and tried to stop the performance on the grounds that the nudity would bring the police. The professor was shouted down with cries of "Hell no, we won't go," but authorities at MIT were concerned by the overcrowding on a stage that at best could hold a hundred people. The Kresge Auditorium could accommodate twelve hundred spectators, but *Paradise Now* had drawn two thousand. Citing the dangers of fire, MIT canceled the final two performances of *Paradise Now*. Performances of *Paradise Now* had already been prevented in so many places, Judith reflected, but the cancellation at MIT seemed to Judith even more significant than Richard Nixon's election.

After a performance of *Mysteries* at Brown University, where students seemed so moved by the "Plague" scene they began administering first aid and mouth-to-mouth resuscitation, the company drove north to perform *Mysteries* in mid-November at Goddard College in Vermont, a small, progressive school where they were received warmly. From Goddard, the company drove to Carnegie Mellon University in Pittsburgh and then to Rutgers University in New Brunswick for more performances. The erratic geographical route of the tour seemed haphazard and poorly planned, and, in fact, Saul Gottleib who had arranged the schedule had little experience in the meticulous care necessary to plan such a tour.

After a day in New York City, the company returned to Vermont in a snowstorm to play at Castleton State College, a small, rural teachers' training school that seemed quite unprepared for a visit from The Living Theatre. The large audience of fifteen hundred people was indifferent, unresponsive, even hostile to *Paradise Now*. The following night, they were invited to perform before a smaller audience of three hundred at Bennington College by faculty member Claude Fredericks, whose *Idiot King* had been staged at the One Hundredth Street loft in 1954. Another faculty member warned Fredericks that if The Living Theatre played there, Bennington would be burned to the ground. A local free-love commune came to see *Paradise Now* and, in the spirit of the play, disrobed entirely, followed by many of the students, outraging some of the more conservative faculty members at the exclusive women's school.

"We are a revolution disguised as a theatre," Julian had told a reporter for *Ramparts,* the West Coast activist magazine. The term "Paradise Now" had been conceived as a street cry, a demand, an urgently immediate necessity calling for a change in moral position and action to support it. Members of the company were reading Abbie Hoffman's *Revolution for the Hell of It,* which added to their own already strong fervor. The company's approach to the audience in *Paradise Now* was aggressive and sometimes even hostile if that was necessary to rouse a response. "I am pure hashish," Steven Ben Israel would sometimes assert, "smoke me!" Their purpose was to provoke or even anger the most comfortably middle-class element of their audience. If the spectators were thus awakened, the actors could "take them to Paradise." Those whose fears, smugness, or sense of helplessness denied any possibility of real change would often leave; the company believed that anyone who stayed could be changed for the better.

Since Julian and Judith were following Artaud's appeal for the release of irrational feeling as the catalyst for change, they could not have been surprised by a reaction from the critics. Also, a large part of the tour was scheduled for university audiences, many of whom would be defensive. Whenever The Living Theatre performed—as with the Bennington free love commune—local activists and revolutionaries came to see them and often were the first ones on the stage, the first to disrobe, the most zealous about going into the streets at the end of the play. These were the people who in the late 1960s assumed social upheaval was imminent. For people such as Robert Brustein at Yale, this cadre from within the audience made the play seem more like a "controlled happening." Large segments of the audience felt manipulated and outraged, while others felt a sense of ecstatic release, leading to considerable polarization.

Paradise Now was a sort of tinderbox waiting to explode, and this occurred at various points during the tour. One explosion was in the city of brotherly love. There, the company performed *Antigone, Mysteries,* and then *Paradise Now* on 26 November at the YMHA before fifteen hundred people, including Arlen Spector, a trustee of the YMHA and the district attorney of Philadelphia. At one in the morning, after a four-and-half-hour performance, during which Julian had been accused of being a "false Jew," an exhilarated spectator ran naked into the intersection of Broad and Pine streets in front of the theatre and began dancing, shouting "I'm free! I'm free!"

Almost immediately, ten police cars appeared. When the police entered the lobby, they saw some two hundred spectators, and they arrested Steven Ben Israel, another actor named Echnaton, and Julian, all in loincloths, on charges of public indecency and disorderly conduct. When Robert Cohen, the manager of the YMHA, held on to Julian, trying to prevent his arrest, two policemen tore Julian away and dragged him by the hair down the front steps of the building. According to actor Mel Clay, Julian was gently chanting "Love the police" and was not seriously injured, but the incident came close to verifying Artaud's theory of the actor as sacrificial victim.

Julian and the other actors were released after being brought to court in handcuffs the following morning. During the night, they had been howled at in derision by police and taunted as "Israelites." Robert Cohen accused the police of brutality and threatened a million-dollar lawsuit, alleging that police had not been called and that they used a degree of force "totally out of proportion to the danger either to the community or to the police themselves." Despite the ordeal of being arrested, incarcerated, and brought before a judge, Julian and the others performed in a lecture demonstration at Temple University that afternoon and then returned to New York.

After performing in Princeton, New Jersey, and in a synagogue in Great Neck, New York, the company drove to Scranton, Pennsylvania, to play *Mysteries*. At this time, nine of them were struggling with flu, and Pierre Davis and Luke Theodore were thinking of returning to Europe to wait until the American engagement was completed. Afflicted by mounting paranoia, Jenny Hecht had already departed.

Traveling through drab, gray mining towns, the company continued west to Cincinnati where they performed in a theatre in a park for the privileged that could only be reached by car or taxi. Moving on to Ann Arbor, where the students enthusiastically received *Paradise Now,* Judith and Julian met John Sinclair who had founded the White Panthers, a militant anarchist group. From Ann Arbor, they went to Detroit to do three plays at the Institute of Art. Some members of the company stayed with the poet Andrei Codrescu and, in the revolutionary spirit of the moment, appeared naked at breakfast. The company then turned east to perform at Cornell University in Ithaca, New York. When several scheduled performances in Boston were canceled because of an article in the *Boston Globe,* students in Roxbury hired a catering hall for them.

Julian had turned down several Broadway possibilities for Christmas in New York City. At the last moment, all that was available was a week in a dilapidated former movie house in the Bronx, which was followed by three performances at Hunter College in Manhattan.

The highlight of the time in New York, however, was a New Year's Day dinner hosted by Salvador Dalí in the wine cellar of the St. Regis Hotel where Dalí lived on his New York visits. Dalí had seen *The Connection* on Fourteenth Street and more recently the company in Spain. Although Dalí represented the glamour of surrealism, Judith heard him tell Allen Ginsberg that "gold was the measure of genius," and he said many things that revealed his ambivalence toward fascism.

Dalí maintained that only two sectors of society interested him: the monarch and the court on the top, and the rebellious anarchists underneath. At an elegant table in the company of three Spanish noblemen, in his velvet suit, wielding a gold cane, he spoke of his hopes for the restoration of the monarchy in Spain—a subject that must have seemed strange to Judith sitting next to him. He also dangled the possibility of a castle in Spain for the company.

When Dalí moved to sit near Julian, the Russian Prince Serge Obolensky—a member of the Romanoff family that had ruled Russia—joined Judith. Flirtatious, speaking English with a perfect British accent, Obolensky praised aristocratic virtues which his rigid hauteur seemed to exemplify. A member of Nixon's Crime Commission, he was interested only in preventing student disorders and incipient anarchy. The incongruity of a meal shared by an actress performing for the sake of revolution and an aristocrat working to suppress it was not lost on Judith.

49. California Dreaming

The company left New York on a somber note. Carol Berger, one of its members, had been diagnosed with cancer and required an immediate operation; large quantities of blood were donated by various members of the company. There was also some dissatisfaction with *Paradise Now,* which needed constant reworking. Too often, Julian, Steven Ben Israel, Rufus Collins, and Mel Clay had been caught in the trap of their own vehement and excessive tirades. Elements in the play seemed too rhetorical, critic Richard Gilman observed, offering as an illustration Julian's lines about the actual number of prisoners in the nearest prison and his question of who in the audience would form a cell to free them. Such gestures, Gilman felt, were painfully hopeless and absurd, especially because nothing was or could be done for the prisoners, even in the event that one seriously wanted to free them.

The eight performances at the University of Chicago were deplored by the daily newspaper critics. Audiences seemed restrained to Judith, caught by a "frozen stillness in the movement, as if the terrible events of the convention could not have taken place here."

From Chicago, the company drove to Madison, Wisconsin, to

perform *Paradise Now* in an angular Unitarian church so poorly designed by Frank Lloyd Wright that the stage was soaking wet. The performance was uneventful, but company members were disturbed because there was no money to pay their salaries. Saul Gottleib, whose Radical Theatre Repertory was arranging bookings and managing finances, said the money had gone to pay income taxes, but hotel bills had to be met. While the necessary funds did come from a performance in Appleton, Wisconsin, it was a disconcerting sign.

Working their way west, the company performed in the flatlands of Kansas City, Kansas, and, after driving through dense fog and heavy rain, at the University of Iowa in Iowa City. There were another four performances in Boulder, Colorado, marred to some extent by a drug bust involving a member of The Living Theatre's entourage in which police seized LSD and a small amount of marijuana. There were a number of people who always seemed prepared to offer drugs to company members, and the incident only reaffirmed the public's perception that The Living Theatre was a collection of peripatetic, pot-smoking hippies. Marijuana was clearly a staple, and the duties of the road manager included obtaining enough for company members to smoke on each stop of the tour.

Already exhausted from the touring, the company continued to Reed College in Oregon, known as the most experimental school on the West Coast, for another four performances. In his third year at Reed, Garrick was talking about dropping out to form a small guerrilla theatre. He was astonished to find his fellow students' reception of *Paradise Now* frivolous and apolitical. A few weeks after the company left—repeating a pattern of student agitation occurring at various universities after performances of *Paradise Now*—Garrick and fifteen other Reed students protested the college rule against men and women staying overnight in each other's quarters. When faculty members refused to hear their grievance, the students stripped and simulated sex in front of them.

The Living Theatre was again stranded without money when

Saul Gottleib failed to forward necessary funds. They had received an invitation from the American National Theatre Academy to perform on Broadway, which could have solved this
financial crisis. At a company meeting, Rufus Collins urged acceptance, arguing that Broadway would provide a meaningful
finale for the American tour and the occasion for a frontal attack
on the middle class in their own bastion. Julian, with the support
of most of the company, adamantly opposed the prospect as a
corrupting sellout and convinced the company to continue to California.

Rejecting Broadway, the company arrived in Berkeley which
was in a state of siege. The Free Speech Movement that had
started in 1964 had created an unresolved conflict whose issues
kept changing, pitting radical students against the police seeking
to contain them. The most recent provocation had been Governor Ronald Reagan's threat to dismiss Professor Herbert Mar-
cuse, the author of *One-Dimensional Man* and an inspiration to
the left, from his tenured position at the University of California,
San Diego.

Telegraph Avenue, torn up for sewer work, looked like an
open trench. Heavily bearded, bundled in army-surplus clothing,
many students resembled fierce guerrillas. They were faced by
the ominous apparition of police in yellow slickers and gas
masks. In Berkeley, the theatre was truly in the streets, and only a
few hundred students came to sit in the three-thousand-seat auditorium to see *Frankenstein* and *Antigone*. When *Paradise Now* was
performed, it had to be stopped midway because of a midnight
curfew. It was the first performance of the play that had not attracted any attention from local authorities. In Berkeley, which
was "terminally hip" as poet Michael McClure has put it, where
marijuana was openly purchased and consumed on Telegraph
Avenue, sentiments like "I am not allowed to smoke marijuana"
may have seemed irrelevant. In the *San Francisco Chronicle*,
columnist Ralph Gleason observed that the Berkeley audience
was a better show than the disappointment onstage which he
termed a "dramatic Siberia, cold, dismal and humorless."

On the day after *Paradise Now* was performed, Governor Reagan came to visit Berkeley, the streets lined with members of the National Guard. Judith and Julian visited Timothy Leary, the psychedelic drug proselytizer who was facing a thirty-year jail sentence. Smiling a lot, speaking softly, Leary said he was sure he would not be sent to jail and spoke about going to India. In the evening, they visited poet Lawrence Ferlinghetti who played them a tape of Ginsberg chanting the Blake poems Ginsberg had set to music. Ferlinghetti owned City Lights, a bookstore and small publishing house that had published Ginsberg's "Howl," and he wanted to publish Julian's *The Life of the Theatre.*

Financial matters seemed more tangled than ever, and Gottleib was not reassuring. All through the tour, advance receipts had been banked under various names, but in California, Mark Amitin, a new road manager, had committed the honest error of listing the accounts under the name of The Living Theatre. These accounts were frozen by the IRS, still seeking restitution of the sum they claimed was owed to it from the Fourteenth Street theatre. Julian was notified that all future receipts from performances would also be seized. When a dean at the University of Southern California agreed to give Julian an advance check for three thousand dollars, the company departed for Los Angeles on roads washed out from a month of rain.

Los Angeles was dank and dreary. Although the *Los Angeles Herald Examiner* critic was disappointed in *Mysteries,* Dan Sullivan in the *Los Angeles Times* admitted he was fascinated. A fire marshal warned Julian that the University of Southern California Bovard Auditorium stage could only accommodate fifty people during the *Paradise Now* performance, even though the three-ton *Frankenstein* set had not caused any strain. *Paradise Now* was performed with thirty helmeted cops carrying gas masks in the lobby, and a number of marked and unmarked patrol cars surrounding the theatre. USC then canceled the final two performances of *Paradise Now,* citing the fire marshal's warning, the fact that spectators dropped out of the balcony on a makeshift rope ladder, and that others were admitted without tickets. However,

Los Angeles Times writer Ray Loynd charged that it was merely a "pretext to clamp down on theatre offensive to some elements." To be fair, the play did encourage the adventurous members of the audience to take risks that overly cautious people thought could cause harm. And, in fact, free admissions had been an unstated policy of the company since its beginning: as an extension of the idea of street theatre, anyone who said he or she could not pay had been allowed into performances without charge.

By the time the company reached San Francisco, morale and funds were low. Advance receipts at Nourse Auditorium had been seized by the IRS and later released after negotiations with lawyers and Saul Gottleib. Half the company was housed with a commune on Haight Street. Judith, Julian, and their daughter, Isha, slept on the floor of Ferlinghetti's unheated three-room office, and others were welcomed into private homes.

Almost as soon as the company was settled, they tried to offer a free performance of *Paradise Now* at the Straight Theatre in Haight Ashbury—the area dominated by hippies known as the "liberated zone." Competing with the loud music, chanting, and dancing, the company instead performed a single scene from *Paradise Now* in various parts of the room as the dancing prevailed.

Doors singer Jim Morrison and poet Michael McClure actively participated in performances of *Paradise Now* at the Nourse Auditorium. For some extra money, afraid now that escrow funds for the return trip to Europe did not exist, The Living Theatre performed a lecture-demonstration at Mills College in Oakland that was filmed by television. On Sunday afternoon, 9 March, the company was scheduled to give a free performance of *Mysteries* on Hippie Hill in Golden Gate Park but arrived two hours late, deterred by a proviolence leaflet that implicated them which caused a company discussion. When cast members finally appeared, they had no chance to perform as they were drowned out by several rock bands.

Late that afternoon, Michael McClure brought Jim Morrison to visit at Ferlinghetti's office. Julian was on and off the telephone to New York, frantically worried about the money to get the troupe back to Europe where engagements had been scheduled. Quietly, Morrison offered to assist with money.

Morrison—who had read Artaud and Ginsberg in college— saw himself as a revolutionary figure. Agreeing that repression was the chief social evil in America and the cause of a general pathology, he was typical of the sectors of support The Living Theatre had received in America. His long improvisational song "When the Music's Over" was a basic statement of apocalypse. Another of his songs proclaims, as in *Paradise Now,* "we want the world, and we want it now." Morrison had seen every perform- ance in Los Angeles and followed the company up to San Fran- cisco.

On the day after his visit with McClure, Jim Morrison gave Julian twenty-five hundred dollars for the trip home. Driving on icy roads and through snowstorms, the caravan took Route 66 with stops in the Grand Canyon, the Painted desert region in Ari- zona, and Taos. On 20 March, they performed *Mysteries* in a disco- theque in Boston, and the next day, they were in New York to begin a week-long engagement at the Brooklyn Academy, which was supposed to settle the tax bill and leave enough for the re- turn to Europe.

Judith and Julian had been invited to participate in the "Theatre of Ideas," a symposium held at the Friends Meeting House on Gramercy Square. The forum, "Theatre or Therapy?" had been organized by Shirley Broughton, who had once helped them with a benefit at the Cherry Lane, and was attended by five hundred people, including writer Susan Sontag, film maker Ar- thur Penn, *New Yorker* film critic Pauline Kael, poets Stephen Spender and Stanley Kunitz, teachers, psychologists, and artists.

Judith, Julian, Robert Brustein, and Paul Goodman were on the panel moderated by columnist Nat Hentoff. Brustein began by asserting that theatre was never therapeutic because it could not heal. In a matter-of-fact tone—punctuated by some heckling— Brustein talked earnestly about the tension between freedom and responsibility. When he turned his attention to The Living Theatre, he asserted that audience members could never be transformed into sublime artists and that the company was anti-intellectual in temperament.

When Goodman was asked to speak, he calmly proposed in a rambling disquisition that the country was not in a cataclysmic revolutionary moment but in one analogous to the Protestant Reformation. His cautious and moderately conservative tone may have surprised members of the company in the audience, who expected a more activist challenge from Judith's teacher. When Judith began to speak, Henry Howard and Steven Ben Israel interrupted her, quoting lines from *Paradise Now*. "Stop analyzing! Start living!" Rufus Collins shouted. Quickly losing his composure, Goodman left the room, and actress Stella Adler screamed.

In the ensuing mayhem, Norman Mailer grimly shouted for order, only to be propositioned by Jim Tiroff, dressed in velvet, with black glasses, violet plumes, and an orange cape. Richard Schechner, pleading for a moment of silence, was insulted by critic John Simon. Shirley Broughton demanded that Julian control the members of The Living Theatre who had started the agitation, and threatened to summon the police. Julian told her that he was no more outraged by what was happening in the room than he was all the time. Later, he seized a woman's fur coat and threw it across the room, shouting that the "weight of your furs makes it impossible for the needs of the people to touch you!" In *The Life of the Theatre*, Julian admitted that the outrages performed by The Living Theatre were an attempt to shatter with urgency the intellectual complacency of an evening devoted only to words. Although the police were not called, order could not be restored. The discussions, however, continued among individuals for several hours, and at two in the morning, some disputants were still talking.

A week later, Judith and Julian arrived at Goodman's apartment to say good-bye before sailing back to Europe. Performances had gone well at the Brooklyn Academy although Julian had collapsed in his dressing room after *Frankenstein*. At the final performance of *Paradise Now*, Judith undressed completely when challenged by a member of the audience. She made this gesture despite paranoia about police, exacerbated by the news that the attorney general had declared that the university disturbances were the result of organized conspiracies and that Abbie Hoffman had been arrested for possessing guns and narcotics, his apartment searched while he was arraigned for the "Chicago conspiracy" trial.

Goodman was disconsolate and discouraged; his son had died in a mountain-climbing accident two years earlier, and he had never really recovered. He acknowledged that he could not stand the hatred expressed by young university students, the V-sign replaced by the clenched fist. Discussing the psychodrama at the "Theatre of Ideas," he claimed that even if The Living Theatre could define its own ideas more precisely, in the end they would fail to find either liberation or paradise.

The American tour had, to a large extent, succeeded in rousing the ire of the critics who, as Clive Barnes wrote, acted as if the actors had stolen their wallets and raped their mothers. In his piece in the *Atlantic,* Richard Gilman had compared the actors to wounded animals trying to escape. Critics were by nature conservative, Barnes admitted, but the distaste and disgust they expressed was unusual. Wherever The Living Theatre had appeared, they met the same mixture "of a largely excoriating press and a largely enthusiastic public." The critics were terribly offended by physical nudity as well as by a naked declaration of purpose that they deemed naive. They had decided the bodies were ugly, disregarding Judith's view that the human form was inherently beautiful and anyone could be a sublime artist.

At the same time, they were reacting to a systematically planned provocation. Some of the critics were aware that members of the company had been freely using LSD and marijuana. While most of the sex during the "body-pile" in the "Rite of Universal Intercourse" involved the rubbing of genitalia, some of the actors had engaged in open sex with spectators. Jenny Hecht, for example, believed she had to be as generous and open as possible in order to convince anyone of her revolutionary stance, and consequently, she would give of herself as often as she was asked. This was clearly beyond all theatrical precedent.

Actually, given the context of *Paradise Now* and the appeal of

The Living Theatre, the critical response should not have been unanticipated. A year earlier, on 29 April 1968, *Hair* had opened at the Biltmore Theatre on Broadway to begin a run that would last almost a decade, earning millions of dollars for its producer, Michael Butler. This musical focused on the loves and antics of a group of hippies on the night before one of them is to be inducted into the army and sent to Vietnam. *Hair* had frontal nudity and performers in the balcony, yet because of its banality, it could both appeal to the values of peace and love and satisfy tourists. The original intention of *Paradise Now* had been to envelop the audience in such joy that the impossible began to seem possible. As a musical, *Hair* may have come closer to a more superficial kind of joy. Its tone was less aggressively alienating, more sassy and good-natured, and as a result much less threatening to critics or Broadway audiences.

On April Fool's Day, Judith, Julian, and a dozen company members embarked on the *Europa,* a liner full of middle-aged German tourists back from a Caribbean cruise. They had sent large parts of their theatre archive to Europe, unsure of when or whether they would return to America. The young people in their own country seemed to have shifted to drugs—following Timothy Leary's route of depoliticization—or violence; and the seething rage of groups like the Black Panthers or the Weathermen only seemed an index to a generalized anger.

> *America*
> *Our parting was: Zero*

Judith wrote in her final *Diary* entry for the American tour, reflecting a pervasive despair she felt in America.

V
Paradise Outlaws

50. Morocco

By the middle of April, the company had reassembled in Paris. The Sorbonne was defaced by graffiti, and the streets seemed full of police. Judith and Julian's hotel room was perpetually crowded with visitors—some of them angry that The Living Theatre would be playing in established theatres—and they spent an evening at Salvador Dalí's salon talking with him about the Spanish film maker Luis Buñuel.

The six-week tour of France began inauspiciously in Chambéry where they were pelted with eggs during a performance of *Mysteries.* In Besançon, members of the audience seated in a balcony hurled vegetables and eggs. The local newspaper derisively referred to the "omelette finale," and the mother of a young girl raised charges of "attentat à la pudeur"—indecent assault. During "The Plague" scene in *Mysteries,* Luke Theodore had rubbed the raw yolk of an egg that had been thrown at him defiantly over his genitals. The young girl, seated near the edge of the stage, interpreted this as masturbation; enraged, she slapped the actor five times.

Although the legal issues were not pursued, the incident was typical of the continuing turbulence in France in 1969. Charles de Gaulle resigned in the beginning of May, and the troupe was back in Paris to see the streets of the Latin Quarter, from Saint-Germain to the boulevard Saint-Michel, lined with police. Often officers would parade five abreast on the broad boulevard, demanding to see identification and harassing students.

Resuming their tour in a caravan of Volkswagen buses, the

company performed *Paradise Now* in a theatre in Mulhouse surrounded by CRS, the French security troops, in black uniforms. During the "Apokatastasis" scene, Judith was thrown to the ground by a maniacal man screaming German poetry, and Jenny Hecht was flung off the stage. After the performance, everyone had to exit through windows because the CRS had blocked the exits. Some of the spectators left the theatre to chant "Désertez! Désertez!" in front of a nearby infantry barracks.

In Toulouse, Julian and Judith spent their afternoons in the garden of the museum, working on the script for *Paradise Now,* which they hoped to publish. The serenity of such work contrasted with the tensions prevalent in Toulouse: a group of long-haired Living Theatre actors were threatened with scissors and attacked in a café by Action Française thugs; another actor was almost hurt when a firecracker thrown onstage exploded near his face; and Jules Sarrazin, director of the theatre in Toulouse for thirteen years, was dismissed for having invited the group.

At the end of May, Georges Pompidou was elected president of France though Judith was sure that that would do nothing to resolve the dissatisfaction of the young. In Saint-Etienne, during a performance of *Paradise Now,* a group of young people objecting to the pacifist position of The Living Theatre took over the stage chanting "All power comes out of the barrel of a gun." It was another example of the shift to violence the company had experienced in America.

On the train from Paris to Calais, the customs officials scrutinized every book and piece of literature. Crossing the English Channel, Judith—full of the loneliness of her pacifist position— argued quite bitterly with Carl Einhorn, who condoned armed struggle, over what direction their purported revolution was taking. This argument had persisted for years between them and, with each further instance, seemed to become an even more insurmountable obstacle.

In London, in a small hotel behind Paddington Station, the company found themselves squeezed six to a room in bunk beds, an uncomfortable arrangement. When a newspaper account of company members smoking marijuana in the hotel caused the manager to threaten eviction, many of them began living in a maze of scarves and pennants dividing the dressing rooms at the Roundhouse Theatre where they were scheduled to perform through June.

Outside the theatre, some of the members of London's Hell's Angels stationed themselves as a protective cordon, though they could do little against the sarcasm of the newspaper critics. One night, an old man in a brown raincoat sprayed an irritant on some actors during a performance of *Paradise Now,* and another night, an Italian photographer who had been following them began writhing and screaming for God, and had to be restrained. On the whole, however, the British run was successful with consistently sold-out houses.

At the end of June, the company visited the influential English psychiatrist R. D. Laing who seemed full of despair, speaking of the riddles in his new book *Knots.* They then drove through Spain to Málaga where they took the car-ferry to Tangiers, although Moroccan customs officials were reluctant to admit men with long hair.

Arriving in Tangiers on the day of King Hassan's fortieth birthday, they were at first unable to distinguish between the officials and the hustlers in their hooded djellabas selling everything from jewelry to mescaline. The caravan of red Volkswagens continued until they reached Essaouira, a market town on the sea surrounded by an earthen wall. Behind the wall were white houses with pale blue window frames, hundreds of curb-squatting beggars, and an assortment of musicians, jugglers, tumblers, and snake charmers. Many of the town's brightly clad women worked in sardine canneries for five cents an hour, staring directly ahead, protected by their veils.

Situating themselves in the upper floors of a house in town, the company met on its roof with views of the sea, the beach, and the sandy hills to begin discussions on the nature of violence that would hopefully lead to a new work. They were also trying to adjust to the perplexing differences of the Moroccan life surrounding them such as the evident subordination of the files of women transporting huge bundles or carrying water. Moroccan women, for the most part, were relegated to housework. One of the few amenities in the house was the cleaning and cooking services of an old Berber woman with ten of her own children; and the company debated whether she should continue to serve them so menially until they realized the enormous benefits to her of her small salary.

In one sense, she was part of a culture that, as foreigners, they would have to learn to accept. Another matter they would have to learn to cope with was the insects: spiders weaving dusty nets in every corner to catch the omnipresent flies that swarmed over any sign of food; the African head lice afflicting many members of the company; the beetles in the shoes; scorpions, centipedes, and giant waterbugs all over the bathroom; hundreds of tiny red termites crawling up the bedroom walls; grasshoppers and mantises leaping out of the beds.

Judith and Julian were studying Arabic and continuing the preparation of a text of *Paradise Now*. They attended services at the synagogue: only four hundred Jews were left from a population of thousands who had emigrated to Israel. Some of their time was spent with their son, Garrick, who had arrived with backpacks and a lover named Karen. Garrick found a tiled room with a single light bulb, no water or toilet, and unfurnished except for a large framed picture of the king who had just used the radio to denounce the influence of hippies. For Judith, hippies were refugees from a plastic culture who sought the beauty of old ways, a definition that fitted her son. Garrick was full of news of the commune of former Reed students he had joined in Portland, Oregon, the free store they had started, and their guerrilla theatre activities.

Another source of news was R. D. Laing, who was traveling in Morocco. Laing came to rehearsals, talking about the mythology of Aphrodite and Atlantis, and the prospects for revolution, advising that LSD would not lead to permanent changes, that people eventually returned to old patterns. Another visitor was the black activist Stokely Carmichael, who had been a leader in the Student Non-violent Coordinating Committee (SNCC) in the early 1960s. Pugnacious and aggressive, full of anger and rejection, Carmichael now abjured his nonviolence, equating it with a theatre of the absurd.

More surprising was the sudden appearance of Anaïs Nin peering out of a Club Méditerranée bus with a face that looked "as if it had pressed up against the glass of the world too hard, and the impression imprinted." Perpetually costumed in gowns and robes, Nin had been the ultimate bohemian in New York City in the early 1950s, but in a summer dress and sandals, and accompanied by a handsome man, she seemed like a tourist exploring the exoticism of North Africa.

A full introduction to that exoticism occurred in the courtyard of the house in which the company members had settled when a group of Gnaoua musicians declared that they wanted to sacrifice a goat in a purification ceremony. Nomadic, tribal, hashish-smoking trance dancers, the mendicant Gnaoua survived by such celebrations. They had been brought as slaves to Morocco by the Berbers, and the belief in Essaouira was that when they left, a huge tidal wave would destroy the city.

The problem for the vegetarian commune was the goat, but when Judith argued that its sacrifice compromised her religious beliefs, the Gnaoua were willing to substitute other rituals. The ceremony started in the afternoon. The music of the skin-faced lute, the drumming, the hauntingly simple repetition of the *qaraqeb,* and the metal castanets began; and the whirling, somersaulting dance continued in a haze of incense until dawn.

The Gnaoua were one source of the marvelous in a country that was so full of astonishing sights. One day, the company members were dazzled by the immense panorama of the market in Marrakesh. On another occasion, they drove to Ouarzazate in the south through 120-degree temperatures, the desert stretching before them like a vast sea.

The majestic expanse of the desert might inspire visions, but the company seemed mired in its discussions, handicapped by what Judith in her *Diaries* categorized as "idiot-philosophies" like astrology, which seemed to her like "smokescreens blurring what we really want to know." In Essaouira, the company continued its daily rooftop meetings, learning Gnaoua songs and working on a play tentatively called *Saturation City*. The plan was to go to a village or city to do plays in the streets, markets, plazas, schoolyards, bus terminals, and in front of public buildings and police stations with the purpose of "leading people into action within the plays." This concept would inform most of The Living Theatre productions through the decade of the 1970s.

A number of the Gnaoua began sleeping on the roof where they taught some company members complicated ritual practices like how to stick knives in their flesh in a trance state without drawing blood. This was a dangerous development. The extended family arrangement, which had seemed threatening to the landlord of the Cherry Lane in the early 1950s and had flourished in the Fourteenth Street theatre, was particularly alarming to the Essaouira police. They were willing to tolerate "the hippies," as they called the company, as long as they did not mix with the local population. Always expecting arrest, the members of the company reached into whatever elements in the community would welcome them partly as compensation for their paranoia—a fear only compounded by their use of a variety of quasilegal hashish preparations—partly as a mutually educational street sociology, and partly out of an idealistic need to help others less fortunate than themselves.

Using as a pretext the noise at a birthday party for Jenny Hecht, the police broke into the house, arrested two young Moroccan boys, and informed the company that they had forty-eight hours to leave. One motivating circumstance may have been the fact that there was an article in the current *Playboy*—one of the few Western magazines available in Essaouria—with photographs of the body pile in *Paradise Now*. Packing in a rush—as they had under police pressure in Avignon—they saw the more desperate side of Morocco as neighbors pounced on any discarded trifle—a hairbrush, a cooking pan, a plastic scrap.

Once again, the company had been routed, and there were inevitable psychic consequences. Rufus Collins declared he was going to India to study trance. Petra Vogt, whom Judith had seen as a sort of Valkyrie, strong and indomitable, broke down on a drug trip and emerged on the other side of madness: breathless, exaggerating everything, prophetic. It seemed like a fissure.

51. Swimming in Dirty Water

I n his book *The Life of the Theatre,* Julian remembers that in the summer of 1969, in Morocco, the time had come to enact a change in the structure of The Living Theatre. The group of thirty-four adults and nine children had become an institution of sorts, and institutions, Julian acknowledges paradoxically, "are made by success and our success made us dependent on the income we received from being an institution."

Since *Saturation City* had not evolved from the daily rooftop discussions in Morocco, The Living Theatre had no new offering. European audiences had already seen the rest of their repertory, so the prospects of new bookings were limited. The process of collective creation itself had lost some of its vitality. As Julian admitted, it had occurred spontaneously with *Mysteries* but subsequently resulted in "long, grinding efforts," full of moments of tedious boredom.

Since *The Brig,* the group had functioned as an experiment in the abandonment of coercive authority, Judith alleged, "so that the idea of what it is exists differently in each individual member's head. Then we each let each other do whatever each of us wants to do to develop that vision." As Henry Howard had put it at Yale a year earlier, "The whole company has thirty political ideologies. And there has to come out of it one front—not one mind because the thirty of us are never going to agree."

In effect, the company was an association of thirty different revolutionaries who had conceived thirty different approaches to that revolution. Julian was excessively tolerant—to the point of absurdity, poet Taylor Mead (an expert in absurdity) believed. Julian and Judith fought to get the group to understand more deeply the principles of anarchism. Some in the company were too individualistic to accept anarchism or any "ism." Others resented the fact that ultimate decisions seemed to be made by both Judith and Julian, and that though they proclaimed there was no hierarchy, in effect it was implicit in their decisions.

Another decisive factor was the position taken by Rufus Collins and some of those who eventually went to India with him: one's own personal spiritual development was the only fundamental contribution a person could make to changing the world. Yet another contingent, who eventually settled in London, subscribed to a psychedelic and pop-art notion of revolution, rather than a political one. Both Judith and Julian believed that change began with the commitment to community action.

Another problem, reflecting a general weakness in the peace movement, was a challenging rhetoric: "What have you done for the third world today, comrade?" Another conflict arose out of the super political correctness of those in the group like Carl Einhorn who were in accord with the principle of violent revolution. Since the members of this contingent felt they had to be at least as militant as their friends who believed in armed struggle—and they could seem as outrageously exaggerated as figures in a film by Jean-Luc Godard—they contradicted the nonviolent basis of Judith and Julian's position.

At a midnight meeting under the bifurcation of a half-moon, on board the *Cristoforo Colombo* in the middle of September 1969, en route from Málaga to Palermo where the company was scheduled to perform *Antigone,* Julian announced that he and Judith were leaving the company, for no anarchist commune could endure when its members became dependent on its leadership. He offered an analogy to Mao who saw his revolution stalled by bourgeois values and encouraged the Cultural Revolution. That night, Julian dreamed of a group of veiled Essaouiran women breaking through walls to get at him, and he awoke screaming. Judith interpreted the dream as a projection of the company split.

Before this could occur, there were contracts to fulfill and commitments to perform. In Ragusa, Sicily, the local authorities prevented any performance of *Mysteries* or *Paradise Now,* but in Taormina, the entire audience in a great commotion got out of its seats during "The Plague" scene in *Mysteries.* In October in Venice, the film actress Paulette Goddard came backstage to praise *Antigone.*

In Turin, a group of leftist students ran through the audience during *Paradise Now* to distribute a leaflet declaring that the pacifist ideas of The Living Theatre were nebulous. When, at one in the morning, the police arrived and the theatre owners lowered the curtain and shut off the lights because of a local ordinance, Julian led the audience into the streets where he and others spoke for an hour. The next day, the local papers were full of reports of nudity and obscenity, but as Julian once observed, "The Italian eye sees everything a little bit like a potential photograph in a scandal magazine."

In Milan, after a performance of *Mysteries* for an audience Judith characterized as full of supercilious aristocrats—she complained of the "sense of forcing something that's tired"—Julian was brought to a police station and asked to identify photographs of actors in earlier performances in Trieste where Jim Tiroff had posed momentarily in the nude. A few days later, Judith wrote in her *Diary* that *"Paradise* is over. There may still be a few great performances, but the times have changed." In Bologna, where striking workers and students had asked them to perform, Judith observed a "prehistoric exhaustion in the company." When Julian addressed a group of two thousand students on the importance of nonviolence, they sat through it as dully as if in a classroom.

In the newspapers, Judith saw a photograph of Jane Alpert who had been arrested in a bombing with four others, on her face the look of jubilant achievement Judith sought as Antigone after burying her brother. From Washington, D.C., she saw photographs of thousands bearing placards with the names of those dead in Vietnam. From France, Judith heard from Jean-Jacques Lebel that intellectuals and activists were being threatened with preventive detention. In one sense, this was not surprising. Lebel had edited a book of interviews with Judith, Julian, and company members, and had insolently ended it with a diagram for a Molotov cocktail.

The company performed in a cramped space in Florence, which was paralyzed because of a general strike. In Rome in November, where police refused permits to stage *Paradise Now,* Judith saw Carl Einhorn, who had previously returned to America because his father was dying. Vague, secretive, urgent, Carl was intoxicated by the movement of underground radicals. Full of rumors of CIA manipulation tactics and suppression of the Black Panthers, he was also gripped by paranoia, fearing that concentration camps would be used in the event of a general crackdown.

At the end of November, in Naples, with anarchist flags covering the stage, a member of the company removed all his clothes during a performance of *Paradise Now.* Plainclothes police who were all over the stage in the body pile tried to arrest "il nudo," but in the confusion of grasping bodies, he escaped to Amsterdam. A few days later, in the candlelit Law Faculty Hall of Rome University, where students had occupied the premises and invited The Living Theatre to perform *Paradise Now,* two thousand armed and helmeted police arrived in a hundred vehicles, and dispersed everyone with tear gas. The police had warned the company not to dare perform in the pope's city, and consequently, the entire company was questioned by police, escorted to the border, and expelled from Italy.

When the company left Rome, Julian had already announced that he and Judith were willing to continue working with what he called the "action" cell, a core of the company who agreed with their vision of the sort of theatre they could attempt in the future.

The company set off for Brussels on roads slippery with snow. The Belgian audience, which had been warned by the critics that The Living Theatre was already anachronistic, seemed passive, polite, and unbudgeable when presented with *Paradise Now.*

Driving into Germany on a freezing night, they were stopped by border guards alerted by the hippie appearance of company members. The guards demanded that all belongings be dumped on the ground while they rigorously searched every coat pocket and under every hat, even inspecting the bindings of their books. The company continued on icy roads to Berlin where, in the face of hecklers and firecrackers, they performed *Mysteries, Antigone,* and *Paradise Now* at the Akademie der Kunst. Judith and Julian were interviewed by *Der Spiegel,* one of the most prominent magazines in Germany, whose reporter could not quite fathom the reasons for the imminent breakup of the company.

On 10 January 1970, in the giant *Sportspalast*—where Goebbels had asked the German people whether they wanted war, and they had answered with a resounding "Sieg Heil!"—the company performed *Paradise Now* for the final time, with groups of actors and audience members who had taken LSD smoking hashish and tobacco joints. At the end, many people disrobed entirely despite the unheated arena. Milling about in the corridors with the departing audience—traces of fervor, delight, disgust, and mockery on their faces—Judith reflected ruefully that "we are still outside the gates of paradise."

The next day Julian distributed money to each of the actors, repeating Garga's words from the end of *In the Jungle of the Cities:* "It was the best of times!" The actors hugged each other, weeping Julian observed, "because the best was not enough." They had all, as Steven Ben Israel suggested, been "swimming in dirty water": that is, they were subject to the human flaws in their conditioning. Some were going to India with Rufus; some, to Amsterdam; others, to Paris or London; and some were staying in Berlin. Parting was traumatic, Judith realized: "This community, so full of tenderness and reflecting for us all the agonies and hopes of our miserable situation, is the hardest to break up."

52. Croissy-sur-Seine

Before departing from Germany, Judith and Julian decided to visit Daniel Cohn-Bendit in Frankfurt to get his advice on how to reach workers with their new activist theatre. A bare room with a mattress on the floor and a bright red painted sink, Cohn-Bendit's home seemed a container for books, among them the complete works of Lenin. When he answered the phone, it was "Lenin speaking." And although Cohn-Bendit was still fully occupied with the movement for social change, he had no words of advice, only asking them to bring some tapes to the film maker Jean-Luc Godard.

Along with Echnaton, Birgit Knabe, Alain Suire, and Pierre Biner who was translating *Paradise Now* into French, Judith and Julian drove to Croissy-sur-Seine, a suburb of Paris, to stay at the home of film actor Pierre Clementi. The small group calling itself the "action cell" began reading everything they could find on various American radical centers, discussing sentence by sentence, for example, a statement of the Black Panther program. In a purported *Last Statement,* Julian argued that theater buildings were only an architectural trap suitable for a privileged elite and his goal would be to reach the man in the street. Art, Julian proposed to the group, was useful only to the extent that it could expose truth: so that "it can become clear to everyone what has to be done and how to do it." Art should lead to direct action; otherwise, "art was simply the cupbearer of oppression."

Invited by Jean-Jacques Lebel to conduct a lecture-demonstration early in February 1970 at Vincennes, the most radical branch of the University of Paris, Judith and Julian were prepared for the hostility of the students. Out of the recesses of a room scarred with graffiti, a student dressed in drab army fatigues shouted, "No more theatre. Only action!" Julian suggested that the time they were spending together might be used to construct a play that could be used as an immediate means to raise public consciousness about some pressing social problem. Agreeing with the students that a rapid escalation of prices in the Paris subway system, the Metro, provided a suitable issue, and the company, together with the students, devised a brief, forty-second agitprop situation called "Death by Metro." They planned to perform this piece in the Metro itself as a first foray into the street or under it, as it were. In the skit, Pierre Biner, disguised as an old woman, would try to purchase a Metro ticket but would faint away when hearing its price, and would be carried off in a processional by the others. Essentially, this was planned to divert the police while the students took over the station.

At seven in the morning in the Châtelet station a week later, when the workers were in the subway, Julian and Pierre Biner went down to the toll booth on the subway platforms while two others began giving out leaflets. The Vincennes students never showed up, but the police were waiting for some sort of demonstration. Julian was assaulted and held for four hours along with twelve others. In *The Life of the Theatre,* Julian expressed his outrage over the police reaction and quoted the policeman who hit him as saying he regretted he had not been in the SS to "take care of people like him."

The first venture of the action cell had aborted, and Judith found herself feeling weakened and distraught. The action cell did not include Carl Einhorn, who had left the company with a new Italian lover; and in Paris, she began to feel the impact of what she regarded as Carl's abandonment. In the beginning of March, she heard that the trial of Abbie Hoffman, Jerry Rubin, and the Chicago Seven had begun. Judith realized the trial would be a form of spectacular public theatre, and she only regretted not being on trial with them.

One source of encouragement was a flamboyant and impetuous Brazilian director named José Celso Martinez Corrêa, known as Zé Celso, who came to visit. Working in an atmosphere of intolerable repression because Brazil was governed by a despotic military dictatorship, Zé Celso said little was possible in terms of political theatre in Brazil and admitted that his last production, Brecht's *Galileo,* had been closed by right-wing commandos. Zé Celso invited Judith and Julian to bring the action cell to Brazil to work with his company, and the invitation had immediate appeal.

Maurício, another Brazilian friend, told them about a union-sponsored group that toured factories with Brecht's *Exception and the Rule.* Each performance was followed by discussions, but the more sophisticated workers would refuse to talk, saying the actors were the sons and daughters of the ruling class. Maurício warned that while they might be able to accomplish something in the cities, if they tried to perform in the countryside, they would be either murdered, arrested, or prevented by some violent means.

Judith and Julian bought Portuguese grammars and began studying. They received a letter from Zé Celso, now back in Brazil, writing in the tone of a close friend and telling them of the possibility of touring mines and poor settlements but emphasizing the grimness of Brazilian military repression. The repression, if less lethal, seemed as endemic in France, and at a May Day march at the Bastille, Judith and Julian were in a crowd that was tear-gassed by the CRS. In the newspaper a few days later, they read about the four students shot at Kent State, a college in Ohio; two black students shot in Jackson, Mississippi; the subsequent burnings of ROTC facilities; and the seizures of hundreds of other university buildings.

In mid-May, Judith and Julian went to the Cannes Film Festival for a screening of Sheldon Rochlin's film of *Paradise Now* which had been shot at the final performance in Berlin. They also wanted to raise money for a film they wanted to do in Brazil. At the festival, they saw documentaries on Eldridge Cleaver and the journalist I. F. Stone, a film of Helene Weigel's *Mother Courage,* and attended the opening of *Woodstock.* Judith thought the counter-culture event demonstrated how easily potentially revolutionary resources like drugs and rock and roll could be co-opted by an establishment. Theatre, Julian thought, if sufficiently provocative, could be used to unchain the energy subdued by the weight of the establishment; it could charge a people with creative impetus, and change perception and the mode of thought. It could entice, cajole, inform, and "it could openly inspire the proletariat, the Lumpenproletariat, the poor, the poorest of the poor" who had become Julian's intended audience in Brazil.

Back in Paris, they heard from Allen Ginsberg, who wrote that it would be difficult to attempt theatre with Brazilian workers because "industrial work is satanic in its nature" and unions were only a form of mafia. They had dinner with old friends John Cage and Merce Cunningham, and another night, they ate in Goldenberg's Jewish Restaurant in the Marais with director Peter Brook. On Radio Luxembourg, the film maker Louis Malle asked Judith and Julian about Richard Nixon and his recent decision to send American troops into Cambodia. From Italy, they received a mock-up of Carlo Silvestro's book of photographs of The Living Theatre and a book by Aldo Rostagno called *We, The Living Theatre,* which only made Judith observe that they had "hardened into history."

Julian was working on corrections for *The Life of the Theatre* and Judith, *The Enormous Despair.* She was still suffering over the end of her relationship with Carl Einhorn. After years of denial, Judith finally had to admit to herself that Carl had been an emotional opportunist who had systematically seduced other women in and out of the company while insisting on his love for her. The pain she felt over Carl was in some sense a displacement of the realization that the peace movement was foundering and no genuine revolution was to occur. Carl's views, always to some extent ambivalent on the question of nonviolence, had shifted to the extent that he was now willing to support armed struggle, and he had joined Eldridge Cleaver's contingent of Black Panthers in Algeria. Like some young man with a gun in a play by Sean O'Casey, he seemed to represent both the weaknesses and strengths of the revolution.

The feeling that the revolution had not fulfilled itself because of human imperfection was endemic in the movement in 1970. During the summer, two of its avatars—Jimi Hendrix and Janis Joplin—would die because of drug overdoses, deepening the general disillusionment. Like the anarchist Bakunin who was said to have habitually mistook the second month of pregnancy for the ninth, Judith, and Julian to a greater degree, were incurable optimists who so wanted the revolution to occur that they had created *Paradise Now* to hasten and announce its arrival. If the revolution they expected was sometimes difficult to discern, the extent of Judith's distress could be measured by a little poem—like one of Stephen Crane's "pills"—that she wrote in June 1970:

> *I cried aloud to my God*
> *And he answered me*
> *And the answer*
> *Is traveling faster*
> *Than light through the vast*
> *Arenas of human alienation*
> *And I haven't yet heard it.*

53. Brazil

The decision to work in Brazil did have its own logic. "I am with the people who sell their labor, their bodies, their lives to escape starvation," Julian would write while in Rio de Janeiro. "I am thinking of the unbalanced world, the polluted planet, the imminent apocalyptic disaster when, madness, the world falls down, and the light goes out, and we drown down, too soon."

Artaud had gone to Mexico to study the Tupamaro Indians. He had postulated, as well, that the theatre had to merge with real life in order to form a genuinely meaningful event, which Julian interpreted as theatre in the streets for the sake of the social class that, ordinarily, would never be able to afford the luxury of admission to a theatre. Instead of Marx's working class, his new audience would be closer to Bakunin's peasantry and *Lumpen-proletariat,* as well as the unemployable and outlawed, those with nothing to lose.

A vast country with ninety million people and enormous, un-tapped resources, Brazil was populated by the descendants of immigrants from Portugal, Spain, Italy, and Germany as well as the descendants of Indian and African slaves, who had only been emancipated in 1888. As in Argentina, Brazil's immigrants brought with them a strong anarchist tradition, and until the 1920s, most Brazilian unions were anarcho-syndicalist in orienta-tion. In 1918, anarchists under José Oiticica had tried to launch a general strike and to seize key points in Rio and São Paulo in an abortive conspiracy.

In part due to the fear of the influence of Fidel Castro's Com-munist Cuba, the military had seized power on 1 April 1964, driv-ing activists underground and dissolving all political parties except for the Arena party and an official, though token, opposi-tion party. The generals insisted on a strict censorship and full control over education and culture. Workers were not allowed to strike, and all forms of assembly were suspect. The military gov-ernment was known for its repression and a reliance on torture, which had only intensified since the 1968 protests of students and workers, and the appearance of urban guerrilla groups. In 1970, to complicate matters for the establishment, Salvador Al-lende, a Marxist physician, had been elected to the presidency of Chile.

At the end of July 1970, Julian, Judith, three-year-old Isha, and Echnaton flew to São Paulo, a sprawling megalopolis engaged in a process of endless construction. A week later, they would be joined by Birgit Knabe, Mary Krapf, and Roy Harris. Zé Celso was away working on a film and had offered them the use of his apartment just across from his Teatro Oficina. *Oficina* means "workshop" in Portuguese, and the group was one of the most political in Brazil, having produced a version of Brecht's *In the Jungle of the Cities* and *Galileo*. In the latter play, the protagonist's problems with the church were an evident parallel to those of Brazilian intellectuals with the military.

Zé Celso had also invited a theatre group of five Argentinians called Los Lobos—"the wolves"—to work with his group and The Living Theatre. Young, high-spirited, the five members of Los Lobos were not particularly political and stressed movement rather than language, so the collaboration had a special potential.

Ruth Escobar, a leading actress who had her own theatre where she had produced Jean Genet's *Balcony*—a play in which the clients in a bordello in a revolution-torn country enact a series of sadomasochistic fantasies—invited Judith and Julian to meet Genet, whose play *The Maids* they had performed all over Europe.

Genet had just come from the Black Panther trial in New Haven and was tired, so he arranged to meet Judith and Julian at his hotel a few days later. Smoking a Havana cigar, a very small man, only five feet two inches, with a benevolent face and gray eyes, Genet invited them into the hotel bar. He was no longer really interested in theatre, Genet told them, but only in politics. With an unwavering, direct gaze, he spoke rapidly in French about the Black Panthers, who were, in his view, the only American group acting directly against repression. He told them about meeting Faulkner, who had insisted that American blacks had to be patient. He warned them of the vanity of Brazilians who would associate with them only to get their names in the newspapers. Brazil was a country of deep sorrows, he said, and most Brazilians disguised this with a mask of great cheerfulness.

Picking up a small bag at the front desk of the hotel, Genet joked that he was on his way to deliver gold to the revolutionaries and entered a taxi en route to the airport and Paris. Although they had spent less than an hour together, for Judith and Julian, the meeting was a sort of annunciation from a god of the underworld, a voice of a great dissident who had profoundly challenged established convention in his plays and in his life.

In the meantime, there was more humbling work to be done, particularly several weeks of long theoretical discussions with Los Lobos and members of Oficina, before any physical work could be begun. Judith and Julian were studying Portuguese and attempting to further their limited knowledge of the language by translating one of Oiticica's essays, "The Principles and Aims of Anarchy." Joseph Chaikin, a former member of the company from the Fourteenth Street days, arrived after teaching a workshop in Rio and visited with them. From Italy, they heard the disturbing news that two former members of their troupe, Carol Berger and Petra Vogt, had been arrested in Positano on drug charges. Judith received a telephone call from Carl Einhorn, who was back in New York and finding it grim, working for the Liberation News Service. Her drawn-out grief over Carl had been alleviated by a liaison—romantically conducted in French—with Osvaldo de la Vega, one of Los Lobos, the pale, thin Argentinian son of a Spanish miner.

At another party at Ruth Escobar's, Judith and Julian heard that a performance of *The Balcony* had been threatened with a bomb scare. Young, blond, quite pregnant, Ruth Escobar told them that fifteen of her friends had been arrested in the past few years and that she had been detained for two days because of *The Balcony*. In Brazil, theater people had been terrorized by a group known as the Communist Hunting Commandos who used chains to beat actors. At the party, everyone spoke about the kidnapping of a Brazilian consul by the Tupamaros, the name taken by the Uruguayan revolutionaries.

Zé Celso returned to São Paulo, his film work completed at the end of August, near the end of the mild Brazilian winter. Immediately, the rehearsal sessions began to degenerate as Zé Celso, his own precarious finances leaving Oficina in a crisis, created an atmosphere of hostility and antagonism. Zé Celso said that he was unwilling to work with Los Lobos and admitted that he had only invited The Living Theatre on a frivolous whim.

Shocked by this declaration, and with an offer of assistance from Ruth Escobar, Judith, Julian, and the members of their group decided to relocate in Rio and settled in a six-room apartment on the four-mile arc of Ipanema Beach.

To learn the extent of Brazilian poverty, and because they wanted to stage plays in the middle of it instead of in theaters, Judith and Julian began to visit the *favelas,* the shantytowns of improvised dwellings without water or electricity. Usually, the tin-roofed shacks were clustered on hillsides. Women with huge tin cans on their heads brought water to their shacks, which then seeped downhill as sewage in crude drainage ditches, a clogging, stinking black sludge. Most of the children were without shoes, and they formed the constituency Frantz Fanon addressed in his book *The Wretched of the Earth,* a book Judith and Julian were reading at this time.

As white aliens from another culture and social class, Judith and Julian were concerned about how they would be received but were consistently greeted with great warmth. Later, they would realize that the warmth was the superficial disguise of resentment of the life-style, dress, and sexual permissiveness of the group.

Another entry into Brazilian reality was through the Yoruba rites of *candomblé,* known in Brazil as *umbanda* or *macumba,* the ritual of a West African religion whose followers danced themselves into a state of trance and could become possessed by their deities. Trance and possession, Julian realized, were states that could inform an actor with power and feeling, enable communication, and overcome inhibition. The entire scene was transcendently dramatic: incense and candles, altars and statues, pictures of Catholic saints and African slaves on the walls; the initiates in white in front at the altar—men smoking cigars on one side; women, some smoking cigars as well, in hooped skirts and turbans, on the other. All of them were singing, clapping hands to the rhythm of the drums. Sometimes they would enact scenes in imitation of their white masters becoming possessed by the Devil. But the cynosure of the pulsating energy was those in trance, their lips sometimes curling up to their noses, their faces twisted into sneers, their bodies convulsed in spasms.

At the end of September, Jimmy Spicer—who had been the general manager of the Fourteenth Street theatre—arrived with the manuscript of Judith's diaries from 1947 to 1957. The son of a domestic, Spicer had been Claude Fredericks's lover in the early 1950s, and Judith had originally met him when he had delivered some of the programs Fredericks had printed for the One Hundredth Street loft. Taught by Fredericks to disguise his proletarian background, Spicer became the perfect young gentleman and what he wanted most was to serve artists. He had a gift for editing, and he planned to help Judith prepare her diaries for publication.

At the same time, Pierre Biner arrived from France to join the small company, most of them crowded in the apartment Judith and Julian had rented. The company was augmented by the selection of five Brazilians. When Osvaldo de la Vega appeared, after Los Lobos had finished a short tour of Brazil, he moved into a small room in the apartment as well. The Brazilians he had seen on his tour, he claimed, were mostly apathetic, quelled, and repressed.

To get financial assistance, Julian wrote to the Ministry of Culture. He circulated a proposal for a film, and met with officials at several television stations and with Glauber Rocha, the Brazilian Cinema Novo film maker who seemed interested in collaboration. Julian had also written a political essay along anarchist lines on the kind of world he wanted and the steps he thought could be taken to achieve it, which he offered as a basis for company discussions.

Judith and Julian were working on the project which in Morocco had been called *Saturation City,* but whose title they had now changed to *The Legacy of Cain.* The new title was drawn from the work of Leopold Ritter von Sacher-Masoch, a nineteenth-century Polish novelist whose name Kraft-Ebbing had used to designate the term *masochism.* Sacher-Masoch's father had been the police chief of Lemberg (now called Lvov), a small city on the

Russian-Polish border, and he was raised in aristocratic circum-stances. Much of what he learned about sadism and masochism was derived from experiencing a violent revolutionary insurrec-tion of Polish peasants in 1846. Two years later, his father was transferred to Prague, where young Leopold saw more evidence of torture and bloodshed.

In Rousseau's *Confessions,* the young man discovered a rela-tionship between concupiscence and physical torment. After get-ting a degree in law and teaching German history at the University of Graz, at the age of twenty-one, he wrote a book about a sixteenth-century rebellion in Ghent and got interested in the history of European flagellation brothels. He ran off with a physician's wife, and he encouraged her to beat him regularly, relishing the role of the martyr-victim. He continued this pattern with a number of other women and supported them all with a se-ries of some eighty melodramatic, mechanical potboilers in which his hero would find a woman, propose to submit to her, and teach her to enjoy his humiliation. The most successful of these garish novels, the classic of the genre, published in 1870 and called *Venus in Furs,* was about an executive who hires a pros-titute to whip him.

In 1956, Judith had come across an illustrated edition of Sacher-Masoch's *Loves of Plato,* one of the first homosexual nov-els, and began translating it from German. Throughout Europe, she had searched for copies of his other novels, in which Sacher-Masoch proposed to document the sickness of society in six sep-arate volumes entitled *Love, Property, State, War, Work,* and *Death.* Sacher-Masoch only wrote the first two of these: *Venus in Furs* (about love) and *Property,* which proposed the moral iniq-uity of private property on any large scale.

Drawing on Sacher-Masoch and Gilberto Freyre's book of Brazilian history, *The Master and the Slave,* Judith and Julian dis-covered the theme of their emerging new play: the essential mas-ochism of the people supported the sadism of leaders who only expressed their collective will and whose power came from the support of those whom they oppressed.

The crucial problem of his age, Julian often asserted, was the inability to feel. Julian called it the "ice age," arguing that the sadomasochism that he had actively experienced in homosexuality was a mechanism for feeling something, even if it was pain. But pain, as Artaud had conjectured, could open the door to other feelings, even those of altruistic love. The masochist, he argued, identified with a slave class; and that identification, as Genet had suggested in *The Maids,* could lead to revolutionary action if the slaves could learn not to imitate their masters.

54. Dark Voyage

Judith's relationship with Osvaldo took a dark turn in October 1970 when he began to talk about his own sadistic proclivities in a romantic and theoretical way. He was afraid, he claimed, of banal love. Curiously, it seemed as if the art she wanted to project in *The Legacy of Cain* coincided with the appearance of someone who wanted to teach her how to fuse love and pain. One afternoon, after another *favela* visit, he tied her hands behind her back with a black nylon brassiere, all the while offering assurances in a soft, calculating tone that he would not hurt her.

Judith had always loathed men who abused women, but she found herself intrigued by the small marks Osvaldo began to leave on her body, which left her with an uncanny excitement. Sometimes, he would seem ferocious, his features distorted demonically. But whenever she began to cry, he became tender and seductive. One night, he scratched her chest and throat with a pin, and she realized that what attracted her was not the pain but the look of intense desire it seemed to bring to Osvaldo's face. Another night near the end of October, by the light of black and red candles, he twisted her amber necklace around her neck, lifting her and ordering her to smile while holding a metal penknife against her body and murmuring that he wished to cut her.

On the following days, working on her diaries with Jimmy Spicer, she felt moments of panic and terror accompanied by nausea. Yet these feelings, like the pain she had experienced with Osvaldo, seemed to intensify all her bodily functions, and currents of sensation flowed through her body. Thinking of Genet's *Maids,* which ends in death, she asked Osvaldo where his practice could lead. His answer was the promise of orgasm without sexual contact. In love notes, Osvaldo began to write of "the voyage," and during rehearsals, he would twist her fingers under a table to remind her of it. At the same time, he was carrying on a flirtation with a fashionable, well-spoken, thirty-year-old actress named Susana de Morais, the daughter of Vinicius de Morais, an internationally known diplomat, poet, and musician. When Osvaldo suggested that he wanted to sleep with Judith and Susana together, Judith remembered that the final anguish in Sacher-Masoch's novels was the torture of watching the beloved make love with a new love.

One night, he drew the dull edge of his knife into the recesses of her sex, and another night, without drawing blood, he left two red gashes on her back during sex. On a third night, he scratched two circles around the periphery of her breasts. On a fourth night, he hit her with his two-pronged leather belt. Judith did not confide any of these events to Julian, though she did show the marks on her body to Mary Mary and Pierre Biner.

The apprehension and fear this acceleration of violence caused Judith was intensified by an atmosphere of political tension as the police in Rio began a wave of preventive arrests of suspected subversives, drug users, and intellectuals. The eight editors of *O PASQUIM,* a weekly satirical newspaper featuring a double-page spread on underground subculture that had interviewed Judith and Julian, had been arrested as well.

Jenny Hecht had a friend, Dorothy Lenner, who taught in the theatre department of the São Paulo State University. She had asked Judith and Julian if they could arrange some kind of lecture-demonstration.

Early in November, Osvaldo showed Judith a rope he had purchased to tie her with. At the same moment, Julian conceived a piece he thought would be suitable for bringing, with a group of the São Paulo students, to a *favela*. In the piece, the first of which would be ultimately integrated into *The Legacy of Cain,* the actors would tie each other with ropes and chains, and lie helplessly on the ground. The performers in bonds would wait, sometimes for twenty minutes, for the people to liberate them. Again, Judith felt the grim conjunction of life and art.

In his workbook, Julian observed that Osvaldo's attitude to the group had been peculiar from the start. While he seemed to admire Judith and Julian, he did not relate to the other actors. One minute, he would try to contribute; the next moment, he would try to destroy.

During rehearsals, Judith and Julian discussed the theories of Sacher-Masoch with the group, and one night in his bedroom, Osvaldo tied Judith's wrists and ankles, and jerked a rope around her neck as they made love. The following night, he showed her a small Japanese knife with a fine, curved blade. "Burning with such desire as I have never seen in any face," he made a diagonal one-inch incision along Judith's left shoulder, and then put his mouth to the wound and made love to her with his tongue dripping with her blood.

Judith realized she had violated an ultimate taboo and reached a turn in her relationship. During rehearsals, Osvaldo began to speak to Judith about Susana de Morais who had joined the group. One afternoon, after rehearsal, the three met in Osvaldo's tiny room. Judith enjoyed Susana's soft skin and the blackness of her long hair that covered the three of them like foliage. But when Osvaldo made love to Susana, he did it with a strength he had not shown Judith, and watching them, she inwardly cowered.

When they tried again, Judith realized that Osvaldo's physical hostility was occurring less to arouse himself than to exclude her and that Susana, fourteen years her junior, had won him. "Nature and time and the rhythms of the universe" had betrayed her, she confided to her *Diaries* in a poem.

In the apartment, however, she was less philosophical, breaking down in hysterical tears; and she soon shared the cause of her pain with Julian and members of the company. Though Julian tried to absolve her of any guilt, Osvaldo accused her of using her suffering as a means of controlling him. Free love, Julian observed in his workbook, had always been a source of conflict within the company because it was still associated with the bourgeois qualities of fidelity and possession. To a certain extent, he believed, Judith's insecurity about being in Brazil—an insecurity which they both disguised with their bravado, he admitted—had resulted in a compensatory power game with Osvaldo.

The company had been to some extent demoralized by the relationship. Jimmy Anderson had arrived just before Judith's divulgence, and his arrival was interpreted as a sign of positive energy. Now, many were tied in knots of uncertainty, and some spoke of leaving Brazil.

Julian believed Judith might be on the verge of a crack-up. She still thought she loved Osvaldo, that her pain was caused not by his Japanese knife which he had already thrown in the ocean but by her loss of Osvaldo to Susana. With Julian, she visited two hypnotists. One of them, a man who looked like Bela Lugosi, told her to repeat the refrain "the name Osvaldo means nothing to me." The hypnosis worked. It was related to the search for the trance state in *macumba,* a passage to deeper levels of consciousness, and helped her understand the love that people can feel for their masters. If the loss of Osvaldo was her final hysteria over failed love—the sort of despair she had felt in Croissy over Carl Einhorn—she knew her liberation hinged on the recognition that she had for years depended on sexual seduction and entanglement as a sign of strength.

Walking on the beach in the middle of November with Luis

Carlos Bellonzi, a Brazilian member of the group who was tutoring her in Portuguese and caring for Isha, Judith saw a group of boys sadistically kicking a wounded seagull. Feeling too weak to intervene but knowing how much she had to rebuild her psychic strength in order to go on with the work of the company, she asked Bellonzi to accompany her to the top of the double mountain nearby called Dois Irmãos, "the two brothers." From the mountain's base, the road wound through a *favela* which grew poorer and poorer as they climbed. At the apex of the *favela,* where the wood shacks were packed with mud and the black children played in the banana and palm trees, they found an overgrown, steep, narrow path. With a fallen branch, Bellonzi beat the way through the brambles and spider webs, and Judith imagined that if she reached the top, she could free herself of her slavery to love. At the peak, with vultures circling over the vast valley below and the ocean stretching before them, Bellonzi removed all his clothing to dance ecstatically near the precipice.

That night, she made love with Osvaldo for the last time, realizing that it had become banal and now all that interested her in Brazil was the work.

55. Ouro Prêto

By 1 December 1970, the group had relocated to Ouro Prêto. An old mining town, with thirty thousand inhabitants, toward the interior, it was the "wild west" of Brazil, Judith declared in a letter to Carl Einhorn. Judith and Julian had decided to work in Ouro Prêto because of an invitation to participate in a theatre festival the town had organized in 1968, which had attracted students from all over Brazil.

Surrounded by red clay hills, Ouro Prêto is an eighteenth-century baroque city with imposing churches, some designed and decorated with works by the sculptor Antônio Francisco Lisboa Aleijadinho. There were many buildings with balconied facades and a central square of asymmetrical perfection built above former mining tunnels. The town's name, Ouro Prêto, means "black gold" in Portuguese, given because originally its gold deposits were located in a dark stone. Now manganese and bauxite were mined for aluminum production, and hundreds of poor people lived in the windowless shafts of abandoned gold mines.

The trip from Rio had not been uneventful. Osvaldo and Susana had not joined them, and en route, there were problems with the Volkswagen bus that Ruth Escobar had loaned them when they left São Paulo. Even more ominous, they had been stopped by military police and detained in a jail room for over an hour for a check of documentation. The check was merely a pretext. The police claimed they were searching for arms and subversives. When Julian naively expressed his indignation—incredulously asking the police whether Brazil was a democracy—the group was freed.

In Ouro Prêto, the group found accommodations in an old inn on a hill overlooking the town. The Pousada de Chico Rei was owned by Miss Lilly, a Danish woman who had moved to Ouro Prêto in the early 1950s. She had created a circle of international artists and intellectuals, among them the American poet Elizabeth Bishop, who now lived in her own house in the town. According to legend, the head of Tiradentes, the eighteenth-century dentist who had led the unsuccessful uprising against the Portuguese that inspired the country's later liberation, was buried on the grounds of Miss Lilly's inn.

Exploring the town, Julian noticed the graffiti—"Down with the Dictatorship!" "Power to the People!" "Long Live the Armed Struggle!"—on the walls of the School of Mines which was located in an old fortress. However, when Julian spoke to some students about pacifism, he was asked whether he was with the CIA.

Every afternoon, the company would meet to work on the part of *The Legacy of Cain* that they were planning to do in a *favela* with the São Paulo university students, beginning with a blindfolded procession. A potential problem was the professor at São Paulo who had invited them with the understanding that their lecture-demonstration would be inside the university theatre.

By the middle of December, after a nine-hour bus trip, the group was back in São Paulo with a contract for the lecture-demonstration. They had found a *favela* soaked in mud with a fine, red powder covering the shacks and its adjoining hills of refuse. To encourage the collective participation of the residents, the company planned to use statements made by the inhabitants in answer to the question "Tell us a little about your life here?" A number of the actors with tape recorders began interviewing residents. All the company members were apprehensive about the dangers of flouting the censorship regulations—particularly because of the part of *The Legacy of Cain* with the actors in bondage.

Dorothy Lenner, the São Paulo professor sponsoring the lecture-demonstration, read in a newspaper that Susana de Morais had left the company because of their drugs and sexual promiscuity. Professor Lenner had never once entered a *favela* and admitted that she would be uneasy at the prospect. When Julian and Judith explained that they intended to bring her students into a *favela,* Lenner explained that her university could not risk such involvement and any students who chose to participate could only do so as a private matter. Actually, São Paulo was rife with political paranoia at that moment. Two members of Zé Celso's group had been recently arrested, and the Swiss ambassador had been abducted, his return offered in exchange for seventy political prisoners.

In the midday sunshine, just before Christmas, the actors carried a huge cake they had baked into a muddy plaza. The blindfolded actors maneuvered across the mud, singing "What is life?" and "What is property?" *(O que e a propriedade?).* In the first sequence, the tape-recorded comments of the residents were played, so that their own voices called the people together.

This was followed by a repetitive song measuring the moments of a laborer's life by the paltry salary he received.

Fusing a Brechtian sense of dialectic with an Artaudian kineticism, the company performed six stories on Sacher-Masoch's categories of enslavement: money, love, property, the state, war, and death. In each case, a storyteller narrated a simple story—for example, the fool who starved to death because he could not eat his money—while a pair of actors mimed the action which ended in some interpretation of the relationship of master and slave. After the actors whirled themselves into a trance state, each master signed a contract with red thumbprints with each slave and then bound the slave with a rope, strap, or chain. When the spectators untied the actors, the cake was eaten—faster than he could cut it, Julian observed, perhaps because the frosting on the cake was a replica of the cruzeiro, formerly the Brazilian monetary note.

Judith had been liberated by a man in his forties with wrinkled skin and bare feet who had whispered, "Tomorrow the people will liberate the whole world." "The ship is now in the water," Julian acknowledged in his workbook, "we have done the only important work of our lives today."

56. Mother's Day

In January 1971, the company gave another performance in the *favela* and one for a larger audience in the nineteenth-century city of Rio Claro, two hours outside São Paulo. A serious young student named José Carlos Temple Troya who wrote an account of the performance for the Rio Claro newspaper decided to join the company. Luke Theodore arrived from Europe, making

Judith reflect that a year earlier they had performed *Paradise Now* for the last time before seven thousand people in the Berlin Sportspalast. From Italy, they received a copy of the Italian version of *Paradise Now*. Andrew Nadelson, a pianist who had been Garrick's roommate at Reed, appeared saying he wished to work with them.

There had been hardly any income during the months in Brazil and resources were low. Living on oatmeal, rice, and tea in a friend's house in São Paulo, the company faced a most pressing problem: the expiration of visas. To resolve this problem, the group decided to take a bus to Montevideo in Uruguay—thirty-six hours each way—where they could get six-month visas and also visit a therapeutic anarchist community called the Comunidad del Sur.

Forty people, including fifteen children, living in three stone houses, with a print shop to prepare anarchist texts, the Comunidad del Sur had been in existence for fifteen years. Plain food and plain people living in a sober harmony, Julian thought. But if this was a preview of the "beautiful non-violent revolution" to which Julian aspired, he felt uneasy when the communards laughed at the actors' long hair and declared them decadent because they used cosmetics.

By the middle of February, Judith and Julian returned to Ouro Prêto. When they had first arrived in December, they were told by Julio Varella, director of the Festival de Iverno, that they would be able to perform there; but now they would learn that they were not welcome. Since the festival was a showpiece for Brazil and closely monitored by the authorities, this was not entirely unexpected.

During the day, Judith and Julian began working on literary projects in a chilly two-room garden apartment behind the Calabouco ("dungeon") restaurant and gallery whose owner was sympathetic to their concerns. Judith resumed editing her diaries with Jimmy Spicer, and Julian returned to the *Paradise Now* text and the idea for a new play about alchemy featuring an association between Richard Wagner and Faust.

Near the end of February, they saw another aspect of Brazilian reality in carnival, which was preceded by a procession of the poor dressed in rags and men dressed in women's clothes, beating tin cans in a parody of the official gilded event. For three nights, they heard the sound of drums and brass horns, and saw the dancers in the streets and the necessary release of what seemed like manufactured joy. A grimmer aspect of Brazilian reality was encountered at the Alcan Aluminum of Canada foundry. Walking along the railroad tracks, they saw the spectacular furnaces in a landscape that seemed like a surreal nightmare: a thousand nonunionized workers earning the equivalent of fifty dollars a month crowded over a few acres, the air thick with dust, with giant ingots and bales of wire instead of trees. One day, they hoped to perform there.

In the middle of March, they found a ten-room house on the side of a hill near a murky, reddish river and a small *favela* which could accommodate the seventeen members of the group—now including Pamela Badyk, Steven Ben Israel, Bill Shari, and Tom Walker who had come from New York. Money was extremely scarce. Sleeping on straw-filled sacks, the community lived very simply, although they would share their meals with those who were desperate. Late every afternoon, there would be a four-hour meeting to discuss ramifications of *The Legacy of Cain,* or reports about the community of Ouro Prêto. Pierre Biner had drawn a very detailed map by going through all the irregular streets of Ouro Prêto and marking each house, noting the social class of its occupants. Teams, including at least one Portuguese speaker, had been sent out to gather information, asking people about the nature of their work and how they made ends meet. This research into the fabric of the community was called the Campaign, and it included advocacy for change. Members of the company always regarded this work as at least as important as whatever theatrical works they would create and as an integral part of the creation of *The Legacy of Cain.*

A week after the new community had assembled and company rehearsals had begun, they received the shattering news that Jenny Hecht had committed suicide in the United States, overdosing with seconals. Jenny had been Judith's closest friend in the company. For years, she had hurt her mind with drugs and pills to discourage herself, she said, from becoming as intellectual as her father, Ben Hecht, and as a way of coping with the suffering she saw. Fundamentally, she found reality too fearsome and did not "want to leave the playground," Judith observed. Sadly, they held the Jewish Passover seder that Judith and Julian led for the company every year; whether or not individual members were Jews never seemed as important as celebrating a passage out of slavery. On this night, however, Jenny was no longer present to ask the four questions, beginning with "Why is this night different from all other nights?"

The news of Jenny's death acted as a sort of catalyst, and the members of the company began a concerted effort to reach the community of Ouro Prêto. The problem was to get the trust of members of the community who ordinarily would have seen the actors as an anomaly—after all, they did not have to toil in a factory for their bread. Birgit Knabe taught yoga to seven prisoners in the small local jail under the supervision of twenty policemen. Steven Ben Israel and Pamela Badyk started a course on breathing at a sports club across the road. Others began working with the children at a local junior high school in Saramenha, a nearby community where miners and foundry workers lived.

The school at Saramenha, built by the developer of the aluminum foundry, asked the company to perform with the children for Mother's Day. Judith proposed a piece based on the children's dreams about their mothers. Six children, bound by crepe paper ribbon to their mothers, would each recite their dreams. They would then be wafted—held aloft by the actors—into a sea of dreams represented by the other eighty children in gym outfits lying on their backs on the floor, kicking their legs, and crying out "Voar, voar" (fly, fly). All the elements of *The Legacy of Cain* were to be integrated into the play as the child wound its body up in the crepe paper cord and the mother assumed the role of the punishing parent. Dressed in violet and riding on Andrew Nadelson's shoulders, Judith played the Dream Mother who whipped the children until they rose to overthrow her. Then the children flew away, snapping their crepe paper cords.

On 14 May, hundreds of women—wives of miners and workers in the aluminum foundry—with gaunt, anxious, passive faces crowded into the workers' recreation hall to see the play. For the most part, they seemed reserved, full of suspicious respect. Also in the audience were two Augustinian monks who, horrified at the scene in which the children lay kicking on their backs, denounced the company to the municipal council for having the children participate in what they regarded as obscene acts, setting off a chain of events ending with imprisonment and expulsion.

Through the month of June, Judith and Julian continued work on their literary projects, now at Casa Mariana, named after Marianne Moore. This was the elegant residence of the American poet Elizabeth Bishop, whom Jimmy Spicer had known since the early 1950s and who was away teaching at Harvard. In Bishop's library, Judith found copies of Dorothy Wordsworth's, Virginia Woolf's, and Franz Kafka's diaries.

Every afternoon or evening, there would be group discussions of the progress of the outreach program. Although they were all constantly pushing at the edge of the danger they felt around them, certain precautions were necessary for general safety. As part of the Orwellian absurdity of the military repression in Brazil, no one could use the word *union* or *revolution,* or pronounce the name of the Tupamaro revolutionaries. For *revolution,* for example, they were forced to use as part of a code the word *decoration.*

Often they invited local residents and students over to the house in the evening. In large measure, it was a magnification of what had occurred in Morocco. The front door was never locked, and although marijuana was never smoked outside, it was used freely in the house.

Some members of the group thought the scene was much too open. There were a number of sexual liaisons and swapping of sexual partners in the community. Judith had had a brief affair with a German actor during carnival, and Luke Theodore was constantly trying to seduce Brazilian boys. They heard that a priest had preached a major sermon against them in Ouro Prêto.

Bill Shari, furious about what he considered to be laxness and a lack of control, threatened to return to New York. When, at the end of June, Andrew Nadelson bizarrely set several small fires in the house, burning Pierre Biner's carefully constructed map of Ouro Prêto, Shari decided he would have to move out of the house. By turns sullen and artificially cheerful, the always-temperamental Paulo Augusto packed his suitcase and left precipitously, claiming he needed to see a dentist.

On the afternoon of 1 July, the day the theatre festival officially opened in Ouro Prêto, officials from the Department of Political and Social Order, the political police known as DOPS, and a dozen local policemen expecting to discover a cache of weapons walked through the unlocked front door with a warrant and dogs. While the rooms were being searched, everyone in the house was herded into the kitchen where Jimmy Anderson, pretending to be the cook, shuffled about preparing dinner. In a two-hour search, the police found no marijuana in the house but later would claim to have uncovered a brick of it in the backyard under a sign that incongruously declared Look! in English. Two nights earlier, Tom Walker recalled, a local student had tried to sell them a supply of marijuana that they refused because they could not afford it and they did not trust him.

Fortunately, Isha was with a babysitter. Nor were Judith, Julian, Jimmy Spicer, and several others in the house; but when they returned for the afternoon meeting, they were arrested as well. "Guerrillas," Julian had written just before leaving for Brazil, become "models of courage in a society that makes cowards of us all," and this was a moment that required considerable resources of courage.

In Ouro Prêto's filthy jail, where Birgit had taught yoga to the prisoners, the men and women were placed overnight in separate cells without mattresses. For most of the night, the members of the two cells sang to each other, mixing blues songs, a Gnaoua chant, and "We Shall Overcome" with the story that would become their common front: they knew nothing about any marijuana.

The next day, they were all driven to the DOPS headquarters in a modern facility in the city of Belo Horizonte, two hours away, where they were greeted by photographers' flashbulbs. In a corridor, while the interrogation was proceeding, members of the group saw pictures and reports of their arrest on television. Everyone was interrogated separately: had he or she ever smoked *maconha?* was he homosexual? did the members of the group promiscuously sleep with one another? Brutal and harsh, the interrogator, a policeman named Ari, would slap the cigarette out of a subject's mouth without warning. During the interrogations, the South American members of the troupe received special attention: Rocky Segura, a Peruvian, was slapped against a wall, and Ivanildo Silvino Araujo received electroshocks to his fingers and penis. After Ivanildo's torture, he was ordered to smile; and when he refused, a DOPS agent threatened to burn him alive with gasoline.

After the interrogations were completed, those who had been in the house during the raid were fingerprinted and separated from those who had not. At four in the morning, in a small locked room that contained only a desk and two broken chairs, with Birgit and Mary Mary, Judith was questioned a second time by Dr. Renato da Silveira Aragao, the attractive white-haired chief of DOPS in the region of Minas Gerais. A few hours later, in Dr. Renato's office with its diploma from the course on Special Warfare from the United States Army, those who had been outside the house during the raid—Judith, Julian, Mary Mary, and Andrew Nadelson—were released.

Driven back to Ouro Prêto by friends, the released group was on their way to their house when they were warned by local underground youths that the police would try to entrap them again with planted marijuana. Full of mounting fear, they did not know where to hide. Julian went to find legal assistance. Mary Mary found friends who would shelter her. Judith first went to see Isha, who was staying with friends. Then, Judith and Andrew fled to an abandoned mine shaft inhabited by two very old mendicants, a *macumba* priest and his wife, whom they had fed at their table. On a piece of paper, the priest wrote down the names of the company members still incarcerated, and then lighting incense in a ceremony of protection, he burned the paper and crumbled its ashes into a cup of tea which they all drank.

Later that evening, Andrew and Judith rejoined Julian. Seeking a public place in the event they were going to be apprehended, they went to the Calabouco art gallery reception to which they had been invited. Drinking *batidas*, a drink of sugarcane rum and fruit, they were arrested again.

57. DOPS Prison

Back in the DOPS jail in Belo Horizonte, Judith noticed that the phrase "suspicion of acts of subversion" had been stamped on their dockets. The police from Ouro Prêto arrived with one blue plastic bag full of marijuana, as well as several large bags of books, journals, letters, and bits of Pierre Biner's map of Ouro Prêto.

Dr. Renato showed them photographs of the marijuana being dug up under the peculiar Look! sign and was particularly disturbed by copies of the writing of Karl Marx and Mao in Portuguese which had been found in the house. When Mary Mary was interrogated by Dr. Renato, he pointed to a picture of a North Vietnamese man. This man, she was told, hated Americans and the implicit though characteristic threat was that he would be her torturer.

Paired in separate cells, Julian with Andrew Nadelson and

Judith with Mary Mary, they were allowed to see an attorney, Ariosvaldo de Campo, a man with a stern expression who told them they would be held in preventive detention until their trial in Ouro Prêto. The usual wait for trial, he advised, was three months. The cells had no mattresses, but an American consul from Rio brought them blankets. There were journalists with questions and many photographers. One of them slipped a newspaper under the door of Judith's cell with the discouraging news that Jim Morrison had died of an overdose in Paris.

Julian was then placed in a cell with six men and a television blaring dubbed American westerns. The DOPS-trained dogs lived behind his cell and contributed to the incessant noise with their barking. While the noise managed to interfere with his reading and writing, it did not prevent him from these activities. Nor did the usual terror of the prison experience keep him from working: as Henry Howard once paradoxically put it, Julian was too terrified to ever be afraid. He was writing additional material for *The Life of the Theatre,* based on his experiences in Brazil, that seemed to cut to the heart of his ideological struggle while retaining an outlook still basically affirmative and optimistic:

> If, as Gandhi says, capital engenders greediness and competitiveness as character traits, might anarcho-communism engender generosity and cooperation? The theory of the revolution is not based on the idea that human character is "good" but that if we change the conditions in which we function, our character will change.

By looking through a three-inch space at the bottom of the thick metal plate that formed her cell door, Judith could see Julian's cell. Judith's cellmate, a twenty-two-year-old Brazilian named Maria Dálcia, had a shortwave radio on which Judith heard two items of interest: First, DOPS had decided not to separate her from Julian but to keep them at their headquarters. The other male prisoners had already been sent to the Colonia Penal, and the women, to a women's penitentiary. Second, Garrick and

Karen in Oregon had had an eight-pound daughter whom they named Eden Star.

After a week's wait and their first showers in the flea-infested DOPS prison, Mary Mary and Andrew Nadelson were released. Assisted by journalists, and with Steven Ben Israel who had been secreted and never arrested, they stayed with the American consul in Rio and flew back to New York to rally support for the others.

On 9 July, Julian's mother, Mabel—with more blankets, pillows, and flea sprays—arrived at the DOPS prison in Belo Horizonte. Confident, untroubled, and cheerful, she told the press that she had come for Isha and that a mother's place was always with her son if he was in trouble.

In the Colonia Penal, the ten male members of the group were confined two to a cell in the same wing. Their diet was so deficient that it meant slow starvation and illness for most of the long-term prisoners, and they were only allowed outside in a gray concrete courtyard for an hour a day. Nevertheless, their spirits were high. They had been allowed to keep their long hair and had been given permission to perform *Mysteries* for over a hundred prisoners; they were also preparing another play based on the dreams of various prisoners.

For most of the members of the group, jail was a sort of terrible triumph, something that they had on some level expected. They felt privileged to be with dedicated revolutionaries, to "pit our ideas," as Judith put it, "against the raw material of our subject matter." Even though most of the revolutionaries were involved in armed struggle like Maria Dálcia, the company members generally admired them and felt a sense of solidarity with their struggle.

In her cell, Judith listened to news broadcasts, Nixon was going to China. Giving Maria Dálcia English lessons, she received Portuguese lessons in return, using a Portuguese version of *The Iliad*. Life in the DOPS jail was more informal than in the other prisons she had experienced—one of the prisoners was trusted with a coffee route—but prison life had its inevitable terrors.

Once, at four in the morning, she was summoned outside of her cell. Dreading torture, she was relieved when she was only asked to help search a new prisoner.

Most of all, she was comforted by Julian's presence. She worked on the manuscripts of her diaries, and every afternoon she was allowed to work with Julian. They were interviewed by *Veja,* the Brazilian equivalent of *Time,* and for television, where they described their work on *The Legacy of Cain.*

In fact, Judith and Julian had become overnight celebrities in Brazil as the news media used the story as a way to test the censorship imposed by the military government. When the trial began at the end of July, after Julian was allowed to withdraw funds from a bank in Ouro Prêto for his lawyer, he was greeted by a cheering throng. Ruth Escobar, who came to the trial, organized a committee of Brazilian artists to gather support.

In New York City, Steven Ben Israel spoke on WBAI, organized a press conference, and established the Paradise Defense Fund. He also sent a petition signed by Bob Dylan, John Lennon, Mick Jagger, and Jane Fonda which appeared on the front page of a number of major newspapers in Brazil. From the United States, Allen Ginsberg, Arthur Miller, Alexander Calder, James Baldwin, and Susan Sontag sent telegrams. From France, Samuel Beckett, Jean-Louis Barrault, Jean Genet, and Jean-Luc Godard all made public statements or sent telegrams deploring the arrests. From Italy, writers Alberto Moravia and Fernando Pivano and film makers Pier Paolo Pasolini and Bernardo Bertolucci sent a joint telegram. The most effective protests, however, were demonstrations organized outside of Brazil's Varig Airlines offices in New York and the Brazilian consulate. And the most sensational publicity was caused by the fact that one large newspaper, the *Estado de Minas,* began publishing excerpts from the diaries Judith had been keeping while in prison.

In August, wearing their blue prison uniforms, the entire group was brought by bus to Ouro Prêto and back—two and a half hours each way—for each day of the trial. Judge Moacyr de Andrade seemed prejudiced against the defendants, a condition that was not alleviated when Jimmy Anderson testified that his elation in Brazil was caused by experiences with *macumba* rather than *maconha,* Luke Theodore sat in the lotus position to testify, and Tom Walker blessed the judge in the courtroom.

The case itself presented its awkwardness for the prosecution with "witnesses" who refused to identify properly the accused, providing contradictory testimony. The evident flaws in most of the evidence were patiently exposed by Ariosvaldo, the defense attorney. The most comic aspect of the trial, however, was its central feature, the blue plastic bag containing the contraband marijuana. Each day of the trial, the evidence, which was set out on a table in front of the judge for all to see, seemed to diminish mysteriously until at the end there were only a few ounces left. The police had been enjoying themselves or selling it.

Finally, at the end of August, the trial was resolved by a presidential order of expulsion for the company. President Emilio Garrastazu Medici, a figurehead for the military, had received a telegram from Jean-Paul Sartre, a name even he recognized, and realized the fiasco of the trial was only becoming an embarrassment to Brazil and threatening the tourist industry. The Living Theatre had been imprisoned for over two months.

Transferred to the Maritime Prison in Rio, in the hands of the federal police, they were held in wet, filthy, basement cells with no sanitary facilities or bedding except for the cement floor and their luggage. There were extradition problems faced by half of the company—all those who were not Americans would have to return to their own countries. Julian was called upstairs to try to resolve the problem, and he asked to consult with Judith. As usual, he wanted all major decisions to be taken in tandem, but the paternalistic Brazilians could not understand this. When a guard laughed at his request, Julian remonstrated. With Judith and the company looking on in horror, Julian was thrown down a flight of stairs, hurled against a wall, and beaten by a group of other policemen. Taking the fall like a Meyerholdian actor, he was only bruised though he could have been badly hurt. It seemed such a painful conclusion to what they had set out to accomplish in Brazil.

Later, Julian would reflect that the mistake The Living

Theatre made in Brazil was that "we stayed in one place too long a time." In Europe, he said, "we had found that if we stayed in one locale for longer than two months, we aroused the ire of certain conservative elements who just either didn't like the way we looked, or had some idea that we were doing something wrong for their community, and they found some way of forcing us out, or making it unpleasant for us." It was a sad reflection, but it spoke quite directly of the difficulty involved in creating the kind of social change he and the group envisaged, and the dynamic of resistance that could be expected in response. It was also an admission that as messengers of revolution, the group was destined to be nomadic.

58. "A Fetish of Revolution"

When Judith, Julian, and eleven other members of the group arrived in New York City on 4 September 1971, they were interviewed by CBS News. They declared they had been freed because of the privileges of class, race, and money. Two days after their arrival, Judith and Julian visited Abbie Hoffman in downtown Manhattan in the rooftop apartment of a commercial building. When they buzzed Hoffman through an intercom labeled REVOLUTION, he came down to greet them. Jovial, without a shirt, holding a joint in his hand, and with a supply of cocaine in his apartment, he told Judith that she had invented the prototype of the hippie. He wanted to know why Judith and Julian had not denounced their captors more forcefully during the television interview. Hoffman was unaware that the Brazilian members of the cast were still in jail and needed to be protected.

Playful and flirtatious all evening, Hoffman persuaded Judith to join him on a fire escape. In a moment of uncomfortable privacy, she made love to him, fulfilling a desire she had long harbored. In its way, the act was a fundamental expression of revolutionary solidarity and a life-style not bound by convention.

After a trip to Washington, D.C., to appeal for help in securing the release of the European and South American members of the troupe, Judith and Julian returned to New York to participate in the Attica demonstrations. Attica Prison in upstate New York had been the scene of an unsuccessful rebellion in which forty-seven prisoners were killed. Carrying red and black banners to Rockefeller Center, the demonstrators shouted, "Free all prisoners!" and "Attica means fight back!"

Covered with play money, a plastic machine gun in its hand, an effigy of Nelson Rockefeller—who had ordered what was called the "Attica Massacre"—burned while Julian addressed the rally. After speaking about Brazil, Julian encountered Tennessee Williams attending his first political demonstration. Bewildered, a bit shy, alarmed at the presence of so many police, Williams asked Julian and Judith to address a "Stop the War" rally at St. John the Divine cathedral in December.

Early that October, Judith and Julian experienced a very different kind of revolutionary ferment when they flew to Oregon to retrieve Isha who was living with Garrick. With long braids and an unabashed enthusiasm, Garrick was with Karen and their daughter, Eden Star, on a commune he had started called Rainbow Farm near the tiny town of Drain, Oregon, thirty miles outside Eugene. As an open community welcoming outsiders, the commune varied in size from twenty to seventy people. The communards grew all their own food and burned fallen trees for fuel and heat. Its members seemed to have cut themselves off from the world deliberately and did not even read newspapers. Garrick was busily planning an enormous gathering of free spirits who would assemble in a national forest.

Judith and Julian lectured at Simon Fraser University in Vancouver, at the University of British Columbia. They then drove south, spending Halloween with Ken Kesey and his Merry Pranksters in Ashland, Oregon. Stoical but optimistic, not especially political, like the young people at Rainbow Farm, Kesey was rooted in family and farm.

Staying in a Chinese hotel in San Francisco, Julian gave Ferlinghetti the expanded version of *The Life of the Theatre.* Judith visited Carl Einhorn, now working for the Revolutionary People's Communication Network and an underground paper called *Babylon.* Carl was no longer enamored of the Black Panthers. Huey Newton, a West Coast leader of the Panthers, was now living in a luxury apartment and talking about black capitalism, Carl acknowledged.

In Los Angeles, in the middle of November, after lecturing at the Davis and Riverside campuses of the University of California, Judith and Julian saw a performance of Ezra Pound's opera *Villon,* and met with Luke Theodore and Steve Thompson, an old member of the company who had been Jenny Hecht's lover. By the beginning of December, they were back in San Francisco to be interviewed for *Rolling Stone* and the *Berkeley Barb,* one of the best alternative newspapers, and to speak about Brazil on public radio. With Paul Krassner, they visited Wavy Gravy whose Hog Farm had departed for India. At San Francisco State, they heard poet Dianne Di Prima read from her book of poems, *Revolutionary Letters.* With an FBI informant in the audience who sent a full report to Washington, they spoke on "Theatre and Revolution" at Ferlinghetti's City Lights Poets' Theatre.

In New York City, in early January 1972, they met Allen Ginsberg recently returned from India, where he had met Rufus Collins and a group of Living Theatre members in Calcutta. Ginsberg invited them to meet a Tibetan lama, Chogyam Trungpa Rinpoche, with whom he had been studying and to participate in a televised discussion on Channel 13 with the monk. Trungpa's message was obedience. When Julian asked him whether that meant that young men should go to Vietnam if drafted, he said yes, and Julian protested.

In the middle of January, they spoke on using theatre as a means of reaching workers and miners at Carnegie-Mellon University in Pittsburgh, a talk that would subsequently bring the entire company to Pittsburgh for a year. Back in New York City, they visited Joseph Chaikin, who told them about his work with prisoners in the Tombs, and saw Jerry Rubin in his Prince Street loft. Somber, Rubin admitted that he used to think anything was possible, even revolution in America, but now he was not so sure. They also visited Murray Bookchin, a mathematician and socialist historian with a Ph.D. in philosophy, who suggested they bring The Living Theatre to workers in the industrial complexes in New Jersey.

To help support the company, Julian and Judith left for another lecture tour in the middle of February. At Smith College, Julian and Judith spoke for three hours on anarchism and the feasibility of revolutionary action. At St. Foy College in Quebec, Julian lectured in French. After another lecture in Toronto, they ran into John Cage and Merce Cunningham, and chatted over a meal about the miseries of touring.

In Detroit, they visited a Ford plant and stayed at an affiliate of Garrick's Rainbow community that they found soaked in idealism with everyone addressing them as "brother" or "sister." At another Rainbow house in Ann Arbor where they were lecturing, they visited with John Sinclair of the White Panthers, who had recently been released from prison.

They spoke at Dalhousie University in Halifax and at Carleton University in Ottawa where the students seemed sure the revolutionary spirit was exhausted although they questioned Judith and Julian for three hours. In Burlington, where they spoke at the University of Vermont, they again met Murray Bookchin, who was planning to publish a magazine called *Anarchos*.

Returning from their tour at the end of March, Judith and Julian had to face the problem of where to situate the company. They found an old house on State Street in Brooklyn, and Steven Ben Israel, Pamela Badyk, Pierre Devis, Luke Theodore, Birgit Knabe (who now went by the name "Gypsy"), Roy Harris, Jimmy Anderson, and Bill Shari—all former members of the company who had rejoined—formed the nucleus of the new company.

Judith, Julian, and Isha settled into a comfortable room at

the top of the house, facing an old public school where Julian's uncle had instituted the Child Guidance Service for the New York City school system. Tacked on the wall of their room was a passage from Christopher Lasch's *The Agony of the New Left* that pointed to their hopes for the movement to which they were committed:

> The experience of the New Left already refutes one of its principal tenets, that a revolutionary movement has no need of theory because theory will spring spontaneously out of the daily struggles of the movement. Struggle itself only leads to more struggle or—as in the case of the labor unions to eventual absorption. Particularly in a society for which no precedent exists, the problems of which, accordingly, are almost entirely novel, a theory of radical social change can develop only if radicals—particularly radical intellectuals—cultivate it systematically.

By the middle of April, with Isha enrolled in a progressive school, Judith and Julian returned to the lecture circuit, flying to Urbana, Illinois, where they spoke at a branch of the state university. They then rented a car to drive to the University of Illinois at De Kalb on whose campus a bomb had just been discovered. At Bowling Green University in Ohio, they spoke, as elsewhere, on the principles of collective creation, their experiences in Brazil, street theatre, and nonviolence. They lectured at Ohio State in Columbus and then flew to Buffalo for another lecture where they met Gordon Rogoff, who told them he had been dismissed from Yale because of his enthusiastic support of their 1968 appearances.

In Brooklyn at the end of April, daily meetings of the company were resumed. On May Day, with Allen Ginsberg, Judith and Julian went to see the dramatic adaptation of "Kaddish," his poem about his mad mother, Naomi. Enormously moving, the play featured Marilyn Chris—who had begun her career with The Living Theatre in the early 1950s—playing Naomi. Later that evening, Judith and Julian watched televised accounts of Columbia University students taking over buildings. They also saw the funeral of FBI Director J. Edgar Hoover on television, with President Nixon announcing that the "age of permissiveness is over." On the following day, Nixon would order the mining of Haiphong harbor and the total embargo of North Vietnam, accelerating the war.

As a response, the company staged "The Plague" scene from *Mysteries* at the ITT building on Park Avenue, where thousands of people rallied against the war. A few days later, The Living Theatre was at the United Nations with the Vietnam Veterans against the War, confronted by construction workers in hardhats throwing bottles and stones. In Alabama, there had been an attempted assassination of George Wallace. It was a moment of particular national turbulence with hundreds of demonstrations all over the country. A bomb was found in a ladies' room in the Pentagon in Washington, D.C., and William Sloane Coffin of Yale and the pediatrician Benjamin Spock were arrested at a rally.

Abbie Hoffman and Jerry Rubin attended a company meeting with the intention of persuading them to come to Miami in support of Senator George McGovern who was running against Richard Nixon. Judith and Julian opposed the invitation, arguing that the reforms promised by McGovern were not revolutionary changes and electoral politics would not, for example, end the economic exploitation of the third world. Before any company decision was reached, Judith and Julian flew to Toledo, Ohio, for another lecture, and then to Goddard College in Vermont to lecture and visit Peter Schumann's Bread and Puppet Theatre, one of the most committed theatrical groups on the left.

At the end of May, the interview for *Rolling Stone* appeared and *The Enormous Despair,* Judith's diary account of the American tour of 1968–69, was published by Random House. Judith's title was drawn from the letter Martin Buber had sent her in 1961, rejecting the idea of the General Strike for Peace because of his fear of failure. Now, a decade later, Buber's fear had a different flavor. There were those who called Judith and Julian counterrevolutionary and even reactionary because of their unswerving pacifism and their insistence that violence only played into the hands of central authority.

Liberal politics traditionally absorbed and co-opted radical energies, Julian believed, vitiating the prospect for change. In a large sense, he realized that he represented a crucial aspect of this problem, living with the contradiction of creating an antibourgeois morality when his own conditioning was thoroughly bourgeois. Although he had always been a "traitor to his class," he had been impelled to continue because "I have seen the bird of paradise flying, like summer, heard her singing her fabled song beginning 'The best government is no government. Moult, moult.'"

In the middle of June, poet Ed Sanders visited the company on his way to Miami. Sanders agreed that McGovern was only a political turnip, and he sympathized with the company decision not to accompany him because there seemed no valid act for them to perform. Instead of going to Miami, the company moved a few blocks away to 131 St. Felix Street at the end of June. In a poor neighborhood in the process of gentrification, the new house faced the backstage entrance of the Brooklyn Academy of Music. Harvey Lichenstein, director of the Brooklyn Academy, gave Judith and Julian a space in which to work. In the new house, Bill Shari hung a black flag from his window, and at meetings, the company continued to explore and discuss the myths preventing liberation surrounding property, money, and the idea of the state.

Early in July, Judith and Julian heard from Garrick that the gathering of the clans he had been planning for over a year was taking shape and culminating on 4 July near the headwaters of the Colorado River. Conceived of as another Woodstock, the Rainbow Family of Living Light attracted some 200,000 visitors, primarily by word of mouth and in spite of mass arrests of longhairs and roads barricaded by the Colorado State Police. To discourage the event, the forest service had closed for repairs every campground for fifty miles around, and the State of Colorado called up five thousand National Guard for maneuvers. Although the event was intended as a Dionysian celebration, it was also a test of federal prohibition of the right of assembly on public land. The event would be repeated every summer in the future—its free spirit of celebration a consequence of the anarchism Judith and Julian had always advocated—even though the Rainbow tribe was constantly harassed by government authorities.

In the beginning of August, Judith heard from Paul Goodman, now sixty years old and recovering from a heart attack in New Hampshire. Goodman had read *The Enormous Despair* and was ready to comment on it. The book made him realize that The Living Theatre had made "a fetish of the word 'revolution' which connotes a total systematic change—and who needs it?" Life should be spent doing what is worthwhile, he wrote, and what could be done to one's best capacity. Political organization was necessary only as a final resort and only to prevent authority from interfering with life. It was the last bit of advice Judith would receive from her old friend and therapist because a few days later she heard that he had died.

59. Revolutionaries between Revolutions

Julian and Judith flew to San Francisco at the end of August, staying in Ferlinghetti's City Lights office to read the galleys of *The Life of the Theatre* and to deliver a lecture to fifteen hundred schoolteachers at the American Theatre Association convention in the grand ballroom of the Hilton Hotel. Judith visited with Carl Einhorn, feeling as she had in the past, bruised by the encounter. With Julian at the convention, she saw Zé Celso, full of comradeship and affection. Celso was showing a film of Oficina performing ritual theatre in Brazilian villages where they had appeared unannounced and without costumes in an extension of what The Living Theatre had done in the *favelas.*

Returning to Brooklyn in September, Judith and Julian introduced the company to Meyerhold's *Biomechanics,* studying photographs of the exercises he taught that had been collected by Lee Strasberg in the 1930s, one of the few reminders of the great Russian constructivist director. The company was now augmented by Rufus Collins, Steve Thompson, Echnaton, Mel Clay, and Pierre Biner—all former members who had rejoined.

Zé Celso showed up with a young Brazilian companion who one night made ardent love to Judith. Most of all, Celso wanted to meet Allen Ginsberg, so Julian and Judith brought him to Ginsberg's flat where they spoke about waning sexual drives till four in the morning while poet Gregory Corso slept peacefully on a mat.

In his workbook later that night, Julian complained that at forty-seven, the inhibitions that had plagued him all of his life had prevented hundreds of potential sexual encounters. He declared himself a "sexual anarchist" to work against such inhibitions. Bleary, the next day, Judith and Julian were at a peace rally in Sheep Meadow, where they saw Ginsberg wearing a T-shirt with the Vietnamese death toll enumerated on it.

In a well-meaning but confused review of *The Enormous Despair* in the *New York Times* at the end of October, Tennessee Williams's friend Dotson Rader lamented that the movement was dead. "The hardest thing of all," Julian commented, "was to be a revolutionary between revolutions." Julian felt no relief with the appearance of *The Life of the Theatre,* the book he had worked on for so long. Edgy, he was disturbed by the fact that even with a fairly strenuous lecturing schedule, he and Judith had failed to earn enough money to sustain the company.

In addition, they felt harried, under pressure to move their group to create further installments of *The Legacy of Cain.* "It is as if we work under the lash," Judith remarked in her *Diary*. "Julian and I feel the pressure of time and life's brevity to a point of hysteria." Julian's book had been subtitled, perhaps clumsily, "The Relation of the Artist to the Struggle of the People." At this time, he felt that his every moment had to be spent working for a revolutionary cause that exposed the falseness of an authoritarian position based on violence, and a competitive system fostering greed and an accumulation of wealth that only polluted the planet. Every member of the St. Felix Street commune fervently shared this attitude, and daily meetings would involve political discussions and inquiries that would last for five or six hours.

Some of this buoyant energy was momentarily deflated on 7 November 1972 when Richard Nixon was reelected to the presidency. The wake for the radicals was at a party at Jerry Rubin's Prince Street loft which Judith and Julian attended along with Ginsberg, Abbie Hoffman, Ed Sanders, attorney William Kunstler, peace activist David Dellinger, John Lennon, and Yoko Ono.

Lennon came in raving drunk and howling, carrying a bottle of tequila. Staggering, Lennon was steered into Rubin's bedroom by Yoko wearing an oversized brown leather coat and a big hat on which was fastened a sheriff's badge. Dropping on Rubin's waterbed, Lennon embraced Rubin, declaring he expected Rubin and Hoffman "to lead us all to kingdom come." In a stuporous rage, Lennon began quoting from Mao's "Little Red Book," drunkenly threatening to join the Weathermen and shoot a policeman. Cursing, crying out that he felt hopeless and useless, Lennon told Julian that he only wanted to share a vision of possibility, that he wanted to be converted, that he wanted to believe in change and be convinced of its future. His voice, however, was full of anger and scorn. In no shape to listen to the patient explanations offered by Julian and Judith, Lennon was drunk and high on cocaine. He asked Judith what her anarchist theories would mean to him if he was only a potato farmer. Suddenly, in a bizarre moment that could have occurred in a play by Eugene O'Neill, he shouted at Judith that he wanted "to cut you with a knife!" The violence of his assertion was piercing, and coming after her experience with

Osvaldo in Brazil, it was as if he had seen into some hidden psychic space.

A few nights later, at the Alternate University in the East Village, Murray Bookchin in a lecture confirmed Lennon's despair over the possibility that there would be neither revolution nor significant change in their lifetimes. The establishment had the compelling argument, Bookchin suggested, that most Americans led better lives than leftists in China, Cuba, or Chile. Marxism, Bookchin observed somewhat prophetically, was in a deep crisis that Marxists refused to recognize. Bookchin's regular lectures became a forum for The Living Theatre during the winter of 1972–73.

Late that November, Judith and Julian spoke at the Hartford Atheneum. Their talk was attended by a recent Yale graduate named Hanon Reznikov. Six foot three, with a narrow waist, a trimmed beard, and a face that Julian thought could have been drawn by Albrecht Dürer, Reznikov had seen *Mysteries* and *Paradise Now* in the fall of 1968 as part of the last all-male freshman class at Yale. Raised in Brooklyn, he was a scholarship student majoring in molecular biophysics. He was immediately drawn to the activism of the group and stunned by the signals of sexual boldness he felt in the company. He shifted his major to drama, took courses with Brustein, Richard Gilman, and Stanley Kaufman, and participated fully in the political intensities of university life at that time. In the spring of 1970, he had watched the Ericka Huggins and Bobby Seale Black Panther trial in New Haven, a historical moment when some of his friends chose to become Weathermen.

Graduating from Yale, he had been living in New Haven, acting at the Long Wharf Theatre, and directing plays. Like many members of his generation, he used psychedelics as a means of exploring alternatives to a cultural situation seemingly frozen in conservatism. A month before Judith and Julian's Hartford talk, he had purchased *The Life of the Theatre,* which convinced him of the depth of the company's commitment, something he felt when he had first seen The Living Theatre. After the talk, he spoke with

Julian and Judith, who invited him to Brooklyn. A month later, he was living in the St. Felix Street house and had become Judith's lover.

Judith had long been drawn to younger men, and all of her lovers since Carl Einhorn had been at least a decade her junior. Now she was forty-seven, and Hanon was half her age, a considerable difference. Furthermore, the relationship was complicated by the active participation of Julian, who now chose to act out a subtle rivalry with Judith that had first manifested itself in the affair with Tobi Edelman twenty years earlier. With a playful aggressiveness, Julian pursued his wife's lover, who thought of himself as pansexual and understood relations with other men as part of the revolutionary discovery of the moment.

Recognizing Hanon's ability to write as well as act, Julian realized how valuable a contribution the young man might be able to make and immediately got him to work on the *Strike Support Oratorium*. Julian had been in touch with Cesar Chavez, whose United Farm Workers were organizing a nationwide boycott of grapes and lettuce. Designed to assist Chavez's strike, the *Strike Support Oratorium* began with a biomechanical processional toward a supermarket, the chanting and singing actors in green and purple (for the lettuce and grapes) mounted on each other's shoulders, using megaphones, choreographed to move together in perfect synchronicity.

In the spring and summer of 1973, Hanon began performing in *Seven Meditations on Political Sadomasochism*. In Brazil, Julian had entered a line from the French anarchist Proudhon in his workbook—"toujours l'esclave a singé son maître" (the slave has always aped his master)—which would become a motivating principle of the play. Their angriest, most agitated and propagandistic play, *Seven Meditations* was an anarchist black mass. In the tradition of *The Brig*, it dramatized the horrible conditions faced by political prisoners and was written in response to the appeal to publicize their plight made by some of the company's fellow prisoners in the DOPS prison in Belo Horizonte.

In *Seven Meditations*, the spectators sat on the floor in a circle around performers dressed in black or red street clothing. Each sequence of the play—on sexuality, on authority, on property, on money, on violence, on death, and on revolution, the seven categories of *The Legacy of Cain*—was preceded by a chant continuing throughout the play that members of the company had learned from the Gnaoua musicians in Morocco. Accompanying the chant was a brief statement; for example, in the first sequence, on sexual dominance, submission, and repression. As the statement was recited, actors would dramatize one of its aspects in a highly ritualized manner. Some of the illustrations were quite graphic and powerful. In the sequence on property, for example, slaves were chained and dragged around the circle by their masters. In the sequence on violence, a victim was hung upside down from a pole while wires from an ITT field telephone generator were pushed inside the anus in simulation of the actual torturers in Brazil. As the victim screamed in agony, a fact sheet from Amnesty International was read aloud.

The reliance on classic or modern texts, from Eldridge Cleaver's *Soul on Ice* or Bakunin, gives the play an overly tendentious and monotonous character. This would especially appeal to an audience which fully shared the company's anarchist assumptions and sympathies, and would sometimes infuriate others. In the sequence on money, for example, part of the text is drawn from Bakunin's argument that all wage labor was forced and therefore tantamount to what he called wage slavery. In the final meditation, where the audience was able to participate in political discussion, audience members were often vehement about their relation or dependence on the wage system.

The play's heavy emphasis on words was in a way a continuation of the company's attention to text, what they called "obedience to the text," in spite of the myth of spontaneity that had made The Living Theatre famous. Composed entirely of these texts, most twenty-five to a hundred words in length, the play has a didactic and rhetorical weight that sometimes seems to support Eric Bentley's conclusion, stated when they were at

Yale in 1968, that The Living Theatre was a bunch of political simpletons. Nevertheless, the play was extremely popular in Europe
throughout the 1970s and was performed more than three hundred times.

60. The Lucha and Joy Cells

We are "lying fallow," Julian wrote in his workbook in
the spring of 1973, "using the time to induce fertility.
We are passing out of the dry salvages, out of the wet Sargasso
into lush isles." The company had performed *Seven Meditations*
at the University of North Carolina in April, and in May, they
staged it again as part of a two-day anarchist conference at
Hunter College in New York.

The play elicited many enthusiastic comments, Julian noted,
but the conference was dominated by a passionate lunatic fringe
who did not understand how to organize a movement among the
people. He was no longer sure that theatre was a viable way, and
he admitted that both he and Judith were concerned about that
realization: "We don't want to do plays anymore, and yet we don't
know how else to proceed."

Julian had been assembling the text for *Seven Meditations* all
spring, and with Judith, Hanon, and the company, preparing *The
Money Tower,* another part of *The Legacy of Cain* cycle. *The Money
Tower* was influenced by the Russian poet Vladimir Mayakovski
and was designed as a form of *ballet mécanique* according to the
principles of the Russian constructivist Meyerhold. In 1931,
Meyerhold had declared that "the actor embodied a new man,
freed from the power of an inert, immovable environment and full

of that vital energy which makes it possible to calculate with utmost precision his every gesture or movement, and to build anew the house of the world."

In the backyard of the house on St. Felix Street, Julian and Bill Shari had built a five-story, forty-foot set made of scaffolding in the form of a tower, with a moving elevator topped by a huge, green neon dollar sign to illustrate the clashes of the class system. At the top level was a plexiglass representation of the World Bank with Hanon and Mary Mary in silver jumpsuits playing the masters of capital. At the bottom were ten miners whose raw material was lifted by the elevator to a blast furnace where eight steel workers turned it into metal, then passed their materials up to the six actors representing the management class on the third level where it became money. Above them, on the fourth level, were four actors with puppets representing the military, police, judges, and clerics. The biomechanical movement that Meyerhold had devised depended on an exact timing that suggested the movement of machines—as in Chaplin's *Modern Times* or Fritz Lang's *Metropolis*—and to synchronize the actors' movements with the elevator, the flow of money with spoken or chanted texts, a metronome was used in rehearsals.

The conflict in the play occurs when the banking class, facing inflation, demands lower wages, longer hours, and layoffs. After a worker is accidentally killed in the elevator, a strike and rebellion ensue; and police intervention is prevented by the introduction of the idea of an anarchistic society functioning without money. This transformation would result from a general strike, which was difficult to dramatize but suggested by the rhythmical dismantling of the tower at the end of the play, a narrative deus ex machina that would certainly prove unconvincing to the moneyed classes, though workers usually admired the skill that was demonstrated.

Near the end of the play, one of the actors makes a brief speech about how The Living Theatre has joined the Theatre Workers Job Branch number 630, an arm of the Industrial Workers of the World (IWW). Formed at the beginning of the century, the IWW had allied itself with the unemployed and set out to eliminate management as a class in order to empower workers. Standing for the autonomy of the worker, the IWW position was the workers could run plants better than middle management and their bosses. While, during the course of the century, the IWW had gradually lost the influence it had wielded during the First World War, it searched for ways to reinterpret the machinery of industrial governance and community action, and the organization of food and housing cooperatives, the models proposed by the play. Many in the audience associated the IWW with a solidarity that may have once existed among the working classes—as evidenced in Steinbeck's *Grapes of Wrath*—but that now seemed more a utopian guideline than a practical step that could be realized on a large scale.

During the summer of 1973, The Living Theatre rehearsed *The Money Tower* at the Brooklyn Academy of Music and performed *Seven Meditations* at the Peace Church on Washington Square in Greenwich Village, at Columbia University, and at the State University in Buffalo. In October, they invented a play composed of the *Strike Support Oratorium* and the "Apokatastasis" scene from *Paradise Now*. This new work was performed once a week in front of the offices of the national Chilean airline on Fifth Avenue in Manhattan to protest the overthrow of Salvador Allende and, after Cambodia was invaded later that fall by American troops, in Federal Plaza in downtown Manhattan.

These performances, however, did not produce sufficient income to support the St. Felix Street commune. Julian was faced with the reality of bills to pay. Financial circumstances had been alleviated by a five-thousand-dollar grant from the National Endowment for the Arts and by Roy Harris, an actor in the company, who decided to contribute $20,000 of his inheritance to The Living Theatre. The contribution was a sign of the zeal of the company and how seriously its members regarded the importance of taking art out of the museums of culture and into the streets.

Roy Harris's gift saw the company through the winter of 1974 and helped create the set of *The Money Tower*. When Julian received word that The Living Theatre had been awarded a Mellon grant to perform for an extended period in Pittsburgh, the news intensified the sense of mission that had unified the company during the more than five hundred ideological discussions and rehearsals which led to the creation of *The Money Tower.* One index of this intensity was the *Red Book,* a large journal into which Julian regularly transcribed the ideological propositions as they developed from 1971 through 1974. At the same time, the marathon discussions had contributed to a growing tension among some of the members of the group—Roy Harris and Brigit Knabe among others—who were tired of the incessant talking and wanted to involve themselves in more direct political action.

In the spring of 1974, the company moved to a rambling former inn overlooking Lake Champlain at Mount Philo, in Charlotte, Vermont, to continue rehearsing *The Money Tower,* where they remained through the fall. At Mount Philo, the emotions among Judith, Hanon, and Julian intensified, and Julian kept a running account of the heated passions of their lovemaking—in the shower, on a beach with Judith watching—in a small, red journal. For Julian, Hanon was "the lodestar of my life," an incarnation of physical beauty, a Michelangelesque figure of grace and intelligence. For the first time in his life, Julian found himself full of a charged sexual initiative. Although Julian approximated that he had had about eighty lovers before Hanon, none of them had flowered into a sustained relationship. In his sexual diary, Julian admitted he had never previously been the real object of another's physical desire, even though he knew that for Hanon he was only a game and Hanon really only "burned for Judith."

After Thanksgiving, the company transported the set of *The Money Tower* to Pittsburgh to begin their Mellon residency. Pittsburgh was a steel town producing one fifth of the nation's steel, although the world market for this material was shrinking, and foreign competitors with more sophisticated technology and lower labor costs were capturing an increasing share of the world's market. Intending to reach the steelworkers, they were aware that they would be unable to perform the play—which had an outdoor set—until warmer weather began.

Judith and Julian rented two houses on the North Side of Pittsburgh. One, in a black ghetto on Bidwell Street, was occupied by what was called the Lucha (Spanish for "struggle") cell, the more hard-core militants in the company who favored a social realist approach in their theatre. The second, near North Park, in a more gentrified area a few blocks away, was a former day-care center occupied by Judith, Julian, and Hanon and what was called the Joy cell.

Early in December 1974, the growing division between the Lucha and Joy cells erupted, and many meetings were ravaged by accusations and screaming. The tension between the two groups was manifested in casting for *The Money Tower* as the Lucha group insisted on taking the roles of the workers on the lower levels of the scaffolding, leaving the upper levels to the Joy cell. Many of the Lucha members had been disillusioned by pacifism and the failure of the movement of the late 1960s to change anything in America; and they were inclined now more than ever to support armed struggle. Some had become adherents of the Progressive Labor party, a hard-core Maoist organization of leftist zealots.

As in Morocco, this group began to contest Judith and Julian's leadership. With an insistent sense of what now is called "political correctness," they insisted on collective decisions, even on the most minute matters of stagecraft. Some of the struggle for creative control may have also been caused by jealousy of Hanon Reznikov's increasing contribution to the writing and directing.

When the Lucha group decided to separate from The Living Theatre, the Joy cell continued the work of the Campaign. The company felt that first they had to reconnoiter unfamiliar territory, and a group of actors with video cameras began interviewing steelworkers and coalminers, as well as workers at Gulf Oil, Alcoa, and Westinghouse. The great fear of the workers, they soon learned, was unemployment as the Pittsburgh area was in the process of losing over 100,000 jobs, mostly in steel and coal.

Throughout the winter of 1975, company members rehearsed *The Money Tower* and created another new work called

Six Public Acts. As in Brazil, company members made inroads into the community as a means of research. The Joy cell established a neighborhood food cooperative. Some of the actors worked with sports clubs, others in schools, and there were several workshops at Carnegie-Mellon University. Judith and Tom Walker joined the neighborhood citizens' police committee. Judith had always been interested in the possibilities of reaching police, whom she regarded as fellow workers, and had opposed those who regarded them as "pigs" since the Democratic Convention in 1968.

The $22,000 Julian had received from the Mellon grant, which he had stretched out over a year to support a group of over thirty people, was running out with no promise of renewal. The winter of 1975 was unusually cold, and there was little heat for long periods because gas bills had not been paid. Julian managed, once again, to keep things afloat by securing loans and gifts from friends, but things looked precarious.

At the end of April, the company performed *Seven Meditations* in Pittsburgh and early in May unveiled *Six Public Acts,* which moved through the city like a medieval mystery play. Since the play was performed in seven different public spaces in Pittsburgh, the audience was able to move in a processional from site to site following an actor carrying a plexiglass sign with the word MURDER written horizontally while actors acrostically painted in the names of the various sections—money, love, property—of *The Legacy of Cain* cycle. Another part of *The Legacy of Cain* series, *Six Public Acts* presented the consequences of a loss of freedom through bondage to a violent culture, but it was much less confrontational than *Paradise Now.*

At a Bell Telephone office, the first site, the implications of Cain's murder of his brother, Abel, were explored. In a Breughelesque mood, performers enacted the agony of death in the manner of "The Plague" ritual in *Mysteries* while other performers lined up the shoes of the victims before the 150 spectators. At a public flagpole representing the state, each performer, and many spectators, pricked a finger and smeared blood on the flagpole, dedicating their drop of blood to some cause. In front of the Mellon Bank, a pharaoh and his consort were transformed into a golden calf. Money was burned, and fake bills distributed, bearing the motto "This note legalizes the exploitation of labor." In front of a high-rise apartment building, a jail structure was erected. At a police station, bread and roses were left for police. Finally, the sixth act occurred in a park where actors tied each other up while reciting a love poem to illustrate the master-slave relationship in love.

During the summer of 1975, the Joy cell continued rehearsing *Six Public Acts* and also grew corn, tomatoes, and green vegetables in the front and back yards of its house. The vegetable garden was unfenced so that any hungry person could take freely from it, but more important it was intended as a demonstration of what could be done even in a city.

Julian had scheduled a series of performances in September for the Three Rivers Festival under the terms of the Mellon grant, but by that time, the festival administrators were horrified by the company. When it rained on the day of their performance, the administrators threatened to break their contract because of an "act of god." In order to get paid, the company performed in the pouring rain without an audience.

Not discouraged by what had happened at Three Rivers, the company erected *The Money Tower* at a railroad crossing outside the Homestead Steel plant, and in six other locations in Pittsburgh, including the Jones and Laughlin steel mill. The company regarded the steelworkers as its genuine audience. In front of the U.S. Steel Building, the entire company was arrested when local police believed one of the actors was using a real gun. There were four performances of *Six Public Acts* and three of *Seven Meditations*. Except for one of these performances which was a benefit, the others were all free in fulfillment of the terms of the Mellon grant.

By then, the company had exhausted its financial resources. When they received an invitation to perform in the Venice Biennale, at the Odin Theatre in Denmark, and at the Sigma Festival in Bordeaux, the Joy cell departed for Europe on the *Queen Elizabeth* at the end of September.

61. The Years of Lead

The Living Theatre would remain in Europe for the next seven years. For much of that time, the company was centered in Italy, which was in a volatile political state as its Communist party—progressive and culturally oriented—assumed considerable regional and municipal power. This period was known in Italy as the "years of lead" because of terrorism from the right and left, with the Socialists in office and anarchist centers of influence throughout Italy.

In the beginning of 1976, The Living Theatre was invited to Reggio Emilia by local anarchist groups. Living in cheap hotels and pensiones, and using local issues, they performed their *Strike Support Oratorium* at a factory occupied by workers. Since all performances in Europe would be in the language of the host country, a good part of their time was spent in language study. By this time, several young European actors had joined the company.

Before leaving Reggio Emilia, Judith and Julian heard that they had been given the Lifetime Achievement Award from the *Village Voice* in New York City. There was also some disquieting news: Jim Tiroff, a former member of the company, had died of a heroin overdose; Jimmy Anderson had been murdered on Fourth Street in Greenwich Village by a crazed cocaine dealer; and Warren Finnerty had dropped dead in the lobby of St. Vincent's Hospital in the same neighborhood. Before their deaths, Anderson had left the company to organize food cooperatives, and Finnerty had been living in a tenement in Hell's Kitchen in a state of poverty and alcoholic dejection after making a name for himself in Hollywood with parts in films like *Easy Rider, Murder Inc.,* and *The Pawnbroker.* It seemed as if many of the first generation of Living Theatre performers were exiting the scene abruptly.

During the winter of 1976, the company spent a week in Florence at the Pitti Palace performing *Seven Meditations,* which they staged another dozen times in Turin, and then again in Milan for two weeks. They were given a residency that spring in the town of Superga, overlooking Turin, to create an Italian version of *The Money Tower.*

In June, in Bologna, they performed scenes from *Six Public Acts* in piazzas for workers and on a strip of lawn in front of an incineration plant with three giant furnaces belching black, odiferous smoke. They were harassed by priests in Cosenza and Genoa who would not permit them to perform in front of their churches, charging that The Living Theatre was desecrating holy ground. There was further harassment when a Korean member of the group who refused to present identification to the police was arrested and then beaten in jail.

In the beginning of July, the company was in Sicily at the Taormino Festival. In the Teatro Antico, one of the most majestic theatre locations in all of Europe, facing the sea and Mount Etna, they performed *Seven Meditations* and *The Money Tower* for audiences of up to seven thousand people. For the rest of the month, they balanced their time between schools, factories, unions, and performed without charge in the streets. Such choices meant a sacrifice of income and an increase in vulnerability. Everywhere in Italy, there were interviews with magazines and press conferences at which they would invariably be asked whether their work was not too intellectual for people in the street. Judith observed that the problem existed only among intellectual journalists and never among the people in the streets.

Some members of the company took a few weeks off during August. They had performed or conducted workshops almost daily since arriving in Europe, and Julian complained that "my whole life, not enough time, not enough sleep." He had abandoned his playful pursuit of Hanon, who was now exclusively Judith's lover, and for the first time formed an enduring relationship with a man. José Carlos Temple Troya, who now called himself Ilion Troya, had rejoined the troupe in Pittsburgh, and in Europe became Julian's lover.

Judith and Julian and other members of the company participated in a series of peace marches at military bases across the island of Sardinia, including a demonstration at La Maddalena, where atomic submarines were stationed. Often, they would perform without charge at midnight for the marchers, recruiting additional cast members from their audience. By the end of the summer, Julian realized that the company was broke again and that a third of its members were not planning to rejoin them.

Throughout Italy in 1976, the company performed in psychiatric hospitals. In such facilities, they could not be accused of being too intellectual as they relied on the patients' responses, using poetry and physical expression to encourage participation, and songs and dances to help the patients release blocked senses and feeling. These workshops ended by taking patients out of the hospital grounds singing through the streets "Essere libero significa essere libero dalla paura" (to be free is to be free from fear). Their purpose, Julian observed, was to create an ecstasy strong enough to rupture the sense of "institutional doom" that pervaded such places.

In each hospital, they visited patients' quarters and sometimes ate with them. At the psychiatric hospital in Cogoleto outside Genoa, for example, after creating a play about liberation, they shared a meal on metal plates with a group of frightened, shabby, gnarled men who seemed molded in their resignation by tranquilizers. As a result of such visits, reaching out with hands and eyes, Judith and Julian exposed themselves to a view of suffering and confinement they had only experienced in jails.

In the fall of 1976, the company spent the month of September in Cosenza performing *Six Public Acts* on the streets and for a much larger audience on Italian television. They then went to Naples and toured a half-dozen surrounding, smaller towns. At the end of October, they went to Genoa, where they performed *The Money Tower* for large audiences and decided to store its cumbersome set.

All through November and December, they were in small Italian towns, performing, giving workshops, meeting with local anarchists, and speaking on radio stations. The company had also created a number of short agitprop plays such as *Why Are We Afraid of Sexual Freedom?*, in which there was a provocative display of various sexual positions; *Is There Something Wrong with the Way We Work?*, and *Brothers, Don't Shoot!* An extension of *The Legacy of Cain* cycle, these were performed on the streets without charge, an important part of what they called "the Campaign." By Christmas, however, funds were so scarce that members of the company were living with friends in Naples, and a collective decision was reached to return to the proscenium stage as a survival strategy.

To raise money, Julian planned a tour which began in Brussels, and then took the company to twelve cities in Spain in February and March of 1977. Even though Franco had died two years earlier, *Seven Meditations* still had to be approved by a board of censors in Barcelona. On the company's first night in Barcelona, an audience of fifteen hundred people, Julian observed, were mostly disconcerted because they came to see avant-garde theatre and got avant-garde politics instead. Some audiences were quite excited by what they saw, and in Madrid, spectators leaped on the stage to stop the torture scene in *Seven Meditations*. In Majorca, during a performance of *Seven Meditations*, Julian's hotel room was ransacked by thieves who stole six thousand dollars and defaced the room with swastikas.

The loss of money was more than compensated for by the large crowds they had entertained throughout Spain and Portugal, and by a performance of *Six Public Acts* for Swiss television. One hour of the three-hour performance was cut by censors who approved of nuclear power plants but were afraid of erotic processions, Julian noted. In Lausanne, in the middle of May, after a performance of *Seven Meditations*, about a thousand people with masks and painted faces occupied the casino with music and dancing; but the occupation only lasted one night. Most of the Swiss in Geneva and Basel were restrained and complacent, Julian thought. They paid high admission prices and tolerated *Seven Meditations* like bad-tasting medicine.

62. *Prometheus*

In the summer of 1977, with some of the money accumulated during the tour, Julian rented two large apartments, a ten-minutes' walk from each other, near the Stazione Termini in Rome. With Hanon, he was preparing *Prometheus at the Winter Palace,* another exploration of the ways that people have been bound by social forms. He remembered that in high school his English teacher had declared that Joyce modeled his life on Dante's and Thomas Mann, on Goethe's. When the teacher asked Julian for his model, his reply had been Prometheus, surely a curious though revealing reply.

At the beginning of *Prometheus,* the audience discovers the actors in their seats tied with ropes. Action starts when the actors are untied. With a Cocteau-inspired dreaminess, the first act retells the classical myth of Prometheus, played by Hanon, who anarchistically steals the fire and is bound on a rock by Zeus, the king of the gods, played by Julian. The implications of the theft are discussed by seminude mythical figures like Orpheus, Pandora, and devout Io, pursued by the Furies and played by Judith. With the kind of declamatory energy used in *Paradise Now,* Aristotle, Pythagoras, and a chorus of doctors explore the principles of order violated by Prometheus.

The style shifts to epic realism in the second act which is set during the Russian Revolution. Zeus becomes Lenin; Io, the anarchist Emma Goldman; Prometheus, her consort, Alexander Berkman; Pandora, the dancer Isadora Duncan; and Orpheus, the poet Mayakovski. In a long monologue, Julian as Lenin re-creates the history of the Revolution, accounting for the imprisonment of the anarchists by arguing that "free speech is a bourgeois luxury . . . a tool of reaction."

Then Lenin explains that in the next act of the play, volunteers from the audience will be asked to stage the storming of the Winter Palace, a central event during the Revolution that led to Lenin's usurpation of absolute power. With the audience volunteers divided into groups—four bolsheviks, a dozen anarchists, four Tolstoyan pacifists, four terrorists, five imprisoned women, some actors in Mayakovski's troupe, and a group of Red Army and White Guard soldiers—each group rehearses with a Living Theatre actor while Lenin reveals the strategy for seizing the palace. Four red ribbons stretching across the stage indicate the entrances to the palace. Each time the volunteers charge, another ribbon is cut until the people occupy the palace and sing the "Internationale."

The play continues with the disenchantment of Emma Goldman and Berkman, who meet with Lenin. There is a gymnastic, biomechanical scene from Mayakovski's *Moscow Is Burning,* which ends abruptly when the disillusioned Mayakovski kills himself. When Lenin dies, he is lifted to the top of a pyramid as the sign of hierarchical oppression, and at his funeral, the anarchist Prince Kropotkin criticizes his ruthlessness.

When the lights go on for the third act, the entire company is glowing in midair in bright rainbow colors, hanging motionless by their arms and legs from the metal-pipe scaffolding which is Prometheus's crag. It is a stark, eerie moment. Orpheus announces that the scene is "Prometheus Unbound," which will be played out with a silent vigil at a prison in the name of the end of all punishment. As in *Paradise Now,* members of the audience have been transformed into actors and led out into the streets.

The tension between oppressive forces and freedom illustrated in the first two acts may be resolved in the minds of some members of the audience as they are brought to face the brick wall of the nearest prison. It is a nonviolent action, not an insurrectionary breaching of the wall, but a meditative confrontation with the strength of the state.

Prometheus rehearsals kept the company busy during the summer of 1977. There were several short pieces created by members of the company, including a short street play called *Can I Kill You?* which they played in the nude at a late July festival organized by Italian radicals and anarchists for ecological balance and against nuclear energy plants. Early in September, Judith, Julian, and Hanon attended the Italian anarchists' annual congress at Carrara, and Julian spoke about nonviolence to a few hundred anarchists who seemed to endorse violence as a necessary tactic.

The question of violence seemed even more urgent when, in mid-October, the company interrupted its *Prometheus* rehearsals to go to Munich to perform *Seven Meditations* in German in an atmosphere of tension and fear. Radical German leftists had kidnaped a former Nazi official—whom they would subsequently murder—and were bargaining for his exchange for prisoners who belonged to the RAF, the Rote Armee Faction, held in the Stammheim Prison. In the Munich performances of *Seven Meditations,* this prison was identified by Julian as a place where "white" torture—the perpetual use of glaring white lights—was employed. In October 1977, five of the RAF prisoners died under mysterious circumstances which most movement people believed was murder but which some suspected were coordinated suicides in the hope of provoking revolution. On 25 October, four days after the final performance of *Seven Meditations,* Julian was arrested and charged with "defamation" of the state and questioned for nine hours. He was only released when a crowd of angry Germans assembled outside the police station and chanted, "Living! Living! Living!" "What is important," Julian declared, "is that in the silence we have spoken."

Back in Rome in November, the company resumed rehearsing *Prometheus*. R. D. Laing and Daniel Cohn-Bendit visited. There were constant meetings with anarchist groups concerned with the European specters of terrorism and counterterrorism, highlighted by the kidnaping and murder of Italian Prime Minister Aldo Moro in the spring of 1978. Judith and Julian refused to swerve from their position on nonviolence, especially when they met Red Brigade members who claimed that they had been inspired by The Living Theatre though they felt the actors were wrong about shunning violence. At the same time, Judith and Julian supported the necessity of revolutionary change and advertised that they were ready to assemble the company to create plays around issues that could publicize worthy causes, as they did in Naples for a group of unemployed workers and in Turin for a group called Soldiers for a Democratic Army.

At the end of January 1978, the company left on tour again, this time beginning with a lucrative engagement to perform *Seven Meditations* at Belfort in French. Crossing borders, they were welcomed to Frankfurt by Daniel Cohn-Bendit, where they gave a series of workshops and another five performances of *Seven Meditations* in German in a jammed theatre to discouraged audiences, Julian felt, of young people with a gloomy outlook.

In Rome in February and March, the company continued rehearsing *Prometheus*, and in April in Florence, they performed *Seven Meditations* in Italian for the first time for an audience of twenty-five hundred people at the Palazzo de Exposizione. Throughout the spring and summer, the company continued to work on *Prometheus*, giving workshops, visiting the *manicomi* (the mental hospitals) and performing their street plays for special occasions.

At the end of September, in Prato, they opened *Prometheus*, and at its second performance, the police refused to allow the final act, the prison vigil. In Rome, at the Teatro Argentina—the famous site of Mozart premieres—there were again problems with the police who apprehended the entire cast after the third performance and released them after identification procedures confirming that no member of the cast was wanted on criminal charges anywhere in Italy.

In November, they traveled to France and Belgium. The company was still "tripping from theatre to theatre and living in Volkswagen buses." They were poets "decoding utopia," Julian asserted in a poem. Behind in his payments as always and still trying to avoid taxes to a corrupt state, he was conscious of the "lebanese nut of cannabis secreted under my balls" as he crossed borders.

The effort to imagine, rehearse, and stage *Prometheus* had taken almost a year. The thirtieth anniversary of the company was celebrated for three days at the end of December in Milan at an homage featuring films of *The Brig* and *Paradise Now,* lectures and round-table discussions, radio and television broadcasts. Despite all the "slag heaps of decadence" Julian found in Europe, he felt at ease there. "I have," he wrote, "no desire to return to the arid land of the U.S.—the prospect is to me like going to jail."

63. Sleep and Dreams

In January 1979 in Rome, there was a wave of bombings set by right-wing sympathizers in theatres and a fire bombing in Feltrinelli's Bookstore. Thirty-six hours after Judith and Julian presented a clear statement of the anarchist-pacifist analysis of the situation on Radio Citta Futura, five women presenting a feminist program were shot and the station vandalized.

It was hoped that both *Seven Meditations* and *Prometheus* would clarify the dangerous polarization between left and right in Italy, and suggest nonviolent resolutions. The company was asked to perform these plays constantly through the winter and spring. In Ferrara that April, when a performance of *Prometheus* ended at a local jail where a large crowd chanted inflammatory slogans, The Living Theatre was denounced by local officials for obscenity and incitement to riot. The news was reported nationally and Julian, while encouraged to see that the protests were recognized, worried that future engagements could be threatened.

At the end of May the company was invited to give a series of workshops at a branch of the University of Paris at Vincennes, and Judith and Julian read their poems along with Allen Ginsberg at the American Artists' and Students' Center. One night they were invited to dinner by Michel Foucault, the French philosopher. Amiable but priestly and somber, Foucault served them a gourmet vegetarian dinner with whiskey, champagne, and marijuana in his high-rise apartment. Curious about their work, Foucault especially wanted to know about Brazil because he had just returned from there. Finally, Judith asked him about his expectations for the future and what one could hope for. Softly, he answered that he had no response. Later, at the elevator as Judith and Julian were leaving, he apologized for not answering, explaining that hope never comes when one searches for it, but it "springs up suddenly between your feet."

In July, the company presented seventeen performances of *Prometheus* at the Roundhouse Theatre in London despite negative reviews. Each night after the play, unhindered, they held vigils at the Holloway Prison for Women. Usually, after the vigils, members of the company would assemble for an ongoing party at R. D. Laing's house.

In the fall, the reviews for *Prometheus* in Greece were especially favorable, and the company toured there in October and November, alternating it with a revival of *Antigone* which was received with special enthusiasm. There was a similar reception for *Antigone* in Italy where they performed it through April.

Throughout the spring of 1980, while they were moving from city to city in Italy, the company was rehearsing its version of

Ernst Toller's *Masse Mensch* which they premiered in German at the Olympia Park in Munich at the end of May 1980. This performance was resisted by authorities in Munich who hated the play, partly because it was set there. In bilingual cities like Bolzano in northern Italy, the play would be done at seven in the evening in Italian and a few hours later in German. The company would later present versions of the play in Italian, French, Spanish, and English. This linguistic facility, unprecedented really in the history of theatre, had to influence the way in which members of the company saw the world and their place in it as international harbingers of peaceful, nonviolent revolution.

Toller had been involved in the establishment of the Bavarian Socialist Republic after the First World War when libertarians seized power in Munich in 1919 and held it for a few weeks until an army massacre. Written in jail, the play was about a middle-class revolutionary who stirs the people to begin a revolution for which they are unprepared. As the Nameless-One, Hanon brilliantly played the anonymous spokesman of a violent nihilism that precipitates disaster, raising the specter of how a revolutionary vision can lead to catastrophe.

In the fall, the company was invited by the Communist Student Union to spend a month in Poland. *The Life of the Theatre* had been reproduced in samizdat. Playing *Antigone* to standing-room audiences in Warsaw, Posnan, Lublin, and Kraców, Julian found the Poles reserved as if holding back. Interviewed on radio and television, Julian and Judith defiantly spoke about anarchism. In Kraców, they performed a version of the *Strike Support Oratorium* with students in an open courtyard under threat of arrest in support of workers in Gdansk whose Solidarity movement was gaining the strength that would, a decade later, represent the first crack in the Iron Curtain.

On a forty-eight hour transit visa in Prague, they staged a clandestine performance of *Antigone* behind the locked doors of a beer hall for an amazed audience of two hundred people who had been assembled through word of mouth. This audience constituted most of the government of the future "velvet revolution"—except for Václav Havel who was in jail—that would replace the Communists. Judith thought this was, perhaps, the most moving of any Living Theatre performance because the audience identified totally with Antigone's resistance. Afterward, most of the audience was questioned by police though no arrests were made.

The company continued to perform *Antigone* and *Masse Mensch* to highly receptive audiences through the summer of 1981, and, except for festivals in Spain, Switzerland, and Austria, they remained in Italy where by now they were a household word. The constant touring was wearying, however, and Julian was relieved when in the fall of 1981, he was contacted by Jack Lang, the Socialist minister of culture in France, who said he was interested in creating a permanent residency for them. Lang had seen the company perform *Frankenstein, The Maids,* and *Antigone.*

As a sign of his eagerness, Lang gave the company funds to create *The Yellow Methuselah,* a spectacle fusing elements of George Bernard Shaw's play on creative evolution, *Back to Methuselah,* and the cosmically surreal *The Yellow Sound* by the painter Wassily Kandinsky. The play was written and directed by Hanon, the first of his attempts to transform nontheatrical texts into plays. It had a set by Julian, featuring a 150-foot painting that moved on a crank mechanism and changed imperceptibly during the course of the performance. Julian designed 140 costumes, sewn by six of Valentino's seamstresses, and the company rehearsed the play in Rome in Cinecittà, where Mussolini had ordered the production of his fascist propaganda films. Playing Shaw, Julian interviewed members of the audience and used their taped responses, and Judith played the serpent in Eden and later Lilith.

Amnesty International in Paris asked the company and the Grateful Dead to play benefits of *Antigone, Masse Mensch,* and *The Yellow Methuselah* in France during the summer of 1982. Negotiations with Lang were continuing with the possibility that the company might get the Vieux Colombier in Paris where Artaud had performed. There was some opposition to using French tax dollars to support a company still considered American, though registered as a French association and with only a quarter of the actors American.

Performing in Paris at the end of July, Julian asked himself in his journal what he was most interested in saying. Underneath the appearance of things, he noted, there is a metaphysical reality, "and if we do not find out what it is we shall die." This "unknown bound thing, this recurrent mummy," revealed itself particularly in dreams, which Julian now intended to express in a play about sleep—the basis, he observed, for human imagination.

The company continued through the summer of 1982 to perform in France and at the famous Volkstheater in Vienna. Judith had learned that Grove Press had agreed to publish her early diaries, and she was occupied with further editing. Julian was writing down his dreams: in Stockholm at the end of August, he dreamed of a little blue pig being sacrificed by priests. In the dream, Julian disturbed the ceremony but realized that it would only continue later, a reflection of his ultimate ineffectiveness and impotence. He wondered whether the pig represented his own penis being cut off.

In the fall, Judith and Julian were in Amsterdam to read at the One World Poetry Festival along with Allen Ginsberg, Yevgeny Yevtushenko, Alex Trocchi, and Paul Bowles's protégé, Mohammed Mrabet. Julian read an imaginary conversation between Martin Buber, Brecht, and himself, and Judith from her book *Poems of a Wandering Jewess,* which had just been published by a small press in Paris.

Back in Rome at the end of October, Julian was wondering whether all drama had to be based on conflict and confrontation since *The Archeology of Sleep,* the play he was imagining, was constructed differently and intended to explore the natural anarchy of the human mind. In November, the company was invited by Jack Lang to come to Nantes for a residency to rehearse *The Yellow Methuselah* and *The Archeology of Sleep.*

By the end of January 1983, the company left the Rome apartments and relocated to a red and white brick former workers' hotel in Tharon Plage, a beach town outside Nantes. The thirty-six rooms were small and cold, and the company resumed its communal meals and meetings. Everyone was transcribing dreams and reading them aloud to each other. Members of the company were studying the scientific bases of sleep and biofeedback mechanisms. Julian, like the rest of the company, was preoccupied with his dreams. He was also rereading Freud's *Interpretation of Dreams,* impressed by the assertion that nothing in dreams is frivolous. In his workbook, Julian noted down a series of them which he realized could be projections of his own death.

In one, doctors were operating with the intention of choking their patient. He woke after the second dream in a sweat, feeling a "gritty malaise." The dream was of a man who had been hung being photographed in a dentist's chair when the photographer notices his eyes are beginning to flutter. In his workbook, Julian speculated that the dream meant he was being executed by the state which initially ignores the artist, then abuses him, then smothers him with honors. The photographer represented fame and the network of artists who could yet save him. A third dream was more disturbing. Exhausted, he had pulled over to the side of a highway and forgot which foot to use to apply his brakes. Examining his feet, he saw that they were made of lead and that furthermore there were three of them. In a fourth dream fragment, he was dancing with a winged creature.

At Tharon Plage, the company was rehearsing *The Yellow Methuselah.* In the middle of March, Judith and Julian took the train to Paris to meet with Jack Lang and to work on the final edit of Sheldon Rochlin and Maxine Harris's documentary *Signals through the Flames.* The night after the meetings, Julian was frightened by a sudden attack of internal bleeding and hemorrhaged with a copious flow of blood. When he returned to Nantes, he was diagnosed with a major tumor in his colon and told he had six months to live.

64. A Death like Chocolate

In a fever of urgent creativity, on a gold velvet divan in a dressing room in a theatre in Nantes, as the company was rehearsing during the month after his diagnosis, Julian wrote most of *The Archeology of Sleep*. On 21 April 1983, the tumor in Julian's colon was removed in a hospital in Nantes.

For over a year, Judith had been suffering from excruciating abdominal stomach pains which doctors in Italy, Spain, and France had attributed to nerves. Hysteria, she noted in her *Diary*, was the role Foucault argued that a male-dominated culture had unfairly assigned to women. Now she was diagnosed with gallstones—Piscator, she remembered, had died of a ruptured gall bladder. A week after Julian's operation, the gallstones were removed, and she was placed in a room adjoining Julian's.

Judith and Julian had always shared the prospects of growing old together, and except for his colitis, Julian had enjoyed good health. Now Judith had to face the overpowering fear of the loss of Julian and the grief of accepting that Julian was in his final stage. In the hospital, it became clear to her that Julian's final play was not really about sleep but about death and that, on some deep level, Julian had been aware of this. That awareness surfaced during the first ten days of recovery as Hanon and Tom Walker brought videos of the rehearsals for Julian and Judith to see. Actors climbed over the garden wall of the hospital to work on scenes with them at a time when Judith and Julian were not given painkillers because of French medical theory which advocated withholding them to encourage the body to recover on its own.

On 1 June, a few days after Julian's fifty-eighth birthday, the company opened *The Archeology of Sleep* in Nantes. With a Joycean stream of consciousness, the play presented the dreams of five sleepers-actors in beds onstage—with sixteen-year-old Isha as the Sleep of the City—their dreams animated by the company. Julian, as the mad doctor representing the corruption of medicine, lectured on the different degrees of sleep consciousness; alpha, beta, and gamma states; and the horrible scientific vivisection of felines used in sleep research.

Hanon had suggested that Julian's play be accompanied by a series of other artistic events on the theme of sleep. Cots with sleepers were set up all over the city; and the artists of Nantes contributed to a sleep museum of concerts, dance performances, poetry readings, painting, and film. Although the play was received well in Nantes, Jack Lang was unable to overcome the opposition to giving the company a permanent place in Paris, and its future in France seemed subject to political pressures and uncertain.

In July, Julian heard that American film director Francis Ford Coppola, who had seen The Living Theatre perform in Los Angeles near the end of their American tour in 1969, wanted him to play the role of a gangster in *The Cotton Club*. Shooting began in August and lasted for seven months. Set in Harlem in 1928, the film was a high-budget production about the psychopathic gangster Dutch Schultz and featured actors Richard Gere, Bob Hoskins, Gregory Hines, and Nicholas Cage. With a hardboiled New York accent, a three-piece suit and hat, his long hair invisible in a bun, Julian played Sol Weinstein, Dutch's henchman assigned to watch his errant girlfriend. Ironically, the pacifist Julian had been asked to play a killer who, early in the film, claims he was found in a garbage pail and, in his final scene, is shot to death falling into a garbage can.

While in New York, Julian arranged for a six-week engagement for The Living Theatre at the recently refurbished Joyce

Theatre in New York. The company arrived to join Julian in November and rehearsals in English continued through December. In January, the company presented a repertory of *The Yellow Methuselah, The Archeology of Sleep, Masse Mensch,* and *Antigone.*

The New York critics were savagely negative, beginning with Frank Rich who in the *New York Times* asserted that Julian had placed his hand under Rich's notebook and near his crotch during the premiere of *The Archeology of Sleep.* Speculating that Julian's act was part of an attempt at self-promotion, Rich dismissed the play as tacky and pathetic, arguing that the company was now a "scraggly collection of indistinguishable riffraff." In the *New York Post,* Richard Watts agreed that Julian's touching of Rich was offensive and disgraceful, and dismissed the play. In another piece in the *New York Times,* Benedict Nightingale claimed that The Living Theatre was "stuck in a time-warp" and that Shaw was a curious figure for them to use since he advocated the death penalty. The play was not dramatic, Julius Novick argued in the *Village Voice,* and the return of the group without its former revolutionary arrogance was merely an exercise in nostalgia.

The reviews of the other productions were equally disparaging, so much so that the Joyce stay had to be curtailed, and a planned American tour never materialized. The reviewers particularly objected to the foreign accents of a number of the actors. "Never in the annals of the New York stage has any work been so virulently attacked," Julian maintained. The commercial press had tried to "wipe us off the face of the earth," but eight thousand people had seen thirty-three performances.

In March, Julian suffered a recurrence of his illness, and many of the company returned to Europe. Hospitalized in Doctors' Hospital in Manhattan, Julian was operated on again. Recovering in the apartment he had inherited from Mabel, cared for by Judith, Hanon, Isha, and Ilion Troya, he became overwhelmed by his health problem and concentrated on his will to recover. On his fifty-ninth birthday at the end of May, he was wracked with abdominal and back pain, debilitated by fatigue and weight loss. He had cultivated cheerfulness "like an amulet," he wrote, but it had been a hard time. Although he was now living in fear, he reminded himself hourly to choose life.

His experience with the illness and hospitals led him to conclude that the main problem of the twenty-first century would be humanization in the face of technology. He was still fully engaged with thoughts about theatre, wondering what acting style could reach an audience and stir them to movement. Most American acting, he argued in his workbook, was insincere, and most theatre, baroque and mechanical.

On 7 June, after a day of vomiting and extreme weakness, Julian was admitted to the Medical Arts Center where he was told that his cancer had metastasized and he now had an abdominal tumor. When Allen Ginsberg came to visit Julian, he found him connected to tubes and fed intravenously. With his Buddhist perspective, Ginsberg asked Julian whether he could now accept the prospect of his own death, suggesting it might be time to relax his resistance to it. Grinning, Julian's answer was that he would resist to the end because "death is the ultimate corruption."

But Ginsberg may have suggested an inevitable process, and in his workbook, Julian called him the "door-opener." Transferred to Mount Sinai Hospital, fed now by hyperalimentation tubes that gave him predigested food, he dreamed of acting in the final scene of Shelley's *Cenci,* a dream that culminated with a dramatically Artaudian gesture of standing with outstretched fingers and crying out "I want to die!"

Still, there were too many things left undone. At the end of July, his condition temporarily better while he was getting chemotherapy and blood transfusions, his hospital room was transformed into a sound studio and he was asked to dub new lines for *The Cotton Club.* By the beginning of September, he was home, sleeping over twelve hours a day. Nursed by Hanon, he was still linked to the hyperalimentation machine, his spirits buoyed by a stream of old friends: among them Martin Sheen, Joe Chaikin, Jack Gelber, Ira Cohen, John Cage, Amiri Baraka, Michael McClure, Gregory Corso, and Nam June Paik.

On the first day of November, he read three poems as part of a poetry gathering at the Museum of Modern Art, and he spent the next few months working frantically on other poems and the essays he was writing for *Theandric,* the title under which his last notebooks were published. A new bilingual book of his poems, *Daily Light, Daily Speech, Daily Life,* arrived from Italy.

He was also preparing for a role in Samuel Beckett's *That Time,* a half-hour monodrama directed by Gerald Thomas in which he played a dying man recalling his life. For three weeks in March of 1985, the audience at La Mama saw only his facial expressions as he reacted to the prerecorded sound of his own voice remembering. In June, Julian went with La Mama to Frankfurt to perform the play three more times. He was baffled by the extraordinary success of the Beckett play which in so many ways was antithetical to his own optimism. With an art of accomplished pessimism, Beckett was telling his audience "with great skill and sadness that life was empty, meaningless and without hope."

Julian and Judith had received Guggenheim Fellowships for 1985, and Judith was teaching a workshop at New York University. During the summer of 1985, with Ilion, Julian went to Miami to do an episode of "Miami Vice." Several times that summer, with Judith, Hanon, Isha, and Ilion, Julian went to Hollywood to play Henry Kane, a minister in a defunct religious sect in *Poltergeist II.* The film was only a second-rate horror film, but it would provide seed money to start The Living Theatre's new work. "I keep thinking about the theatre in New York," he wrote in his workbook, "not only how to find it, raise the finances for it, run it, but what its programme is, what it is saying. What is needed is only a way to say what the angels have always said—but even they have had a hard time making it known."

By the end of July, Julian was again debilitated by the chemotherapy and had lost twenty pounds. Despite his weakness, he flew to Europe with Judith and Hanon to film a video for Nam June Paik. One sequence was shot at La Casa Anatta, on Monte Verità near Ascona where Kropotkin had stayed, as well as Isadora Duncan, D. H. Lawrence, and a host of Theosophists and anarchists.

Judith, Julian, and Hanon were filmed lunching in a restaurant on the ground floor of the house where Einstein had lived when he conceived the theory of relativity. Another sequence showed Julian and Judith sharing a joint at Bakunin's grave in Bern. It was a supreme, final symbol of ultimate defiance. This last sojourn in Europe made Julian realize, more than ever, that he was an "incurable Europhile," that he reveled in its cultivation of intelligence and art and that in the United States he felt "alien and far from home."

However invigorating the Swiss climate seemed at the time, the trip exhausted him. "Nomads," he had written in *The Life of the Theatre*, "lead shorter lives, but the wide range of their experiences is their compensation." He had had sixty years of such compensation.

Early in September, Julian began bleeding internally, and he returned to Mount Sinai Hospital for transfusions. At the end, he was dictating new poems to Hanon until he lapsed into a coma. His heart stopped on 14 September, the anniversary of the day he had met Judith in Genius Incorporated in 1943, the day he had always regarded as his real wedding anniversary. Death, he had written in his final poem, was "deliberately chosen as if it were all chocolate."

65. An Enduring Legacy

Buried next to Judith's parents in New Jersey, Julian was identified on his gravestone as poet, painter, actor, and anarchist. His funeral was filmed by Nam June Paik, and his death was commemorated by articles all over the world: in a dozen papers throughout Italy, in others in France, Spain, Germany, and Brazil. In New York, there was a three-column obituary in the *New York Times,* an elegiac remembrance in the *Village Voice* by Eric Bentley, and a piece by Jerry Tallmer in the *New York Post* called "Farewell to a Tom Paine."

At the Joyce Theatre, there was a tribute with poems read by John Cage, John Ashbery, Allen Ginsberg, Amiri Baraka, and many others. Julian's drawings were shown in a gallery in Greenwich Village while former company members performed Julian's poem "Daily Life." The art historian Dore Ashton curated a larger show of his paintings and costumes at Cooper Union.

Like the mythological phoenix, however, his theatre was in the process of resurrection. In 1986, various members from the past including Martin Sheen and Joe Chaikin assembled in the Great Hall of Cooper Union—where Lincoln and Emma Goldman had spoken—to perform in a "retrospectacle" of scenes from former productions, featuring a re-creation of the storming of the Winter Palace from *Prometheus.* In 1987, Judith performed in Joseph Papp's Central Park production of *Richard II* and directed Karen Malpede's *Us* at the Theatre for the New City, run by a former member of the company, George Bartenieff. In this play about a relationship between a man and a woman, their marriages juxtaposed to the lives of their respective parents, two actors play all six roles.

In 1988, Judith and Hanon were married. They had been lovers since 1973, and before his death, Julian had asked Hanon to protect Judith. Hanon was exactly the age of Judith's son, Garrick, and Judith was the same age as Hanon's mother. However, Hanon was prepared not only to cope with the difficulties of an age difference that would seem more important as the years passed but was willing to accept the challenge and burden of the stewardship of The Living Theatre. In the spring of 1988, Hanon directed Jerome Rothenberg's *Poland/1931,* a poetic tale of the migration of the Rothenberg family. That summer, he directed a street play called *Turning the Earth* which was performed in all five boroughs of New York City and which encouraged inner-city inhabitants to plant gardens in empty lots. Later that year, Judith directed Michael McClure's *Vktms,* a version of the Orestes myth in which Hanon played Orestes.

In 1989, an affordable theatre was found in what is known as Alphabet City on the lower East Side of Manhattan at Third Street and Avenue C. Essentially a deep storefront, the space had been the Happy Days Bar and Grill since the end of Prohibition but had most recently existed as an after-hours drug location where local police reportedly stopped every hour to collect their dividend.

Although they knew that only their most dedicated followers would come to such a neighborhood, to a small theatre operating on the margins, they felt they were in a vital part of the city where their kind of theatre could be galvanizing. The opening of the new space occurred with Armand Schwerner's *Tablets* on 31 May 1989. With this play, The Living Theatre continued its experimental path. Dense, elliptical, self-referential, a highly metaphysical investigation of the roots of language, the play explored the reactions of a scholar to his discovery of a body of Sumerian poetry dating from 4000 B.C. Essentially about the beginning of poetry, it was staged as a long, thin triangle with the audience seated in three sections along the lines of the triangle and the actors in mud-colored mesh performing between them.

In the summer of 1989, when the Tompkins Square difficulties began because of the occupation of the park by the homeless, The Living Theatre used twelve members of the company and twelve homeless people to create *The Body of God,* a play which dramatized their plight. In *Tumult,* they created a half-hour street play about the right to public space, paralleling the eviction of the homeless to what was happening in Tiananmen Square in Beijing. As in Italy, their intention had been to design open forms where ordinary people could create their own actions and write their lines within a dramatic context.

There were several other productions in 1989. In *Waste,* Hanon suggested that Western systems were based on the waste of natural resources and that alternatives were possible. His method was to reinterpret scenes from *Seven against Thebes* (a character becomes mayor of New York), a medieval miracle play, a No play, a play from the commedia dell'arte, *Hamlet,* and from the works of Brecht, David Mamet, and Robert Wilson. Since *Waste* was performed outdoors, the theatre space was transformed into a museum with participation from community artists, poetry readings, concerts, and dance performances as in Nantes.

By performing Else Lasker-Schuler's play *I and I,* a version of the Faust story, The Living Theatre was continuing in the direction it had begun with Gertrude Stein's *Doctor Faustus Lights the Lights* in 1951. A Weimar poet who had fled the Nazis to settle in Jerusalem before the war, Lasker-Schuler had imagined a situation where Faust and Mephistopheles were lovers and Hell was populated by Nazis. *I and I* was played in a little black-box cabaret, Judith's design a tribute to Valeska Gert in whose Beggar's Bar she had worked during the Second World War. This was another demonstration of how each play staged on East Third Street would use the space in an entirely different manner.

In the spring of 1990, Judith directed Eric Bentley's *German Requiem,* an adaptation of a version of *Romeo and Juliet* by von Kleist. In the summer and fall of 1990, the company took *The Tablets* and *I and I* on tour, playing in Italy, Spain, Germany, and Czechoslovakia. These plays were particularly well received by the press and the public, and, five years after Julian's death, this tour established the continuing vitality of The Living Theatre in Europe.

During the winter of 1990–91, Judith lived in Los Angeles to play Granny Addams in *The Addams Family* with Raul Julia and Anjelica Huston, a slick Hollywood film based on Charles Addams's famous cartoons. Judith was deeply concerned about the imminence of the Gulf War and tried to rally people on the set to participate in a protest organized by Ron Kovic and Martin Sheen. On the morning after the war actually began, the teamsters on the set gave all the actors except Judith tiny American flags to wear in their lapels. During a kitchen scene with Anjelica Huston, when Judith was at the center of attention, she also was offered a flag which she refused, saying "Don't give that flag to me unless you give me a book of matches to go with it." The remark cost Judith a role in the sequel.

In the spring of 1991, the company performed Hanon's *Rules of Civility*, a play ironically animating 110 rules of social propriety postulated by George Washington when he was thirteen and tracing them to the moral choices of the Gulf War era. Isha played the thirteen-year-old Washington, and Tom Walker played him as an adult. When the company was invited to perform the play in Rome, they ended the play with a candlelight vigil in front of the American embassy on the Via Venetto to protest what had happened in Iraq. When embassy officials called the police, the company was forced to disperse; but they had shown the Italians that The Living Theatre was still agitating and relevant.

In 1992, with the threat of curtailed grants and economic recession, Hanon wrote *The Zero Method,* a two-character play in which he and Judith—against the counterpointed theorems of Ludwig Wittgenstein—remember how they had met and what kept them together. Learning the play in Italian, they performed it for two months in Italy, every night in another city or town. The tour was so successful it supported the company for a year.

Until the Third Street location was closed by the New York City Fire Department in the spring of 1993, all these productions were mounted on tiny budgets of approximately $20,000 in grant money a year, some touring income, and some $10,000 in contributions, with half of the box-office receipts going to the actors. Two nights a week, performances were free though the audience was asked to contribute what it could.

A further source of financing were the films Judith was making: *The Addams Family* and *Household Saints.* As always, everything she earned was dedicated to her dream of a theatre whose strong social vision would transcend entertainment. The dream was pursued in *Anarchia,* a play written by Hanon Reznikov and produced during the winter of 1993–94. *Anarchia* is a quintessential Living Theatre production. Its subject matter—the impact of the theories of Malatesta, a late-nineteenth-century Italian anarchist, on the lives of six characters in New York at the end of the twentieth century—reflects the core of a commitment and a dream that has inspired the group for more than forty-five years, leaving an enduring legacy.

The degree of success was never as important as the pursuit of the dream itself. As Julian frequently used to say, quoting the sages and rabbis of the Talmud, "Our struggle is our glory!"

Acknowledgments

I have been helped by the good will and cooperation of a number of people. First of all, I would like to thank my wife, Mellon, for her continual inspiration and for more mundane matters like teaching me how to use a computer. For his faith in this project, I am indebted to my agent, Tom Connor, and for invaluable editorial suggestions, to Jim Moser of Grove Press. I also wish to thank Rachel Berchten for excellent copy editing.

My greatest debt is to Judith Malina, who gave me full access to The Living Theatre Archives and hours of interview time, and who diligently commented on my manuscript as it evolved. Along the way, many people allowed me to interview them, and this list is in the order in which I saw them: Franklin Beck, Leonard Price, Maurice Edwards, Sally Goodman, Jackson MacLow, Claude Fredericks, Steven Ben Israel, Mary Krapf, Dorothy Shari, Marilyn Chris, Jackie McLean, Tom Walker, Hanon Reznikov, Ilion Troya, Ira Cohen, Mark Amitin, Isha Manna Beck, and Garrick Beck.

Ilion Troya offered particular assistance with the photographs. Isha Manna Beck, Erica Bilder, Joanie Fritz, and Lisa Chin gave me important help with The Living Theatre Archives. I am especially grateful for a faculty research grant from Queens College for the spring of 1993. Morris Dickstein, Richard Schotter, Debbie Geis, and Paul Avrich, my colleagues at Queens College, were particularly helpful. I was also assisted by letters and conversations with Allen Ginsberg, Gary Goodrow, Berenice Hoffman, Anthony Hecht, Michael McClure, Jack Gelber, Jean-Claude Van Italie, Pamela Badyk, Paul Williams, and David Wieck. Kenneth Brown let me read "Finding Out," an unpublished memoir. My coeditors at *American Book Review,* Ron Sukenick, Rochelle Ratner, and Barry Wallenstein, helped me in various ways.

Notes

Notes

The material in this book is based on extensive interviews; Judith Malina's published and unpublished diaries; Julian Beck's unpublished journals and workbooks; comprehensive theatre logs; and The Living Theatre Archives, most of which is located in Judith Malina's home in New York City and the remainder in the Billy Rose Collection of the New York Public Library. Unless archival material is identified as part of the Billy Rose Collection, it is housed in Judith Malina's home in New York City. Since 1947, Judith Malina has been writing her diary in little notebooks. Two segments of this diary have appeared in print: *The Enormous Despair,* which covers from August 1968 to April 1969, was published by Random House in 1972; and *The Diaries of Judith Malina,* which covers from 1947 through 1957, was published by Grove Press in 1984. In these notes, I refer to material taken from the *unpublished* diaries as from "Unpublished Diary."

1. Genius Incorporated

1. Opening pages. Judith Malina, interview with author, 15 November 1991. Judith Malina, *The Diaries of Judith Malina: 1947–1957* (New York: Grove Press, 1984), pp. 47–57. See also entry for 18 April 1957, p. 432. This book will be referred to as *Diaries* in future notes.

2. Since most actors were unemployed. This would be especially true for young actors. Jason Robards, in a remembrance of Colleen Dewhurst and their time as students in the American Academy of Dramatic Art, said most young actors only got to do summer stock and had other jobs to support themselves during the year. Dewhurst worked as a secretary in the Screen Actors Guild. See Robards's piece in the *New York Times,* Sunday, 1 September 1991, Arts and Leisure section.

3. William Marchant. Malina, interview with author, 15 November

1991; and Julian Beck, Journal, 16 April 1957. Beck's journals and workbooks are part of The Living Theatre Archives.

4. Poet with "golden flashing tongue." Beck, Journal, 4 April 1957.

5. Unfettered freedom. *Diaries,* 14 December 1949, p. 91.

2. An Immigrant Childhood

1. Information on Rosel and Max Malina is from Judith Malina's unpublished essay "A Recollection of Rosel Zamojre and Max Malina," dated 15 March 1979; and from Judith Malina, interview with author, 8 October 1991. Some of the material in this chapter is drawn from Judith Malina, interview with Marcia Gail Black, March 1986, included in an appendix to her Smith College master's thesis, "Jewish Sources in the Work of The Living Theatre.

2. Broadway Central Hotel. A distinguished building designed by Stanford White and located on lower Broadway near Bleecker Street, the hotel catered to immigrant Jews, and several of its floors were reserved for Chasidim who had their own strictly kosher dining room where the Malina family would sometimes eat.

3. A saintly figure. *Diaries,* 6 April 1950, p. 105. Max Malina's itinerant congregation found a home in the lower chapel of the Central Synagogue, founded by the renowned reform rabbi Stephen Wise. The chapel was available because reform Jews did not assemble for daily morning prayers. Max Malina's followers, however, were like unwanted stepchildren, adopted out of conscience but still resented.

4. A constant procession. Max Malina wrote a book on the German Jewish community in New York, and he edited two newspapers, *Der Zeitgeist* and *Das Judische Familienblatt,* which published his appeals for the rescue of Polish and German Jews. He tried to diminish the hostility that German Jews felt for their Polish brethren—the more educated Germans assuming superiority over Yiddish-speaking Polish *shetl* dwellers—and to awaken both camps to the enormous peril faced by all European Jewry.

5. Organized committees. *Diaries,* 28 March 1948, p. 30. Judith told me that she remembered Einstein visiting her father several times at the Broadway Central. Malina, interview with author, 8 October 1991.

6. Rosel went to work in a factory. A collection donated by the congregation was invested and lost by one of its members, leaving Rosel destitute. A wealthy acquaintance, an eccentric physician who lived in a swank Central Park West building, invited Rosel and Judith to stay with her, and they spent several months in her terraced apartment. When the physician of-

fered to adopt Judith provided that she left Rosel, they moved to a crowded slum tenement in the Bronx and then to a grim furnished room with an electric hot plate for cooking on Sixteenth Street in Manhattan.

7. Wooster Street basement and read some poems. *Diaries,* 1 June 1948, p. 42.

8. Isamu Noguchi. *Diaries,* 1 May 1948, p. 36.

3. Privileged Childhood

1. Operation for a mastoid infection. Leonard Price (Julian Beck's first cousin), interview with author, 11 December 1991.

2. Material on Irving and Mabel Beck from Leonard Price and Franklin Beck, interviews with author, 28 October 1991.

3. He began a log book. At eleven, he saw *Carmen* and *I Pagliacci,* and the next year, he saw *Tännhauser* with Lotte Lehmann, *Faust,* and *La Bohème.* The log exists in The Living Theatre Archives.

4. Material on Horace Mann culled from Living Theatre Archives, where, in a folder, copies of the Horace Mann *Record* are catalogued.

5. Lady Augusta Bracknell. Anthony Hecht, the poet, played John Worthing. This was not Julian's first performance in drag: in the fall, he had played a matronly, overblown nouveau riche woman in the Frederick Jackson comedy *The Bishop Misbehaves.*

6. Camp in Brandon, Vermont. At Camp Twin Lakes, Julian wrote articles on sports, campfires, and a cracker-eating contest for the camp paper.

7. Yale. Yale file, Living Theatre Archives. Julian saved some of his finals and papers, and they reflect how seriously students were tasked before the war. In his classical civilization course, he wrote a paper on Virgil's debt to Homer. In his English literature final, he was asked to comment on passages from Shakespeare, and to discuss the relation between Milton's Satan and the Byronic hero. During the war years, students were asked to take classes that could benefit them as future combatants, a factor that may have contributed to Julian's pacifism.

8. "The sexual ride in my life." J. Beck, Journal, 7 August 1960. Sex with other young men during his senior year in high school. Transcript of Julian Beck, interview with Andrew Nadelson, 28 December 1984, Living Theatre Archives. Masochist fantasy; and he could no longer serve. Julian Beck, *The Life of the Theatre* (San Francisco: City Lights Books, 1972), p. 151 (I am using the 1991 Limelight reprint which conveniently numbers the pages).

9. Rejection from the army. Actually, Julian's case was not isolated,

and more than five million men were rejected for the draft, over three million for what was diagnosed as some form of emotional instability. Such a diagnosis reflected the biases of the prewar era, although some of the rejected men may have suffered from what the author Philip Wylie called "Momism," overprotective mothers like Mabel Beck who admired her son's air of sophistication and his poised elocution, often at poor Franklin's expense.

4. The Beggar's Bar

1. Attended the theater frequently. This was only an acceleration of what for Julian had already become habitual. In his log book, he entered every play, concert, opera, ballet, or film he saw. In 1941, he saw fifty-one plays, including Judith Anderson in *Macbeth* twice; in 1942, he saw fifty-eight plays.

2. She did not want to work in conventional theatre. Beck, *Life of the Theatre*, p. 13.

3. Information on Valeska Gert is from my interview with Judith Malina on 15 November 1991; and her unpublished essay on Gert in The Living Theatre Archives. The Beggar's Bar was closed after the war because the eggnog contained alcohol for which Gert had no license.

4. Bill Simmons. Judith Malina, interview with author, 21 January 1992.

5. The two became close friends. In the interview with Andrew Nadelson, 28 December 1984, Living Theatre Archives, Beck maintained that he was never Simmons's lover.

6. Son of a Provincetown fisherman; and Julian told Léger. 1940s folder, Living Theatre Archives.

5. A Provincetown Summer

1. Julian's painting threatened. The painting may well have challenged Judaic principles that she associated with her late father. Max Malina shared in a centuries-long tradition of Talmudic scholarship that sanctified words and, while instilling a reverential appreciation of culture in Jewish families, did not particularly respond to painting, which was close to the forbidden graven image and related to idol worship.

2. "The sale of beauty." Franklin Beck to Julian Beck, 20 August 1944,

1940s folder, Living Theatre Archives. Even though Franklin wrote the letter, it was in his father's voice. In Julian Beck's *Life of the Theatre,* Julian describes an Oedipal fantasy of murdering his father.

3. "What your heart shrieks for." Some of Mabel's letters to Julian in Provincetown are in the 1940s folder. Her lush magniloquence irritated her son but subtly influenced him as well. On the 1940 trip to Mexico, he remembered how she labeled every vista ecstatically. Beck, Journal, 25 October 1960. Irving Beck sent Julian a check for twenty-five dollars a week, a generous amount in an era when the average salary was fifty dollars a week, and one could purchase an Electrolux for sixteen dollars and a new car for a thousand.

4. Sometimes, Julian cooked for Williams. Beck, Journal, 27 February 1983.

5. "My then rising comet burst over the world." Beck, Journal, 10 July 1955. Julian was back in Provincetown in 1955 and remembered what had transpired eleven years earlier.

6. "Could make a mark without drawing something." Beck, Journal, 27 September 1956.

7. The balcony was reserved for sexual encounters. See Steven Naifeh and Gregory White Smith's massive biography, *Jackson Pollock* (New York: Harper Perennial, 1991), p. 487.

8. To repress homosexual inclinations. Naifeh and Smith, (*Jackson Pollock,* p. 249) quote Pollock's friend Peter Busa who was convinced Pollock had encounters with men. Naifeh and Smith also cite Lee Krasner who told several close friends that Pollock liked men, though the subject of homosexuality made him nervous. Naifeh and Smith (p. 480) claim that homosexuality was on his mind in the summer of 1944 and that after his opening at Peggy Guggenheim's, he frequented a gay bar called George's Tavern in the Village where he met Tennessee Williams.

9. Drunken sexual idylls. The admission occurs in Beck, Journal, 27 February 1983; and it is repeated in the Beck interview with Nadelson, 28 December 1984, Living Theatre Archives.

6. An Athenian Gallery

1. Some of the details about Peggy Guggenheim are from her autobiographical *Out of This Century: Confessions of an Art Addict* (New York: Universe Books, 1957); and from Jacqueline Bograd Weld, *Peggy: The Wayward Guggenheim* (New York: E. P. Dutton, 1986).

notes

2. Adolph Gottlieb's comments are from an interview with David Sylvester in David and Cecile Shapiro, eds., *Abstract Art: A Critical Record* (New York: Cambridge University Press, 1990), p. 266; and Barnett Newman's is from Alwynne Mackie, ed., *Art/Talk: Theory and Practice in Abstract Expressionism* (New York: Columbia University Press, 1989), p. 69.

3. "Ingratiating" is the term Beck used in his interview with Nadelson, 28 December 1984, Living Theatre Archives.

4. "In changing your sex." Guggenheim's letter is in The Living Theatre Archives. After the war, when Peggy Guggenheim returned to Europe, Bewley got a Ph.D. in literature, taught at Fordham University, and became known as a James scholar with his book *The Complex Fate.*

5. Angry and calculated. See Gore Vidal's preface to Guggenheim's autobiography, *Out of This Century.*

7. Piscator

1. The New School. One of Piscator's students was Tennessee Williams, who also worked as a waiter at the Beggar's Bar.

2. Erwin Piscator. See Ronald Hayman, *Brecht* (New York: Oxford University Press, 1983), p. 117; and Mordecai Gorelik, *New Theatres for Old* (New York: Samuel French, 1947), pp. 378–83.

3. To hitchhike to New Orleans. *Diaries,* 24 June 1950, p. 113. Before leaving for New Orleans, Judith Malina had been working as an usher in the Broadway Theatre. The play was *Carmen Jones,* and the actor who played the toreador, a part-time policeman, issued an eight-state alarm. See *Diaries,* 11 May 1951, p. 160.

4. Worked with a Dadaist group. The Berlin Dadaists had utter contempt for their audiences. Like Brecht, Piscator believed that theatre was an opportunity to recondition spectators only partially capable of seeing or listening, who only wanted a mild emotional reminder of life. Julian Beck felt that Piscator's flaw was underrating his public and speaking down to them in platitudes. Beck, Journal, 5 May 1953.

5. "Vanguard army." *Diaries,* 17 February 1950, p. 100.

6. Classes in acting. Judith Malina compiled a 140-page Piscator Notebook while studying at the Dramatic workshop that is preserved in The Living Theatre Archives. Cassandra; and Lope de Vega. Judith Malina, *The Enormous Despair* (New York: Random House, 1972), p. 67. Many of her classmates were interesting. One of them, Chandler Cowles, showed her a

letter from Henry Miller while they were rehearsing Shaw's *Androcles and the Lion. Diaries,* 15 March 1950, p. 103.

7. "Staying power." *Diaries,* 17 June 1947, p. 3. "Rough edges." *Diaries,* 15 June 1948, p. 45. Piscator told Alfred Kreymborg that "Malina has some rough edges that life will have to wear off."

8. "One eye in her hand." *Diaries,* 3 January 1948, p. 15. Malina's admission that she was stubborn is in the Piscator Notebook.

9. Hurt rage. Beck, Journal, 5 May 1953; see also *Diaries,* 17 October 1950, p. 127.

10. Could never express herself to him. Malina, *Enormous Despair,* p. 8.

11. *The Flies.* Simone de Beauvoir spoke to Piscator's students about Sartre's intention to capture the plight of the existential man in the prisoner's dock. This would become a primal pattern for The Living Theatre.

12. Too much technical training. *Diaries,* 21 July 1947, p. 6.

13. Art was treacherous and dispensable. Beck, *Life of the Theatre,* p. 87. *Diaries,* 25 January 1951, p. 146.

14. Slight and much too short. *Malina,* Piscator Notebook. Later, Piscator would refuse to allow her to play Lady Macbeth because of her slight build and small stature. See *Diaries,* 8 December 1950, p. 136.

15. Brecht felt he needed famous actors. Brecht wanted well-known performers in order to attract the largest possible audience. Like Piscator, he had no belief in the sanctity of art and would constantly revise his plays. The incident is remembered in *The Enormous Despair,* pp. 230–31.

16. A studio where Julian could paint. Julian Beck's studio was located at 1112 Second Avenue, at Fifty-ninth Street, and the rent was eighteen dollars a month.

17. City College. Julian Beck's transcript, 1940s folder, Living Theatre Archives. Registered as an English major, he was reprimanded by the registrar for taking electives without necessary prerequisites in a letter dated 15 February 1949. While most of his English and German grades were A's, he did not do well in the sciences.

18. Humiliated. Beck, Journal, 25 October 1960.

19. "Corrupt and infectious." Beck, Journal, 14 April 1955. Julian knew his views were immature but formed, in part, by the ongoing revelations in the winter of 1945–46 in the pages of the *New York Times* of the horrors of Nazi concentration camps.

20. *Antigone. Diaries,* 18 February 1948, p. 24. Judith Anderson's performance as Medea would become a model experience for Judith.

21. They wrote some fifty letters to artists. All these letters are in the Billy Rose Collection in the Lincoln Center branch of the New York Public

Library. Like Pound, Julian Beck kept carbons of letters, though he would sometimes use the reverse sides of fashion illustrations to make his copies.

22. Rachel. See Rachel Brownstein, *Tragic Muse: Rachel of the Comédie-Française* (New York: Knopf, 1993).

8. Searching for Love

1. Julian was off hiking in the Sierras. Julian left New York by train on 8 July, slept unlawfully on a Yosemite meadow on 15 July, and tramped the Sierras with a friend named Joe Turner until the end of the month. One day, he was guided on horseback by the wife of the Speaker of the California State Legislature.

2. First serious sexual relationship. See *Diaries*, 15 May 1948, p. 38, where Malina explains that the "mysterious ways of sex" were first revealed to her by Robert Jastrow, later an eminent nuclear physicist, at his bar mitzvah party. Malina described Brixel to me on 28 April 1992. He instigated the *Diaries* and is mentioned several times in them.

3. Returned to Vienna. Malina did not know that Brixel had a Swedish wife and two children. Later, he would become a prominent conductor at Salzburg.

4. "The same end." *Diaries*, 21 July 1947, p. 6.

5. Marriage was something Judith wanted and Julian dreaded. *Diaries*, 14 August 1947, p. 7.

6. Peculiarities. The word is Malina's. *Diaries*, 25 September 1950, p. 10. Judith used the word "pampered" and told me Julian was raised as a "Jewish prince" when I interviewed her on 28 April 1992. Another difference was religious commitment. The Becks were assimilated and secularized Jews, and Julian found Judith's desire to attend synagogue services naive.

7. The letter to Robert Edmund Jones, dated 11 October 1947, is in The Living Theatre Archives in the Billy Rose Collection.

8. Cummings lived in a cramped apartment. *Diaries*, 1 November 1947, pp. 12–13. *Him* was one of the famous Dadaist plays like Alfred Jarry's *Ubu Roi* which Judith and Julian were reading. *Him* had been staged at the Provincetown Playhouse in the Village in 1928. It featured twenty-one scenes of dizzy repartee among its characters: Me, Him, Mussolini, and the three Weirds.

9. Matters with Kreymborg. Details on Kreymborg are from his autobiography, *Troubador* (New York: Boni & Liveright, 1925). Malina describes their encounters at various interstices of the *Diaries.*

9. To Have or to Have Not

1. Malina uses the term "breach" in her *Diaries,* 13 December 1947, p. 14; she refers to a "strained situation" on 5 January 1948, p. 15.

2. Hartford Institute for Living. Details from *Diaries,* pp. 18–31.

3. "A strong phantom." Unpublished entry in Judith Malina's diary for 7 June 1948. "Diplomatic" and "coquettish" are both in an unpublished diary entry for 28 May 1948. "Dark veil" is Malina's metaphor and used in *Diaries,* 8 June 1948, p. 44.

4. Pierre Garai. Berenice Hoffman, telephone conversation with author, 5 March 1992.

5. "Loved ourselves." *Diaries,* 24 September 1950, p. 126.

6. "All the glory." Beck, *Life of the Theatre,* p. 13.

7. "Effects that belong to it alone." *Diaries,* 7 July 1948, p. 50.

8. Quarreled again. Most of the material critical of Julian was edited out of the published *Diaries* but exists in original entries for 8 August, 15 August, and 23 August 1948. "There seems to be little else left open for me" was written on 8 September 1948.

9. *Neurotica,* edited by Jay Landesman, was a precursor of the Beats, one of those seismographs signaling new attitudes to sex, psychoanalysis, and drugs that was an important part of the cultural underbelly in the 1950s.

10. A Child Bride and a Little Boy A-Wooing

1. Her head in the oven. Judith Malina, interview with author, 16 May 1991.

2. Live-in domestic. A good part of The Living Theatre Archives is housed in what formerly was the maid's small room. See *Diaries,* 16 October 1948, p. 57; and 21 and 22 October 1948, p. 58. "Bleached" is used in the entry for 27 October 1948, p. 59. The published diary omits the detail of Judith's tears at dinner with the Becks, though it appears in the original entry for 22 October 1948.

3. Truman's victory. Wallace received very few votes. The votes in the Beck-Malina family mirrored the closeness of the race between Truman and Dewey. In an original entry for 2 November 1948, Judith revealed that she reluctantly voted for Wallace, her mother and Julian for Truman, and Julian's parents for Dewey. This was the last time that either Judith or Julian

voted. When they left the voting booth, they decided they no longer could delegate their power to a structure in which they did not believe. Judith Malina, interview with author, 22 March 1993.

4. Basement on Wooster Street. Coincidentally, this was the same basement where Judith read her poems in the summer of 1943 and was introduced to anarchism by Edwin Honig.

5. Julian observed that Williams consistently condescended to Flossie during the entire visit. His version of the event is in a journal entry on 18 March 1957. See *Diaries,* 4 October 1948, pp. 55–56. The "little boy a-wooing" phrase, with its hint of suppressed irony, exists only in the original entry for 1 January 1949, another illustration of how Judith systematically sought to protect Julian's image in the published version of her memories.

6. "Chamber drama." *Diaries,* 10 November 1948, p. 61.

7. "How else can one run a seeryous teeater." See *Diaries,* 18 February 1949, p. 72. Later, Malina would favor the myth that the police had actually closed the Wooster Street theatre. Actually, Beck and Malina gave the space up because the struggle seemed too great for so small a space.

8. "Too eager to see the good." *Diaries,* 28 January 1949, p. 66. Julian's Candide-like affirmation could both annoy and buoy Judith. In his journal, he would later relate her militance to physical appearance, claiming that she was the "ugly duckling." Beck, Journals, 27 September 1960.

11. Anarchists and Babies

1. "Prisoner of family life." *Diaries,* 18 February 1949, p. 72.

2. "Anonymous messages." Beck, *Life of the Theatre,* p. 12. At one of the performances of the Peking opera, Julian remembered seeing a giant mechanical lotus open onstage during a forty-five minute time period while an actress, crouched in its matrix, sang and slowly rose. It was the sort of movement he would seek to emulate in future productions in the 1960s. See *Life of the Theatre,* p. 163.

3. Annotated by Julian. Judith wrote two of Julian's last term papers at City College: one, on Pound; the other, on Karen Horney. Judith Malina, interview with author, 11 January 1991.

4. Simmons's visit. Judith Malina, interview with author, 16 January 1991.

5. "Brilliant flashes." *Diaries,* 17 October 1949, p. 87.

6. Julian had been introduced to Fredericks in 1944 by John Simon who had been Beck's Horace Mann classmate.

7. Subject of anarchism. Judith and Julian considered writing a book called *The Free Society* discussing the daily problems of living without the delegation of authority. See *Diaries,* 31 August 1949, p. 85; but Judith was smart enough to realize that "not having solved my own life, I wish to go out and solve everyone's" (26 October 1949, p. 88).

8. Group of demonstrators. *Diaries,* 18 August 1949, pp. 84–85.

9. Marginal in America. Walter Bridge in Evan Connolly's *Mr. and Mrs. Bridge* refers to the economist Thorstein Veblen as a "socialist crackpot," so one can imagine the way anarchists were regarded by those in the mainstream. The word *anarchism* is generally misused to describe a state of mayhem, riot, or extreme social disorder when pillage, looting, and rape prevail.

12. Broken Love

1. Baziotes . . . came over. *Diaries,* 22 February 1950, p. 101.

2. Motherwell visited. *Diaries,* 14 January 1950, p. 96.

3. "Hell Bomb." *Diaries,* 30 January 1950, p. 97.

4. The words "emotional" and "tense" are not used in the published version but exist in an unpublished entry for 12 February 1950; on 19 February, she complained about her inadequate sexual outlet.

5. The cigarette incident and the phrase "broken love" are only in the original entry for 27 February 1950. "Distant and unknowable" is from *Diaries,* 1 March 1950, p. 102.

6. "Pacifism as a tactic" is only in the original diary entry Judith made for 11 April 1950.

7. "Spent light." *Diaries,* 14 May 1950, p. 109.

8. Owen Lattimore. Formerly the trusted adviser to Chiang Kai-shek, Lattimore was accused by McCarthy of being a Russian spy responsible for allowing Mao to gain control of China, even though he had no evidence to support charges that dominated the newspapers all that spring. Eventually Lattimore's career was aborted. See Robert B. Newman, *Owen Lattimore and the Loss of China* (Berkeley: University of California Press, 1991).

9. "Bingo in a bomb shelter." *Diaries,* 29 June 1950, p. 114. In later years, Judith and Julian would often quote Abbie Hoffman's comment that "we are shouting theatre in a crowded fire!" Julian's shout was an early example of that.

10. "You are crazy." *Diaries,* 1 August 1950, p. 117.

11. Possibly even to tragedy. "Possibly tragedy" is in Judith's original entry for 19 September 1950.

13. Séances and Mumbo Jumbo

1. Judith described Walter McElroy as "satanic" in the original entry for 12 February 1950. Some of the commentary on McElroy and Glenn is drawn from my interview with Claude Fredericks on 10 October 1992. The séances are described at various points in the *Diaries* for the summer of 1950 and also by Harold Norse in *Memoirs of a Bastard Angel* (New York: William Morrow, 1989), pp. 180–90.

2. The dianetic therapist's sexual advances are unmentioned in the published *Diaries* but are accounted for in original entries on 28 October and 4 December 1950. The therapist told Alex Burdett, a friend of Julian's, that he suspected Julian and Robin were having an affair.

3. "Mumbo-jumbo." *Diaries*, 31 December 1950, p. 138.

4. "Dictatorship of the psychiatrist." *Diaries*, 2 December 1950, p. 135.

5. "Galvanized her." This is not in the published *Diaries* but in the original entry for 22 December 1950.

6. Canterbury. See Norse, *Memoirs of a Bastard Angel*, pp. 202–3.

14. The New Musicians

1. "The future is a dream." *Diaries*, 31 December 1950, p. 139.

2. Lou Harrison. *Diaries*, 25 March 1951, p. 152.

3. Muse and lover. Judith Malina, interview with author, 15 December 1991.

4. Yeats in an essay. *Diaries*, 9 May 1951, p. 162.

5. Evolutionary scale. *Diaries*, 4 March 1949, p. 73.

6. John Cage. Some of the details are from Mary Emma Harris, *The Arts at Black Mountain* (Cambridge: MIT Press, 1990), which was a valuable resource throughout this chapter. Cage's theory of chance was influenced by the I Ching, which he had discovered listening to D. T. Suzuki lecture on Zen Buddhism at Columbia University. His music would influence a generation of composers, leading to minimalism and performance art.

7. Abruptly rejected him. Cage was married to Xenia Kashvaroff, a painter. One hot summer night, after a party, Peggy Guggenheim, her husband Max Ernst, Cage, and Xenia decided to undress to see how detached they could remain. Apparently, Ernst was more aroused by Xenia than Cage was by Peggy. See *Out of This Century*, pp. 279–80.

15. The Saintliness of the Beaten

1. "Dumb as a pantomime." *Diaries,* 8 June 1951, p. 172. Twenty-five in June. The lack of accomplishment is a recurrent lament. At a lecture once, Julian remembered, Judith was in anguish when she learned Eleonora Duse had achieved stardom at twenty. "Blind alleys." *Diaries,* 20 July 1951, p. 178.

2. Bohemian ghetto. Norse, *Memoirs of a Bastard Angel,* p. 184.

3. An idiotic poet. *Diaries,* 14 August 1951, p. 183.

4. Unhappy and alienated. *Diaries,* 30 October 1951, p. 196.

5. Loss of three teaching positions. Goodman was fired from the University of Chicago; from the Manumit School, a preparatory school in New Hampshire where he met his second wife; and from Black Mountain where a conservative Quaker faction on the faculty disapproved of the way he consorted with male students. The difficulty at Black Mountain was triggered by two No plays Goodman wrote while in residence during the summer of 1950, *The Quiet House* and *The Magic Flight,* which drew on relationships between students and faculty.

6. Wilhelm Reich. Reich had discovered that the incidence of cancer among mental patients was lower than that of the general population and speculated that repression was eventually reflected in the cellular structure of the body, an armor restraining feelings that needed release. He devised the orgone box, a small meditation room the size of a telephone booth, constructed of alternating layers of organic and inorganic material, which could deliver, he asserted, a cosmic sexual charge leading to spontaneous orgasm. Sent to a federal prison in Maine for using the mails fraudulently—he was trying to explain his orgone theories—he died of humiliation. Julian was outraged by the circumstances of Reich's death in a federal penitentiary and called it an example of vigilantism in a letter to the *New York Times.* Julian thought the persecution of Reich signaled a fear of openness and of fundamental change.

7. "Acts and words." See Taylor Stoehr's illuminating preface to *Nature Heals: Psychological Essays of Paul Goodman* (New York: Free Life Editions, 1977). See also Paul Goodman, "The May Pamphlet," in *Nature Heals.*

8. People were swamped. Many of these ideas are derived from Goodman's one popular book, *Growing up Absurd.* Written in the 1950s, it was only published by Jason Epstein at Random House in 1960 after having been rejected by sixteen other publishers. Some of the material on Goodman comes from my interview with Sally Goodman, his second wife, on 15 December 1992.

16. The Gypsy Path

1. Faust myth is a modern archetype. Julian Beck to Donald Gallup, 22 August 1951, Living Theatre Archives, Billy Rose Collection. Stein was the best playwright. Beck, Journal, 17 October 1952.

2. William Carlos Williams's letter is reproduced in *Diaries,* 15 December 1951, p. 196; as is Rexroth's letter advising that his play not be done on one night (*Diaries,* 10 October 1951, p. 191–92).

3. Rexroth's reputation. See Linda Hamalian's sober and circumspect *A Life of Kenneth Rexroth* (New York: Norton, 1991); and Kenneth Rexroth and James Laughlin, *Selected Letters,* ed. Lee Bartlett (New York: Norton, 1991).

4. Collection of beautiful moments. Beck, Journal, 27 December 1954.

5. The worst loss, however, was personal. Harold Norse offers another version of the incident in *Memoirs of a Bastard Angel,* p. 223. He claims that Judith's voice "broke" over the lines "I freeze! I burn! I am hot! I am cold!" and that the "breaking" occurred because she was unconsciously critical of Rexroth's stilted dialogue.

6. Altercations. *Diaries,* 6 February 1952, p. 208. Harold Norse, in *Memoirs of a Bastard Angel,* describes Richard Stryker demanding payment for composing the music for *Beyond the Mountains,* and getting slapped in the face and struck with a flute by an irate Judith.

7. *Sweeney Agonistes.* The inclusion of Eliot's play caused Anaïs Nin to withdraw as an official sponsor of The Living Theatre, claiming that Eliot was already dead as a literary force.

8. Free community of artists and friends. This was more an expression of anarchism than a search for originality. Theatre as a basis for a larger artistic center encompassing dance, music, and literature was an idea for which Harold Clurman proselytized with the Group Theatre in the 1930s. First to apply Stanislavsky's theories of "emotional memory" in America, the Group Theatre was a collective dedicated to presenting drama of moral significance and social import. See Wendy Smith, *Real Life Drama* (New York: Knopf, 1990), pp. 231–32. Another source for Julian was Paul Goodman who formally proposed a community of friends through art in his essay "Advance-Guard Writing" in *The Kenyon Review* (Summer 1951).

9. Tacitly agreed. Judith Malina, interview with author, 7 January 1992. Details about Philip Smith from an interview with Judith Malina on 15 September 1992. Smith later became a Hollywood prop master, working on films like *The Godfather* and *The Exorcist.*

10. New York had become "the most creative place." Julian Beck to Robin Prising, 26 January 1952, Living Theatre Archives, Billy Rose Collection.

11. "Easy to find lovers." *Diaries,* Easter Sunday, 1952, p. 221. "Our child and our theatre." *Diaries,* 3 April 1952, p. 219.

12. "I lie in bed at night." *Diaries,* 16 May 1952, p. 226.

13. She had not made love with Julian. Beck, Journal, 8 August 1952.

14. Affront an audience. Julian Beck, "Storming the Barricades," in Kenneth Brown, *The Brig* (New York: Hill and Wang, 1965), p. 13.

15. Julian's design. Julian Beck to Daniel Longwell (editor of *Life*), 7 May 1952; and Julian Beck to Robin Prising, 21 May 1952, both in Living Theatre Archives, Billy Rose Collection.

16. "Humiliating agony" and "madhouse tornado farce." Beck Journal, 8 August 1952.

17. Gypsy path. *Diaries,* 27 July 1952, p. 238.

18. Faults as an actor. Judith Malina's original diary entry for 23 July 1948.

19. "Barefoot and barechested bohemian theatre." Beck Journal, 8 August 1952. "The wrong element." Julian Beck to Robin Prising, 13 October 1952, Living Theatre Archives, Billy Rose Collection. Jack Gelber, in his article "Julian Beck, Businessman," in *Tulane Drama Review* 30, no. 8 (Summer, 1986), p. 11, says he was told several times that Paul Goodman was observed buggering a neighborhood youth by Village neighbors who demanded that the landlord "throw out the perverts."

17. Unspeakable Cries

1. "Broken by the system." Julian Beck to Robin Prising, 13 October 1952, Living Theatre Archives, Billy Rose Collection.

2. Resumed her sessions with Paul Goodman. Malina, interview with author, 7 January 1992.

3. "Happening." See Harris, *Arts at Black Mountain.* Ronald Hayman, in *Artaud and After* (London: Oxford University Press, 1977), p. 158, asserts that Cage, prompted by Pierre Boulez, had been reading Artaud, who became a direct influence.

4. Superficial dilettante. Beck, Journal, 26 December 1952.

5. "Constricting system." Beck, Journal, 5 October 1952.

6. "The lie of Authority." These lines from Auden's "September 1, 1939" were excised from the *Collected Poems,* much to Judith's consternation.

7. "Vile function." Beck, Journal, 4 November 1952.

8. "Destroy the outer law." *Diaries,* 14 November 1952, p. 253.

9. Erdman's dancing. Beck, Journal, 15 January 1952.

10. Her unrequited infatuation with Lou Harrison was perennial. Campbell instructed Judith on black magic techniques which proved to no avail. According to Judith, Christopher Isherwood had sternly admonished her in the San Remo against any use of black magic. See *Diaries,* 15 March 1952, p. 216.

18. In Praise of Love

1. "Monstrous" was a favorite adjective of Julian's. Beck, Journal, 21 January 1953.

2. "Ugly and wicked temper." Beck, Journal, 25 March 1953. Judith omits any mention of the incident in the *Diaries,* so Julian may have given it more importance than it merited.

3. James Agee. Some of the details here are from Laurence Bergreen's *James Agee: A Life* (New York: E. P. Dutton, 1984), which only identifies Judith as a married mother. Malina, interview with author, 7 January 1992.

4. Like Paul Goodman. Beck, Journal, 13 March 1953. Sexually, he was a "suicide." Beck, Journal, 17 May 1953. To block pain. Beck, Journal, 1 June 1953.

5. Mouse being played with by a giant. *Diaries,* 20 November 1953, p. 303.

6. Prophetic tone of blame. Beck, Journal, 11 July 1953.

7. Lecherous, with a perpetual cigar in his mouth, Weegee. Beck, Journal, 5 July 1953. In an interview on 10 January 1992, Judith Malina told me Weegee was a role model for The Living Theatre because of the way he followed his instincts and yet had the discipline to create superb art.

8. "Heart of his love." Beck, Journal, 4 August 1953.

19. Circling the Moon

1. "Pink chic" and "preened their windows." Beck, Journal, 19 November 1953.

2. Engaging Judith. Beck, Journal, 13 September 1953.

3. Michael Harrington. Malina, interview with author, 7 January 1992.

In Harrington's defense, we should remember that both he and Agee were nominally Catholics and the year was 1953. Harrington founded the Young Socialist League in 1954. His book *The Other America* would have a profound effect on social theory in the United States in the 1960s.

4. "Flower among us." *Diaries*, 10 November 1953, p. 302.

5. Women who "circled him like the moon." *Diaries*, 28 October 1953, p. 299. "Too torn for me to lean on." *Diaries*, 31 December 1953, p. 305.

6. "Breaking down of hierarchies." *Diaries*, 22 October 1953, p. 298. It is an accurate observation of the primary reason for the fear of anarchism which intends to eliminate all hierarchies. Goodman recommended that Nina be placed in Lore Perls's care.

7. Mask of joy. Beck, Journal, 15 November 1953.

8. An open sexual community. Judith Malina, interview with author, 6 April 1993.

9. Agee reading from *A Death in the Family* is recalled in Judith Malina's original diary entry for 5 May 1958.

10. "My life's fire." *Diaries*, 22 February 1954, p. 313. "Nobility of the sun." Alan Hovhaness to Judith Malina, 15 June 1955, Living Theatre Archives.

20. The Broadway Loft

1. The tambourine was Jackson MacLow's; he composed the music which annoyed Julian, no doubt because it was on a tape recorder which failed to function at the opening. Judith Malina, interview with author, n.d.

2. "Alternate mind." Beck, Journal, 4 June 1954.

3. Tobi posed. Beck, Journal, 21 June 1954.

21. A Death in the Family

1. Alien life pattern. Beck, Journal, 2 August 1954. "Never cold or distant." *Diaries*, 17 May 1956, p. 404.

2. Wildly passionate. Beck, Journal, 5 January 1955. Insincerity. Julian Beck to Tobi Edelman, 8 August 1954, Living Theatre Archives.

3. Tobi's reluctance to continue the relationship prevented. Beck, Journal, 14 October 1954.

4. Too vigorous. *Diaries*, 21 October 1954, p. 344.

5. The play lacked. Beck, Journal, 27 December 1954.

6. Tennessee Williams was indifferent to any notion of drama other than his own. See *Diaries*, 21 October 1947, p. 11. Dotson Rader, in *Cry of the Heart* (New York: Doubleday, 1985) asserts that Williams made a habit of turning away from many of his friends, often ignoring them in public as an affront. Beck felt it was a case of ingratitude. In his autobiography, *Memoirs of a Bastard Angel,* Harold Norse claimed that there was a startling change in Williams's personality after the success of *The Glass Menagerie.* He became callous, insensitive, and often obnoxious, going out of his way to humiliate former friends. Beck felt Williams began to dislike him after he criticized Williams's play *You Touched Me* in the summer of 1944. See Beck, Journal, 20 December 1952.

7. "Wounded by ambition." Beck, Journal, 31 May 1955.

8. Agee had once explained that they were not in love. *Diaries,* 19 May 1955, p. 363.

9. *Phaedra* had special significance for Judith because the French actress Rachel had used it as her vehicle, and this was the first time Racine's play had been staged in English in New York.

22. Halls of Bedlam

1. Catholic Worker. See Dwight Macdonald in the *New Yorker,* 4 October 1952; and his *Memoirs of a Revolutionist* (New York: Farrar, Straus and Cudahy, 1957).

2. Contained anger. Jackson MacLow, interview with author, 25 Febraury 1952. O'Neill's lover. See Dan Wakefield, *New York in the Fifties* (New York: Houghton Mifflin, 1992). In *Exile's Return* (New York: Viking Press, 1951), Malcolm Cowley observed that all the gamblers in the Village respected Day because she could drink them under the table. She became less bohemian after the birth of her daughter: when she published an autobiographical novel, she purchased all the printed copies and destroyed them.

3. Day and her followers believed. This is based on a statement by Connie Bowers of the Fellowship for Reconciliation, dated 25 June 1955, Living Theatre Archives.

4. Judith had brought Saint-Simon's memoir. See *Diaries,* 20 June 1955, pp. 367–75, for Judith's version of the incident. She states that Julian advised her not to bring her diary, so the possibility of arrest must have been pronounced from the outset. Ammon Hennacy had his Bible in his bookbag, as well as books by Shelley and Tolstoy. Day had her Bible and read psalms aloud to the others. The *New York Times* account of the incident appeared on 18 June 1955.

5. Five hundred dollars for bail. Several weeks later, Judith received a suspended sentence. The former judge Julian hired to facilitate Judith's release was Morris Ploscowe, who had served as director of the American Medical Association-Bar Association Committee on Narcotics. He would advise them in the future.

6. Mrs. Cornelius Vanderbilt's home. Beck, Journal, 10 July 1955.

7. Sexless. Beck, Journal, 24 April 1955. Shied from sexual encounters because he felt inadequate. Beck, Journal, 29 November 1955. Fear of feeling. Beck, Journal, 4 December 1955.

8. Hovhaness's letters are quoted in *Diaries,* 20 August 1955.

9. "But yu can do nowt." *Diaries,* 28 September 1955, p. 384.

10. Local police. *Diaries,* 14 October 1955, p. 385. The problem revolved about a line in which one of the disciples said, "Our master is fucking me."

11. A licensing inspector. *Diaries,* 19 November 1955, pp. 386–87. Ironically, the inspector was a member of the War Resisters League who knew Dorothy Day and Ammon Hennacy.

12. "Every law there was to break." Beck, Journal, 18 November 1955.

13. Ganymede Gallery. Beck, Journal, 21 November 1955; and *Diaries,* 23 November 1955, p. 338.

23. Naughty Bliss

1. "La gloire." *Diaries,* 31 December 1955, p. 389.

2. Lester. Judith Malina, interview with author, 15 January 1992.

3. John Cage. *Diaries,* 7 May 1956, p. 401. Stoney Point. *Diaries,* 27 June 1956, p. 409.

4. "Inundated with love." Beck, Journal, 9 July 1956.

5. "Naughty bliss." Beck, Journal, 19 February 1956.

6. "Virtuous daredevil." Beck, Journal, 12 August 1956.

7. What she had tried to do as an actress had been for her mother. *Diaries,* 13 June 1957, p. 437.

8. Irving Beck. *Diaries,* 17 March 1955, p. 357.

24. Celebrations

1. "Mischievous kids." *Diaries,* 14 January 1957, p. 425. Caressed and embraced. *Diaries,* 4 February 1957, p. 427.

2. "My devotion." Beck, Journal, 3 March 1957.

3. "Julian was ambivalent." When Kupferman's operas opened in June, they received mediocre notices though Julian's setting was praised as inventive by Ross Parmenter, a music critic for the *New York Times*.

4. "Gild the lily." Beck, Journal, 20 March 1957.

5. "Roi-soleil." Beck, Journal, 21 February 1955. "Our taste." Beck, Journal, 20 May 1957.

6. Julian defended it. *New York Times,* Sunday, 7 April 1957.

7. Letter from Jean Cocteau. Beck, Journal, 4 April 1957; and *Diaries,* 25 April 1957, pp. 433–34.

25. Prison

1. Dorothy Day's account of the protest is in *Loaves and Fishes* (New York: Curtis Books, 1963) pp. 160–77. Julian Beck's account is in his Journal for 8, 9, and 13 August 1957; and in an essay, "All the World's a Prison," *Village Voice,* 4 September 1957. See also *Diaries,* pp. 441–62. There are six prison letters from Julian to Judith in The Living Theatre Archives. Each published accounts of the incident and prison life in a Greenwich Village magazine called *Phoenix.*

2. A judge who angrily sentenced them. Magistrate Walter J. Bayer told the demonstrators they were a group of "heartless individuals who use their religion as an excuse to break the law." See *Catholic Worker* 24, no. 1 (July/August 1957).

3. He had never been more touched or satisfied. In the Horace Mann *Alumni Bulletin* (Spring 1958), Julian claimed that the protest was his only act of public consequence and "the only thing of which I can surely say that it was not performed in the service of Mammon."

4. They possessed an unusual degree of altruism. Julian makes much of this in his *Village Voice* piece without offering any specific examples. He does note with surprise the incidence of homosexuality, even among heterosexual prisoners.

5. "Little crusaders." Beck, Journal, 14 August 1957. The Women's House of Detention was demolished in the early 1960s.

26. Cage's Drums

1. Pawlet, Vermont. Fredericks, interview with author, 10 October 1992; and Beck, Journal, 20 August 1957.

2. Julian attended high holiday services at Rabbi Carlebach's ortho- dox temple. Carlebach had been Max Malina's teacher and a year earlier had helped bury Rosel Malina. Beck, Journal, 26 October 1957. As the rabbi's daughter, Judith had a pronounced Jewish identity, but Julian's was only emerging.

3. "Emblem of hope." Beck, Journal, 14 September 1957.

4. "Subconscious world." Beck, Journal, 29 September 1957.

5. Art should be in a state of imbalance and imperfection. Beck, Jour- nal, 14 September 1957. This became one of the crucial aesthetic principles of Living Theatre productions in the late 1960s. On the jacket of his journal for 1957, Julian queried whether art ever changed life, a Wildean formula that explains one element of ritual the group employed in works such as *Mysteries* and *Paradise Now.*

6. "Burdened by failure" and "fat applause." Beck, Journal, 25 Octo- ber 1957.

7. Anaïs Nin. Beck, Journal, 30 November 1957.

27. Pledging the Temple

1. Larry Rivers. Beck, Journal, 2 January 1958.

2. Seven hundred dollars in January. Beck, Journal, 26 January 1958.

3. Hazel McKinley. Beck, Journal, 26 January 1958. See also *Diaries,* 17 February 1958. Note that the published *Diaries* only proceed through the Women's House of Detention imprisonment. From 1958 to August 1968 and from April 1969 to the present, Judith Malina's small notebook entries re- main only in their unpublished version which I have read and which I refer to in these notes as "Unpublished Diary."

4. Oscar Serlin. Unpublished Diary, 28 February and 3 March 1958. Julian and Judith should have realized that anyone who praised Rodgers and Hammerstein was unlikely to support them. Rodgers and Hammerstein presented a make-believe world of happy endings for those who conformed to the rules and behaved in a genteel manner. Thoroughly middle-class, they represented the exact opposite of the world The Living Theatre wanted to explore and create.

5. Frank O'Hara. Unpublished Diary, 16 February 1958.

6. Eric Gutkind's *Absolute Collective* is subtitled "A Philosophical At- tempt to Overcome Our Broken State" (trans. Marjorie Gabain [London: C. W. Daniel Company, 1937]).

7. "Orgone energy." Beck, Journal, 2 March 1958.

8. Entanglement with Lester. Beck, Journal, 17 March 1958; and Unpublished Diary, 3 and 20 March 1958.

9. Illuminated black and white wine cases. Unpublished Diary, 25 March 1958. The idea would become a major influence for the set of *Frankenstein,* eight years later.

10. Cry of distress. Unpublished Diary, 25 March 1958.

11. Peace march. *New York Times,* 5 April 1958, described the march as a page-one story and stated that five thousand demonstrated in London. Atmosphere of vitality. Unpublished Diary, 4 April 1958.

12. "Vast significance" and "scream of anguish and beatific love." Unpublished Diary, 6 April 1958.

13. Unfeigning realism. Judith Malina makes the comment in Sheldon Rochlin's documentary film on The Living Theatre, *Signals through the Flames* (Mystic Fire Video, 1982).

28. *Communitas*

1. Mysterious sums. Unpublished Diary, 16 April 1958. Lester was then working for Irving Beck.

2. Eyes drawn tight in anger. Unpublished Diary, 4 May 1958.

3. Sitting next to Judith, Julian, and Jasper Johns. Julian felt good about the fact that his painting *Four Horsemen of the Apocalypse* was hanging in the Pittsburgh International Exhibition of Contemporary Art along with work of Francis Bacon, Chagall, Ernst, Rauschenberg, and Larry Rivers.

4. "Eternity beats." Unpublished Diary, 1 March 1958. The Buber lecture is described in Unpublished Diary, 30 April 1958; and by Julian Beck in his Journal, 30 April 1958.

5. In front of the Atomic Energy Commission. Unpublished Diary, 7 May 1958. Day and the others received a thirty-day suspended sentence.

6. Eisenhower should have appeared. Unpublished Diary, 30 May 1958.

7. "Monstrous wars." Beck, Journal, 17 May 1958.

8. "Blind and bruised." Beck, Journal, 2 July 1958.

9. Volunteer labor. Some of the other workers were Al Saltzman, Larry Kornfeld, Hans Hokanson, Jerry Raphael, Henry Proach, and Mel Clay. Kornfeld later managed the Judson Theatre and became a talented director. Proach and Clay became members of the company. Joseph Chaikin, Ray Johnson, Jackson MacLow, and Spencer Holst also helped. The plumbing and electrical work was contracted out to the De Wees brothers, two black SIA anarchists.

10. Goodman's review appeared in the *Nation* on 29 November 1958.

11. Artaud's premise that the plague. Anaïs Nin, in Paris in 1933, attended Artaud's Sorbonne lecture "Le Théâtre et la peste" and reported that he began acting out dying from the plague: "His face was contorted with anguish, one could see the perspiration dampening his hair. His eyes dilated, his muscles became cramped, his fingers struggled to retain their flexibility. He was in agony. He was screaming. He was delirious." Quoted in Hayman, *Artaud and After,* p. 89. Artaud's performance must have shocked Nin because she knew him as such an exceptionally mild, sweet-tempered man.

12. Carl Solomon. Unpublished Diary, 9 October 1958. Solomon recalled the event in a little essay called "Meeting Julian Beck during the Papacy of John the Twenty-third," *Exquisite Corpse* 4, no. 11–12 (November/December 1986), p. 12. When I asked Solomon in a telephone conversation on 9 August 1991 why he chose to appear at The Living Theatre in the first place, his reply was that "living meant surviving" to him at that time. Judith Malina, on 14 February 1992, told me that he had been brought to the theatre by poet Spencer Holst. Solomon returned to his mother in the Bronx who informed Pilgrim State Hospital, to which he was returned. Like Artaud, he was released after spending eight consecutive years in lunatic asylums.

13. "Illegitimate." Unpublished Diary, 17 December 1958.

29. A Poet's Theatre

1. Another wall for James Waring's dancers. This time Julian used illuminated egg crates. Filled with objects like Joseph Cornell's boxes, this "bright piece of magic" was praised in the *Village Voice* by Allen Ginsberg in his review. See the *Village Voice,* 17 December 1958. While doing the wall, Julian met Nicola Cernovich, who did the lighting for the production. Cernovich had won an award for lighting *Ulysses in Nighttown,* a celebrated off-Broadway production, and he would later work with The Living Theatre.

2. Casting and rehearsing. Julian also built a set, found the necessary props, counseled on makeup, and resolved the myriad issues that occur with any dramatic production.

3. *Many Loves and Other Plays* was published by New Directions (New York, 1968).

4. Failure of communication. Years later Julian wrote that Williams told him the play was about accuracy. The play was, Julian observed, a palimpsest with layers of interconnected meanings. See Beck, "Storming the Barricades, pp. 4, 25.

5. Williams had declared. William Carlos Williams to Yale critic Norman Holmes Pearson. See John Thirlwall, ed., *Selected Letters of William Carlos Williams* (New York: McDowell, Obolensky, 1957).

6. Julian had noticed Atkinson rushing out. Beck, Journal, 14 January 1959. With the beginning of the Fourteenth Street theatre, Julian discontinued making regular entries in his journal, only writing in it sporadically. A decade later, he would resume making entries in what he then called "workbooks."

7. His review was respectful. The *New York Times* review appeared on 14 January 1959. Subsequent reviews were more sobering. Judith Crist in the *New York Herald Tribune* found Williams's play full of a disappointing glibness. In the *Nation* on 7 February, Harold Clurman was more impressed with the potential of the Fourteenth Street space than with Williams's play. Gerald Weales, in the Spring 1959 issue of *Kenyon Review,* a fastidiously conservative magazine, found the play pretentious.

8. Goodman had previously expressed his jealousy. Judith Malina described Goodman's antipathy to Ginsberg in an account of the party after the opening of *Many Loves.* Unpublished Diary, 14 January 1959. Howard Smith described the reading itself in the *Village Voice* on 4 February 1959. "Gallivanting" is Julian's term in Journal, 7 February 1959.

9. Baroness Wedell Wedellsberg's husband was chairman of the board of Canadian Club.

10. Julian's article "Why Vanguard?" appeared on the cover of the Arts and Leisure section of the *New York Times,* Sunday, 22 March 1959.

11. Corso reading. Unpublished Diary, 16 March 1959. Further details provided by Judith Malina in conversation with me on 5 December 1992. One notorious member of the audience was the journalist Hunter S. Thompson, who at that time was living in the Village and working as a copyboy at *Time.* According to Thompson's friend Gene McGarr who was with him at the time, the two men had several bags of beer between their legs. As they finished a can, they would kick it down the aisles like a hockey puck. This disturbed Corso enormously who ended up shouting at them. See the material excerpted from E. Jean Carroll's oral biography *Hunter* (New York: Dutton, 1992) in *Esquire,* February 1993, pp. 66–67. Another account is provided by Brad Gooch in *City Poet,* his biography of Frank O'Hara (New York: Knopf, 1993), pp. 324–25.

12. Mechanical and flat. Unpublished Diary, 4 April 1959.

13. A young actor. See Joseph Chaikin, *The Presence of the Actor* (New York: Theatre Communications Group, 1991), p. 47. Son of a man who studied the Talmud in Chicago, Chaikin was afflicted with a rheumatic heart condition as a child that continued to limit his options as an actor but never made him stop. Later, he founded the Open Theatre.

30. Jazz

1. Jack Gelber. Some details from Unpublished Diary, 16 April 1958; and others from Jerry Tallmer's piece "The Boy Who Broke the Circle—and Unsquared It," *Village Voice*, 4 November 1959.

2. "Deep freeze." Jerry Tallmer, *Village Voice*, 29 July 1959.

3. "We had to show." Beck, "Storming the Barricades," p. 27.

4. Toothpaste commercial. Donald Malcolm, *New Yorker*, 10 October 1959.

5. Julian's surrealist background mural. In an era of hyperinflated Broadway budgets, it seems almost anachronistic to note that Julian's set, and all expenses for props and incidentals, cost under a thousand dollars. See Maurice Zolotow's feature on The Living Theatre, front page of the Arts and Leisure section of the *New York Times*, 10 September 1961.

6. Jamming. Jazz, as many commentators have noted, was the music of revolt before rock and roll. As novelist Ronald Sukenick puts it in *Down and In: Life in the Underground* (New York: William Morrow, 1987), p. 84, "Digging Bop is one of the main ways subterraneans can express their cultural radicalism."

7. This was a crucial principle of the play. McLean told me he learned this when, in an emergency during the London production of *In the Jungle of the Cities,* an actor walked out and Julian asked him to fill in as a Chinese bartender. Jackie McLean, interview with author, 22 January 1993.

An equally important psychological principle was created by Judith's staging. Stage left was for the white actors pretending to be junkies; stage right was for the black musicians who were junkies. If a white or a black crossed the stage, a certain symmetry was violated, causing a subtle uneasiness, an unbalancing which the audience longed to see rectified (Judith Malina, interview with author, 20 November 1992). There were a number of black actors in the cast of *The Connection,* including Leroy House, who is still with the company as Rain House, and Carl Lee, who played Cowboy and was the son of Canada Lee who had appeared in the Broadway production of *Native Son.* Two black actors, Jimmy Anderson and Rufus Collins, would become permanent members through the 1960s. Julian, who had learned from the tactics of the civil rights movement, wrote that it was important to bring blacks into the theatre and to "learn to communicate, black and white, each learning about what goes on in the other's heads and lives." See Julian Beck to Karl Bissinger, published in the *New York Times* as "Thoughts on Theatre from Jail," 21 February 1965.

8. Permanent feature of the acting. This was frequently misunderstood by the professional critics as amateurism. It is analogous to the way

William Carlos Williams, Kerouac, and Ginsberg replaced a purified literary speech by what they called natural speech in their work which was equally misunderstood or disparaged by the literary critics. At the same time, The Living Theatre exercised a bias for relatively inexperienced or untrained actors. "Political leaning, sexual inclination, and willingness to follow Judith's direction in developing a new acting style were more important than previous experience," according to Jack Gelber in his article, "Julian Beck, Businessman," p. 8.

9. The musicians were less reliable. Unpublished Diary, 3 and 17 June 1959. McLean once disappeared to retrieve a monkey that had escaped from its cage in his kitchen at home. The monkey was an actual creature though it could have had metaphorical significance (McLean, interview with author, 22 January 1993). Steven Ben Israel told me that Tina Brooks, McLean's understudy, was so strung out that he would sometimes forget about the play, go off on his own, and play for fifteen minutes or so (Ben Israel, interview with author, 25 November 1992).

10. Sense of family and community. McLean told me that both Judith and Julian were also his teachers, that he was greatly influenced by their humanist philosophy and politics, and that their cumulative impact "made me more sympathetic to the world" (McLean, interview with author, 22 January 1993). This was a general refrain among those whom I interviewed. In an interview with David Rosenthal, McLean stated that he thought Judith and Julian were "people who were looking far into the future, for a better way. You had to love them to be with them, because The Living Theatre was like a big commune. Mostly everybody lived together, ate together, and were together working out each person's problems. I didn't live with them because I had my wife and kids, but I was part of it because certainly I lived with them when we left New York, when we went to Europe." See David Rosenthal, *Hard Bop: Jazz and Bop Music, 1955–65* (New York: Oxford University Press, 1992), pp. 80–81. An actress who particularly emphasized the aspect of family and community created by Judith and Julian was Marilyn Chris whom I interviewed in an ABC studio on 15 December 1992. Chris said that after seeing *The Connection,* she approached Julian in the lobby of the theatre to ask if she could join the company. Wearing his sandals without socks, a black leather jacket, a chartreuse shirt, and a pink tie, Julian responded that "if you embrace us, we will embrace you." Chris went on to perform in *Many Loves, In the Jungle of the Cities,* and *The Apple* though she had had no real experience before.

11. Lester had become involved. Unpublished Diary, 24 February 1959 and 4 May 1959. "Defected." Unpublished Diary, 11 June 1959.

12. Demons. Beck, Journal, 1 August 1959. "Exotic pleasures." Beck,

Journal, 13 August 1959. "Knew he could not satisfy her" and "confused mixed-up life." Beck, Journal, 14 August 1959. Julian's "confused" needs no overinterpretation. The program for *The Connection* included a brief essay by Artaud, "The Theatre and Culture," in which he asserted that "confusion is the sign of our times." Julian would have declared that for artists it was normative.

13. A number of whom experimented with heroin. Malina, interview with author, 20 November 1992. Some tried it for a day, some for a week or longer. Larry Rivers's comment, based on what he says Garry Goodrow told him, is from his autobiography, *What Did I Do* (New York: Harper Collins, 1992), p. 354.

14. The daily reviews appeared on 16 July 1959. Tallmer's only appeared on 29 July 1959. To some extent, the reaction of the daily reviewers was predictable, and even some of the actors found the play troublesome. Joseph Chaikin at first thought it morbid, burdened by a sense of "unrelieved dread."

15. "Theatre of poverty." Beck, Journal, 3 August 1959. The comment was prophetic.

16. Mailer's letter appeared in the *Village Voice* on 12 August 1959, and Ginsberg's, on 2 September. Kenneth Tynan's comments were originally written for *Harper's* and were used as the preface to the Grove Press edition of *The Connection* (New York, 1960), pp. 7–11. Brustein's review was in the *New Republic* on 28 September 1959, and Hewes's in *Saturday Review* on 26 September 1959. Brustein commented on the significance of the play in his interview with Julian Beck and Judith Malina in *Yale/Theatre* 2 (Spring 1969), p. 18.

31. A Dream of Transformation

1. *Show Business,* 23 December 1959. Louis Calta's article, "1958–9 Season in Retrospect," in the Arts And Leisure section of the *New York Times,* Sunday, 28 June 1959, records the off-Broadway boom. Along with The Living Theatre would be the Café Cino which began in 1959, the Judson Poets' Theatre founded in 1961, Ellen Stewart's La Mama which started in 1962, the Open Theatre and Theatre Genesis in 1963, and the American Place Theatre which opened in 1964.

2. Audiences for *The Connection.* The play attracted a highly responsive, sometimes outspoken, working-class audience, mixed with Village intellectuals and "tourists" from uptown. Members of the audience were

known to return several times. Since one had to climb twenty-two steps to enter the second-floor lobby, it was not a Broadway audience. In 1960, tickets cost $3.75 and $2.50.

3. "Bourgeois money" and "mutilating power." Beck, Journal, 12 December 1959.

4. Ephemeral. In *Tonight We Improvise,* Dr. Hinckfuss states that "theatre does not endure, it is a miracle of form and motion, and a miracle can be momentary." Julian saw his journal as a way to "extend if not preserve forever the moments and events of the life one has had." Beck, Journal, 28 December 1959.

5. *Time,* 25 January 1960. Williams was so excited. Jerry Tallmer in a piece on Warren Finnerty's Obie award, *Village Voice,* 25 May 1960.

6. Shirley Clarke. The film was made although Judith and Julian felt betrayed when Clarke did not give The Living Theatre appropriate credit. In 1962, the Board of Regents of the State of New York attempted to censor the film on the grounds of obscenity, but this was overturned by the Apellate Division of the State Supreme Court. See *New York Times,* 3 July 1962.

7. "Wild beast." Beck, Journal, 16 January 1960.

8. Strangers. Beck, Journal, 20 September 1959.

9. He entered a declaration. Beck, Journal, 31 January 1960.

32. Mammon's Revenge

1. Marijuana and hashish. Beck, Journal, 11 February 1960.

2. "Harried genius." Unpublished Diary, 20 January 1960.

3. "Oriental delight." Unpublished Diary, 31 December 1959. The reference is more likely to opium than to Chinese food.

4. Pound's revolutionary genius. Beck, Journal, 5 and 6 July 1960.

5. "Gibberish." *New York Times,* 23 June 1960. "Absurd and pathetic." Jerry Tallmer, *Village Voice,* 7 July 1960.

6. Path of folly. Beck, Journal, 18 July 1960.

7. More community. Malina, interview with author, 20 November 1992. It should be pointed out that each actor was only being paid forty-five dollars a week from which $7.50 was sometimes deducted for taxes. Many of the actors resisted Julian's demand: one of them, Bill Shari, told Julian he was "pushing too many of the production problems" on the actors. See Michael Smith, *Theatre Trip* (New York: Bobbs Merrill, 1969), p. 139. By 1964, many of the production demands were routinely met by actors.

8. "Mammon's revenge." Beck, Journal, 10 July 1960. Beck noticed

Gelber's new attitude as early as March. In his article, "Julian Beck, Businessman," Gelber argues The Living Theatre was kept alive by three separate $25,000 contributions though he does not specify the contributors. According to Gelber, "Julian's genius" was for "defusing angry, unpaid actors and crew, for deflecting the landlord and the city marshals bent on seizing theatre property for unpaid bills, and for delaying government action on tax problems." Gelber remembers that actors would clamor at the box office for back pay, and Julian would dole out just enough to placate them. He also maintains that most of the company, including Julian, stayed on the payroll only until they became eligible for unemployment assistance. In a time when government assistance to the arts was unknown in the United States, Beck had invented an indirect form of subsidy. See Gelber, "Julian Beck, Businessman," pp. 14–15.

9. Grim and taciturn. Unpublished Diary, 5 August 1960.

10. Polaris submarines. Ironically, Charley Solin, the building inspector who had closed the One Hundredth Street loft, was also a participant. Judith and Julian toured the *Ethan Allen,* the new submarine built to house the missile. Unpublished Diary, 29 August 1960.

33. Europe

1. Martin Sheen. Actors usually did not formally audition for The Living Theatre, but Sheen incandescently read Hickey's speech from O'Neill's *Iceman Cometh.* Sheen's roommate at that time was Al Pacino who had some small roles, swept floors, and tried to make himself useful. Much to Judith's regret, she admitted to me, she had not recognized Pacino's talent. Malina, interview with author, 20 November 1992.

2. Sex with men. Beck, Journal, 11 November 1960.

3. Nonprofit status. Unpublished Diary, 26 December 1960.

4. "Demolished" is Judith's term. Unpublished Diary, 1 January 1961. Julian . . . in a night of heroin. Unpublished Diary, 28 January 1961.

5. New rehearsal atmosphere. Beck, "Storming the Barricades," p. 30.

6. The play seemed to baffle. Howard Taubman, in the *New York Times* on 21 December 1960, admitted he was "bewildered." Richard Watts in the *Post* praised Judith's direction as vigorous, imaginative, and inventive.

7. State Department assistance. Beck, Journal, 8 March 1961; and Unpublished Diary, 9 March 1961. Brecht had been investigated by the House Un-American Activities Committee in 1947, and any company that performed his plays was suspect. According to John Lindsay, Max Isenbergh of

the State Department told him that if money was available, it would never go to The Living Theatre. See article in the *New York Post,* 20 July 1962. Helen Hayes had been given a million dollars by the State Department to tour Europe that summer, so some funds had been available.

8. Fellini grotesque. Beck, Journal, 2 May 1961. The work was sold at ridiculously low prices. The *Times* covered the auction on 3 May 1961.

9. Boarded a French ship. Judith feared air travel but was unhappy when she learned the ship was war booty, a German ship which the French remodeled after the war. Unpublished Diary, 29 May 1961.

10. Shackles of bourgeois prejudice. Julian was not naive enough to believe that France was without bourgeois prejudice, but he frequently quoted Gertrude Stein's comment that "it was not what France gave you, but what she did not take away from you."

11. The Grand Prix. The Living Theatre was the first American company to win it and the first off-Broadway company to tour Europe.

12. They took a train to Rome. De Chirico attended *The Connection,* and Julian met the surrealist master. Rome, Julian thought, was a city of greed and death. Full of excessive baroque decoration, he compared it to a calloused lover. Beck, Journal, 5 June 1961.

13. They played in Milan. Georgio Strehler of the Piccollo Theatre saw The Living Theatre at this time and was influenced by them.

14. Berlin. The Berliner Ensemble, Brecht's company, attended *In the Jungle of the Cities.* Julian found German men fiercely sexual, "with high proud bodies and thick, curling lips." There was a sadomasochistic edge that attracted him. He said he was able to forgive but not forget what the Nazis had done. The company stayed in an old pensione run by a "mad Jew" who asked Judith to find him an American wife. When one of the members of the company lay on a bed after check-out time, however, he summoned the police. Unpublished Diary, 3–7 July 1961; and Beck, Journal, 19 June 1961.

34. Militants

1. It marked a milestone in the American peace movement. The 1960 Mississippi lunch counter sit-ins of the civil rights movement led by members of the Southern Christian Leadership Conference were certainly an earlier model. The attempts to register Southern black voters from 1961–64 by the Student Nonviolent Coordinating Committee were another model.

2. "Becoming a woman." Beck, Journal, 26 August 1961.

3. "Sodomic yen." Beck, Journal, 4 December 1960.

4. "Palpable spirituality." Jack Gelber, telephone conversation with author, 30 November 1992.

5. Letter from Bertrand Russell. Russell's letter was dated 25 November 1961 and is in The Living Theatre Archives.

6. Actors Equity. Judith believes her appeal may have hindered her career. Judith Malina, interview with author, 25 June 1993.

7. The reviewers were respectful. Jerry Tallmer stated in the *Village Voice* on 14 December 1961 that Gelber was "farther out on the space frontier" than anyone writing for the American theatre. Richard Watts, writing in the *Post* on 24 December 1961 under the headline "An Evening of Vast Perversity" said the play displayed Gelber's "frenzied distaste for bourgeois audiences" and had the flavor of a "studious esoteric stunt." Robert Hatch, in a general discussion of The Living Theatre in *Horizon,* in March 1962, astutely observed that the play worked like group therapy, constantly posing the question of whether what was transpiring onstage was more real than life itself.

8. "Maniac on a cliff." Beck, Journal, 7 December 1961. "Privilege of failure." In Maurice Zolotow's *New York Times* feature on 10 September 1961.

9. A letter by Martin Buber from Jerusalem. Judith chose the term "the enormous despair" as the title for the first published book of her *Diaries,* recording the American return in 1968–69. Buber's letter is in The Living Theatre Archives and dated 17 December 1961. Judith applied Buber's comment to those in the movement who chose violence.

10. General Strike. Reported in the *New York Times,* 30 January 1962. Soviet mission. Saul Gottlieb's account in The Living Theatre Archives. Bob Dylan. Judith Malina, interview with author, 13 November 1992. In Unpublished Diary, 22 October 1972, Judith remembered smoking a joint with Dylan in a telephone booth.

11. Tactical Forces Division. The Duffy Square police attack was reported on page 4 of the *New York Times* on 4 March 1962. Judith Malina was arrested for "resisting arrest." Forty-one others were also arrested. In a cold rain, thirty-two people were arrested at a sit-in at the Atomic Energy Commission offices. Two useful articles appeared in the *Village Voice* on 8 March and the *Guardian* on 12 March 1962. Julian described the events leading to his beating in the April *Liberation* and in its fullest form in *Evergreen Review* (May 1962), pp. 121–24.

12. Bill Shari. An important member of the company, Shari was unconscious after being beaten, and was so battered and bruised that while in jail for two days, he could barely stand. A chemistry major at St. Peter's, a Jesuit college in New Jersey, where he had also studied stage management, he had

been radicalized by a Jesuit professor who gave him the *Catholic Worker* to read. He worked as a lighting technician on *In the Jungle of the Cities* and played in *The Connection*. My interview with Dorothy Shari on 5 December 1992; and Michael Smith's in *Theatre Trip*, pp. 136–41.

35. A Mad Gambler

1. Telegram to Governor Nelson Rockefeller. Julian, to little avail, also filed a complaint with the New York Civilian Complaint Review Board.

2. Linus Pauling. See Committee for Non-Violent Action, *Bulletin* (16 March 1962). Pauling collected the signatures of over eleven thousand scientists in a petition to the United Nations to stop testing by international agreement. See Joseph Roddy's article on the peace movement in *Look,* 17 July 1962.

3. Merton's perceptive comments appeared in the *Catholic Worker* (29 January 1962).

4. Julian managed to hire ambulances. Jackie McLean as told to David Rosenthal in *Hard Bop,* p. 81. "Mad gambler." Beck, Journal, 14 April 1962.

5. Touring twenty-two cities. The only mishap, besides scrapes in hotels, was the loss in Zurich of a bag containing the manuscript of *The Life of the Theatre.* Characteristically, Julian rewrote it from scratch. Judith Malina, interview with author, n.d.

6. "Under their wing." Chaikin was quoted in a *New York Post* article, appearing on 20 July 1962; he charged that the State Department maintained a bias against The Living Theatre.

7. "Disobey as much as you can." Beck, Journal, 1 May 1962.

8. Human will is weak and malleable. Julian's version of the play he directed was more optimistic. In an article in the *Village Voice* on 11 October 1962, he argued that Brecht meant "man could be turned from materialistic and selfish beings into men who could also see clearly, look at the facts, and save one another."

9. New York critics were respectful. The daily reviews appeared on 19 September 1962. Walter Kerr in the *Herald Tribune* said that it was "wantonly overlong." In the *Post,* Richard Watts found the play "repeats its points until it becomes wearisome." John McClain in the *Journal-American* claimed it left him feeling bored and weary. In the *Nation,* Harold Clurman found the production "wretched." His review appeared later, on 6 October 1962, as did the favorable piece by Michael Smith in the *Village Voice* which appeared on 27 September 1962.

10. Rival production. The Living Theatre version was based on Gerhard Nellhaus's translation authorized by Brecht's son Stefan who lived in the Village. The famous 1931 production in Berlin had Peter Lorre as Galy Gay. In The Living Theatre production, Joseph Chaikin played Galy Gay, and Judith played the Widow Begwick, a part that Olympia Dukakis had in Bentley's production.

11. Civil rights agitation. Early in October, President Kennedy had ordered four thousand National Guard troops to maintain order and enforce integration at the University of Mississippi in Oxford.

12. Note from Joseph Campbell. Campbell's note is quoted in a verse section of Unpublished Diary, 13 October 1962.

13. Judgment for $6,800 in back rent. Actually, the first Alternate University had been housed in the Fourteenth Street location although this, of course, was never intended as a money-making venture.

14. Supreme Court judgment. There were articles in the *New York Times* and the *Herald Tribune* on 8 November 1962. In the middle of this financial crisis, Garrick was bar mitzvahed at the Society for the Advancement of Judaism on 24 November 1962.

15. Auction by the city sheriff. In "Julian Beck, Businessman," Jack Gelber claimed that Julian had pledged the five-thousand-dollar air-conditioning system repeatedly to secure loans or placate creditors, although he had never even paid for it in the first place. Gelber maintained that Julian turned down a Broadway offer for *The Connection,* and Julian had frequently stated that he would never consider staging a play because it might make money. See, for example, the symposium including Edward Albee, José Quintero, and Julian in *The Second Coming* (October 1960), p. 25. Actually, Shelley Winters had wanted to play a Sister Salvation who would save the junkies at the end of the play in a perfect Hollywood ending which no one in the company was willing to accept.

36. The Fluorescent Tunnel

1. "Brilliant connection" and "hideous fluorescent tunnel" are images Julian Beck used in "Storming the Barricades," his introduction to Kenneth Brown's *Brig* (p. 4).

2. "Street kid with a rose." Some of the details here come from Kenneth Brown's unpublished memoir, "Finding Out." Brown had worked at the Copacabana and was tending bar in a fancy restaurant near Sutton Place patronized by the Kennedy clan and the Sulzbergers when Julian called to tell him he wanted to produce his play.

3. Sane prisoners had been conditioned to behave like madmen. In *The Brig*, all the characters except one try to remain sane in an insane world. Several other American writers had recently described characters driven mad by society. Julian read William S. Buroughs's *Naked Lunch* on the ship returning from Europe in 1962. Joseph Heller, and Ken Kesey in *One Flew Over the Cuckoo's Nest*, explored the relativity of madness in the early 1960s. The photographer Diane Arbus romanticized freaks and insane people in a desperate search for innocence. In accord with Artaud's idea that society had conspired to prevent the madman from revealing "intolerable, unbearable truths," psychiatrists such as R. D. Laing praised the unique insights afforded to the insane, and "madness" itself began to be reinterpreted by many in the 1960s and given saintly connotations. Luke Theodore, one of the actors in The Living Theatre, told Michael Smith that he deliberately sought the breakthroughs afforded by madness. See *Theatre Trip*, p. 118.

4. Theatre so violent. Artaud's notion that depicted violence discourages us from committing it may represent more of a moral hope than the result of any scientific inquiry. Artaud's hope is based on Aristotle's notion of a catharsis that cleanses by the depiction of horror. The supposition in the United States is that media violence only encourages violence, but of course that is usually not art. In "Storming the Barricades" (p. 24), Julian said that Artaud was his mentor and that the problem was "how to create that spectacle, that Aztec, convulsive, plague-ridden panorama that would so shake people up, so cause feeling to be felt, that the steel world of law and order which civilization had forged to protect itself from barbarism would melt."

5. Noise level. Beck, "Thoughts on Theatre."

6. "The venerable line." Judith Malina's "Directing *The Brig*," which is an afterword to Kenneth Brown's *The Brig* (p. 88). The actors read the manual onstage as well.

7. "Examined with care." Malina, "Directing *The Brig*," p. 100.

8. Consensual spirit that began to govern the group and unify it. See Michael Smith's interview with Rufus Collins in *Theatre Trip*, p. 93. Kenneth Brown, in an interview with Richard Schechner in the *Tulane Drama Review* (Spring 1964), p. 213, stated that *The Brig* caused the group to become "a family in that we all began to love one another. We became so involved in the play that we stayed in the theatre long into the night and sometimes long into the next day discussing what we had done, what were the possibilities, what was to be done the next night. After a while we lost sight of the play completely and we discussed only its universal meanings."

9. Special programs. These were a crucial part of the artistic community Beck had envisaged. The reputation of The Living Theatre had been

greatly augmented by these gatherings, especially by the poetry readings. For example, a few weeks earlier, Ginsberg, LeRoi Jones, and Ray Bremser had read in a benefit for *Yugen,* Jones's magazine; another night, John Ashbery read, and just before Christmas, one-act plays by Frank O'Hara and Jones were presented. Revolutionists like Jones, who would write such savagely vitriolic plays as *The Slave* and *The Dutchman,* were attracted to The Living Theatre and formed an important part of its ambiance. Ray Bremser was a Beat poet who had served a prison sentence. When I met him at the Kerouac Conference in Boulder in 1982, he had a stick of dynamite in his boot, an old miner's habit that in his case was a function of paranoia.

10. "I began to feel." Chaikin, *Presence of the Actor,* p. 52.

11. Jenny Hecht. Malina, interview with author, 20 November 1992.

12. Steven Ben Israel. Successful on the coffeehouse circuit in the Village, Ben Israel performed on bills with Bob Dylan, Tom Paxton, Theodore Bikel, and Peter, Paul, and Mary. He worked the opening of the Bitter End but was also in a Brooklyn production of *Tonight We Improvise.* The Lord Buckley imitation he did at the Village Gate benefit for the General Strike was called "Jonah and the Whale" and was about smoking marijuana (Ben Israel, interview with author, 25 November 1992.)

13. "Pot and perversion." The details of the draft card burning are in a poem called "Violence," written on 3 March 1963 and included in a section of the unpublished diary that is entirely in verse. On the hawkish mood of Americans, a Lou Harris poll in the summer of 1963 reported that by a two to one margin, Americans favored sending troops to Vietnam on a large scale. Ed Sanders was a friend of The Living Theatre who maintained the principle of "total assault on the culture." In a former kosher butcher shop near Avenue D on the lower East Side, he ran the Peace Eye Bookstore and mimeographed *Fuck You: A Magazine of the Arts* which was one of the beginning points of the samizdat alternative publishing scene. Later, he formed the Fugs, a rock group, and wrote Charles Manson's biography.

14. Living in the dressing rooms. Brown, "Finding Out." An expression of anarchist libertarianism, inhabiting the theatre is what caused the downfall of the Cherry Lane.

15. Critics generally did not know. Daily reviews of *The Brig* appeared on 16 May. Michael Smith's review appeared in the *Village Voice* on 23 May. To a certain extent, the reaction was predictable. Robert Brustein remembered finding *The Brig* ugly and uncomfortable: "I don't remember a more unpleasant evening in the theatre. But it made a point" (Brustein, "Interview with Julian Beck and Judith Malina," p. 19).

16. Right-wing groups. See the *New York Times,* 16 May 1963, for an article on censorship. "The Establishment." See the *Village Voice,* 23 May

1963. When *Evergreen Review* number 32 (June 1963) was seized, photographer Edward Steichen declared that if "human beings in the act of making love are indecent, then the entire human race stands indicted."

17. "Phantom Cabaret." Wavy Gravy became the organizer of a famous California commune called the Hog Farm in the 1960s. Selling his poems and begging, Moondog and his German shepherd were familiar features on the streets of New York all through the 1960s. A grotesque purveyor of nostalgia, Tiny Tim became a minor pop celebrity in the 1960s.

18. At least one of them had a genuine breakdown. This was Henry Howard, an actor who had previously played in several Hollywood films and fifteen off-Broadway shows, including *The Three Penny Opera* during the last two years of its record-breaking 2,700 performance run. Howard was a friend of Steven Ben Israel's who introduced him to the company. He claimed that the "concentrated energy" demanded by *The Brig* resulted in a psychosis that made him leave the play for four months. See Michael Smith's interview with Henry Howard in *Theatre Trip,* pp. 103–4. Another time, Steve Thompson, an actor playing prisoner number eight, lost a button that was found onstage during a performance by Henry Howard who had rejoined the company. When Howard spit in his eye, an improvised act, Thompson went berserk and had to be restrained with a straitjacket. (Ben Israel, interview with author, 25 November 1992).

37. *The Brig* Bust

1. Press conference. Details are drawn from Julian Beck's essay, "How to Close a Theatre," *Tulane Drama Review* 8, no. 3 (Spring 1964), pp. 184–88. Most of this issue was devoted to the trouble described in this chapter.

2. None of the large foundations had been willing to assist. Kenneth Brown asserted the reason was entirely political: "If you spit in a man's eye, you can't seriously expect him to pay for it, no matter how well you do it." See his article *"Frankenstein* and the Birth of the Monster," *City Lights Journal,* no. 3 (1966), p. 53. The largest individual donors were the architect Paul Williams, and the playwrights Tennessee Williams and Edward Albee.

3. "Something more sinister." This was spelled out by Robert Brustein who in a piece in the *New Republic* suggested the seizure of the theatre was ordered by a conspiracy of high-echelon government officials. Jack Gelber in his article "Julian Beck, Businessman" offers a very different set of circumstances. He argues that the role of embattled revolutionaries and mar-

tyred, misunderstood artists was deliberately cultivated to mask box-office failure. At the point of ultimate crisis, when Julian knew he could no longer forestall the various creditors, Gelber alleges "he decided to call the Internal Revenue Service and rouse the beast of government into action." Unfortunately, Gelber provided no substantiation for these charges. See "Julian Beck, Businessman," pp. 11, 18. Michael Harrington's wife, Stephanie, reporting in the *Village Voice* on 3 June 1964, alleged that Julian said he had called the IRS "because he thought that they would help him."

4. Pretext. Malina, interview with author, 13 January 1992.

5. IRS seizure. Judith Malina, interview with author, 13 January 1992. Michael Smith's front-page story in the *Village Voice,* 24 October 1963. Brown, "Finding Out," pp. 23–26.

6. Liberation. Brustein, "Interview with Julian Beck and Judith Malina," p. 69.

7. Two actors with Marine Corps training. These were Tom Lilliard and Chic Ciccarelli. Both of them became Hollywood film actors.

8. IRS agents removed the fuses. Julian pointed out that the intensity of the light, as in Gertrude Stein's *Doctor Faustus Lights the Lights,* was integral. The two plays had a lot in common: both minimized narrative, both were about hell, and both minutely examined a moral sensibility and the question of identity. See "Storming the Barricades," pp. 8–9.

9. Civil disobedience. Beck, "How to Close a Theatre," p. 189.

10. Moving men. The contents of the theatre were sold at public auction the following week for $225. Karl Bissinger, a friend of Julian's, bought *The Brig* set and stored it in his basement so that it could be used in the future. Brown, "Finding Out," p. 27.

11. Later, in a poem. Judith's poem was called "Last Performance of The Living Theatre Invective" and was published in the June 1964 issue of *The Evergreen Review* (pp. 49–52). Kerouac, Richard Brautigan, and Harold Pinter also had work in the issue.

12. Bail. Julian denounced the $500 bail as the "privilege of the rich," but he took advantage of it. The *New York Times* report on 22 October 1963 was by Louis Calta who had trashed *The Connection.* Jerry Tallmer covered the matter for the *New York Post* on 21 October 1963.

13. Jim Tiroff. Judith Malina, interview with author, 4 December 1992. Brown, "Finding Out," p. 33.

14. Henry Howard. Malina, interview with author, 4 December 1992. Brown, "Finding Out," p. 33.

15. Carl Einhorn. Malina, interview with author, 4 December 1992. An early notebook. Living Theatre Archives.

38. Demeaning the Court

1. "O my America." Unpublished Diary, 23 January 1964.

2. Lenny Bruce. Steven Ben Israel, interview with author, 25 November 1992. Ben Israel knew Bruce from the Village coffeehouse circuit.

3. "Devotion of artists." Unpublished Diary, 23 January 1964.

4. First names. The trial was described to me by Judith Malina in the interview on 13 November 1992. Depositions by Tennessee Williams and Edward Albee, who were both out of the country, were read testifying to the moral character of Julian and Judith, and the importance of their work.

5. Fellatio. Unpublished Diary, 25 June 1964. This page contains the cinders collected at another draft-card burning Judith attended that week on Union Square.

6. Another long poem. "Last Performance of The Living Theatre Invective." Considering Judith and Julian's performances, the courtroom could hardly have been boring. After the conclusion of the trial, a dramatized version was presented at the Café Cino with Lee Worley playing Judith and John Coe playing Julian. Both Judge Palmieri and Peter Leisure came to see whether it was libelous.

7. "I can assert my innocence." As quoted in the *New York Herald Tribune,* 26 May 1964. There were accounts in the *New York Times,* the *Daily News,* and the *Village Voice.*

8. "Grey and grim." Unpublished Diary, 6 June 1964.

39. *Mysteries*

1. "Refugees." Unpublished Diary, 6 August 1964.

2. Germans. Unpublished Diary, 28 and 29 July 1964.

3. London. Unpublished Diary, 2 and 22 September 1964. Brown, "Finding Out," pp. 36–38. Warren Finnerty returned to the United States to work in such films as *Murder, Inc.* and *Easy Rider.*

4. Reviews were mixed. The English reviews were summarized in the *New York Times* in an Associated Press dispatch on 4 September 1964. Bernard Levin, the reviewer for the *Daily Mail,* called the play "horrifying, inescapable and brilliant." Herbert Kretzmer in the *Daily Express* admitted he was so moved that his stomach clenched like a pounding fist. In New York, Jonas Mekas's filmed version of *The Brig* opened at the second Lincoln Cen-

ter film festival. The following spring, it would win the Gold Medal at the Venice film festival. A half-hour version of the play was shown on CBS which Paul Gardner, television critic for the *New York Times,* admitted was revolutionary for television, and the most "intelligent and mature dramatization" of the season. See the *New York Times,* 3 August 1964. In Berlin in November of 1964, *The Brig* was performed on West German television for twenty million people. In addition to this attention after the fact, Jack Gelber's novel *On Ice* was published by Macmillan in the fall of 1964.

5. Mark Duffy. Bernard Miles. Brown, "Finding Out," p. 38. See also Gelber's "Julian Beck, Businessman," p. 19. In Smith, *Theatre Trip,* p. 95, Rufus Collins repeats the rumor that the American embassy had exerted pressure to close *The Brig.*

6. Kenneth Tynan. Unpublished Diary, 22 September 1964.

7. "Dreamed of a stage." Unpublished Diary, 16 March 1958. In an interview on 5 November 1992, Judith told me that the title for *Mysteries* was derived very spontaneously and its original title had been "One Night of Love." The Eleusinian mysteries were dramatizations of Greek myth. The Eleusinian ceremonies were called *orgia,* and a highlight was the revelation of certain sacred objects by the Hierophant, a high priest of Demeter whose daughter, Persephone, had been abducted while she was gathering narcissi by Hades, master of the underworld. The Eleusinian mysteries were performed for two thousand years with a secrecy enforced by the Athenian state. Other cities in Greece performed Orphic and Dionysian mysteries. See George Mylonas's *Eleusis and the Eleusian Mysteries* (Princeton: Princeton University Press, 1961).

8. "To aid the audience." Beck, "Storming the Barricades, p. 21.

9. "Pierce the shell" and "Break down the walls." Beck, "Storming the Barricades," pp. 16, 18.

10. Social action. Julian Beck, interview by columnist Joseph Barry, *Paris Gazette,* 18 October 1964.

11. "Ritual games." Julian Beck, quoted by Saul Gottlieb, "The Living Theatre in Exile," *Tulane Drama Review* 10, no. 4 (Summer 1966), p. 140.

12. An Indian raga. Nona Howard used to sing ragas, and she contributed to this piece.

13. Incense. Julian got the idea for this from a happening directed by Nicola Cernovich, the lighting director at the Fourteenth Street location. Pierre Biner, *The Living Theatre* (New York: Horizon Press, 1972), p. 86.

14. "The Plague." As a young woman, Judith had been impressed by *Things to Come,* a film based on a story by H. G. Wells, which depicted the plague in a world in ruins as the "wandering sickness." See *Diaries,* 19 August, 1947, p. 8. In some early versions of *Mysteries,* particularly in Amster-

dam, "The Plague" was followed by a jazz coda performed by a trio with Steven Ben Israel on drums as the dead danced onstage.

15. Brussels. Trieste. Vienna. Rome. See Gottlieb, "Living Theater," p. 145. An actor appeared nude. This was Jim Tiroff, one of the daredevils of the group. The taboo of nudity onstage had been broken a few months earlier in London by Peter Brook's *Marat/Sade.* The tableaux vivants were the only part of the play that relied on scenery. There were four large, open boxes onstage, and in each, an actor improvised a pose in intense light for two seconds, followed by a four-second blackout, and then another vignette until the entire cast had been displayed several times. The tableaux vivants were Julian's idea, probably derived from Artaud.

40. Heist-sur-Mer

1. "Surrender immediately." Malina, interview with author, 5 November 1992. The telegram was sent because their lawyer had not appeared at a scheduled hearing.

2. They sailed back. Judith and Julian were met at the dock by Garrick who had been living with Mabel Beck. At the Foley Square courthouse, they surrendered to United States marshals and were interviewed by reporters from all the New York dailies.

3. Passaic County Jail. Unpublished Diary, 13 January 1965; and Stephanie Harrington's piece "A Short and Unhappy Visit to America," *Village Voice,* 21 January 1965. Ironically, Stephanie Harrington had warned Judith to be more serious during the trial.

4. "Month of silence." Unpublished Diary, 15 December 1964. The government had a boarding arrangement for women at the Passaic County Jail.

5. "Chaste as a cell." Unpublished Diary, 23 January 1965.

6. Optimistic view of life in prison. See Beck, "Thoughts on Theatre."

7. Heist under conditions. My interviews with Judith Malina, 23 November 1992; and Steven Ben Israel, 25 November 1992. Also my interview with Dorothy Shari, 5 December 1992. Married to Bill Shari, Dorothy Shari felt particularly besieged in Heist because she had to care for her two small children. She would give birth to another two on the road in Germany in the 1960s. Another source for life at Heist is a film using The Living Theatre actors made by Allan Zion and Thomas White called *Who's Crazy,* a story

about a group of asylum inmates taken out for a drive who create a disordered utopia in an abandoned farmhouse. Much of the action was improvised and the actors were asked to explore whatever seemed most absurd or obsessional about themselves. See Brown, *"Frankenstein,"* pp. 71–72. This sense of the absurd was a defining characteristic of the company. Garry Goodrow told me that on occasion he would hang a sign reading Mixed Nuts on the side of a bus in which the company traveled, much to Julian Beck's consternation. Garry Goodrow, conversation with author, 19 May 1994.

8. "Too smooth." Henry Howard interviewed by Eleanore Lester for her piece "The Final Decline and Fatal Collapse of the American Avant-garde," *Esquire,* May 1969.

9. Subtle tribalism. See Beck, *Life of the Theatre,* p. 104.

10. Luke Theodore as interviewed by Michael Smith in *Theatre Trip,* pp. 115–16. A big, muscular man raised in Oklahoma City where his Cypriote father owned a café, Theodore was stage manager of *The Fantasticks* when he was introduced to the company by Joseph Chaikin. Drawn to The Living Theatre because he had wanted to bring his "naked experience" to a stage "that isn't false, isn't a lie," he became stage manager of *The Brig* and then acted in it.

11. "Horde" and "Becoming statues." Unpublished Diary, 12 March 1965.

12. Mary Krapf. Mary Mary told me she was in jail because of a drug deal she had nothing to do with and so she was released. Mary Krapf, interview with author, 3 December 1992. Born in Brooklyn in 1939, she attended a Catholic high school in a maroon uniform and escaped to a basement apartment on Sullivan Street in the Village, right under *The Fantasticks.* She played the guitar, sang folk songs, and worked as a cashier in the Commons, a café across the street from the Gaslight. Friendly with Mary Travis, Dylan, and a bunch of artists who were experimenting with amphetamines, she had always intended to become an actress but felt inhibited by the presumptions of most theatre.

13. New acting style. Beck, "Thoughts on Theatre"; and Julian Beck "Broadway and The Living Theatre Polemic," *Kulchur* 2, no. 6 (Summer 1962), pp. 21–24.

14. Inhabitants of Sodom. *New York Times,* 7 May 1965.

15. "Simple, classical, austere." Julian Beck to Judith Malina, from Danbury Penitentiary, 9 January 1965, in *Yale Theatre* 2 (Spring 1969), p. 12.

16. Fulfilling Genet's intention. Conversation on the maids between Julian and Judith in Biner, *Living Theatre,* pp. 108–10.

41. *Frankenstein*

1. "Dominated our stages for so long." Julian Beck, to Dr. Wladimiro Dorigo, 27 March 1965, in *Yale Theatre* 2 (Spring 1969), p. 13. In spite of Julian's declaration that there would be no text, the final version would have a very set text.

2. A villa in Velletri. At the end of March, artists in Rome conducted an auction at the Feltrinelli Bookstore for the benefit of The Living Theatre. See Rome's English-language *Daily American,* 25 March 1965.

3. *Community.* Beck, "Storming the Barricades," p. 5. Collective creation in Rome and Berlin was described to me by Mary Krapf on 3 December 1992. "Worthy of our ideas" is from my interview with Judith Malina on 4 December 1992.

4. A dollar fifty a day. This money was for extras like cigarettes or alcohol; lodging, food, and travel expenses were paid for by Julian. By 1966, there was enough money to raise the allowance for extras to four dollars a day. Of course, in the 1960s, one could live quite adequately in Europe on five dollars a day.

5. Uniquely American character. Pamela Badyk, an Australian who joined the company when they performed *The Brig* in London, told me on 18 December 1992 that no matter how many Europeans were involved, the company was perceived by its audiences as American.

6. Wait and wait. Peter Hartman, interviewed by Michael Smith in *Theatre Trip,* p. 159.

7. The final act. Originally, it began with fifteen climactic scenes from Ibsen, repeated simultaneously in the various cubicles, while the monster moved from cubicle to cubicle strangling the actors. The point was to illustrate the elimination of the effete upper class that was Ibsen's subject, but the actors realized this was much too obscure. *Frankenstein* was perpetually in process and was changed so considerably that no two of the fifty-one European performances were alike.

8. Dr. Frankenstein starts a fire. At the end of Mary Shelley's novel, the monster immolates himself in a funeral pyre. An excellent discussion of *Frankenstein* and The Living Theatre's work of the late 1960s is found in Margaret Croyden's *Lunatics, Lovers and Poets* (New York: McGraw-Hill, 1972).

9. "Communal effort" and "Leap into the abyss." Julian Beck and Judith Malina, "Notes on the Direction of *Frankenstein,"* *City Lights Journal* no. 3 (1966), p. 70.

10. According to Peter Hartman. Smith, *Theatre Trip,* p. 161.

11. Informed by police. See Saul Gottleib, "The Living Theatre In Europe," *Evergreen Review* no. 45 (February 1967), p. 25. Italian courts decided the ban was unconstitutional and lifted it.

42. Beggars and Stepchildren

1. In Vienna, an informant. Federal Bureau of Investigation Memorandum, 8 December 1965. According to Judith, the account is exaggerated.

2. Sixth Fleet. Unpublished Diary, 2 February 1966.

3. Ezra Pound. Malina, interview with author, 6 April 1993.

4. "I trembled." Unpublished Diary, 11 April 1966.

5. "Seeds of divine discontent." Unpublished Diary, 10 May 1966.

6. Liaisons with other women. Malina, interview with author, 4 December 1992.

7. Reggio Emilia is a Communist town with an exemplary historical record of resistance to fascism. A small town with merciless church bells, its inhabitants were uneasy about the presence of The Living Theatre. The group had the use of the local theatre situated on a central piazza with its monument to the Resistance as a rehearsal space, so they were quite visible. When Garrick visited, he swam nude with some of the actors and a few teenagers, causing a local scandal. The visit made Judith homesick, sad about not having a permanent home. Unpublished Diary, 6 July 1966.

8. *Sipario,* an Italian theatre magazine, to offer an evening of "free theater." See Beck, *Life of the Theatre,* pp. 82–83. Fundamental question. Judith Malina as interviewed by Pierre Biner, *Living Theatre,* p. 143.

9. Jean-Louis Barrault. Unpublished Diary, 25 June 1966.

10. "Communal to the point of sameness." Taylor Mead remembered the performance of *Mysteries* at Cassis in a brief essay, "Too Much, I think," *Exquisite Corpse* 4, no. 11–12 (November/December 1986), p. 12.

11. Maligning them with implications of drug use. Some members of the company used drugs habitually. See interview with Roy Harris in Smith, *Theatre Trip* (p. 131) who states he used 250 micrograms of LSD for the performance of *Frankenstein* in Venice and for a rehearsal of *Antigone.* Harris, whose real name was Roy Levine, was a cousin of Henry Howard's. This use of LSD was not unanticipated among American artists in the 1960s. The most notorious example is Ken Kesey and his Merry Pranksters, who drove an old school bus painted in Day-Glo across country, stopping at universities and distributing thousands of LSD tablets to students during the winter of 1963–64.

12. Berlin never loved him. Unpublished Diary, 11 September 1966.

13. "Beggars and stepchildren." Unpublished Diary, 3 October 1966.

14. The play was still changing. Smith, *Theatre Trip,* pp. 7, 10. "Freedom to fail." Smith, *Theatre Trip,* p. 14. Michael Smith was sent to Europe to cover avant-garde theatre in the fall of 1966.

15. *Frankenstein* set had arrived smashed. Sets were too cumbersome and heavy for the Volkswagen buses, so they were shipped by truck.

16. "Without sleep." Unpublished Diary, 14 December 1966.

17. Police demanding to see papers. Unpublished Diary, 10 January 1967. Bill Shari was dragged by his handcuffs, burning his wrists; Jimmy Anderson suffered a deep gash under one eye; and most of the others were scratched or bruised. Bill Shari and Rufus Collins were again beaten by police after being released from a hospital where they had received some first aid. One of the actors had a ball of hashish in his pocket which he flipped over a partition in the holding cell. Steven Ben Israel, interview with author, 5 November 1992.

18. Judith's pacifism. Unpublished Diary, 10 January 1967.

43. A Deaf Man Answers Unasked Questions

1. Any two chairs. Unpublished Diary, 12 March 1967.

2. *Antigone* opened in Krefeld. Brecht's adaptation, translated by Judith Malina, was published by Theatre Book Publications (New York, 1984). Judith and Julian discussed their version with Lyon Phelps in *Drama Review* 12, no. 1 (Fall 1967), pp. 125–31. Judith received high praise from critic George Steiner who, in a book discussing the history of the play's many performances, stated that Judith's was "the embodiment of millennially outraged, patronized, excluded womanhood." See George Steiner, *Antigones* (Oxford: Clarendon Press, 1986), p. 150.

3. Still on probation. The tax problem for which the Internal Revenue Service had closed the Fourteenth Street theatre was still being negotiated and would result in a token one dollar penalty. In Europe, American members of the troupe paid no United States taxes, since Americans abroad were permitted to earn $20,000 annually free of taxation, a sum which they could never achieve on their fifty-dollar-a-week allowances in 1967.

4. Interviewed . . . by Leonard Lyons. The interview appeared in the *New York Post* on 19 April 1967, and in it, Judith raised the hope that the company would one day be able to perform in America. In Rome, Roger Eustis, owner of the old Loew's cinema on Second Avenue and Sixth Street, who

called himself a radical capitalist and had engaged in Timothy Leary's psychedelic celebrations, had discussed the possibility of The Living Theatre's coming to New York for a five-week run.

5. Pasolini was possessed. See Julian Beck, "Tourner avec Bertolucci," *Cahiers du cinema* (October 1967).

6. "Saintly group of theatrical geniuses." Peter Hartman interviewed by Michael Smith in *Theatre Trip*, p. 162. Hartman told Ira Cohen that he once made love with Julian in the Black Forest (Ira Cohen, interview with author, 1 April 1993).

7. "Art was not enough." Unpublished Diary, 30 May 1967.

8. Renewed revolutionary ferment. In *Time,* the group read about race riots in Newark—in which LeRoi Jones, by then called Amiri Baraka, had been arrested in the back of a truck carrying guns—and Detroit which had to be occupied by eight thousand National Guardsmen. Black demonstrators marched on Washington, disrupting congressional proceedings.

9. Garrick. When he returned to the United States, Garrick burned his draft card, and in the summer of 1968, he was arrested for chaining himself to an army recruiting station.

10. Grotowski. Beck, *Life of the Theatre,* p. 124. While Julian was in Rome, he and Judith received the International Olimpio Prize presented in Sicily by the Italian actor Vittorio Gassman.

11. "Anarchists of the Anti-Word," *Time,* 1 December 1967.

12. Allen Ginsberg. When arrested, he shouted, "Pentagon, Pentagon, reverse consciousness. Apokatastasis!" Related to the word *apocalypse,* this Greek word means "a transformation of satanic forces into celestial." The end of the third scene in *Paradise Now* is based on this concept.

44. *Paradise Now*

1. Act of persuasion. Julian was helped by Christian Maurel, drama critic for *Le Nouvel Observateur,* who had praised the work of The Living Theatre.

2. Cefalù. Unpublished Diary, 15 February 1968.

3. Discussions on the idea of paradise. Krapf, interview with author, 3 December 1992.

4. Daily exercises. Unpublished Diary, 21 February 1968.

5. "Wither away." *Time,* 1 December 1967. After the revolution of 1917, of course, the Bolsheviks rounded up as many anarchists as they could find and summarily shot them. Instead of withering, the Soviet dictatorship of the proletariat solidified in the persons of Lenin and Stalin.

6. "Theatre and Revolution" first appeared in *The Evergreen Review* in May 1968 and was reprinted in *The Life of the Theatre*. "You cannot be free if you are contained within a fiction." Beck, *Life of the Theatre,* p. 81.

7. Instead of an enactment and premise of the first scene. Richard Schechner's interview "Containment Is the Enemy," *Tulane Drama Review* 13, no. 3, pp. 25, 29. See also "Julian Beck to Saul Gottleib, 25 April 1968," *Yale Theatre* 2 (Spring 1969), pp. 16–17.

8. Sequestered themselves inside one of the huts. Krapf, interview with author, 3 December 1992. The map was included in the program for *Paradise Now.*

9. What to clarify. Michael Smith's interview with Julian in *Theatre Trip,* p. 102.

10. Judith Malina and Julian Beck, eds., *Paradise Now* (New York: Vintage Books, 1971). The play was transcribed only six months after its first production. The copyright page announces that it is not private property, and any community that wishes to perform it may do so without paying performance royalties. *Paradise Now, Frankenstein,* and *Mysteries* are available through Mystic Fire Video.

11. In a pile of practically naked figures on the stage floor. In some performances, all items of clothing were removed by some of the actors. The climate at Cefalù had been so perfect that many of the actors had lived in a state of nudity for three months. Judith commented on the nakedness in an interview with Robert Brustein, claiming it was an attempt to break down the barriers of role playing in and out of the theatre. *Paradise Now* was an attempt to break through false exteriors. Clothing, masks, and much social behavior are expressions of the "knot of basic corruption" that prevents us from finding a way back to paradise. See Brustein, "Interview with Julian Beck and Judith Malina," p. 23.

12. Beck, "Theatre and Revolution." The end of the play is pure Piscator. Judith remembered that at his Dramatic Workshop, he had asked her to read a play called *La Muette de Portici* which ends with the audience leaving the theatre singing "L'amour sacre de la patria" and which began the uprising that eventually freed Belgium from the Dutch. See Malina, "Directing *The Brig,"* p. 87. The ending is also Brechtian. Brecht, who constantly revised his plays because he had no belief in their sanctity, often left his endings unresolved so audiences might seek solutions in the world.

45. The Events of May

1. "Dictate to the rest of the world." Daniel Cohn-Bendit, *Obsolete Communism: The Left Wing Alternative* (New York: McGraw-Hill, 1968), p. 32.

Cohn-Bendit is now an elected official in Frankfurt responsible for multicultural affairs. See article on him in the *New York Times,* 21 April 1993.

2. Nanterre. See "The March 22nd Movement," in *The Student Revolt: Activists Speak,* ed. Hervé Bourges (London: Jonathan Cape, 1968).

3. Similar disturbances in many universities. Although for the most part these were smaller in scale, they occurred at many American universities. At Queens College of the City University of New York, where I have taught since 1963, I was unable to give any final exams during the spring semesters of 1967 through 1969. As early as 1966, over a hundred students lay down on the Long Island Expressway blocking rush-hour traffic to protest the war. There were many arrests.

4. "High school football squad." James Jones, "The Events of May," in Allan Priaulx and Sanford J. Ungar, *The Almost Revolution* (New York: Dell, 1961), p. 1.

5. After his country's humiliating defeat at Dienbienphu, Pierre Mendès-France ended French participation in the war to subjugate Vietnam as a colonial possession in 1954. He is quoted by J. J. Servan-Schreiber in *The Spirit of May* (New York: McGraw-Hill, 1969), p. 31.

6. "A place of live theatre in which anyone could become an actor." Brustein, "Interview with Julian Beck and Judith Malina," pp. 26–27.

7. "Theatre as a major instrument of combat." Daniel Cohn-Bendit, quoted in Priaulx and Unger *Almost Revolution,* p. 77. Cohn-Bendit was addressing what American and German Students for a Democratic Society members were calling "participatory democracy." A more liberal slant in France was provided by J. J. Servan-Schreiber who compared this to the old Roman Forum where all community problems could be discussed by concerned citizens, a prospect he admitted seemed utopian to him in 1968.

8. "Greatest theatre I've ever seen." Brustein, "Interview with Julian Beck and Judith Malina," pp. 26–27.

9. Jean Vilard. Founder of the Théâtre Populaire whose mission had been to bring theatre to the people, Vilard was in Piscator's lineage and a cultural hero for the French.

10. *Enragés* moved in. See Schechner, "Containment Is the Enemy," p. 33.

11. "Ragged fanatics." Paul Ghali, *New York Times,* 3 August 1969.

12. De Gaulle promised wage increases. These were largely an illusory offer as inflation reduced purchasing power. Not all the workers were easily bribed. At Flins, in the Renault plant, a thousand CRS dragged off 150 resistant workers.

13. The press began writing about normalization. There was considerable control of the press in France, and the Ministry of Information did not allow television journalists to report on the activities of the students.

14. Kennedy assassination. A few days later, Valerie Solanis shot Andy

Warhol in the face. She had sent The Living Theatre a play about lesbians called *Up Your Asses* when they were at Fourteenth Street.

15. "Theatre is the Wooden Horse." Beck, *Life of the Theatre,* p. 121.

16. The Living Theatre would withdraw. Except for Maurice Béjart and his dance company, all the other scheduled groups had already withdrawn and left France because of the turbulence. Tensions were high for artists all over Europe. In Belgium, playwright Hugo Claus was sentenced to four months in prison for representing the Holy Trinity by nude men; in France Jean-Jacques Lebel received seven months for staging a happening in which four nudes appeared.

17. "Life style or an artistic tendency." Schechner, "Containment Is the Enemy," p. 44.

46. Naked in New Haven

1. Garden of Voltaire's house. Judith Malina, "Full Moon," in *Living Theatre Poems* (New York: Boss, 1968). Geneva performances were covered in the *New York Times,* 22 August 1968.

2. Jenny Hecht. In *The Enormous Despair,* in an entry for 31 August 1968, p. 4. Judith Malina used Martin Buber's phrase about his fears of the General Strike of 1961 as the title of her diary account of the American tour published by Random House in 1972.

3. The ship's captain offered Julian a Campari. Malina, *Enormous Despair,* 1 September 1968, pp. 4, 8.

4. At a press conference. Malina, *Enormous Despair,* 9 September 1968, p. 17.

5. Julian lean and haggard. Brown, "Finding Out," pp. 185–86.

6. Ambivalent review. New Haven *Register,* 17 September 1968. *Time*'s reviewer. *Time,* 27 September 1968. Judith feels that the argument in *Time* is particularly flawed and that it is based on the fear that "good" becomes evil when it tries to further its cause aggressively. Nonviolence cannot be confused with violence, she maintains.

7. Brustein found that the group acted as a sort of cult. See Ron Frutkin's 27 September 1968 interview with Robert Brustein in *Yale Theatre* 2 (Spring 1969), pp. 102–3. Harold Clurman would subsequently use the cult charge in his *Nation* piece on 28 October 1968. Kenneth Brown alleged that most of those who rejected The Living Theatre at Yale wanted to teach rather than act or direct ("Finding Out," p. 188).

8. "Hustled offstage." Robert Brustein in the *New York Review of*

Books, 13 February 1969. Judith claims that this was Brustein's paranoia and that the woman was a friend of the company who had been encouraged to speak in the first place. Judith Malina, interview with author, 28 October 1993. In *The Enormous Despair,* 24 January 1969, p. 170, Judith admitted that the company never warned the audience that "they would be beleaguered for what they say."

9. Bentley commented. Michael Feingold, "Interview with Eric Bentley, 27 November 1968," *Yale Theatre* 2, pp. 106–11.

10. Destroy the values. Judith Malina, quoted in Stephen Schneck's article in *Ramparts,* 30 November 1968.

11. "Rite of Universal Intercourse." The New Haven *Courier Journal* in a front-page piece on 27 September 1968 entitled "Bedlam in Review" said the stage was a "mass of writhing, nearly naked bodies."

12. Chapel Street. Ira Cohen, conversation with author, 5 December 1992. Ira Cohen was there because he had known Mel Clay in Morocco in the early 1960s when Cohen was editing *Gnaoua.* He became a close friend of The Living Theatre—a *Paradise* addict like many others who were admitted without paying. He later lived with Petra Vogt, a member of the company. Kenneth Brown wrote he was blinded by mace, and he saw others similarly incapacitated (Finding Out," p. 194). Judith Malina described events at Chapel Street in *The Enormous Despair,* 26 September 1968, pp. 43–45.

13. Intellectually dishonest. See composer William Balcolm's comments in "The Last Discussion," conducted at Yale on 30 September 1968, *Yale Theatre* 2 (Spring 1969), p. 45.

14. "Emotional swamping." *Yale Theatre* 2, p. 50. "Brustein hated the play." Malina, *Enormous Despair,* 26 September 1968, p. 43. In November 1968, the Yale *Alumni Magazine* called it "an orgy of self-pity and infantile release." Another related view was later expressed by critic John Lahr who called the play a "gorgeous and horrendous masturbation." See *Up against the Fourth Wall* (New York: Grove Press, 1970), p. 264.

15. Shame the audience. Feingold, "Interview with Eric Bentley," p. 111. Even friends of The Living Theatre like Kenneth Brown thought that *Paradise Now* was an "exercise in futility" and that society would be oblivious to their appeals for justice or peace. Brown found the play presumptuous and self-serving, and thought it resulted from having been too insulated and isolated in Europe ("Finding Out," pp. 192–96).

16. "Unwobbling pivot." *Yale Theatre* 2, p. 32. The phrase was Ezra Pound's borrowing from Confucius.

17. "Outside the gates of paradise." William Borders's piece in the *New York Times,* 28 September 1968.

47. Religion and Rigidity in New York

1. *Frankenstein* opened. New York Reviews appeared in the *Times* and the *Post* on 3 October 1968. In the *New York Times,* Clive Barnes was impressed by the actors' movements which incorporated a fluidity and resilience more often associated with dance than with theatre. Richard Watts of the *Post* was bored, complaining that sound and electrical effects had replaced dramatic intelligence. In the *New Yorker,* on 12 October 1968, Edith Oliver found the piece overdone and numbing though "technically the production was remarkable." Jack Kroll's *Newsweek* piece appeared on 14 October 1968.

2. Judith danced with Allen Ginsberg. Malina, *Enormous Despair,* 2 October 1968, pp. 55–59.

3. Krishnamurti. Malina, *Enormous Despair,* 8 October 1968, pp. 67–69.

4. Confucian calm. Frutkin, "Interview with Brustein," p. 20. "Wasteful day." Malina, *Enormous Despair,* 4 October 1968, pp. 60–61. See also William Borders's report in the *New York Times,* 5 October 1968.

5. Richard Avedon. Malina, *Enormous Despair,* 23 October 1968, p. 98.

6. Jack Kroll's comment appeared in his *Newsweek* piece on 28 October 1968.

7. When *Mysteries* opened. The *New York Times* review of *Mysteries* appeared on 10 October 1968. Jerry Tallmer merely summarized the action in the *Post,* impatiently adding that he wished it had been edited more severely. Lewis Funke's nasty review of *Antigone* in the *New York Times* on 11 October 1968 agreed The Living Theatre was "desperately in need of editing." In the *Village Voice,* Yale professor Gordon Rogoff treated both *Mysteries* and *Antigone* in a respectful, long, literary piece. Rogoff noted that innovativeness had assumed a political character with Brecht in East Berlin, with Joan Littlewood and Peter Brook in London, with Roger Planchon in Lyons and Giorgio Strehler in Milan, and with Joseph Chaikin and Peter Schumann in New York.

8. Review of *Paradise Now. New York Times,* 15 October 1968. Edith Oliver, in the *New Yorker* on 26 October called *Paradise Now* both portentous and fatuous. Richard Gilman, in the *New Republic* of 9 November 1968, called the play flaccid, crippled by an excess of pompous, self-righteous talk. The comments here are from his piece, "The Theatre of Ignorance," which appeared in the *Atlantic* in May 1969. Robert Pasoli's piece appeared in the *Village Voice* on 17 October 1968. Ross Wetzsteon's "Theatre Journal" appeared in the *Village Voice* on 24 October 1968. Another particularly il-

luminating piece is novelist Leslie Epstein's "Walking Wounded, Living Dead," *New American Review* (April 1969).

9. "Hurt me beyond my capacity." Malina, *Enormous Despair*, 21 October 1968, pp. 94–95. On 25 June 1993, Judith Malina told me she now believes the entire thing was a setup by troublemakers determined to disrupt and possibly prevent the performance.

10. Fillmore East. See Emanuel Perlmutter's piece in the *New York Times* on 23 October 1968. In the *Village Voice* on 31 October 1968, Richard Goldstein reported that when Julian was asked how he could support the violent threat of burning down Graham's theatre, he claimed that it was passion not violence, and that it was "a bourgeois myth to confuse the two."

11. Brustein's comment about Judith and Julian's appearance on the Merv Griffin show, quoted in the *New York Review of Books*, 13 February 1969.

12. Stony Brook. Malina, *Enormous Despair*, 29 October 1968, p. 108.

48. A Revolution Disguised as a Theatre

1. Kresge Auditorium. Malina, *Enormous Despair*, 31 October through 8 November 1968, pp. 108–18. See also report in *Variety* on 13 May 1968 on the cancelation by MIT.

2. The erratic geographical route. Mark Amitin, interview with author, 3 April 1993. Amitin worked for the Radical Theatre Repertory and became road manager on the western swing of the tour. Judith Malina argues that the contingencies of any tour depend on where and when a company is wanted and that the geographical zigzagging was usually unavoidable.

3. Another faculty member. Arthur Sainer later became a drama critic at the *Village Voice*. Malina, *Enormous Despair*, 21 November 1968, p. 125. Another source for the American tour, though sometimes impressionistic, is Renfreu Neff's *The Living Theatre: USA* (New York: Bobbs-Merrill, 1970).

4. "We are a revolution disguised as a theatre." Julian Beck, quoted in Schneck, *Ramparts*, 30 November 1968.

5. *Revolution for the Hell of It*. Abbie Hoffman was not exactly mainstream. When journalist Jack Newfield reviewed the book in the *New York Times* on 29 December 1968, he called it a "recipe for private amusement and public catastrophe." Hoffman, he asserted, was a combination of Ernie Kovacs, Artaud, and Prince Kropotkin. This was not a revolutionary country or a revolutionary period, Newfield added, and "to act as though it is, and ignore the consequences, is dangerous."

6. Exhilarated spectator. Malina, *Enormous Despair*, 29 November

1968, pp. 126–128. *Philadelphia Inquirer,* 27 November 1968; and Philadelphia *Evening Bulletin,* 27 November 1968. This was actually Ralph Jarmon, who drove a truck transporting the *Frankenstein* set. Julian had a crush on him.

7. Echnaton. Mel Clay, "Julian," *Exquisite Corpse* 4, no. 11–12 (November/December 1986), p. 5. Echnaton's real name was Hans Shano.

8. Taunted as "Israelites." Malina, *Enormous Despair,* 29 November 1968, p. 130.

9. Threatened a million-dollar lawsuit. Philadelphia *Evening Bulletin,* 27 and 28 November 1968; *Philadelphia Inquirer,* 28 November 1968. The lawsuit was never filed; Julian and the others returned to court and received a nominal fine.

10. Salvador Dalí. Malina, *Enormous Despair,* 1 January 1969, pp. 151–53. Dalí made the remark about gold being the measure of genius at the Russian Tea Room where he had invited Judith, Julian, and Ginsberg—who had brought Jack Kerouac along—to lunch. Beck, Journal, 11 November 1960.

11. Prince Serge Obolensky. Malina, *Enormous Despair,* 1 January 1969, pp. 154–56.

49. California Dreaming

1. Elements in the play. Richard Gilman, *Atlantic,* May 1969. Judith argues that several prisoner support groups were formed which got lawyers to help at least ameliorate conditions in various prisons.

2. "Frozen stillness." Malina, *Enormous Despair,* 7 January 1969, p. 163.

3. Small amount of marijuana. *Boulder Daily Camera,* 6 February 1969. The duties of the road manager. Amitin, interview with author, 3 April 1993.

4. Rufus Collins urged acceptance. See Neff, *Living Theatre USA,* pp. 145–46.

5. The company arrived in Berkeley. Malina, *Enormous Despair,* 18 February 1969, pp. 175–77. Michael McClure's "terminally hip" is from his remarks on The Living Theatre in *Third Rail* no. 7 (Los Angeles, 1985–86), p. 36.

6. "Dramatic Siberia." Ralph Gleason, "Not So Revolutionary," *San Francisco Chronicle,* 21 February 1969.

7. Marked and unmarked patrol cars. *Los Angeles Times,* 5 March 1969. "Offensive to some elements." *Los Angeles Times,* 6 March 1969.

8. Jim Morrison. Malina, *Enormous Despair,* 10 March 1969, pp. 213, 216. The influence of The Living Theatre was damaging for Morrison. A few months after seeing them in San Francisco, at a concert in Miami, drunk and

stoned on cocaine, he exposed himself, masturbated on stage, and was charged with lewd behavior and convicted by the district attorney. After that, his career was broken: promoters would not book his band, and radio stations stopped playing his music.

9. "Theatre of Ideas." Malina, *Enormous Despair,* 21 March 1969, pp. 221–25. Julian Beck's account is in *The Life of the Theatre,* pp. 166–69. Frank Moses reported the imbroglio in the *New York Times* on 25 March 1969; and Robert Pasoli in the *Village Voice* on 26 March 1969.

10. Judith and Julian arrived at Goodman's apartment. Malina, *Enormous Despair,* 30 March 1969, pp. 232–34. Judith and Julian also visited Joseph Chaikin, ailing because of his heart condition, and Eric Bentley before their departure.

11. The American tour. Clive Barnes. *Holiday Magazine,* January 1969.

12. Barnes admitted. Beck, *Life of the Theatre,* pp. 167–69.

13. Open sex with spectators. Malina, interview with author, 25 June 1993.

50. Morocco

1. Anaïs Nin. Most of the details in this chapter come from Judith Malina's Moroccan Diary, a 150-page handwritten account only dated August 1969. Also called Mogador, Essaouira was the place where the Allies defeated Rommel.

2. Gnaoua. The utter abandon of the Gnaoua in their dance—in which they sometimes slashed themselves with knives—was a source of fascination for Judith and Julian. Judith told me about the Gnaoua teaching company members to cut themselves without drawing blood on 9 September 1993.

3. "Smokescreens." Unpublished Diary, March–April 1967. Note that this comment was made two years earlier—"I loathe the sentimentality of the occultists," Judith had written—which by 1969 represented a hardened position.

4. *Saturation City.* See Beck, *Life of the Theatre,* pp. 220–21.

51. Swimming in Dirty Water

1. "Long, grinding efforts." Beck, *Life of the Theatre,* pp. 84–85.

2. The group had functioned. Judith Malina, quoted in Beck, *Life of the Theatre,* p. 122.

3. Henry Howard. *Yale Theatre* 2 (Spring 1969), p. 40.

4. Taylor Mead. Mead, "Too Much, I think," p. 12.

5. Anarchism or any "ism." Krapf, interview with author, 3 December 1992.

6. Another problem. Judith Malina, interview with author, 20 December 1992.

7. Julian announced. Unpublished Diary, 19 September 1967.

8. "The Italian eye." Beck, *Life of the Theatre,* p. 82.

9. "Sense of forcing something that's tired." Unpublished Diary, 27 October 1969.

10. *"Paradise* is over." Unpublished Diary, 2 November 1969.

11. "Prehistoric exhaustion." Unpublished Diary, 11 November 1969.

12. Jean-Jacques Lebel. Jean-Jacques Lebel, ed., *Living Theatre: Entretiens* (Paris: Editions Pierre Belfond, 1969).

13. Rome. *New York Times,* 2 December 1969.

14. "Outside the gates of paradise." Unpublished Diary, 10 January 1970.

15. "It was the best of times." Beck, *Life of the Theatre,* p. 220.

16. "Swimming in dirty water." Ben Israel, interview with author, 25 November 1992.

17. "This community, so full of tenderness." Unpublished Diary, 11 January 1970.

52. Crossy-sur-Seine

1. "Clear to everyone." Living Theatre Action Last Declaration, Living Theatre Archives.

2. "The cupbearer of oppression." Beck, *Life of the Theatre,* p. 94.

3. "Death by Metro." Beck, *Life of the Theatre,* p. 38–39. Also Judith Malina and Hanon Reznikov, interview with author, 23 March 1993. The police were in the Châtelet station because an informer had taped the class at Vincennes.

4. "Theatre ... could openly inspire ... the poorest of the poor." Beck, *Life of the Theatre,* pp. 178–79.

5. "Industrial work is satanic." Unpublished Diary, 4 June 1970.

6. "Hardened into history." Unpublished Diary, 22 June 1970.

7. Her relationship with Carl Einhorn. Malina, interview with author, 22 March 1993. Some of Cleaver's contemporaries, according to Alice Walker on the Op-Ed page of the *New York Times,* 5 May 1993, saw him only

as a "psychotic opportunist." Curiously, in the 1980s, Cleaver became a salesman and then a preacher.

8. "I cried aloud to my God." Unpublished Diary, 29 June 1970.

53. Brazil

1. "I am with the people." Beck, *Life of the Theatre,* p. 188.

2. Brazil's immigrants brought with them a strong anarchist tradition. See Paul Avrich, *Anarchist Portraits* (Princeton: Princeton University Press, 1988), pp. 255–59. Oiticica died in 1958.

3. To meet Genet. Unpublished Diary, 5 August 1970; and Beck, *Life of the Theatre,* p. 102. Genet chose to romanticize the strutting violence of the Panthers.

4. When Carol Berger died on a prison operating table on 13 October 1970, four days after pleading for treatment of her growing cancer, Petra Vogt and a number of others who had been arrested were released.

5. Frivolous whim. Unpublished Diary, 1 September 1970.

6. Superficial disguise. A good source for this is Marcel Camus's acclaimed film *Black Orpheus,* based on the work of playwright Vinicius de Moraes.

7. Trance and possession. Beck, *Life of the Theatre,* pp. 62–63.

8. Jimmy Spicer. Fredericks, interview with author, 10 October 1992; Amitin, interview with author, 3 April 1993; and Malina, interview with author, 6 April 1993.

9. Sacher-Masoch. See James Cleugh, *The First Masochist* (New York: Stein and Day, 1967). Malina, interview with author, 22 March 1993.

10. Gilberto Freyre's *The Master and the Slave* had been published in an English translation by Knopf in 1946. Its original title was *Casa grande e senzale,* which means "the big house and the slave quarters." An article in the *New York Times* on 23 May 1993 reported on the rise of slavery in contemporary Brazil.

11. The crucial problem. Beck, *Life of the Theatre,* p. 146.

54. Dark Voyage

1. Details of the relationship with Osvaldo de la Vega are drawn from the Unpublished Diary, for October and November 1970; and interviews with Judith Malina on 22 and 23 March 1993.

2. Judith had always loathed men who abused women. In Beck, *Life of the Theatre,* there is a letter from Judith Malina to Carl Einhorn in which she emphasizes this (p. 185).

3. Osvaldo's attitude. Instead of a journal, Julian had begun to keep what he called "workbooks." Often, he would transcribe highlights of rehearsal discussions. The observation is from the entry for 26 September 1970.

4. "Nature and time." Unpublished Diary, 8 November 1970.

5. Free love. Beck, Workbook, 10 November 1970.

6. Knots of uncertainty. Beck, Workbook, 18 November 1970.

7. On the verge of a crack-up. Beck, Workbook, 19 November 1970.

55. Ouro Prêto

1. "Wild west." Judith Malina to Carl Einhorn, n.d. (ca. 1970), Living Theatre Archives.

2. Detained in a jail room. Beck, Workbook, 23 November 1970. Judith demonstrated a similar naivete in Ouro Prêto when, on a day of photographing churches, she decided to take a picture of the facade of a bank and was prevented by a policeman. South American banks are the favorite targets of revolutionaries.

3. Tiradentes. He was hung in the central square and, according to legend, parts of his body were sent to each province in Brazil. Judith thought the story was similar to Polynices' in *Antigone.*

4. Graffiti. Beck, Workbook, 4 December 1970.

5. Dorothy Lenner. Four students participated in the *favela* play. To fulfill their contract, the company performed what they called an "acting exercise" without words—to avoid the censor—based on *The Legacy of Cain* material in the artistic community of Embu, fifteen miles outside of São Paulo.

6. Master and slave. Pozzo and Lucky in Beckett's *Waiting for Godot* (1947) give us the classic formulation of this relationship in contemporary theatre.

7. "Liberate the whole world." Unpublished Diary, 23 December 1970.

8. "The ship is now in the water." Beck, Workbook, 23 December 1970.

56. Mother's Day

1. José Carlos Temple Troya. The son of a Spanish immigrant who raised rice and oranges, Troya was studying social sciences in Rio Clara and living with Tom Miller, an American anthropology professor who had translated Ginsberg's "Howl" into Portuguese and who introduced him to the counterculture. Troya had read an article by Frances Quadri in *Sipario* about The Living Theatre.

2. Plain people. Beck, Workbook, 8 February 1971.

3. Ten-room house. The rooms were divided by hanging cloths. Bill Shari had left the group in Morocco when he contracted tuberculosis. Tom Walker was the Yale student who carried Judith Malina on his shoulders after the New Haven premiere of *Paradise Now*. Walker had come to São Paulo to visit a boarding-school friend and was invited to remain with the group.

4. Teams, including at least one Portuguese speaker. There were two Brazilian members besides Troya. Paulo Augusto, who had been in Zé Celso's group, was from a wealthy and politically connected São Paulo family. Ivanildo Silvino Araujo was more of a representative Brazilian as he was descended from African, Indian, and Portuguese families.

5. "Leave the playground." Unpublished Diary, September 1969.

6. To perform with the children for Mother's Day. Unpublished Diary, 14 May 1971; and, Malina, interview with author, 22 March 1993. The full name of the school is L'Ecole Amerigo Rene Giannetti de Saramenha.

7. Elizabeth Bishop. Called a "poet's poet's poet" by John Ashbery, Bishop had fallen in love with a land-poor Brazilian aristocrat named Lota de Macedo Soares while on a freighter trip to South America. Like Jimmy Spicer, she drank to excess.

8. Pushing at the edge of the danger. Tom Walker, interview with author, 24 March 1993. Judith Malina, interview with author, 13 September 1993.

9. Nadelson bizarrely set several small fires. Judith blamed the fires on self-hatred (Unpublished Diary, 29 June 1971).

10. Expecting to discover a cache of weapons. Troya overheard this when he was placed in the police car. José Carlos Temple Troya, interview with author, 26 March 1993.

11. "Models of courage." See Beck, *Life of the Theatre*, p. 92.

12. Ivanildo received electroshocks. Judith thought Troya had not re-

ceived any electroshock only because he was white, while the other two were black. Judith Malina, interview with author, 11 November 1992. Information on Ivanildo is from a letter from Echnaton published in *Tulane Drama Review* 15, no. 3 (1971), p. 28.

57. DOPS Prison

1. Blue plastic bag. Judith Malina, interview with author, 14 September 1993. According to Tom Walker, the police were unaware of the "windowpane" LSD stashed in books which were ultimately delivered to the prisoners in jail. Walker, interview with author, 24 March 1993.

2. North Vietnamese man. Krapf, interview with author, 3 December 1992.

3. Henry Howard. See Michael Smith's interview with him in *Theatre Trip*, pp. 103–4.

4. "If, as Gandhi says." Beck, *Life of the Theatre*, p. 177. This entry is dated 16 August 1971.

5. Maria Dálcia. She had participated in a bombing, and received electroshock and had her fingernails removed during the period that she was in Judith's cell. She is now considered a "disappeared" person. Judith Malina, interview with author, 10 November 1992. In the DOPS prison, prisoners with money were able to purchase food and to bring in televisions or radios. Maria Dálcia's sister-in-law, for example, brought her home-prepared meals twice a day. When Maria Dálcia learned that Mary Mary was going to be released, she pleaded with her to expose the Brazilian death squads who assassinated civilians suspected of leftist activity. Krapf, interview with author, 3 December 1992.

6. Mabel Beck was brought to Brazil by Karl Bissinger, a former *Vogue* photographer who was then working with the War Resisters League.

7. Colonia Penal. My interviews with Walker, 24 March 1993; and Troya, 26 March 1993. See also Echnaton, Letter, 20 July 1971, pp. 25–29. See also Paul Ryder Ryan's sketchy account, "The Living Theatre in Brazil," *Tulane Drama Review* 15, no. 3 (1971), pp. 21–25.

8. "Pit our ideas." Malina, interview with author, 14 September 1993.

9. Dreading torture. Malina, interview with author, 22 March 1992.

10. Withdraw funds. Walker, interview with author, 24 March 1993.

11. Petition. Over one hundred telegrams were received in Brazil. Jack Gelber wrote a letter that appeared in a Brazilian newspaper, and Stefan Brecht, Brecht's son, sent a check directly to the DOPS prison. Yoko Ono

contributed two thousand dollars to the Paradise Defense Fund, and there were a number of poetry reading fund-raisers. There was also coverage in the American press. The *New York Times* sent a reporter to interview Judith and Julian; the *Village Voice* did a story on 19 August; and there were a number of stories in the underground press, particularly in the *Berkeley Barb*. All of these are included in the FBI folder on The Living Theatre which, under the Freedom of Information Act, I was allowed to read.

12. The most sensational publicity. At that time, the Brazilian newspapers were run by what was called self-censorship which meant that if they published what the government did not like, they were closed. Judith's ambition was to describe the prison situation in order to help the other prisoners, most of whom had been involved in armed struggle because their lives were in danger. Judge de Andrade's wife admired Judith. As in some novel by Anthony Trollope, when she read in the newspaper Judith's diary account of the hardness of her husband, she stopped having sex with him. Ariosvaldo, Judith's attorney, appeared one night in her cell insisting that Judith soften her account of the judge in a future entry. Malina, interview with author, 14 September 1993.

13. Presidential order of expulsion. Ironically, when Judith was invited to return to Ouro Prêto in August 1993, she was treated like a cross between Queen Elizabeth and Elizabeth Taylor, interviewed on the two leading television talk shows in Rio, and presented with the key to Brazil.

14. Julian was called upstairs. Unpublished Diary, 3 September 1971.

15. "We stayed in one place too long a time." Julian Beck and Judith Malina, Interview, *Berkeley Barb,* 3 December 1971.

58. "A Fetish of Revolution"

1. Arrived in New York City. Articles in the *New York Times;* and the *Daily News* on 4 September 1971. In September, Judith and Julian had letters in the *East Village Other,* an alternative newspaper, and in *Win,* the magazine of the War Resisters League.

2. Visited Abbie Hoffman. Unpublished Diary, 6 September 1971.

3. Julian encountered Tennessee Williams. In December, Julian telephoned Williams regretting that he could not attend the St. John's protest but claiming that the only real way to stop the war was "to bring down the entire military-industrial structure." Unpublished Diary, 5 December 1971. When the event occurred, Williams was disturbed by obscenities in a play by Norman Mailer. See Dotson Rader's account in *Cry of the Heart.* Rader

claims Williams became attracted to the antiwar movement because young people made him feel alive.

4. Rainbow Farm was purchased with a legacy of $20,000 that Garrick had received from Mabel Beck.

5. City Lights Poets' Theatre. See *Berkeley Barb,* 10–16 December 1971, which also exists in the FBI file.

6. Chogyam Trungpa Rinpoche. He would establish Naropa, a Buddhist institute in Boulder, Colorado, where Ginsberg would set up the Jack Kerouac School of Disembodied Poetics.

7. Julian's uncle. This was Leon Goldrich who also became superintendent of schools. Goldrich was the uncle whose $6,000 bequest to Julian was used to begin The Living Theatre in 1947.

8. Christopher Lasch. Quoted in Paul Ryder Ryan's article on *The Money Tower* in *Drama Review* 18, no. 2 (June 1974), p. 12. It would be inaccurate, by the way, to dismiss The Living Theatre as narcissists. Lasch, in *The Culture of Narcissism,* defines the narcissist as someone who lives only for the moment and denies the continuity of history.

9. Gordon Rogoff. Unpublished Diary, 15 April 1971.

10. J. Edgar Hoover. Unpublished Diary, 2 May 1971. See recent biographies such as Curt Gentry's *Hoover: The Man and the Masks* (New York: Norton, 1991) that claim Hoover was homosexual and not quite the all-American boy.

11. "Traitor to his class." Beck, *Life of the Theatre,* p. 155.

12. Rainbow family of Living Light. See Garrick Beck's account in Alberto Ruy Buenfil, *Rainbow Nation without Borders* (Santa Fe: Bear and Co., 1991), pp. 67–82. Also Garrick Beck, interview with author, 9 April 1993. A number of the children of sixties' radicals continued in that tradition. Abbie Hofmann's son, Andrew, for example, has been arrested in Chicago because of his work with a needle exchange program to prevent AIDS and has been organizing soup kitchens for the homeless in Boston. See the *New York Times* Style section, 10 April 1993.

13. "A fetish of the word 'revolution.' " Unpublished Diary, 2 August 1972.

59. Revolutionaries between Revolutions

1. Comradeship and affection. Beck, Workbook, 23 August 1972.

2. "Sexual anarchist." Unpublished Diary, 13 October 1972. "Inhibitions." Beck, Workbook, 13 October 1972.

3. "The hardest thing." Unpublished Diary, 28 October 1972.

4. Failed to earn enough money. The budget for the St. Felix Street commune came to $1,750 per month. Julian's workbooks occasionally break it down: rent was $400 a month; Isha's school, $35 a week; and a garage for the car was $50 a month.

5. "Under the lash." Unpublished Diary, 28 October 1972. Also Malina, interview with author, 4 December 1992.

6. John Lennon. Unpublished Diary, 8 November 1972; Beck, Workbook, 8 November 1972.

7. Murray Bookchin. Beck, Workbook, 11 November 1972. The Alternative University was an offshoot of the late 1960s and existed in many American and European cities. Its adherents proposed many of the notions that we now recognize as New Age.

8. Hanon Reznikov. His given name was Howard Reznick. Reznikov was his grandfather's last name, and Hanon is a Hebrew name that means "graceful." Hanon Reznikov, interviews with author, 12 December 1992 and 23 March 1993.

9. Processional toward a supermarket. Although they could have performed off-Broadway or off-off-Broadway, The Living Theatre was committed to street performance. In spirit, they were close to the German Workers' Theatre League which after the First World War sent dozens of agitprop troupes composed of proletarian amateur actors to perform *Lehrstücke*—didactic teaching plays—in union halls, summer camps, and strike headquarters. By 1973, there were a number of theatres established on the off-Broadway circuit, including Robert Kalfin's Chelsea Theatre Company, the American Place Theatre, the Open Theatre, and the companies controlled by Joseph Papp. Off-off-Broadway featured groups like Ellen Stewart's La Mama, Lynne Meadow's Manhattan Theatre Club, André Gregory's Manhattan Project, Richard Schechner's Performance Group, and George Bartenieff and Crystal Fields's Theatre for the New City.

10. Horrible conditions faced by political prisoners. Krapf, interview with author, 3 December 1992. Also Judith Malina, "Making and Breaking the Traditions" (Lecture given at the New York Public Library, Celeste Bartos Forum, 14 February 1989).

60. The Lucha and Joy Cells

1. "Lying fallow." Beck, Workbook, 14 May 1973.

2. "We don't want to do plays anymore." Beck, Workbook, 19 May 1973.

3. *The Money Tower.* The play was finally entitled *The Destruction of the Money Tower.* The green neon dollar sign was contributed by lighting artist Rudi Stern. There was also a score by Carlo Altomare, Mary Mary's lover, who later founded the Alchemical Theatre in New York. Hanon Reznikov, interview with author, 10 December 1992; and Judith Malina interview with author, 17 September 1993. See scenario in *Drama Review* 18, no. 2 (June 1974). Also see Ross Wetzsteon's piece "The Living Theatre at the Pittsburgh Station," *Village Voice,* 21 April 1975.

4. Meyerhold had declared. Quotation is from an exhibition on the Russian avant-garde at the Guggenheim Museum in the fall of 1992.

5. Workers usually admired. Working-class people admired the capability and skill of members of the company who were able to erect the scaffolding in fifteen minutes and bring it down in eight while singing.

6. Emotions among Judith, Hanon, and Julian. Beck, Sexual Diary, covering the spring through fall of 1974. I particularly drew on entries for 18 April, 4 July, 7 September, and 8 October.

7. Pittsburgh. See *National Geographic,* December 1991.

8. Lucha . . . cell. Joy cell. Reznikov, interview with author, 10 December 1992; and Tom Walker, interview with author, 29 March 1993.

9. Company was arrested. Walker, interview with author, 29 March 1993. The FBI file on The Living Theatre states this occurred on 16 September 1975.

61. The Years of Lead

1. In Europe for the next seven years. A crucial source at this point is Julian Beck's performance log which he kept from 1976 through 1983. Also Malina and Reznikov, interviews with author, 23 March 1993; and Walker, interview with author, 24 March 1993.

2. Warren Finnerty. See obituary by Kenneth Brown, *Village Voice,* 20 January 1975. I was also helped by Brown, "Finding Out," pp. 384–85. At a memorial service at the Peace Church on Washington Square, actor Rip Torn emotionally blamed Finnerty's death on the crass commercialism of Hollywood which had stopped giving him work because of his independence.

3. Further harassment. The Korean member of the troupe was named Kim-sek-Jong though he called himself Chris Creatore. He was the adopted son of an Italian-American businessman.

4. "Not enough time." Julian Beck, *Theandric: Julian Beck's Last Notebooks,* ed. Erica Bilder (Philadelphia: Harwood Publishers, 1992), p. 147.

5. "Institutional doom." Beck, Performance Log, 13 October 1976. Cogoletto. Unpublished Diary, 22 October 1976.

6. Cosenza. While the company earned very little in Cosenza, Julian persuaded Italian television RAI to give them one and a half million lire. Unpublished Diary, 2 October 1976.

7. Barcelona. Beck, Performance Log, 21–23 February 1977.

8. Erotic processions. Beck, Performance Log, 2 May 1977.

9. In Lausanne. Hanon was not performing with the company but hospitalized because of a major problem with his sternum which was pressing on his spine. In Lausanne, the operation resulted in complications that left him paralyzed for a month.

10. Restrained and complacent. Beck, Performance Log, 31 May 1977.

62. *Prometheus*

1. Two large apartments. They were located on the Via Gaeta and the Via Ferruccio.

2. High school. See Beck, *Theandric,* p. 30.

3. Actors are untied. If the audience was too uninventive to untie them, there were always technicians and stagehands to do it. Walker, interview with author, 24 March 1993. Hanon Reznikov told me that the Russian director Evreinov used to stage the storming of the Winter Palace annually with a cast of thousands in Leningrad. See also discussion in Theodore Schank, *American Alternative Theatre* (London: Macmillan, 1982), pp. 32–34. Music for the play, which was originally entitled *Prometheus at the Winter Palace,* was composed by Carlo Altomare who played Orpheus, and it was choreographed by Jessica Sayer—who had been Hanon's lover at Yale—a leading dancer with Alwin Nicolais.

4. Munich. Beck, Performance Log, entries from 21–28 October 1977.

5. Red Brigade members. Malina, interview with author, 23 March 1993.

6. Discouraged audiences. Beck, Performance Log, 23–26 January 1978.

7. Teatro Argentina. During the third performance, Renato Nicolini, the Roman commissioner of culture, volunteered to play a terrorist bomb thrower. The arrests occurred around midnight after the prison vigil as the cast was eating *cornetti,* an Italian version of the croissant, in a bakery. Later, this would be referred to by company members as the *cornetti* bust.

8. "Tripping from theatre to theatre." Julian Beck, *Living in Volkswagen Buses* (Seattle: Broken Moon Press, 1992), p. 8. This was the final in-

stallment of a series of poems called *Songs of the Revolution*. The first thirty-five songs had been published by Interim Books in New York in 1963. Numbers thirty-six through eighty-nine were published in a bilingual edition in Paris by Union Générales Editions in 1974, and in Spain by Ediciónes Jucar in 1978.

9. "Slag heaps of decadence." Beck, *Theandric*, p. 155.

63. Sleep and Dreams

1. Julian . . . worried. Beck, Performance Log, 18 April 1979.

2. Michel Foucault. Unpublished Diary, 2 June 1979.

3. *Masse Mensch*. Judith first made production drawings for the play as a student in Piscator's Dramatic Workshop in 1946, and the play was on the first projected list for Living Theatre productions in 1947. Judith Malina, "Notes on Ernst Toller's *Masse Mensch*," 21 March 1981, Living Theatre Archives.

4. Audience was questioned by police. Reznikov, interview with author, 10 December 1992. The name of the beer hall was Orechevko. The home of a magazine called the *Jazz Section*, it was a liaison place for the Czech resistance.

5. Remained in Italy. Julian and Judith also returned to New York to deliver a eulogy for Mabel Beck who died on 30 December 1980.

6. Jack Lang. When The Living Theatre was awarded the Prix des Nations in Paris in the early 1960s, the students presented an ostrich egg as their own prize; the sallow-faced young man who presented the prize was Jack Lang.

7. Underneath the appearance of things. Beck, Workbook, 26 July 1982.

8. Grove Press. Jimmy Spicer, who had helped so much with the initial editing in Brazil, died in 1979 of a diseased liver.

9. A little blue pig. Beck, Workbook, 29 August 1982.

10. Left the Rome apartments. Before The Living Theatre departed, in the middle of January, a group of Roman intellectuals including Alberto Moravia, Paolo Milano, Geraldo Guerrieri, and the film maker Bernardo Bertolucci assembled at the French cultural center in Rome to bemoan Italy's failure to support The Living Theatre.

11. Tharon Plage. Isha Manna Beck, interview with author, 8 April 1993; Reznikov and Malina, interviews with author, 23 March 1993; and Walker, interview with author, 24 March 1993.

12. Doctors were operating. Beck, Workbook, 10 January 1983.

13. Second dream. Beck, Workbook, 24 January 1983. "Julian speculated" was a paraphrase of Cocteau.

14. Third dream. Beck, Workbook, 3 February 1983.

15. Hemorrhaged. Unpublished Diary, 15 March 1983; Reznikov, interview with author, 23 March 1993.

64. A Death like Chocolate

1. Gold velvet divan. Unpublished Diary, 10 April 1983; Isha Beck, interview with author, 8 April 1993.

2. Prospects of growing old together. Malina, interview with author, 17 September 1993.

3. Received well in Nantes. Before the play opened, there was a change in municipal government from socialist to conservative, and the group suddenly found itself in hostile territory.

4. Joyce Theatre. The invitation came from Cora Cahane and her husband, Bernard Gersten, who owned the Joyce.

5. Frank Rich's review appeared in the *New York Times,* 19 January 1984, as did Watts' piece in the *Post.* Julius Novick's *Village Voice* review was on 7 February 1984, and Benedict Nightingale's in the *New York Times,* on 23 February 1984. She also reviewed Judith Malina's *Diaries* in the *Times* on 12 August 1984, adding that the company was now a group of "dilapidated gurus making histrionic gestures of dogmatic defiance."

6. "Wipe us off the face of the earth." Quoted by Ilion Troya in *Exquisite Corpse* 4, no. 11–12 (November/December 1986), p. 4. Later, Julian claimed the critics reaction was a sign of the "closure" that came with the Reagan era (Workbook, 2 June 1985). Two weeks after the Joyce engagement, at the opening of a play at the Lucille Lortel Theatre on Christopher Street in the Village, Julian approached critic John Simon, a high-school classmate, and asked him to explain his hatred. When Joseph Chaikin tried to hit Simon with an ice cream cone, Judith pushed Simon out of the way. See "Page Six," *New York Post,* 27 February 1984.

7. "Like an amulet." Beck, Workbook, 31 May 1984.

8. Humanization. Beck, Workbook, 19 May 1984.

9. Ginsberg asked Julian. Allen Ginsberg, telephone interview with author, 21 June 1993. "Door-opener." Beck, Workbook, 30 July 1984. Believing that Julian was close to death, Ira Cohen helped to organize benefits in Los Angeles and San Francisco where Michael McClure and Lawrence Ferlin-

ghetti read. In London, Al Pacino donated the proceeds of one night's receipts from *American Buffalo,* the play in which he was performing. Ira
Cohen, interview with author, 1 April 1993.

10. "I want to die." Beck, Workbook, 23 June 1984.

11. "I keep thinking about the theatre in New York." Beck, Workbook,
20 July 1985. This is the final workbook.

12. "Incurable Europhile." Beck, Workbook, 8 August 1985.

13. "Nomads." Beck, *Life of the Theatre,* p. 53.

14. Death . . . "as if it were all chocolate." *Exquisite Corpse* 4, no. 11–12
(November/December 1986), p. 4.

65. An Enduring Legacy

1. Gardens in empty lots. Garrick Beck, who works for the Board of
Education in New York, conceived of a project to teach inner-city kids the
mysteries of botany and agriculture by planting vegetables and flowers in
abandoned lots.

2. Happy Days Bar and Grill. This and much of the information in this
section is drawn from my interviews with Hanon Reznikov on 8 April 1993;
and with Judith Malina on 17 September 1993.

3. "Don't give that flag to me." Malina, interview with author, 17 September 1993.

4. 1992. There were also a number of special productions including
Erica Bilder's production of *The Maids,* a production of Walter Hasen-
clever's *Humanity,* and Ilion Troya's direction of Julian Beck's autobiographical *Enigmas.* On 29 April 1992, the night of the Los Angeles riots, The Living
Theatre opened Xavier Mohammed's *Echoes of Justice,* a play based on the
Larry Davis case where a former police informer shot seven policemen
whom he thought were planning to kill him. There were also poetry readings, concerts of new music organized by Patrick Grant, and dance by Johnson Anthony.

5. Fire Department. See Jerry Tallmer's story in the *New York Post,* 6
February 1993.

6. Contributions. Some were quite generous like Yoko Ono's 1984 gift
of five thousand dollars.

7. Films Judith was making. Judith had previously played Al Pacino's
mother in *Dog Day Afternoon,* in *Awakenings,* and in Paul Mazursky's *Enemies: A Love Story. Household Saints,* a Nancy Savoca film, opened in the
spring of 1993. Judith won high praise for her performance as the Italian

mother of a lower East Side butcher whose granddaughter becomes a saint. Other members of the cast included Tracey Ullman and Lili Taylor.

8. Enduring legacy. Two recent doctoral dissertations in Europe, where the reputation of The Living Theatre has always been stronger than in America, reflect this legacy. In 1989, Graziana Maria Lucia Felli completed her dissertation on The Living Theatre in Italy and France in the 1960s at the Universita Degli Studi Dell Aquila; and in 1991, Fanette Vander completed hers at the Université de Paris, VIII.

Index

Index